Foundations of Sustainable Business

THEORY, FUNCTION, AND STRATEGY

Nada R. Sanders, Ph.D.

D'Amore-McKim School of Business
Northeastern University

and

John D. Wood, J.D.

Environmental Studies Program
Lasell College

WILEY

VICE PRESIDENT & EXECUTIVE PUBLISHER	George Hoffman
EXECUTIVE EDITOR	Lisé Johnson
PROJECT EDITOR	Jennifer Manias
ASSISTANT EDITOR	Katherine Bull
EDITORIAL ASSISTANT	Amanda Dallas
DIRECTOR OF MARKETING	Amy Scholz
SENIOR MARKETING MANAGER	Kelly Simmons
MARKETING ASSISTANT	Elisa Wong
DESIGN DIRECTOR	Harry Nolan
INTERIOR DESIGNER	Tom Nery
ASSOCIATE PRODUCTION MANAGER	Joyce Poh
SENIOR PRODUCTION EDITOR	Yee Lyn Song
SENIOR PRODUCT DESIGNER	Allison Morris
PRODUCTION SERVICES	Lavanya Murlidhar/Laserwords (SPi Global)
COVER DESIGNER	Kenji Ngieng
COVER PHOTO	© AleksandarGeorgiev/iStockphoto

This book was typeset in 10/12 ITC New Baskerville Std at Laserwords and printed and bound by Courier Westford. The cover was printed by Courier Westford.
This book is printed on acid free paper.

Founded in 1807, John Wiley & Sons, Inc. has been a valued source of knowledge and understanding for more than 200 years, helping people around the world meet their needs and fulfill their aspirations. Our company is built on a foundation of principles that include responsibility to the communities we serve and where we live and work. In 2008, we launched a Corporate Citizenship Initiative, a global effort to address the environmental, social, economic, and ethical challenges we face in our business. Among the issues we are addressing are carbon impact, paper specifications and procurement, ethical conduct within our business and among our vendors, and community and charitable support. For more information, please visit our website: www.wiley.com/go/citizenship.

Evaluation copies are provided to qualified academics and professionals for review purposes only, for use in their courses during the next academic year. These copies are licensed and may not be sold or transferred to a third party. Upon completion of the review period, please return the evaluation copy to Wiley. Return instructions and a free of charge return shipping label are available at www.wiley.com/go/returnlabel. If you have chosen to adopt this textbook for use in your course, please accept this book as your complimentary desk copy. Outside of the United States, please contact your local representative.

Library of Congress Cataloging-in-Publication Data

Sanders, Nada R.
  Foundations of sustainable business : theory, function, and strategy / Nada R. Sanders, Ph.D., Lehigh University; John D. Wood, J.D., Econautics Sustainability Institute.
      pages cm
  Includes bibliographical references and index.
   ISBN 978-1-118-44104-6 (pbk.)
 1. Management–Environmental aspects. 2. Industries–Environmental aspects. 3. Business enterprises–Environmental aspects. 4. Sustainable development. I. Wood, John D., 1980- II. Title.
  HD30.255.S265 2015
  658.4'083–dc23
                                                                                    2014023327

Printed in the United States of America.
10 9 8 7 6 5 4 3 2 1

PRAISE FOR
FOUNDATIONS OF SUSTAINABLE BUSINESS

"This is an excellent, well-informed, thorough introduction to why sustainability is important in business and how best to achieve it."

Daniel Fiorino, American University

"It is a sustainability book for business people; it addresses the issues of business and sustainability today without being overly political."

Richard Grogan, Antioch University New England

"An introduction to sustainability that is well integrated with business topics and provides a proactive and practical approach to greening companies."

Susan Cholette, San Francisco State University

"This book assembles the various and often interdisciplinary aspect of sustainability in a very readable and understandable fashion."

Beate Klingenberg, Marist College

"It is complete, easy to read, it flows from one topic to another, it is extremely well organized. This would make a great text for [a] management course in sustainability."

Gregory Graman, Michigan Technological University

To business leaders working to make the world a better place for generations to come.

-Nada R. Sanders

To everyone who wants to do the right thing and still get paid.

-John D. Wood

Nada R. Sanders, Ph.D.

Nada R. Sanders is an internationally recognized thought leader and expert in forecasting and supply chain management. She is author of the book *Supply Chain Management: A Global Perspective* and is co-author of *Operations Management*, in its 5th edition. She was ranked in the top 8 percent of individuals in the field of operations management from a pool of 738 authors and 237 different schools by a study of research productivity in U.S. business schools, is a Fellow of the Decision Sciences Institute, and has served on the Board of Directors of the International Institute of Forecasters (IIF), Decision Sciences Institute (DSI), and the Production Operations Management Society (POMS).

Dr. Sanders holds the title of Distinguished Professor of Supply Chain Management at the D'Amore-McKim School of Business at Northeastern University. Prior to that, Dr. Sanders served as the Iacocca Chair at the College of Business and Economics at Lehigh University and as the West Chair at the M.J. Neeley School of Business, Texas Christian University, as well as Research Director of the Supply and Value Chain Center. She holds a Ph.D. in Operations Management and Logistics, and an MBA, from the Fisher College of Business at The Ohio State University, as well as a B.S. in Mechanical Engineering.

Throughout her career, Dr. Sanders has successfully held a range of leadership roles in both academic and professional organizations and has served on numerous executive boards. She has provided training and consulting to a range of Fortune 500 companies, including IDG, Nike, AT&T, CIBA Corning, Mattel, Schottenstein Corp., Cognitive TPG, MTC Corp., Dell, and many others, and is a frequently called upon keynote speaker and expert witness. Dr. Sanders has received numerous research and teaching awards, including the Carl Beidelman Research Award (2012) at Lehigh University, a university award given for highest quality research.

Dr. Sanders has authored over one hundred scholarly works and has served on the editorial boards of prominent journals in her field, including the *Journal of Operations Management, Production and Operations Management, Decision Sciences Journal, Journal of Business Logistics,* and *International Institute of Forecasting.* She is co-editor for the *Journal of Business Logistics'* special issue on interdisciplinary research and was co-founder and Associate Editor of *Foresight: The International Journal of Applied Forecasting.*

In 2008 she was invited to serve as a participant at *The Gordon Cook Conversations* at Windsor Castle, UK. This retreat brought together a small, diverse group of international leaders identified to have 'star quality' in the development of strategies that will impact society in the coming decade.

John D. Wood, J.D.

John D. Wood is a Member of the New York State Bar and Executive Director of Econautics Sustainability Institute (ESI), a 501(c)(3) non-profit dedicated to promoting sustainability in the private sector through research, education, and advising. Wood also serves as Legal Counsel for Suncoast Claims, Inc., a public insurance adjusting firm that has represented over $50 million in claims on behalf of property owners recovering from environmental catastrophes in the Atlantic and Gulf Coast regions. He is an Adjunct Professor of Green Business in the Environmental Studies Program at Lasell College.

Prior to founding ESI, Wood worked with an array of non-profits on land use, energy policy, and industry regulations. He worked on a campaign to promote sustainable land use as a consultant with the American Conservation Association, a Rockefeller trust dedicated to sustainable land use in North and South America. As a Legal Fellow at the Natural Resources Defense Council, he worked on regulatory, environmental, and public health issues related to natural gas drilling in the Marcellus Shale, as well as legal mechanisms to promote environmental justice in urban environs. As a Research Associate at the Institute for Policy Integrity, a non-profit organization founded by the Dean of NYU School of Law, he was part of a team of lawyers and economists that use cost-benefit analysis to advocate for smarter government regulations.

Wood is a legal scholar with publications in the *Environmental Law Reporter*, the *NYU Environmental Law Journal*, the *NYU Journal of Law and Liberty*, *The New York Environmental Lawyer*, and the *Torts, Insurance, and Compensation Law Journal*. He is an expert in risk management, environmental law, climate change, and the energy-water nexus. Wood earned his J.D. from New York University School of Law and his B.A., *summa cum laude*, in English and Philosophy from Texas Christian University.

PREFACE

Consumer and regulatory pressure for sustainable performance has grown rapidly over the past few years, pushing the economy into a new era where the bad guys finish last. However, the competencies and proficiencies required to develop and manage a sustainable organization are not easy to come by. "While a growing number of business schools teach some ethics and corporate social responsibility, the management and organizational development skills and perspectives required to run a sustainable business are rarely taught."[1] This textbook is designed to meet the need for a comprehensive introduction to sustainable business from a managerial point of view.

We designed this book to show how and why business is evolving—first introducing business topics as they are traditionally presented in an MBA program, then explaining how each topic has changed in light of sustainability. By integrating cases of social and environmental leadership in the private sector, we present the various managerial-class disciplines in a new light. We eschew the traditional economic single-mindedness of managerial decision-making and instead foster an appreciation for the social and environmental ramifications of business decisions.

Although there exist many great resources on sustainable business, this textbook is unprecedented in its scope and content. Not only do we marshal the most influential concepts and perspectives from interdisciplinary research in sustainability, we also integrate sustainable business policies into strategy for core functional areas, such as accounting, management, marketing, and operations. "Integration of sustainability into core business functions remains the most important leadership challenge facing business."[2] By integrating policy into practice, we prepare students to engage in this important topic in the workplace. It is our hope that this book inspires future business leaders to be the change agents that many of our industries need.

---

[1]Pat Hughes & Kathleen Hosfeld, *The Leadership of Sustainability: A Study of Characteristics and Experiences of Leaders Bringing the "Triple-Bottom Line" to Business,* Center for Ethical Leadership, page 4 (2005).

[2]BSR/GlobeScan, *State of Sustainable Business Survey 2013*, page 8 (October 2013), available at https://www.bsr.org/reports/BSR_GlobeScan_Survey_2013.pdf.

Organizing Framework for the Textbook

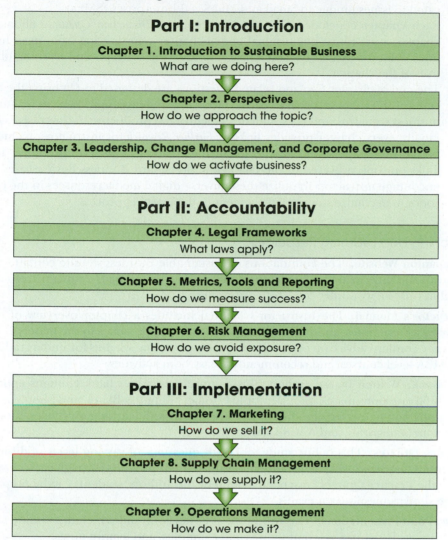

Part I: Introduction

Chapter 1. Introduction to Sustainable Business

What are we doing here?

Chapter 2. Perspectives

How do we approach the topic?

Chapter 3. Leadership, Change Management, and Corporate Governance

How do we activate business?

Part II: Accountability

Chapter 4. Legal Frameworks

What laws apply?

Chapter 5. Metrics, Tools and Reporting

How do we measure success?

Chapter 6. Risk Management

How do we avoid exposure?

Part III: Implementation

Chapter 7. Marketing

How do we sell it?

Chapter 8. Supply Chain Management

How do we supply it?

Chapter 9. Operations Management

How do we make it?

Pedagogical Features

➢ Every chapter begins with a vignette in the *Chapter Opener* that introduces a central concept of the chapter with one or more business example.

➢ *Cross-Linkages* between chapters refer readers to other portions of the text that expand upon the topic under discussion. This feature allows readers to approach concepts from more than one perspective, highlighting the interdisciplinary nature of the subject.

➢ Every chapter includes at least one of all of the following call-out boxes: *Leadership, Ethical Decisions, Global Insight,* and *Managerial Insight.* These boxes provide concrete examples, quotes from industry decision-makers, and thought-provoking statistics that motivate the text. At least one call-out box in every chapter is dedicated to issues unique to Small and Mid-Sized Enterprises (SMEs).

➤ Each chapter concludes with *Key Terms*, general *Discussion Questions* about the chapter, and at least one original end-of-chapter *Case* drawing from news headlines, followed by case questions that implicate the concepts and learning objectives of the chapter.

➤ The end-of-chapter *Case* and related questions are designed to (1) bring the concepts of the chapter "down to earth" by having students apply them to real-to-life business scenarios, and (2) stimulate engaging and productive in-class discussions.

➤ Finally, every chapter provides links to *Further Research* for instructors; including books, whitepapers, and articles for further reading, interactive websites, TED-Talks on topics covered in the chapter, and Harvard Business Review cases. We encourage instructors to utilize these diverse digital media resources in the classroom to maximize student engagement in the learning process.

Teaching and Learning Resources

Companion Website. The Foundations of Sustainable Business website contains myriad tools and links to aid both teaching and learning, including the valuable resources listed in this list. www.wiley.com/college/sanders

Instructor's Manual. The Instructor's Manual includes a chapter overview of each chapter, lecture notes, and suggested and alternative approaches to the material. This resource contains advice on course development, a sample syllabus for undergraduate- and MBA-level courses, and recommended classroom activities.

Test Bank. Written by the authors, this comprehensive test bank contains approximately 60 questions per chapter. Multiple Choice, Fill-in-the-Blank, and Short Answer questions vary in degree of difficulty and are tagged with learning objectives, Bloom's Taxonomy categories, and AACSB standards.

Practice Quizzes. This online study tool, with questions of varying levels of difficulty and immediate feedback, helps students evaluate their progress through each chapter. Since the Practice Quizzes have been written by the authors, students can be prepared to see similar questions on exams.

PowerPoint Presentations. This robust set of PowerPoint slides includes outline material from each chapter, relevant figures and examples, and lecture notes.

ACKNOWLEDGMENTS

We are grateful to the many faculty reviewers who provided excellent feedback through-out the drafting process; some of whom reviewed multiple chapters, encouraged us to introduce this book to the market, and provided invaluable suggestions from their own teaching experience. Thank you to the following reviewers:

Melvin Blumberg, *Pennsylvania State University*
Edith Callaghan, *Acadia University*
Joseph Cazier, *Appalachian State University*
Susan Cholette, *San Francisco State University*
Daniel Fiorino, *American University*
Gregory Graman, *Michigan Technological University*
Richard Grogan, *Antioch University New England*
Carol Hee, *University of North Carolina at Chapel Hill*
Beate Klingenberg, *Marist College*
John Mahon, *University of Maine*
Deborah Steketee, *Aquinas College*
Madhubalan Viswanathan, *University of Illinois*
Margaret White, *Oklahoma State University*

BRIEF CONTENTS

CONTENTS

Part II Accountability

9   Operations Management   259

Ancient Air Conditioning in Modern Building Design

9.1 The Role of Operations Management in Sustainability 260

9.1.1 The OM Function 260

9.1.2 How OM Impacts Sustainability 262

9.1.3 Water-Related Operations Management Risks 263

9.2 Operations Strategy 264

9.2.1 Sustainable Operations as a Competitive Priority 264

9.2.2 Sustainable OM Strategy 265

9.2.3 Stakeholder View of Operational Output 267

9.2.4 Striking the Right Balance through Quality Management 267

9.3. Operations Design 268

9.3.1 Product Design 268

9.3.2 Process Design 272

9.3.3 Process Performance Metrics 273

LIST OF FIGURES

LIST OF TABLES

Chapter 1

Table 1.1: Drivers of Sustainability
Table 1.2: Five Stages of Sustainable Business
Table 1.3: Evolution of Attitudes Toward the Business Case for Sustainability
Table 1.4: Sustainable Take Over of Market Share Across Industries
Table 1.5: Business Implications of Global Environmental Trends
Table 1.6: "Green Shoots" By Market Sector

Chapter 2

Table 2.1: The Costs of Neglecting Stakeholders

Chapter 3

Table 3.1: Virtues and Vices of Main Leadership Strategies
Table 3.2: Becoming a Sustainable Leader: The Five-Fold Path
Table 3.3: 2012 Shareholder Resolutions on Sustainability Issues

Chapter 4

Table 4.1: Characteristics of Evolutionary Stages of Business Attitudes
Table 4.2: Operative Definition of Human Trafficking

Chapter 5

Table 5.1: The Role of Finance Officers
Table 5.2: The Role of Accounting Professionals
Table 5.3: Applying Natural Capital to a P&L Statement
Table 5.4: ISO 26000 Guidance on Social Responsibility

Chapter 6

Chapter 7

Chapter 8

Chapter 9

LIST OF FEATURES

Global Insight: Provides perspectives on international aspects of sustainable business, including global market trends, global development challenges, and business risks presented in the context of international trade.

Managerial Insight: Provides snapshots of operational risks, examples of management success, and managerial strategies that provide business decision-makers with a competitive edge.

Leadership: Highlights pioneers and exemplars of sustainable business practice, and describes success stories of private sector leadership addressing sustainable development challenges.

Ethical Decisions: Illustrates various inflection points where business decisions have ethical ramifications, especially where business-as-usual approaches raise questions of fairness, responsibility, and integrity.

Global Insight

Chapter 8
Global Insight: Talking on Toxic Cell Phones?
Global Insight: Nestlé Creates "Shared Value" for Rural Suppliers

Chapter 9
Global Insights: Creating a Safe Working Environment at SMEs Overseas

Managerial Insight

Chapter 1
Managerial Insight: Balance and Stewardship Are Not Anti-Business Ideas

Chapter 2
Managerial Insight: Patrik Frisk on CSR in Practice

Chapter 3
Managerial Insight: View from the Top: Executive Opinions on Sustainability
Managerial Insight: Kevin Kruse, We: How to Increase Performance and Profits through Full Engagement
Managerial Insight: Chief Sustainability Officers Weigh In

Chapter 4
Managerial Insight: Compliance Challenges at Legacy Facilities

Chapter 5
Managerial Insight: Natural Capital Accounting from Alcoa to Xerox

Chapter 6
Managerial Insight: Traditional Risk Management Is Not Good Enough

Chapter 7
Managerial Insight: Market Trends for Small Businesses
Managerial Insight: Does Red Bull Really Give You Wings?
Managerial Insight: FIJI Water Battles With Greenwashing

Chapter 8
Managerial Insight: Sustainable Supply Chain Management for SMEs
Managerial Insight: The Role of Retailers in Sustainable SCM
Managerial Insight: Herman Miller Engages Over 200 Suppliers

Chapter 9
Managerial Insight: Water Is a "Critical Business Need" for Dow
Managerial Insight: Human Resource Management and SME Sustainability

Leadership

Chapter 1
Leadership: Ray Anderson, Revolutionary Carpet Salesman
Leadership: Statoil ASA Provides Sustainable Oil
Leadership: Coloplast A/S Provides Sustainable Health Care

Chapter 2
Leadership: Timberland, LLC. Engages Workers and Communities
Leadership: Seventh Generation Takes CSR to the Next Level

Chapter 3
Leadership: Chemical Manufacturers Association and 'Responsible Care'
Leadership: LJ Building Maintenance, LLC, SME Leader
Leadership: CLIF Bar Founded on Product and Organizational Innovation
Leadership: Eli Lilly Promotes Sustainability through Corporate Governance

Chapter 4
Leadership: Safeway Takes on Human Trafficking

Chapter 5
Leadership: Using the GRI to Rank the World's Clean Capital Giants

Chapter 6
Leadership: Got an Oil Spill? "Dawn" to the Rescue
Leadership: The Insurance Industry Addresses Climate Change Risk.

Chapter 7
Leadership: SME Markets Organic Eggs
Leadership: UTZ Certified and the Roundtable on Sustainable Palm Oil

Chapter 8
Leadership: United Parcel Service (UPS) Greens Transportation Fleet
Leadership: Tesco Tries to Feed the World Sustainably

Chapter 9
Leadership: Avaya Takes on Climate Change Impacts from Operations
Leadership: Hewlett-Packard Pioneers Recycled Hardware
Leadership: The Rodon Group: Sustainable Plastics Manufacturing
Leadership: Mountain Equipment Co-op Discloses Sustainable OM Metrics
Leadership: Major Sports Leagues Measure Footprint of Stadiums
Leadership: National Resource Defense Council (NRDC) Greens Offices

Ethical Decisions

Chapter 1
Ethical Decisions: Business Externalities Threaten Natural Capital

Chapter 2
Ethical Decisions: Nike Deals with Risks from Suppliers' Labor Practices

Chapter 3
Ethical Decisions: The Sustainability Leadership Gap
Ethical Decisions: Unilever CEO Weighs in on Corporate Governance

Chapter 4
Ethical Decisions: Stephen Meyer: Does Environmental Regulation "Kill Jobs"?

Introduction

You Are Here

Introduction to Sustainable Business

SUSTAINABLE COMPANIES GAIN THE UPPER HAND

According to research in *Harvard Business Review*, sustainability is now the primary driver of business innovation.[1] Sustainable business means balancing social, economic, and environmental considerations in business decision-making; stewarding the natural resource base upon which the business depends; giving back to the communities in which business is done; and promoting long-term value-creation for the company's investors. If sustainability were merely a business fad, the global economic recession of 2008 would have caused sustainable investment to decline as business leaders looked to cut unnecessary expenditures. However, according to research in *MIT Sloan Review*, sustainability spending not only survived the downturn, but from 2009 to 2010, the number of companies increasing investment into sustainability more than doubled, growing from 25% to 59%.[2] Indeed, all industries have shown an increased interest in sustainability in recent years, especially in commodities, chemicals, consumer products, industrial goods, machinery retail, and conglomerates.[3]

Of the companies investing in sustainability, researchers have divided them into two categories according to commitment level: "embracers" and "cautious adopters." Embracer companies are "implementing sustainability-driven strategies widely in their organizations and have largely succeeded in making robust business cases for their investments."[4] Cautious adopters put into place sustainability initiatives without integrating sustainability into core strategy. Regardless of investment level, business leaders from virtually every industry sector agree, "acting on sustainability is essential to remaining competitive."[5] Some of the competitive advantages enjoyed

> *"Sustainability can be about much more than our response to a crisis: It is an opportunity; it is a set of behaviors integrated into an organization's culture[.] Sustainability is about much more than our relationship with the environment; it's about our relationship with ourselves, our communities and our institutions."*
>
> —**Dov Seidman, LRN (2007)**

LEARNING OBJECTIVES

After reading this chapter, you should be able to:

1. Define sustainability and explain its relevance to business.
2. Articulate how global trends drive sustainability in the private sector.
3. Distinguish between the levels of commitment to sustainable business.
4. Make the business case for sustainability.
5. Explain the role of entrepreneurialism and innovation in sustainability.

by companies driven even in part by sustainability include improved resource efficiency, waste management, and (perhaps most critically) brand improvement and reputational benefits.

1.1 What Do We Mean By "Sustainability"?

1.1.1 Sustainability Is a Loaded Word

The term *sustainability* means different things to different people. It is all too easy to fall into the trap of using *sustainability* or *sustainable* in a vague or an ambiguous manner, ultimately signifying either too much or nothing at all. The term also risks being overused. Nonetheless, it is necessary to apply this term to a wide range of social, economic, environmental, and industry-specific issues. Therefore, it would be useful to put forward a general definition of the term, then to explain how the general meaning of the term pertains to business in particular.

The classic definition of sustainable economic development comes from the 1987 World Commission on Environment and Development's so-called Brundtland Report, *Our Common Future*. **Sustainable economic development** "meets the needs of current generations without compromising the ability of future generations to meet their own needs."[6] Although the classic definition of sustainability is broad, it entails two key premises that offer normative guidance: (1) Economic activity should promote social welfare and protect the natural resource base, and (2) Economic activity should take into account impacts on future generations and steward the natural resource base so it is productive for future uses.

The definition of sustainable development will mean different things in different regions of the globe. For instance, Africa has distinct natural resources, population concerns, cultural norms, and political institutions than Asia. Therefore, what it means to "meet the needs of the present" will be different from region to region. Furthermore, the definition of sustainable development will have distinct ramifications for different industries because each sector can be responsible for such wide variations in social, economic, and environmental impacts. Coal mining presents different sustainability challenges than the apparel industry. Yet, despite all the variation across regions and industries, there are two common principles of sustainable development that apply to all businesses.

These two premises of the classic definition of sustainability can be translated into practical terms for business decision-makers. **Sustainable business** calls for measures of business success that include social, economic, and environmental factors and intergenerational stewardship of resources that creates lasting value and opportunity from one generation to the next. Let's call these normative premises the "balancing needs" principle and the "stewarding resources" principle.

These terms capture the importance of accounting for the environmental and social costs of economic activity, and create an expansive duty to consider the interests of future generations by stewarding the resources used by business.

Sustainable Economic Development Economic activity that meets the needs of current generations without compromising the ability of future generations to meet their own needs.

Sustainable Business The private sector trend managing business success in terms of social, economic, and environmental performance.

Principle of Balance The normative principle of balancing social, economic, and environmental factors when making business decisions.

Principle of Stewardship The normative principle of maintaining natural resources at sufficient quality and quantity to remain viable for use by future generations.

This rubric therefore addresses a wide range of moral issues in business, including labor standards, community impacts, deforestation, climate change, water shortage, and more.

The "balancing needs" principle can be applied through a **triple-bottom-line** approach to measuring business performance. John Elkington, founder of Sustainability, a British consultancy, coined the phrase "triple bottom line" in the 1990s. Elkington argued that companies should care about three unique measures of performance: (1) profits and losses; (2) the organization's effect on people; and (3) pollution and resource depletion.[7]

These tripartite social, economic, and environmental concerns act as an organizing principle for the topic of sustainable business.

The stewarding resources principle can be applied through a variety of means in the contexts of supply chain management and operations management. For instance, sourcing raw materials from suppliers using proper harvesting methods can avoid a variety of environmental risks flowing from agriculture and land use. Recycling the constituent parts of old products not only diverts volume from the waste stream, it also reduces the need for new materials. Both practices contribute to stewarding resources.

Triple-Bottom-Line Approach to measuring business performance that includes (1) the traditional financial bottom line measured in terms of profits and losses; (2) an account for social responsibility measured in terms of the organization's effect on people; and (3) an account for environmental stewardship measured by pollution and resource depletion.

GLOBAL INSIGHT: Sustainability at Small- and Mid-Sized Enterprises (SMEs)

Chances are, more students reading this textbook work for SMEs than for Fortune 500 companies. Indeed, SMEs constitute over 90% of global businesses, accounting for half of Gross Domestic Product for all countries, and providing 63% of all employment opportunities.[8] While individual small businesses may not have a significant impact on their own, aggregate SME impacts make up 60%–70% of industrial pollution globally.[9] Still, SMEs have been slow on the uptake when it comes to integrating sustainability. This may be due in part to the unfortunate fact that "SMEs have been relatively marginalized in the debate on sustainability and corporate social responsibility and relatively ignored in academic research on CSR and high-level policy initiatives."[10]

Many resources exist to educate and empower SMEs to make an impact with sustainability.[11] Led by dedicated management and driven by empowered employees, SMEs can be pioneers in ways that larger, more established firms cannot. SMEs may have more discretion in setting their agenda than publicly traded corporations, enabling them to dedicate resources toward sustainability as conscience (rather than shareholder vote) dictates. What it means to be a successful enterprise has changed, and SMEs have the opportunity to set the tone. It's not just about quarterly profit margins anymore, but about creating meaningful, positive impacts in communities; maintaining a happy, healthy, and engaged workforce; and creating a legacy of lasting value.

The smaller a company is, the more intimately it can engage the community in which it does business to maintain a valuable reputation and rapport. The smaller a company's operating budget is, the more significant are efficiency gains from waste reduction and resource conservation. The smaller the business is, the more vulnerable it will be to external shocks and business risks. For these reasons, the business case for sustainability—from the value creation, cost saving, and risk reduction points of view—applies with even greater force to SMEs than to large companies. Unique challenges faced by SMEs in their endeavor to become sustainable enterprises are discussed throughout the chapters of this book.[12]

CROSS-LINKAGE

The triple-bottom-line concept rears its head in various forms. For example, Chapter 2: Perspectives is organized according to a rubric of social, economic, and environmental perspectives; Chapter 5: Metrics, Tools, and Reporting: The Role of Finance and Accounting includes measures of social and environmental performance to supplement traditional finance and accounting practices that concern economic performance.

CROSS-LINKAGE

Practices that promote environmental stewardship are discussed in Chapter 2: Perspectives; Chapter 8: Supply Chain Management and Chapter 9: Operations Management.

An overwhelming majority of business leaders agree with the statement, "We believe substantial opportunities exist to improve both sustainability and profitability," with 81% in agreement and only 5% disagreeing.[13] This textbook explains the various ways in which that statement—that sustainability and profitability are consistent, not conflicting, goals—is true.

There are many "how" questions that arise at this point. How does one integrate sustainability considerations into the traditional responsibilities of running a successful enterprise? How can businesses invest in the welfare of communities and ecosystems without departing from their professional obligation to act in the best interest of the company and shareholders? How can principles of balance and stewardship be brought home to effect action? How do we promote lofty sustainable principles within the material world of business? We can answer the "how" questions of sustainability by integrating best practices into the foundations of business management across functional areas.

Given cost considerations and the competing priorities and pressures faced by business leaders, there is also the inevitable "why" question that the definition of sustainability leaves open. *Why* is sustainability a concern to my company? We can answer that question by discussing business successes, setbacks, opportunities, and costs that have turned on sustainable performance, to understand why these issues deserve consideration. In short, sustainability presents material risks and opportunities affecting business strategy across multiple functional areas.

1.1.2 Running Out of Space

Every decade it seems, the world becomes a more complex place in which to do business. The global economy has been in a recession since 2008, and global ecosystems are in decline. Natural resources are becoming scarce and companies are increasingly constrained in their use of energy and water. Climate change is exacerbating extreme weather events, droughts, loss of crops, and supply chain disruption. These changing environmental conditions affect all of us, as the results are higher prices for goods and services, shortages of food items, environmental catastrophes such as uncontrollable wildfires, and ferocious hurricanes that spell untold disaster. At the same time as global climatic and economic instability, the human population and consumption levels continue to grow rapidly. See Figure 1.1.

Sustainability is not "somebody else's problem." According to a 2011 Ernst & Young survey, 76% of respondents anticipate their company's core business objectives will be affected by natural resource shortages in the next 3–5 years.[14] According to the Center for Strategic & International Studies (CSIS)—a bipartisan non-profit think-tank—the major wildcard for political and social unrest over the next 20 years in the Middle East and South Asia will be water scarcity.[15] The resulting population dislocation,

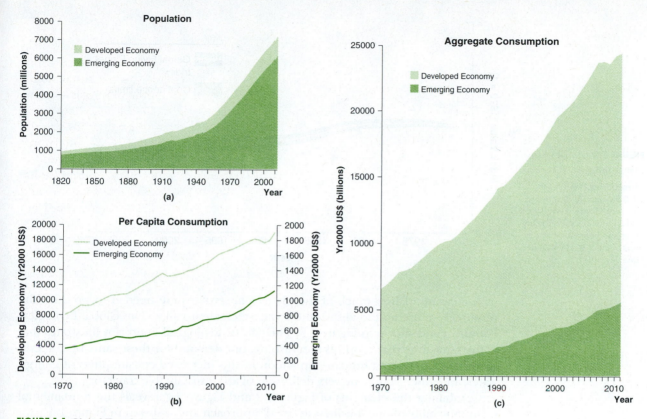

FIGURE 1.1 Global Trends in Population and Consumption

Source: David F. Drake & Stefan Spinler, *Sustainable Operations Management: An Enduring Stream or a Passing Fancy?*, Discussion Paper 13–49, Harvard Environmental Economics Program, page 3 (July 2013). Figures based on World Development Indicators Database, World Bank (2013).

regional conflict, and spillover impacts of water shortage on other national staples could present profound challenges to the private sector.

Even without governmental mandates to reduce consumption, businesses are running into nature's own barriers to growth: scarcity. With global natural capital in jeopardy, the time is overdue for a concerted effort to conserve those resources on the part of businesses whose success depends on their continued availability. **Natural capital** is the available stock of natural resources upon which human life and economic activities depend. The relationship between company profit and natural capital depletion is discussed in Section 1.2.1: What Do Externalities Have to Do with It?

Scientists have measured the health of the Earth's ecosystems through a method called The **Global Living Planet Index**, which is a science-based analysis of the health of the planet and the impact of human activity.

This index, shown in Figure 1.2, indicates that global ecosystems have gone through a steady decline since the mid-1980s. The latest Living Planet Report concludes with the key finding that "Humanity's demands exceed our planet's capacity to sustain us."[16]

Natural Capital The available stock of natural resources upon which human life and economic activities depend.

Global Living Planet Index Scientific analysis of the health of the planet that assesses the vitality of life systems given the burdens imposed by human activity.

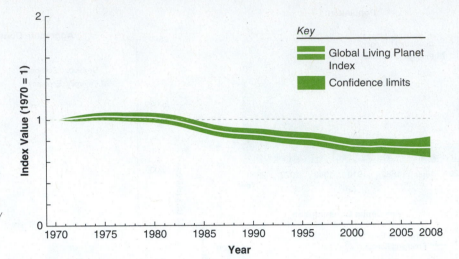

FIGURE 1.2 Global Living Planet Index

Source: Living Planet Report 2012: Biodiversity, Biocapacity, and Better Choices, WWF, page 9 (2012). http://wwf.panda.org/using_site_content/. Used by permission of World Wildlife Fund.

A measure of how much of the planet's ecosystems are needed to produce the resources we use and to absorb the waste we create is called The Global Ecological Footprint and shown in Figure 1.3. The Global Ecological Footprint illustrates that at the same time that supply is diminishing, our demand for these same resources is increasing. A growing human population means increased consumption of energy, water, and food. This is the very definition of an unsustainable trajectory.

Combining the elements of Figure 1.2 and Figure 1.3 reveals the fundamental unsustainability of our "business as usual" approach and is shown in Figure 1.4.

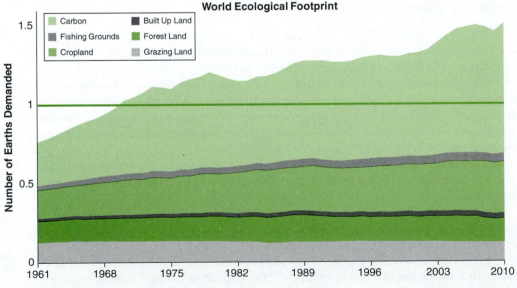

FIGURE 1.3 Global Ecological Footprint

Source: Living Planet Report 2012: Biodiversity, Biocapacity, and Better Choices, WWF, page 9 (2012). http://wwf.panda.org/using_site_content/. Used by permission of World Wildlife Fund.

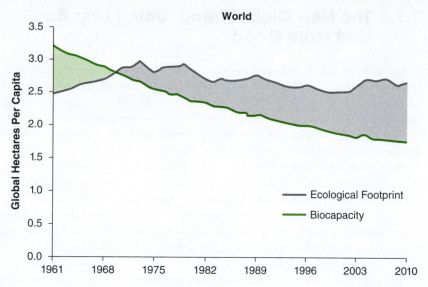

FIGURE 1.4 Human Civilization's Overconsumption

Source: Living Planet Report: Biodiversity, Biocapacity, and Better Choices, WWF, page 40 (2012). http://wwf.panda .org/using_site_content/. Used by permission of World Wildlife Fund.

It appears that the demand on the planet's living resources is already 30% greater than its capacity to regenerate those resources. If these trends continue, by the mid-2030s human society as a whole will demand twice as much as our planet can support, meaning it would take *two Earths* worth of resources to satisfy demand. To be sure, these metrics are not without controversy. Some scientists have criticized the ecological footprint metric because it does not adequately represent the extent of environmental degradation.[17] In other words, the reality of our situation may be worse than the ecological footprint indicates. If the ecological footprint metric is accurate, we are exceeding the Earth's carrying capacity.[18] Reversing course on this unsustainable trajectory is going to take innovation, leadership, and accountability from a lot of businesses, large and small. It is not exaggeration to conclude that humanity is faced with the daunting challenge of ensuring its own future. Let's look at the story of Ray Anderson for some inspiration.

LEADERSHIP: Ray Anderson, Revolutionary Carpet Salesman[19]

In 1973, Ray Anderson founded Interface, Inc., a free-lay carpet tile company, which became the world's largest modular carpet manufacturer. Under Ray's vision, "Mission Zero" became the ambitious, long-term plan to reduce the company's environmental impacts to zero by the year 2020. The idea behind Mission Zero is for the company to take nothing from Earth that cannot be replaced by natural processes. Between 1994 and 2009, Interface reduced material waste, pollutant emissions, and energy consumption; specifically, the company accomplished an impressive 24% reduction in greenhouse gas emissions, 60% reduction in fossil fuel consumption, 82% reduction in waste being sent to landfills, and over 80% reduction in the amount of water used.[20] The financial effects of these pioneering innovations in sustainability were an avoided $450 million in costs, an increase in sales by 63%, and the doubling of corporate earnings.[21] Ray Anderson passed away in 2011, but not before leaving a profound example that seriously challenges contemporary business leaders to take responsibility for their company's environmental impacts and to take ambitious strides toward improving corporate sustainability.

1.1.3 The New Global Trend: Doing Less Bad and More Good

Sustainability is a megatrend for business,[22] on par with globalization in its scope and ramifications for business strategy, cutting across all sectors of the economy and changing the competitive landscape. The sustainability megatrend is the result of a slow-forming convergence of large social, economic, political, environmental, and technological changes which influence a wide range of activities, processes, and perceptions in business, government, and society.

Sustainability emerges from a confluence of factors that include increasing business competition for scarce resources, population growth, industrialization in developing economies, and pressure from consumers, regulators, and shareholders in developed economies. For the last decade, environmental and consumer health issues such as water scarcity, greenhouse gas emissions, industrial pollution, food safety, and others have grown so significant that they have impinged on the ability of companies to focus solely on creating value for shareholders. Executives must now balance these external forces with the traditional imperative to promote their own financial bottom line.

What is emerging from this crucible is an enlightened view on the social responsibility of business. Doing right by stakeholders and doing right by shareholders can and should amount to the same thing.

Sustainable business provides a way past the apparent necessity to sacrifice people and planet for company profits. According to this view, value creation in a competitive landscape defined by resource constraints does not require tragic trade-offs, but rather innovative thinking and a willingness to challenge the status quo. Consumers in the United States and Europe are increasingly concerned about the ingredients of products they consume as well as the processes by which consumer products are manufactured overseas. Governments around the world are interceding into the means of production at greater levels in order to root out unsustainable practices. Public-interest advocacy groups may resort to litigation and publicity campaigns against an industry or business with particularly poor sustainable performance in order to make an example of them. When it comes to the sustainability trend, there are costs for being slow on the uptake.

For those businesses that are not taking on sustainability challengers in an affirmative manner, the risks and liabilities that come from failing to operate sustainably can become so material that investors may demand that they are disclosed in order to forecast the company's financial performance.

During the early stages of the transition into sustainable economic development, sustainable business will basically mean, "doing less bad to people and planet." This is a necessary first step to reverse the trends of resource depletion and excessive contaminant loads of ecosystems, and to take affirmative action to eradicate modern day slavery in the form of human trafficking and labor abuse. The move toward

CROSS-LINKAGE

The resolution to the shareholder vs. stakeholder dilemma is discussed in Chapter 3: Leadership, Change Management, and Corporate Governance. The related concept of shared value creation is discussed in Chapter 8: Supply Chain Management.

CROSS-LINKAGE

We discuss financial disclosure laws related to sustainable performance in Chapter 4: Legal Frameworks. We discuss sustainability reporting in general in Chapter 5: Metrics, Tools, and Reporting: The Role of Finance and Accounting. We discuss materiality assessment in both Chapter 5 and Chapter 6: Risk Management.

sustainability initially gets off the ground with basic risk-minimizing and cost-saving measures such as social responsibility for workers and waste reduction, which have the ancillary benefit of protecting people and the environment.

The next step is transformative, not just corrective. Sustainable business is not just about doing less bad, but also about "doing more good." According to Jeffry Hollender, Co-Founder of Seventh Generation, "Rather than simply emit less CO_2, create less waste, and establish a more equitable workplace, we must find a way to add value to the world in everything we do, from each step in our supply chain and every partner we do business with to every consumer we touch."[23] At this transformative stage, the resources of the private sector are mobilized to address the social and environmental challenges of our time. For managers of a sustainable company, making a positive impact on the world and society is just part of running a profitable business.

Leading companies as well as SMEs from virtually every industry around the world are investing in energy efficiency, renewable energy sources, eliminating waste, maximizing resource productivity, curbing pollution, improving the quality of life for employees, and making strides to benefit local communities through philanthropy and outreach programs. Sustainable performance that adds value along the triple bottom line is the new global trend pervading the private sector, and portends to become the new normal.

1.1.4 The Unsustainable Status Quo: Fisheries[24]

Dealing with unsustainable consumption from one generation to the next has always been a challenge. In 1215 A.D., the Magna Carta prohibited taking "from the land of the heir" more than is reasonably due to the current generation, and required the guardians of an estate to steward the property that was to be passed on to future generations "without destruction and waste."[25] Today we take more from the land and sea than what could reasonably be allocated to any one generation, and we destroy and waste natural resources, forever depriving future generations of access to and enjoyment of the natural wealth of our planet. One example is the problem of unsustainable fishing that is depleting the world's fisheries.

Hunting of wildlife will inevitably drive the hunted species to extinction when kill rates exceed reproduction rates. Fishing is the only form of wildlife hunting that takes place on an industrial scale, so it should come as no surprise that we are indeed overfishing. This is not a new phenomenon. For thousands of years humans have had a major impact on the target species of fishing as well as the ecosystem that supports the target species. Over time, the average size of caught fish diminished as we killed off larger species.

This trend quickened pace rapidly in the 19th century as fishing became industrialized. Large-scale fishing vessel fleets equipped by steam-powered trawlers, then power winches, then diesel engines, then freezer trawlers, then radar and acoustic fish finders, began to prowl the waters of the world for an ever-receding target. Instead of limiting catch to maximum sustainable yield, fishing vessels subject to little or no oversight expanded their reach, fishing deeper waters and more remote seas. See "Ending Overfishing" in Further Research.

As fish populations dwindle, humans have resorted to increasingly aggressive and destructive fishing practices. Trawlers that scrape the bottom of the sea are sometimes used in areas covered in sea grass or coral beds where they can cause irreversible destruction to marine ecosystems. Explosives create blast craters at the bottom of the sea that destroy coral reefs in an instant—reefs that take decades to regenerate. Indiscriminate trawling, poisoning, and blasting are only increasing in use as fishers reach farther down into the barrel, so to speak, in search of fish.

According to the Food and Agricultural Organization of the United Nations, "To satisfy the needs of 9.2 billion people in 2050, overall food production will have to increase by about 70% and production in the developing countries will virtually need to double."[26] Increased food production will depend on productive fisheries, which are critical to global food security and poverty alleviation. Threats to fish populations are especially troublesome because "people have never consumed so much fish or depended so much on the sector for their livelihoods as they do today."[27] Half of oceans' fish stock is fully exploited; one-third of the oceans' stock is over-exploited, depleted, or in a state of recovery; and only 15% of the oceans' marine fish stock remains under- or moderately exploited.[28]

Fish provides a highly nutritious animal protein and source of important micro-nutrients, especially important for pregnant women and young children.[29] In the most food-insecure areas of the globe, fish protein is essential for survival. Further, millions of small-scale fishermen depend upon fishing for their livelihood. Yet in other parts of the world, fishermen are exploited by unscrupulous foreign charter vessel owners and subjected to harsh labor conditions with little compensation and no hazard pay.[30]

Increasing the amount of fishing will continue to push fish species to the brink of extinction, but limiting the amount of fishing could jeopardize the livelihoods of small-scale fisher-men and communities that depend upon fish to meet nutri-tional needs. The principles of sustainable business practices try to find a way through this impasse. A variety of steps could be taken in the fishing industry to promote sustainable solutions to these challenges. Examples include lim-iting the use of intensive fishing practices such as trawling, monitoring vessels for fair labor compliance, more effective industry self-regulation, and so on.

The economic, social, and environmental impacts of overfishing range from the prices on the menu at your local seafood restaurant, the livelihood of fishing vessel workers, and the health of ocean ecosystems. These impacts are what economists call *negative externalities*. We discuss these next.

> **CROSS-LINKAGE**
>
> For more on supplier labor conditions, see Chapter 8: Supply Chain Management.

Negative Externality
A cost generated by business activity, which is shifted from the business onto natural resources, populations, or third parties without consent or compensation.

1.2 Causes and Consensus Around Sustainable Business

1.2.1 What Do Externalities Have to Do with It?

The practice of shifting the cost of business away from the operator and on to natural resources or populations is described in economic terms as *externaliz-ing* the costs of business. A simpler term for such a practice is *bad*. By pushing the costs of environmental destruction onto ecosystems, communities, or future generations without a say in the matter, companies may profit from their activities, but only at the expense of others. A practice of destroying more value than what is created can only be perpetuated if what is consumed is not stewarded appropriately and if the costs of risky activity are shifted to innocent bystanders. Recall that the triple bottom line "aims to measure the financial, social and environmental performance of the corporation over a period of time. Only a company that produces a TBL is taking account of the full cost involved in doing business."[31] Sustainable businesses own up to these externalized costs, creating the appropriate incentives to eliminate waste and overconsumption and to protect employees and surrounding communities from exposure to risks created by the company's activities.

Some sectors of industry cause harm to the environment and public health at levels in excess of their own profits.[32] This means that more value is destroyed than created by economic activity in these sectors. This value destruction comes in the form of lost natural capital, defined earlier.

For instance, coal-fired power generation in East Asia costs an estimated $452.8 billion in natural capital impacts, which outweighs the industry's $443.1 billion in revenue.[33] Cattle ranching and farming in South America causes an estimated $353.8 billion in natural capital costs, which dramatically outweighs the regional sector's $16.6 billion in revenue.[34] Coal-fired power generation in North America causes an estimated $316.8 billion in natural capital costs, whereas it generates substantially less at $246.7 billion in revenue.[35] Although coal production powers a large portion of industrial activity, its results in billions of dollars of environmental and public health costs that render it inefficient. How is this massive inefficiency possible? How could an industry destroy more value than it creates?

The major problem with externalizing costs of commercial activity is not just that it is unfair. Rather, the major problem posed by externalizing environmental and social costs is that the party responsible for the harm never feels the pain they are causing. Touching a hot stove with a bare hand teaches a curious child the lesson of being careful with heat. If a child touched the hot stove and it burned someone else's hand, that child would never learn the lesson of caution. As long as businesses are able to externalize operating costs with impunity, there may be little hope for practices to improve without the intervention of outside agency, such as governmental regulation or consumer activism. However, business innovation can leapfrog outside influence, allowing sustainable companies to determine their own success in a changing regulatory landscape.

> **CROSS-LINKAGE**
>
> For information on natural capital accounting, see Chapter 2: Perspectives.

The basic effort of sustainable business across all functional areas is to **internalize** externalities, that is, for the party that creates the risk to bear the cost of that risk instead of forcing it on someone else. In economic terms, sustainable organizations internalize the negative externalities they create.

> **Internalize** When the party that creates a risk ultimately bears that risk instead of externalizing it.

To internalize externalities is to end the practice of allowing harm to go uncompensated and to begin restoring appropriate incentives for the responsible stewardship of natural and human resources. This is accomplished by (1) offsetting harm through conservation and philanthropy and (2) innovating to perform traditional business functions in ways that reduce or eliminate adverse impacts traditionally associated

ETHICAL DECISIONS: Business Externalities Threaten Natural Capital

Global primary production and processing sectors generate $7.3 trillion in externalities annually, measured by six environmental key performance indicators: water use, greenhouse gas emissions, waste, air pollution, land and water pollution, and land use. These externalities amounted to 13% of global economic output in 2009.[36] Highlighting the social and environmental costs of economic activity helps move toward better balance between economic, social, and environmental factors. Unless externalities are measured, they will not factor into business decision-making. Primary production methods used in, for example, agriculture, forestry, fisheries, mining, oil and gas exploration, and utilities such as electricity generation are highly resource intensive and can be inefficient, neither of which is reasonable in a world of dwindling natural capital. Primary processing methods used in, for example, cement, steel, pulp and paper, and petrochemicals industries, can generate enormous quantities of air and water pollution as well as toxic waste. To the extent that innovation can reduce the impacts of primary production and processing, these industries have the potential to be sustainable. But it will take some effort.

The total externalized costs of global primary production and processing literally decimate global economic output. By internalizing these costs, businesses would be incentivized to improve environmental performance. The answer to the high environmental cost of business is not necessarily to cease the practice, but to improve it. "Don't nix it, fix it." Sustainability does not require the cessation of economic activity, but rather that economic activity must balance environmental and social factors and to steward resources.

with those functions. Businesses promote sustainability, to greater and lesser degrees, according to these two methods: offsetting and innovating around harm.

1.2.2 Shareholder Pressure

An early objection to corporate sustainability was the notion that business leaders should ignore external stakeholders and focus instead on the wealth of corporate shareholders. As it turns out, shareholders have increasingly called attention to the social and environmental impacts of business and demanded that corporate governance take these impacts into account. So-called environmental, social, and governance (ESG) issues are material factors for investors, demonstrated by an increase in ESG shareholder resolutions over the last decade.[37] See Figure 1.5.

According to preliminary research, financial performance measured with Tobin's Q ratio (market value divided by the book value of assets) *declines* when shareholder activists file a resolution related to a company's environmental performance.[38] We might infer from this finding that average investors believe a company is riskier, and therefore a less appealing investment, when it is faced with shareholder resolutions concerning the environmental impacts of corporate conduct. Proactive business leadership may be able to obviate ESG challenges from shareholders by establishing policies of transparency and accountability for these issues. From the stock market to the board room, shareholder pressure is a driving factor in the sustainable business transformation.

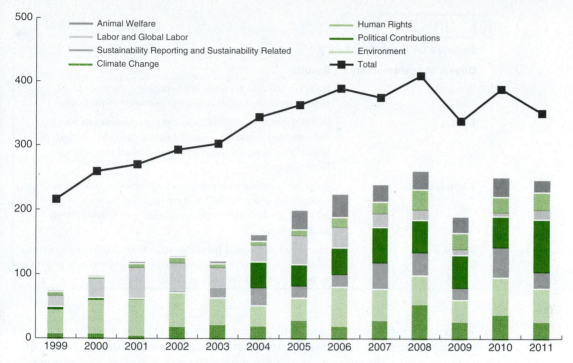

FIGURE 1.5 Trends in Shareholder Resolutions Targeting ESG Issues

Sources: Deloitte, Drivers of Long-Term Business Value: Stakeholders, Stats, and Strategies, page 7 (2012). Institutional Shareholder Services, a division of MSCI, Inc., Deloitte analysis.

1.2.3 Multiple Drivers, One Destination

Whether out of a sense of moral obligation, because of investor or governmental mandates, or simply because Mother Nature is forcing our hand, industries around the globe are making strides to become sustainable. Among those companies pursuing sustainability, the field is diverse across industry sectors, commitment level, and means of implementation. The drivers of sustainable business are multiple, and each is a force unto itself. They include increasingly stringent government regulations, standards promoted by industry and NGOs, public interest and consumer advocacy campaigns, various litigation, expanding marketing opportunities, cost reduction in supply chain and operations, risk management protocols, and natural resource constraints. SMEs are driven to sustainability for different reasons than large businesses. Compared to large firms, the personal values of the owner-manager of an SME are a more important driver than marketing, strategy, or public relations.[39] In general terms, the drivers of sustainable business can be categorized as economic, ethical, institutional, and technological. See Table 1.1.

1.2.4 Baseline Shift Toward Sustainability

A common theme in the regulatory arena, consumer advocacy campaigns, and public interest NGOs and non-profit initiatives, is to bring about the internalization

TABLE **1.1**	
Drivers of Sustainability	
Drivers of Sustainability	**Results**
Economic	Increase efficiency, create opportunities, increase profit, reduce costs, and meet consumer/investor expectations
Ethical	Fulfill social responsibilities to the communities in which the company operates, respect human rights on the part of laborers working for suppliers, and steward resources for future generations
Institutional	Improve standing with regulatory agencies by maintaining compliance track record, and create alliances with NGOs and non-profits to increase credibility and collaboratively problem-solve
Technological	Inspire technological breakthroughs that enable a company to compete in new ways, use less resources, develop new products or processes, and reduce operating costs

of externalities through regulation, voluntary standards, collaboration, and in some cases, litigation. Increasingly stringent standards are reducing waste, reducing energy and water consumption, eliminating the use of toxins, and prompting companies to play a larger role in the betterment of the communities in which they do business. Although sustainability improvements happen incrementally, this remains an area of business competence where it pays to be ahead of the curve.

The number of sustainability indices has grown substantially over the last decade.[40] Today, a majority of Fortune 500 companies publish annual sustainability reports disclosing environmental impacts and explaining sustainability strategies and goals to external stakeholders, and a majority of Fortune 100 companies and two-thirds of Fortune Global 100 companies have committed either to using renewable energy or to reducing greenhouse gas emissions or both.[41] The tipping point of making voluntary commitments to sustainable business practices occurred between 2011 and 2013. Now, among the largest companies, those that are not committed to sustainability are in the minority.

Rio+20 Summit on Sustainability International forum where private sector leaders committed to sustainable principles and practices.

Business representatives attending the **Rio+20 Summit on Sustainability** voted to support certain propositions related to sustainable business.[42] These principles are a common ground of consensus that will assist business decision-makers in moving the conversation forward in their organization as well as in discussions with government. The following business prescriptions are supported by leaders in the private sector:

- Addressing global social and environmental challenges is essential for future business success.
- Leadership is urgently required from businesses to achieve sustainable and equitable economic growth.
- There is a clear economic case for doing business more sustainably.
- Businesses should reduce their focus on short-term performance and focus on long-term competitiveness.
- Businesses should use their power to act quickly and decisively to drive change where government policymakers cannot.

- Drive change by working with customers, consumers, and suppliers.
- Proactively engage with governments to define solutions for sustainable growth.
- Adopt stretching sustainability targets (for example to reduce water, energy, and material use) in order to drive innovation.

These statements of principle and action find expression throughout this text in respective chapters on marketing, supply chain management, operations, risk management, metrics and tools, and leadership.

1.3 The Forms and Stages of Sustainable Business

1.3.1 Sustainability Marginalized

Sustainability was not always the popular kid on the playground. The main problems with sustainable business over the last few decades boil down to a few issues: (1) it was *peripheral* to the core business activities; (2) it proceeded *incrementally* in fits and starts; and (3) it was *uneconomical* according to existing incentive structures. Not too long ago, sustainability was popular among a relatively small group of academics, scientists, NGO officials, non-profit public interest organizations, and community activists. Although it has grown tremendously in relevance and popularity among large companies, there are still a few hurdles to clear before sustainability has its day in the sun.

LEADERSHIP: Statoil ASA Provides Sustainable Oil[43]

Statoil ASA is an international energy company with operations in 35 countries, headquartered in Stavanger, Norway. The company is one of the world's largest suppliers of oil and gas and has contributed to make Norway a modern industrial nation. The company's goal is to meet energy needs worldwide in a responsible manner through innovation and technology. Statoil's corporate sustainability mission is "to ensure sustainable development and help improve the environment."

Climate Change – Industry leadership in carbon efficiency is a strategic corporate objective. Each facility has a quota on greenhouse gas emissions. The company's commitment to addressing climate change leads to operational excellence and development of technical expertise, demonstrated by energy efficiency improvements in projects and facility installations.

Environmental, Health, Safety (EHS) Policies – The company ensures safe operations that protect the public, environment, surrounding communities, and assets. They have a commitment to integrating good health, safety, and environment practices in all areas of the business.

Clean Air – Statoil's on- and offshore facilities use gas and oil for operation. This generates SO_x and NO_x emissions, harmful air pollutants. To proactively combat these emissions, the company installed scrubbers at its refineries before the European Union had imposed the requirement to do so.

Sustainable Performance Initiatives – Statoil has been the top ranked oil & gas company in the world four times according to the Dow Jones Sustainability Index. The company prides itself in obtaining consistently high ratings in socially responsible investing indices.

Sustainability is at risk of remaining peripheral to the mindset of running a business. This will continue to be the case for companies that have not added sustainability as a competitive priority and committed to the practice at the leadership level. Otherwise, sustainability concerns will tend to be relegated to the public relations department, and not frequently integrated across business functions. Further, sustainability appears to be economical only for the largest companies that can afford capital-intensive innovation or perhaps longer periods of amortization from their ROI on sustainability initiatives. Additionally, sustainable business might be uneconomical in the short-term as long as markets continue to reward companies that externalize their costs. Although sustainable business can realize long-term profits, not all companies have such long time horizons. Further, not all governments are taking strides to create the proper economic incentives for sustainable business, and the lack of a suitable legal environment can frustrate the good intentions of any company.

For the time being, sustainability improvements are incremental, following the quality management model, with companies committing to a small-percentage reduction of resource consumption or pollution over a period of years, benchmarked against their own consumption or emissions levels from some arbitrary period of time in the last 20 years (which levels may not have been sustainable then). Incremental improvements are better than none, and a snail's pace is still progress. However, the urgency and scale of sustainability problems, such as global water shortage, demand more than incremental improvements.

1.3.2 Sustainability Grows Up

The following table compares the five levels of sustainable business practices, ranked by increasing degree of transparency and accountability with respect to corporate conduct across the Four M's: motive, manner, method, and medium. Each level is described in terms of (1) the motive for pursuing sustainability, (2) the manner in which the company relates to sustainability principles, (3) the method most commonly used to achieve sustainable goals, and (4) the medium across which those goals are accomplished. See Table 1.2.

TABLE 1.2

Five Stages of Sustainable Business

Motive	Manner	Method	Medium
1. **Profit**	Defense	Ad Hoc	Investments
2. **Philanthropy**	Charity	Programmatic	Projects
3. **Marketing**	Promotional	Public Relations	Media
4. **Control**	Strategy	Management	Codes
5. **Responsibility**	Systemic	Business Model Integration	Products and Services

Source: Adapted from Wayne Visser, "The ages and stages of CSR," Table 1, page 18 from *The Age of Responsibility: CSR 2.0 and the New DNA of Business* (2011). Used by permission of the author.

Stage 1 The profit motive drives the most basic and fundamental level of sustainable business. At this level, businesses pursue sustainability as a defensive strategy to protect profits; sustainability is pursued in a limited fashion, and even then, only when doing so will increase value for shareholders. For instance, ad hoc investments into pollution controls are understood as a means of fending off regulatory delays or violation fines, rather than as a means of protecting the environment. Initiatives such as reducing electricity use are understood primarily as a method for reducing operating costs—not as a means of mitigating corporate impact on climate change. In other words, if it were not for the threat of financial penalty, or the promise of financial gain, sustainable investments would not be forthcoming for businesses at the first level.

> **CROSS-LINKAGE**
> For more on the role of legal compliance in sustainable business, see Chapter 4: Legal Frameworks.

Stage 2 The desire to promote philanthropy through charity events and collaborations with non-profits on various social impact projects characterizes businesses at the second level of sustainability. Corporate philanthropy is responsible for efficiently and strategically allocating resources to support noble causes throughout the world as well as within the communities in which businesses operate. In the United States (but not in some European nations), donations made to non-profit charitable organizations are tax deductible, which provides a financial incentive to pursue philanthropy. Successful businesses are in a financial position to donate money from surplus to improve education in low-income areas, or to promote breakthrough medical research for public benefit, for example. Philanthropic projects can either focus on social or environmental needs outside the scope of corporate conduct, or they can be pursued through direct action. For instance, a business specializing in medical products can donate their own products to low-income areas to meet healthcare needs. Alternatively, a company that sells insurance products may simply set aside funds to fight childhood obesity. Philanthropic efforts allow room for creativity in the pursuit of sustainable business. Contributions, sponsorships, grants, and other funds dedicated to social impacts or environmental conservation provide companies an opportunity to make a positive difference even where product and service innovations seem out of reach. For example, many companies collaborate with the PGA Tour's non-profit golf tournaments to promote social impact causes through corporate sponsorships. Because of corporate philanthropy, the PGA Tour has donated over $2 billion to support over 3,000 local and national charities throughout the United States.[44] Philanthropy allows companies to improve lives they otherwise may not reach through direct operations. A company that generates pollution might not be in a position to modify their production process to reduce those emissions, however they may be able to offset the damage they create by making a donation to an environmental conservation organization that can promote in-kind environmental benefits.

Stage 3 At this level, companies realize the marketing value created by their preventative and philanthropic sustainability efforts from the previous two stages. Committing to social betterment or to natural resource protection can be used in promotional material to enhance brand loyalty and corporate reputation if they are genuine, steadfast commitments rather than one-off projects. That said, if all a company has done to promote sustainability is avoid regulatory violations or make a single contribution to a charity, then using media to spin their efforts into PR material can be perceived as deceptive or self-aggrandizing. While there is a risk of marketing sustainable performance prematurely, once a company has made legitimate and substantial investment into sustainable business, it must accompany these efforts with effective marketing. The marketing function allows companies to capture value created by their efforts and provides a critical window of communication between businesses and their customers that promotes a responsive business strategy.

> **CROSS-LINKAGE**
>
> For more on the opportunities and risks of marketing sustainable performance, see Chapter 7: Marketing.

Stage 4 Here, businesses go beyond mere compliance, philanthropy, and marketing by establishing superior control over risks to their operations and supply chains and embedding environmental management systems and corporate codes of conduct into business strategy. At this level, sustainable performance is benchmarked, goals are set, and performance is monitored and reported throughout the organization and its supply chain. Many companies are arriving at this level of sustainability performance because of its strategic value. At this level, businesses support social and environmental values that align with corporate strategy. For instance, Coca-Cola has made substantial commitments to conserving global water supplies in part by developing a program to monitor water quantity and quality across the globe. Water is the life-blood of any bottling company. For Coca-Cola, if there is no water, there is no product. For Coca-Cola, sustainable water use is a matter of strategy, not just philanthropy.

> **CROSS-LINKAGE**
>
> For more on metrics and tools to promote sustainability, see Chapter 5: Metrics, Tools, and Reporting: The Role of Finance and Accounting.

Stage 5 Businesses driven by responsibility are conceived to address the needs of civilization through their product or service offering. Innovative business models, revolutionary production processes, and lobbying to enhance environmental and social protections offered by government policies typify the few businesses at this advanced level. Here, the company's strategy is molded to address the root causes of unsustainability, environmental protection is integrated into the company's business model, and innovative products and services disrupt markets. At this level, businesses are willing to change their strategy to solve global and civilizational problems.

Each subsequent level transcends but includes previous levels—that is, companies driven by responsibility are still able to improve profits when they commit to sustainable business. A company intent on solving the global water crisis will not do anyone a favor by going bankrupt. At any stage of maturity, sustainable business decisions can improve environmental, social, and economic conditions, but they must provide for corporate profitability.

> **CROSS-LINKAGE**
>
> For more on leadership and the strategy of trailblazing sustainability companies, see Chapter 3: Leadership, Change Management, and Corporate Governance.

1.3.3 Sustainability Gears Up

The idea that business, not just government, has some share of responsibility for the welfare of the environment and society, has been around since at least the 1980's, and each decade the concepts and degrees of responsibility have evolved to address new problems and a greater role for business in solving them.

An alternative way of understanding the evolution of corporate sustainability is the "gearing up" metaphor for organizational transformation. "Like a manual transmission, the framework is designed to take a company from a level of bare compliance with applicable law to a place where sustainability is a systemic, integrated part of its strategy that transforms its business model and markets."[45] See Table 1.3.

To be sure, although the attitude toward sustainability changes with each stage in this evolution, the priorities are not jettisoned along the way. Each stage includes the priorities of the previous stages, but these priorities are looked at from a more enlightened point of view. For example, a company that is concerned with integrating sustainability into core business strategy is still taking measures to ensure that corporate activities comply with applicable laws and regulations, still benchmarking sustainability performance, and still partnering with other stakeholders in the search for sustainable solutions.

TABLE 1.3

Evolution of Attitudes Toward the Business Case for Sustainability

Attitude Toward Sustainability Policies	Business Case for Sustainability	Response
Complying	Sustainability concerns are viewed with skepticism, as is the business case for sustainability.	Generic corporate philanthropy, mere compliance with applicable labor and environmental regulations.
Benchmarking	Sustainability is appreciated as a legitimate concern of external stakeholders, and incorporated into operations for PR benefits.	Focus on measuring, benchmarking, and reducing adverse impacts on the environment.
Partnering	Sustainability is a significant concern for the organization and requires solutions that work for all stakeholders.	Partner with government, customers, suppliers, and others from industry to create innovative solutions.
Integrating	Sustainability is a paramount concern of the organization and provides a competitive advantage in the organization's sector enabling the creation of value for stakeholders.	Sustainability principles have been integrated into business strategy, product and service development, supply chain, operations, and marketing.

Source: Adapted from SustainAbility LTD., *Gearing Up: From Corporate Responsibility to Good Governance and Scalable Solutions*, 34–37 (2004) (explaining the U.N. Global Compact "gearing up" metaphor). Used by permission of SustainAbility.

LEADERSHIP: Coloplast A/S Provides Sustainable Health Care[46]

Coloplast A/S is an international company founded in 1957 that develops, manufactures, and markets medical devices and services related to ostomy, urology, continence, and wound care. The company is headquartered in Humlebaek, Denmark, operates in over 55 countries worldwide and employs over 8,000 people. Europe constitutes the largest market (73% of sales), followed by North America (17% of sales), and the rest of the world (10% of sales). The company's signature offering is intimate healthcare services and products. The company supplies products to hospitals and institutions as well as wholesalers and retailers. In some markets, Coloplast is a direct supplier to consumers. The company prides itself on carefully listening to end consumers and understanding their needs in order to make their lives easier since these patients are battling difficult diseases of a personal and private nature. Coloplast has several sustainability initiatives that involve all of its stakeholders:

End user – provide products that are free of phthalate (a potentially biologically disruptive plastic).

Healthcare professionals – train all white-collar employees in Code of Conduct regarding relationships with prescribers.

Employee – Promote gender equality in management positions; avoid repetitive work; employ active work injury prevention.

Business Partners – 100% of raw materials covered by "Supply chain responsibility programme" which pertains to human rights, labor rights, and business ethics.

Environment – absolute reduction of CO_2; increase recycling.

Society – Reduced cost access to products in emerging markets.

As a result of these sustainability initiatives, the company has gained a great reputation. For instance, Coloplast is noted on the Danish Stock Exchange and has for a number of years been represented among the 20 most traded shares in the country. The company was also included in Ethisphere's 2012 edition of the "World's Most Ethical Companies" listing. In Europe, Coloplast is a market leader in its segment. The access-to-care initiative gives the company market presence in emerging nations as the middle class grows in those countries.

1.4 The Business Case for Sustainability

1.4.1 There Is Actually Just One Bottom Line

Sustainability is not a departure from the traditional business imperative to promote profit—it is rather a refinement. The benefits of sustainability may include flourishing ecosystems, improved public health, and increased consumer satisfaction, but the underlying driver is profit for the company involved. If profit did not accompany sustainability, it would flounder as a movement, yet it has only grown. Companies are taking sustainability seriously not just to save the planet but simply because it is a good investment.

It should be clear that although environmental and social concerns are pressing, there are powerful economic motives behind the sustainable business trend. The many business examples in this textbook show the payoff of sustainability across industries and around the world. The notion that sustainability pays is also supported by scientific research. Consider the research around the adoption of ISO 14001 standards for environmental performance. High-adopters of environmental management systems (EMS) are more likely to report increased recycling activity as well as

> **MANAGERIAL INSIGHT:** Balance and Stewardship Are Not Anti-Business Ideas[47]
>
> Recall the two principles of sustainable business, discussed in Section 1.1.1: balance and stewardship. Roberto C. Goizueta, former Chairman of the Board of Directors and Chief Executive Officer of Coca-Cola Corporation, explained how the interests of society and the interests of corporate profitability are aligned. "The creation of unique value for all stakeholders, including share owners, over the long haul, presupposes a stable, healthy society. Only in such an environment can a company's profitable growth be sustained. Thus, the exercise of what is commonly referred to as 'corporate responsibility' is a supremely rational, logical corollary of a company's essential responsibility to the long-term interests of its share owners." In this way, balance and stewardship of social and environmental resources is consistent with the basic economic imperative to improve profit.

reductions in air emissions, solid waste, and energy usage.[48] A study of Italian firms identified economically quantifiable benefits from EMS adoption including raw material conservation, productivity improvements, energy conservation, smoother production operations, waste reductions, improved access to government regulatory incentives, and reduced insurance costs.[49] The study also found less easily quantifiable benefits, including risk reduction and improved company image.

Growth rates of sustainable market segments are rapidly increasing and taking over market share from conventional products in the food, consumer product, construction, finance, energy, and automotive sectors.[50] See Table 1.4.

TABLE 1.4

Sustainable Take Over of Market Share Across Industries

Food (Environmental)	Between 2002 and 2011, the organic food market grew by 238%, compared to a 33% growth in the overall food market.[51]
Food (Social)	Between 2002 and 2011, there was a 1,442% increase in Fair Trade certified food imports.[52]
Consumer Products	Between 2003 and 2011, the organic non-food market (including linen, clothing, personal care products, pet food, household cleaners, flowers, and nutritional supplements) grew by 400% compared to the 33% growth in the overall non-food market.[53]
Construction	Between 2005 and 2011, the green building market grew by 1,700%, compared with the −17% *contraction* in the overall building market.[54]
Finance	Between 2001 and 2010, Socially Responsible Investing (SRI) portfolios saw an asset growth of 32%, greater than the 27% increase in overall investment asset growth, and during the economic recession of 2007–2010, SRI portfolios grew by 13.2% when overall investment grew only 0.4%.[55]
Energy	Between 2002 and 2011, consumption of renewable energy increased by 456% while non-renewable energy consumption *decreased* by −3.2%.[56]
Transportation	Between 2002 and 2011, hybrid vehicles saw a 646% increase in sales,[57] while the overall vehicle market experienced a −15% *contraction*.[58]

This chapter has framed innovation as the primary means by which businesses make the transition into sustainable performance. We explore this important transformation process next.

1.4.2 Environmental Changes and Business Implications

Several environmental trends have implications for all sectors of the economy. These implications are risks to traditional businesses, yet also opportunities for sustainable enterprises capable of innovation. See Table 1.5.

Among these environmental trends and business implications, there are three common denominators: (1) *Innovation* to avoid the costs resulting from natural resource degradation and to increase the efficiency of resource use; (2) *Transparency* with and responsiveness to stakeholders; and (3) *Stewardship* of natural and human resources to enable long-term growth. Innovation, transparency, and stewardship are the mechanisms of sustainable business.

1.4.3 Green Shoots and Blue Oceans

In addition to the trends and implications common across all sectors discussed earlier, environmental changes pose sector-specific risks and opportunities. These new market niches and opportunities for sustainable development are green shoots of growth emerging in the global economy. See Table 1.6.

The common risks posed to all sectors by a changing physical environment (see Table 1.5) present parallel opportunities unique to each sector (see Table 1.6). Balancing these risks and opportunities is part of sustainable business strategy.

The sustainability trend invites companies to pursue a blue ocean strategy (BOS). **Blue ocean strategy** is the "simultaneous pursuit of differentiation and low cost. The aim of BOS is not to outperform the competition in the existing industry, but to create new market space or a blue ocean, thereby making the competition irrelevant."[59]

Product and process innovations of sustainable businesses can reduce costs and increase revenue regardless of what the competition is doing. By using BOS companies can make lemonade from the lemons of environmental limitations. Sustainable innovation carries the promise of new products, new services, and even new markets. Sustainability is the new hallmark of a competitive enterprise.

Blue Ocean Strategy
The simultaneous pursuit of differentiation and low cost with the goal of rendering competitors irrelevant.

1.4.4 Overview of the Textbook

Part I: Introduction includes Chapters 1–3, and provides the theoretical overview of sustainable business from social, economic, environmental, and organizational perspectives.

Chapter 1: Introduction to Sustainable Business explains what sustainability means and why it is important to business leaders. This chapter provides a factual big-picture overview of the topic, including the evolution of sustainability within the business community, and environmental, social, and economic drivers of that evolution. This chapter

> **TABLE 1.5**

Business Implications of Global Environmental Trends

Environmental Change	Implication for Business
Greenhouse Gas Emissions. Over the next 50 years, greenhouse gases (GHG) may double, increasing global average surface temperature by 3 to 6 degrees Celsius by 2100.	Low-carbon products come into favor; operational and supply chain disruptions increase; costs increase for energy, natural resources, and commodities; changing local conditions require adapting means of production and transportation.
Extreme Weather Events. Between 1980 and the 2000s, flood disasters increased by 230% and drought disasters increased by 38%. This trend is expected to continue.	Operational and supply chain disruptions increase; operations and materials costs increase; public infrastructure such as roadways deteriorate; demand for reconstruction services grows.
Land Use. Over the next four decades, land required for urban uses may increase by 100–200 million hectares.	Access to land-based resources will be restricted; ecosystem services will diminish; arable land will be highly sought-after; pressure will grow to protect natural resources.
Water Quantity. Over the last five decades, global water withdrawals tripled to meet agricultural, industrial, and domestic demands. This trend is expected to continue.	Demand will grow for water-efficient products; water scarcity will constrain growth; operational and supply chain disruptions will increase; stakeholder conflicts will increase due to limited water supply; water costs will increase.
Water Quality. Ninety percent of global water bodies are contaminated by persistent toxic chemical pollutants.	Demand will increase for pollution control systems and technology; water treatment costs will increase; water quality regulations may become stricter; health impacts will grow, demand for healthcare services will increase.
Biodiversity. Thirteen million hectares of forests were lost between 2000 and 2010. High rates of species extinction are expected to continue as critical habitats such as forests and wetlands decline.	Pressure will increase from market, consumers, and regulators to reduce biodiversity impacts; natural resource scarcity will increase operating costs; product re-design will be constrained by limited access to materials; access to land will be limited.
Chemical Exposure. We lack information on human health impacts of cumulative and synergistic exposure to chemicals; despite that more than 248,000 such products are commercially available.	Pressure will increase from regulators, consumer advocates and customers for increased transparency; market preferences will shift to low-impact products and services.
Waste. Raw materials are increasingly produced in one region, used in a second, and managed as waste in a third. 20–50 million tons of e-waste is generated every year, containing hazardous substances and strategic metals.	Pressure will increase from regulators and customers to reduce waste, to increase recycling and materials recovery, and to properly manage hazardous waste; waste management may become a reputational factor; e-waste recovery may be worth the cost.

Source: Dave Grossman, Jeff Erikson, & Neeyati Patel, Impacts of a Changing Environment on the Corporate Sector, *United Nations Environment Programme,* page 3 (2013). Used by permission of United Nations Environment Programme (UNEP).

TABLE 1.6	
"Green Shoots" By Market Sector	
Market Sector	**Opportunity**
Buildings and Construction	Demand for sustainable infrastructure, retrofits, materials sourcing, and skilled design and construction workforce create opportunities for increased building value and reputational benefits.
Chemicals	Demand for sustainable chemical inputs into technology, water treatment, and agricultural products, and phase-out of restricted chemicals create opportunities for green chemistry and reputational benefits.
Resource Extraction	Demand for cleaner fuel sources, sustainable material inputs into industrial processes, and recycling programs to reduce e-waste creates opportunities for exploration and production, carbon capture and sequestration, and create closed-loop supply chains.
Finance	Increased demand for property insurance coverage against extreme weather events creates markets for insurance products that encourage sustainable building design. Financial instruments for major environmental solutions projects will allow large-scale sustainable commercial development.
Food and Beverage	Demand for climate-resilient food supplies creates opportunities for geographically new food supply chains. Demand for organic and sustainable agricultural products creates new markets for growers.
Healthcare	Increase in health problems resulting from pollution and climate change creates new markets for medical products that do not require water or climate-controlled storage.
Information and Communication Technology	The ability to capture and process environmental performance data creates opportunities for IT companies to market products that use data analytics to optimize environmental performance. IT services may displace physical processes, resulting in decreased impacts.
Tourism	Environmental changes impact the desirability of tourist destinations, and increasing demand for eco- and agro-tourism creates local partnership opportunities for the tourism industry.
Transportation	Demand from business customers for cleaner transport options and costs of logistics create opportunities for innovation in the logistics sector. Increasingly stringent fuel economy standards for personal vehicles will also drive innovation in this sector.
Electric Power	Demand for low-carbon powered indoor climate control and renewable electricity generation creates opportunities for smart-grid technology, energy storage products, and energy efficiency services.

Source: Dave Grossman, Jeff Erikson, & Neeyati Patel, Impacts of a Changing Environment on the Corporate Sector, *United Nations Environment Programme*, pages 4–5 (2013). Used by permission of United Nations Environment Programme (UNEP).

motivates the book by ending with a discussion of the business case for sustainability and the role of innovation in addressing the risks and opportunities of sustainability.

Chapter 2: Perspectives explores frameworks for sustainable business, organized under the rubric of environmental, social, and economic perspectives. From biomimicry to stakeholder theory and ecosystem services, this chapter provides key concepts and frameworks that inform subsequent chapters.

Chapter 3: Leadership, Change Management, and Corporate Governance provides examples of the powerful impact companies can have in society when they pursue corporate sustainability. A commitment to sustainability from leaders, and buy-in from employees, is essential to manage the transition from a traditional to a sustainable enterprise. This chapter illustrates how sustainability leadership is distinct in its style, methods, incentives, and goals from traditional leadership. Mechanisms of corporate governance, from the structure of the Board of Directors to Executive Sustainability Committees and shareholder resolutions, can play a large part in shaping organizational sustainability.

Part II: Accountability includes Chapters 4–6, unified by the theme of accountability for the adverse social, economic, and environmental impacts of business.

Chapter 4: Legal Frameworks explains the many ways in which law permeates the business environment, providing outer boundaries for corporate conduct across a wide range of functional areas. From international law to local land use regulations, this chapter provides a comprehensive introduction to the role of law in making the business case for sustainability. Laws provide normative guidance for consumer product design, industrial process design, and supply chain management. Legal frameworks typically aim to reduce risk by instilling accountability.

Chapter 5: Metrics, Tools, and Reporting: The Role of Finance and Accounting provides methods for measuring the social, economic, and environmental impacts of business, and the reporting standards to promote transparency. This chapter introduces helpful analytical tools (such as life-cycle assessment) to enable objective, comprehensive impact analysis to support sustainability-related business decisions. Emphasis is placed on environmental performance metrics and the use of information to drive strategic decisions. Under certain conditions, reporting sustainable performance is a legal duty.

Chapter 6: Risk Management identifies sources of business risk, with emphasis on water resources and climate change; explains the risk elements of exposure and vulnerability; and introduces strategies for reducing risk through organizational resilience. Using the enterprise risk management continuum aligns risk management practice with a company's over-arching sustainability strategy.

Part III: Implementation includes Chapters 7–9, and integrates sustainable principles and practices into the core functional areas of business—marketing, supply chain management, and operations.

Chapter 7: Marketing explains how the marketing function is responsible for driving innovation and capturing the value created by sustainability initiatives. Departures from traditional marketing strategy are explored. The chapter lays out ethical marketing guidelines specifically related to environmental attributes of consumer products. This chapter concludes with a discussion of the role of third-party certification.

Chapter 8: Supply Chain Management addresses the centrality of the supply chain to the environmental and social impacts of business, from carbon emissions to human trafficking. This chapter explores the many opportunities to promote sustainability within supply chain management, from product sourcing decisions to transportation modality.

Chapter 9: Operations Management discusses issues such as product and process design, production methods, and inventory management. Companies can use sustainable operations to improve social and environmental performance by creating new products and improving the way facilities are managed.

Key Terms

sustainable economic development 4	principle of balance 4	Global Living Planet Index 7	internalize 13
sustainable business 4	principle of stewardship 5	negative externality 12	Rio+20 Summit on Sustainability 16
	triple-bottom-line 5		blue ocean strategy 24
	Natural capital 7		

Discussion Questions

1. When did you first learn about sustainability? What was your impression?

2. Do you agree with the idea that businesses have social responsibilities?

3. Have you ever worked for a company that promotes sustainability?

CASE 1

BMW Pioneers Sustainable Automotive Technology[60]

Bavarian Motor Works Auto Group (BMW Group) is a German automobile, motorcycle and engine manufacturing company incorporated in Munich, Bavaria, Germany. The company publishes a Sustainability Value Report every 2 years to inform its stakeholders in a transparent manner about the company's sustainability strategies and how the company intends to incorporate them in the future. For 6 consecutive years, the Dow Jones Index has named BMW as the world's most sustainable automotive company.

BMW uses self-regulation to promote sustainability. For instance, BMW complies with all ten principles of the Global Impact and Cleaner Production program under the United Nations Environment Programme. The company was awarded a Green Power Leadership Award by the U.S. Environmental Protection Agency for using landfill gas to power operations at one of its manufacturing plants. BMW continuously strives to manufacture more fuel-efficient automobiles by pioneering electric and hybrid power engines. The BMW group set voluntary environmental global targets for 2020 in the areas of production, products, and value chain:

- Reduction of resource consumption (water, energy, waste, solvents) per vehicle produced by 45% (base year 2006).

- Reduction of product CO_2 emissions by 50% (base year 1995).

- Leading in renewable energy usage in production and value chain.

- Pioneer in innovative mobility services.

The company benefits from the sustainable initiatives by making them a part of its strategy and continuously informing stakeholders about their progress through annual reporting. BMW sales reached a record high in March 2012 in part as a result of its sustainability leadership.

Recently, BMW launched a new product line, the company's first electric vehicle, the *BMW i*. BMW is attempting to establish a corporate profile "that is defined by renewable resources and innovative means of production that have the least possible impact on the environment."[61]

The engineers at BMW developed an engine that eliminated all tailpipe-emissions common to vehicles, such as carcinogenic volatile organic compounds, smog, and greenhouse gases. The *BMW i* frame is constructed using Carbon Fiber Reinforced Plastic (CFRP) as a substitute for steel, which is as strong but uses half the weight. The lighter the weight, the further the vehicle can travel with less fuel. CFRP technology allowed BMW to "set new standards in both lightweight vehicle construction and safety."[62] BMW is spearheading this technology by becoming the first auto-maker to mass produce cars using CFRP. This innovative technology allows for sustainability innovation in the automotive sector, but it is also produced in a sustainable manner. An ultra-modern plant in Moses Lake, Washington, that produces CFRP is completely powered by renewable hydroelectric power.

Questions for Case 1

1. Using concepts from Section 1.2.1 of this chapter, what are the externalities typically associated with automobile manufacture and design that are avoided by BMW's product and production process innovations?

2. Using concepts from Section 1.4 of this chapter, spell out the business case for an automobile company to pursue sustainable innovation. What would be the primary drivers of innovation? What would be the benefits to the company?

CASE 2　# Greening the Game of Golf

Dixon Golf is the world's first high-performance, environmentally friendly golf ball manufacturer. Based in Tempe, Arizona, the company has been around since 2008, and in 2012 Dixon Golf became the fastest-growing company in the golf industry, hiring 250 people and donating $400,000 to charities.[63] In fact, 10% of all Dixon Golf profits are donated to charity. According to Dixon Golf CEO William Carey, "Nothing makes us more proud than our ability to support the three things that matter to us most: the environment, the economy and charities. We had this idea of saving the world one golf ball at a time, and it has really blossomed."[64]

Dixon Golf makes every effort to use materials from recycled or renewable sources. Their golf balls are both high-performance (they conform to USGA standards) and 100% recyclable. Dixon Golf hats are made from recycled water bottles, shirts are made from renewable bamboo, product packaging is made from recycled paper and recycled styrene, the office complex is powered by solar panels, and their manufacturing plant emits less air pollutants and uses less water than similar facilities.

In addition to giving to charities, Dixon is also trying to clean up golf's impact on the environment. Dixon offers a golf ball recycling program through its retail locations that gives golfers credit for returning their old golf balls. Approximately 300 million golf balls, many made from synthetic rubbers and plastics, are lost around golf courses every year, resulting from wayward swings that find a water hazard or similarly irretrievable lie. The typical golf ball will take anywhere from 50 to 500 years to biodegrade.

Entrepreneurs are finding ways to make a profit from cleaning up the environmental impacts of golf. Lost-golf-ball-retrieval companies are sprouting up, finding and reclaiming millions of golf balls every week. Gary Shienfield founded Knetgolf.com, a Toronto-based company that sold 20 million reclaimed golf balls in 2010.[65] According to Shienfield, "In the recession, people are still playing golf, but they're not so quick to pay $40 for a dozen new, high-end golf balls. Instead, they come to us on the Internet for that ball at $20 a dozen. They are preowned golf balls. They probably bought a preowned BMW, too."[66]

Shienfield has partnerships with 2,200 golf courses to recover lost balls and has seen recent sales bolstered by customers in India, Vietnam, and Southeast Asia, where the golf industry is growing rapidly and customers are looking for brand name golf balls at a good value.

Questions for Case 2

1. Describe the sustainability commitment of Dixon Golf using the concepts from Section 1.3 of this chapter.

2. Using concepts from Section 1.4 of this chapter, what environmental changes have implications for the golf industry? What kinds of sustainable innovations could be motivated by these changes?

Further Research

Check out "The Business Logic of Sustainability," a TED-Talk by Ray Anderson, former CEO of Interface Carpet. Anderson was a leader in sustainable business before his death in 2011. His legacy will endure for his personal transformation on the subject of corporate responsibility for environmental impacts, and making the business case for sustainability.

For a short documentary-advocacy video explaining the global overfishing problem, see the YouTube video "Ending Overfishing."

A classic book on the business case for sustainability is Daniel C. Esty & Andrew Winston's *Green to Gold: How Smart Companies Use Environmental Strategy to Innovate, Create Value, and Build Competitive Advantage* (John Wiley & Sons, Inc., 2009).

The non-profit Carbon Disclosure Project website hosts a series of video interviews with professionals at businesses from a variety of sectors, explaining their company's climate change strategy.

Harvard Business Review Case: Michael Valente, PepsiCo's Turning Point: Establishing a Role in a Sustainable Society, Prod. #: W11097-PDF-ENG (April 20, 2011).

Endnotes

[1] Ram Nidumolu, C.K. Prahalad & M.R. Rangaswami, Why Sustainability Is Now the Key Driver of Innovation, *Harvard Business Review* (September 2009).

[2] Knut Haanaes, David Arthur, Balu Balagopal, Ming Teck Kong, Martin Reeves, Ingrid Velken, Michael S. Hopkins, & Nina Kruschwitz, Sustainability: The 'Embracers' Seize Advantage, *MIT Sloan Review* (February 10, 2011).

[3] *ibid.*

[4] *ibid.*

[5] *ibid.*

[6] United Nations World Commission on the Environment and Development, *Our Common Future*, 43 (1987). This document is commonly known as the "Brundtland Report" after Norwegian Prime Minister Gro Harlem Brundtland, who led the Commission.

[7] J. Elkington, *Cannibals with Forks: the Triple Bottom Line of 21st Century Business, Capstone*, 1997.

[8] *Embedding Sustainability in SMEs*, The Association of Chartered Certified Accountants, page 3 (November 2012).

[9] *ibid.*

[10] *ibid.*

[11] See, for instance, the U.S. Small Business Administration website on Sustainable Business Practices, available at http://www.sba.gov/category/navigation-structure/sustainable-business-practices.

[12] For examples, see *Sustainability Challenges 2013*, Network for Business Sustainability (NBS) (2013), available at http://nbs.net/wp-content/uploads/NBS-SME-Challenges-2013.pdf.

[13] Darrell Rigby and Barbara Bilodeau, *Management Tools & Trends 2013*, page 1, (Bain & Company, 2013).

[14] *Six Growing Trends in Corporate Sustainability*, An Ernst & Young survey in cooperation with GreenBiz Group, page 22 (2011).

[15] John Alterman & Michael Dziuban, *Clear Gold: Water as a Strategic Resource in the Middle East*, v (2010); Nick Langton & Sagar Prasai, *Will Conflicts over Water Scarcity Shape South Asia's Future?*, Vol. 2 Issue 1 CSIS Issue Perspective (2012).

[16] *Living Planet Report 2012: Biodiversity, Biocapacity, and Better Choices*, WWF, page 9 (2012).

[17] L. Blomqvist, B.W. Brook, E.C. Ellis, P.M. Kareiva, T. Nordhaus, et al., *The Ecological Footprint Remains a Misleading Metric of Global Sustainability*, 11(11) PLoS Biol e1001702 (2013) (concluding that we would be better off developing a more ecological and ecosystem process framework to capture the impacts humans currently have on the planet's natural systems).

[18] W.E. Rees & M. Wackernagel, *The Shoe Fits, But the Footprint is Larger than Earth*, 11(11) PLoS Biol e1001701 (2013).

[19] *See generally* Erica Gies, "Interface Founder Ray Anderson Leaves Legacy of Sustainability Success," *Forbes*, accessed August 10, 2011, available at http://www.forbes.com/sites/erica-gies/2011/08/10/interface-founder-ray-anderson-leaves-legacy-of-sustainability-success/.

[20] Ray Anderson (with Robin White), *Confessions of a Radical Industrialist: Profits, People, Purpose—Doing Business by Respecting the Earth* (St. Martin's Press, 2009).

[21] *ibid.*

[22] David A. Lubin and Daniel C. Esty, "The Sustainability Imperative," *Harvard Business Review* (May 2010), last accessed April 29, 2014, available at http://hbr.org/2010/05/the-sustainability-imperative/ar/1.

[23] *In Search of Revolutionary Responsibility: A Letter from Co-Founder Jeffry Hollender*, Seventh Generation Corporate Consciousness Report 2.0, available at http://www.7genreport.com/introduction/.

24 Daniel Pauly, 5 EASY PIECES: HOW FISHING IMPACTS MARINE ECOSYSTEMS (Island Press, 2010).

25 The Magna Carta (1215 A.D.). Available at http://www.archives .gov/exhibits/featured_documents/magna_carta/

26 *FAO in the 21st Century: Ensuring Food Security in a Changing World*, Food and Agriculture Organization for the United Nations, page xx (Rome, 2011).

27 *FAO in the 21st Century: Ensuring Food Security in a Changing World*, Food and Agriculture Organization for the United Nations, page xx (Rome, 2011).

28 *FAO in the 21st Century: Ensuring Food Security in a Changing World*, Food and Agriculture Organization for the United Nations, page 169 (Rome, 2011).

29 *FAO in the 21st Century: Ensuring Food Security in a Changing World*, Food and Agriculture Organization for the United Nations, page 167 (Rome, 2011).

30 E. Benjamin Skinner, *The Cruelest Catch: In the Waters Off New Zealand, Scores of Indentured Workers are Trawling for Seafood—And You May be Buying It*, Bloomberg BusinessWeek, 70–76 (Feb 27– March 4, 2012).

31 "Idea: Triple Bottom Line," *The Economist*, Nov. 17th, 2009.

32 *Natural Capital At Risk: The Top 100 Externalities of Business*, The Economics of Ecosystems and Biodiversity Business Coalition (2013).

33 *ibid.*

34 *ibid.*

35 *ibid.*

36 *ibid.*

37 Deloitte, *Drivers of Long-Term Business Value: Stakeholders, Stats, and Strategies*, page 7 (2012). Source: Institutional Shareholder Services, a division of MSCI, Inc., Deloitte analysis.

38 Ion Bogdan Vasi and Brayden King, "Social Movements, Risk Perceptions, and Economic Outcomes: The Effect of Primary and Secondary Stakeholder Activism on Firms' Perceived Environmental Risk and Financial Performance," Vol. 77 No. 4 *American Sociological Review* 573–596 (2012).

39 *Embedding Sustainability in SMEs*, ACCA Global Forum for SMEs, Page 4 (November 2012).

40 Deloitte, *Drivers of Long-Term Business Value: Stakeholders, Stats, and Strategies*, page 7 (2012). Source: World Federation of Exchanges, Deloitte analysis.

41 Deloitte, *Drivers of Long-Term Business Value: Stakeholders, Stats, and Strategies*, page 7 (2012). Source: World Federation of Exchanges, Deloitte analysis.

42 KPMG, *Business Perspectives on Sustainable Growth: Preparing for Rio + 20 Summit Recap*, 16 (2012).

43 Statoil, *Annual Report: Sustainability Report* (2012).

44 *PGA TOUR Reaches $2 Billion in Charitable Giving*, January 22, 2014, available at http://together.pgatour.com/stories/2014/january/pga-tour-announces-2-billion.html.

45 Judd F. Sneirson, "Green Is Good: Sustainability, Profitability, and a New Paradigm for Corporate Governance," 94 *Iowa Law Review* 993–994 (2009).

46 Coloplast, *Corporate Responsibility Report 2011/2012* (2012).

47 Roberto Goizueta, *Annual Report of the Coca-Cola Corporation* (1996).

48 Florida & Davison (2001).

49 Alberti et al. (2000).

50 Small Business Sustainability Report: The Big Green Opportunity for Small Business in the U.S., Green America, Association for Enterprise Opportunity, and Ecoventures International, pages 22–31 (2013).

51 *U.S. Organic Industry Survey Overview,* (Organic Trade Association, (2012).

52 Fair Trade USA 2011 Almanac.

53 *U.S. Organic Industry Survey Overview. (Organic Trade Association, 2012).*

54 McGraw-Hill Construction Green Outlook (2012)

55 Small Business Sustainability Report: The Big Green Opportunity for Small Business in the U.S., Green America, Association for Enterprise Opportunity, and Ecoventures International, page 28 (2013).

56 *Annual Energy Outlook 2012* (and 2013), U.S. Energy Information Administration, available at www.eia.gov.

57 *U.S HEV Sales by Model*, Alternative Fuels and Advanced Vehicle Data Center (U.S. Department of Energy).

58 *U.S. Sales or Deliveries of New Aircraft, Vehicles, Vessels, and Other Conveyances,* U.S. Bureau of Transportation Statistics (U.S. Department of Transportation).

59 Ten Key Points About Blue Ocean Strategy, last accessed April 29, 2014 , available at http://www.blueoceanstrategy.com/10-key-points-about-blue-ocean-strategy/.

60 See *Adding Value: Sustainable Value Report*, BMW (2012).

61 BMWi, BMW North America (2013), available at http://www.bmwusa.com/standard/content/vehicles/2014/bmwi/bmwi.aspx#intro.

62 *ibid.*

63 See Dixon Golf, Company Information website, last accessed April 29, 2014, available at http://www.dixongolf.com/Company/CompanyInfo/tabid/389/Default.aspx.

64 *ibid.*

65 Bill Pennington, *The Burden and Boon of Lost Golf Balls*, The New York Times Golf Blog (May 2, 2010).

66 *ibid.*

CHAPTER 2

Perspectives

ECOSYSTEM SERVICES

Ecosystems provide humans with a wide range of valuable, even vital, benefits, called ecosystem services. **Ecosystem services** are the benefits that humans realize because of healthy ecosystems, including productive yields, buffers against natural disasters, and biological filtration of air and water. Ecosystem services exemplify the profound interdependence of the human population on natural resources. The benefits of ecosystem services can be calculated in terms of monetary value, which exemplifies the interconnection between natural resources and wealth.

Ecosystem services can be categorized as provisioning (they produce food supplies, fiber materials, genetic resources, biochemicals, and clean water), regulating (they stabilize climate, air quality, water quantity and quality, erosion, disease, pests, and natural hazards), supporting (they circulate nutrient cycles and pollinate crops) and cultural (they provide spiritual and religious values, aesthetic values, and recreational or ecotourism benefits).

In 2005, a global coalition of United Nations organizations, governments, NGOs, academics, businesses, and indigenous peoples commissioned the first ever global assessment of ecosystem services, called the Millennium Ecosystem Assessment, to enable us to make more responsible decisions about the stewardship of natural resources and to understand the many ways in which humans depend on—as well as interfere with—natural systems. The Millennium Assessment Reports provide a breakthrough scientific appraisal of the condition and trends of the planet's ecosystems and the services they provide civilization, including the basis in scientific fact for conserving

> *"Any vision of sustainable development fit for the 21st century must recognize that eradicating poverty and achieving social justice is inextricably linked to ensuring ecological stability and renewal."*
>
> —*Oxfam*, **A SAFE AND JUST SPACE FOR HUMANITY (2012)**

LEARNING OBJECTIVES

After completing this chapter, you should be able to:

1. Explain corporate social responsibility, stakeholder theory, and the business consensus around ecosystem services.
2. Explain the Environmental Kuznets Curve and critique it.
3. Describe environmental perspectives on sustainability, including regenerative capacity and biomimicry.
4. Discuss ethical conflicts, environmental ethics, and environmental justice.
5. Explain the role of Natural Capital Accounting in preserving and conserving natural resources.

Ecosystem Services The benefits that humans realize because of healthy ecosystems, including productive yields, buffers against natural disasters, and biological filtration of air and water.

them and using them sustainably. The Millennium Ecosystem Assessment reached several conclusions:[1]

- Ecosystem services provide the conditions for human existence. A growing human population has led to dramatic changes to ecosystems in all parts of the world.
- While exploiting natural resources improves the lives of billions of humans, over-exploitation weakens nature's capacity to provide those very services.
- The worst of all threats to ecosystem services are the depletion of the world's fish stocks in seas and oceans, the diminishing availability of water supplies in arid regions, and the disruption of ecosystems by climate change and nutrient pollution.
- The activities of mankind have led to massive plant and animal species extinctions; the loss of ecosystem services from pollution, degradation, and other human activities exacerbates poverty, hunger, and disease.
- The pressures faced by ecosystems throughout the world will continue to mount without substantial changes in human attitudes and behavior.
- Until ecosystem services are ascribed some sort of price due to their value and limited availability, extant technology capable of reducing human impacts on ecosystems will not be adequately deployed. Expenses will not be justified to protect ecosystem services that are erroneously perceived as free and limitless.

The implications of these conclusions about the state of global ecosystem services for business leadership are significant.[2] The private sector must take decisive socially responsible acts, pioneering less wasteful methods, reducing consumption of water, energy, and raw materials, and innovating in process and product design to reduce pollution at the source. The private sector must do so in order to ensure that ecosystem services and raw materials upon which supply chains and operations depend, remain in existence. The situational awareness required to run a sustainable enterprise demands an understanding a variety of environmental, social, and economic perspectives.

2.1 Introduction: Perspectives on Sustainability

This chapter is intended to provide a fuller understanding the subject of this book by presenting perspectives from the three main focus areas of sustainable business: social, economic, and environmental. See Figure 2.1. This chapter provides a theoretical overview of descriptive and normative perspectives that have emerged from scholarship over the last two decades to address the various challenges posed by the sustainability megatrend.

Social perspectives look at how human beings ought to relate to one another (ethics) and the priority level that managers should give to societal interests external

FIGURE 2.1 Perspectives on Sustainability by Focus Area

to the business (corporate social responsibility). Economic perspectives look at whether the powerful role global businesses play in the economy is attended by responsibilities for their own conduct (corporate social responsibility), and the economic influences on a population's toleration for industrial pollution (environmental Kuznets curve). Environmental perspectives explain how to base materials sourcing decisions on environmental system conditions (biomimicry), and how human society is interdependent with natural systems (human ecology).

Sustainability theory is only increasing in depth and nuance as academic, investment institution, government, corporate, NGO, and non-profit interest in the subject continues to grow. This chapter provides managers a broader perspective for understanding and addressing sustainability.

2.2 Social Perspectives

This section provides insight into the social dimensions of sustainability, ranging from how human and environmental systems are interdependent, to the ways in which society self-regulates through laws and ethics, to the complexity of human interactions.

2.2.1 Stakeholder Engagement

Stakeholder theory suggests that businesses can be successful only if they create value for customers, suppliers, employees, communities, and financiers. The theory prescribes that managers cannot consider the interests of these stakeholders in isolation, but rather must find ways to align corporate activities with maximizing the interest of all stakeholders.

According to stakeholder theory, it is a mistake to focus solely on financier interests in strategic business decisions because other critical value sources will be forfeited, and liabilities may be incurred. See Table 2.1.

By satisfying customer expectations, forming mutually beneficial collaborative relationships with suppliers, fostering the development of employees, and giving back to the community in which the business operates, a company will be much more likely to realize a long-term profit, thereby proving their worth to financiers.

> **Stakeholder Theory** Theory contending that business success requires creating value for customers, suppliers, employees, communities, and financiers.

> **CROSS-LINKAGE**
>
> For an expanded discussion of stakeholders, see Chapter 3: Leadership, Change Management, and Corporate Governance.

TABLE 2.1

The Costs of Neglecting Stakeholders

Stakeholder	Issue	Impact on Business
Customers	Products and services fail to satisfy customer expectations.	Lost sales lead to less profit and additional marketing expenses to regain customer base.
Suppliers	Suppliers merely take orders but do not contribute to company growth or innovation.	Business remains in a holding pattern, and success is contingent upon supplier performance.
Employees	Employees are not fully engaged and do not contribute maximum productivity.	Low employee morale can lead to inefficiency, lack of commitment, employee turnover, and management problems.
Communities	Violation of local custom or applicable law, ignoring quality of life, failure to take responsibility.	Risk of incurring additional government regulation, loss of public trust, revocation of operating permits, fines and penalties.
Financiers	Failure to create profits for shareholders and investors.	Poor credit, inability to obtain future financing, and bankruptcy.

2.2.2 Corporate Social Responsibility

Corporate Social Responsibility A form of self-regulation that integrates into the business strategy a process for monitoring and managing corporate conduct relative to external stakeholders.

Corporate social responsibility (CSR) is a form of self-regulation that integrates monitoring of and accountability for corporate conduct into the business model. Emerging as a central theme in sustainability alongside the 1987 publication *Our Common Future* (the Brundtland Report), the idea that corporations owed certain duties to their employees, their customers, and the general public began to gain traction in public policy discussions.

Having a CSR policy means that a business ensures its activities are, at a minimum, consistent with applicable law, ethical principles, international norms, and ideally, promote value creation for stakeholders including beneficiaries of environmental integrity, consumers, employees, communities, and others affected by corporate conduct.

Apparel, electronic, and toy companies often outsource manufacturing to the lowest-cost country to keep production costs down. One of the trade-offs from such arrangements is the severely limited accountability over the factory labor conditions. In certain circumstances, the more the parent company looks into the matter, the more remote these practices become, intentionally removed far from the vigilant eye of watchdog groups and international norms. But where some aspects of CSR (such as engaging employees or monitoring suppliers) may be out of reach for some, Nike does have successful programs that benefit communities. One of Nike's initiatives is the "Reuse-A-Shoe" program. By collecting old athletic shoes of any type in order to process and recycle them, Nike reduces the amount of waste resulting from product disposal and provides inexpensive materials for the construction of basketball courts, running tracks, and playgrounds.

The scope of integration of CSR into a business depends upon the nature of the business as well as having a long-term vision. CSR plans should be employed over

"Our initiatives have proven that corporate responsibility doesn't need to be an add-on, but instead can be a powerful competitive advantage. We have saved money by reducing energy costs and greenhouse gas emissions and are creating top line growth by meeting consumers' growing desire for eco-friendly products."

Sustainable business is smart business that decreases costs and increases revenue. "Timberland's corporate responsibility leadership was one of the drivers in the company's acquisition by VF Corporation in 2011. When a $9 billion apparel and footwear powerhouse is attracted to a brand (in part) due to its innovative approach to sustainability, you know there's business value."

longer time horizons than routine tactical business decisions, as the benefits tend to take longer to realize than quarterly reporting would let on. There are at least four different "business cases" to be made on behalf of CSR: benefits to human resources, risk management, brand differentiation, and license to operate.

CSR and Human Resources. Having a CSR program can help a company attract and recruit the most competitive graduates who tend to inquire about these matters during interviews. CSR can also lead to higher rates of employee retention, which saves money by decreasing time and resources spent training employees due to high turnover rates, and which promotes greater productivity by providing employees with a sense of moral gratification from their work. Employees are more committed to their employer when the business promotes employee involvement in the community through volunteering, philanthropy, and community fundraising.

> **CSR and Human Resources**
> The benefits of CSR to human resources functions such as employee recruiting, retention, and promotion.

LEADERSHIP: Timberland, LLC. Engages Workers and Communities[5]

Timberland's commitment to social responsibility does not end at the factory walls. Community service is a central part of what it means to be a Timberland employee. Factory managers, workers, and members of the local community form partnerships to address the needs of the local community. For instance, one factory in India collaborated with the local community after an employee raised the concern over lack of access to clean drinking water within the region. The company partnered with a non-profit to monitor the water infrastructure project and based the installation on feedback from the local community, taking every opportunity along the way to integrate community feedback and add

value, such as ensuring the freshwater infrastructure was sited in appropriate locations and helping develop educational opportunities about the connection between clean water and human health. These social impact projects promote employee development, increased attraction and retention of quality workers, strengthened business partnerships, and reinforced goodwill with affected communities. To incentivize community service, Timberland provides full-time staff an annual benefit of up to 40 paid hours and part-time staff up to 20 paid hours for community service. In order to assist employees in using these hours, Timberland sponsors a global day of service to celebrate Earth Day.

Timberland relies on the input and concerns expressed by factory workers to engage and empower them and their communities. Employee feedback plays a meaningful role in the Timberland's factory working conditions as well as in the selection of social impact causes that the company champions. Workers are at the heart of Timberland's assessment and remediation process and are provided with the conditions for empowerment that allow them to provide meaningful input into the management process.[4] All factory workers are formally trained on their rights and responsibilities and are provided with avenues for raising and resolving any negative issues that might come up in the course of employment. Workers are also members of committees that are set up to conduct ongoing factory assessments, providing a sense of ownership over a factory's performance unlike the experience of many factory workers who have a limited role in big-picture decisions. These practices improve employee morale, increase retention, lower absenteeism, and increase the quality and productivity of labor.

CSR and Risk Management
The benefits of CSR to risk management functions such as maintaining corporate ethos and avoiding risks.

CSR and Risk Management. CSR assists in risk management by building a bona fide culture within the company of "doing right by stakeholders" without external mandates from government. CSR promotes the reputation of the firm, which can take quite some time to develop, and mitigates the risk of tarnishing that hard-earned reputation by preempting corruption, environmental disasters, or bad press from incidental scandals. While there is a legitimately strong role for government in regulating business, any effort that reduces unwanted attention from regulators, courts, media, and government officials is generally good for business as bad press and compliance costs can be avoided.

CSR and Brand Differentiation
The benefits of CSR to brand differentiation such as creating a unique sales proposition.

CSR and Brand Differentiation. When competing for customers in a crowded marketplace, it is imperative for businesses to have a unique selling proposition that separates their product or service from the pack. Taking ethical issues seriously encourages customer loyalty as many customers are eager to reward value-oriented companies rather than what would be perceived as the cutthroat competition that has little regard for such efforts.

CSR and Social License to Operate The role of CSR in meeting informal requirements of the community in which business activities take place.

CSR and Social License to Operate. **Social license to operate** in this context means the informal requirements placed upon a company by the community in a given location, over and above legal requirements for doing business. The social expectations on how a company performs make up its social license to operate: even if a manufacturing plant has a legal permit to operate, if the surrounding community protests the noxious fumes emitted by the plant, the company may not have a social license to operate.

Substantial voluntary steps to promote employee health and safety, workforce diversity, and environmental conscientiousness provide companies with a license to operate in a given area by assuring governments and consumers alike, that the business is an upstanding corporate citizen. Companies that maintain good standing with the communities in which they do business have earned trust to do things right and have demonstrated their reliability in fixing problems when they arise. These companies are poised to avoid interference from regulators or boycotts when accidents happen. When a company meets or exceeds the expectations of the communities affected by corporate activities, it has maintained social license to operate.

ETHICAL DECISIONS: Nike Deals with Risks from Suppliers' Labor Practices[6]

Nike is an Oregon, USA-based athletic apparel and sports equipment company that has outsourced manufacturing to factories in 45 countries outside the United States, particularly in developing countries including India, Vietnam, Thailand, China, Vietnam, Pakistan, Philippines, Malaysia and Indonesia. At such distances and given the markedly distinct social and economic conditions of these countries when compared to the home base, problems with implementing CSR at the factories across the globe have plagued the company. Over a decade ago, Nike was widely criticized for reliance on sweatshops and child labor practices on the part of their suppliers of products bearing the signature "swoosh" logo in developing countries. In 2005 Nike responded to this criticism by becoming the first major apparel company to disclose the names and locations of the plants where their products are manufactured, even while admitting to physically and verbally abusive conditions on the part of their suppliers. Almost two of every three factories making Converse products (168 across the globe) failed to comply with Nike's own standards for contract manufacturers; twelve factories are in the most troubling category because they impose illegally long work hours or deny Nike inspectors access to the facility; almost 100 factories have made no progress on issues such as the verbal harassment of, or paying less than minimum wage to, employees.

The company has since taken steps to improve conditions at its 1,000 overseas factories. However, the risks of poor labor practices of overseas suppliers has not been completely addressed. Nike took over Converse five years ago, and has run into legacy problems. In 2011, Nike made inquiry and found workers at two Converse factories were subjected to "serious and egregious" physical and verbal abuse, including the punishment of forcing workers to stand in the sun, reported Hannah Jones, a Nike executive who oversees the company's efforts to improve working conditions. She said, "We do see other issues of that similar nature coming up across the supply chain but not on a frequent level. We see issues of working conditions on a less egregious nature across the board." Nike contends these lapses in social responsibility in their global supply chain are difficult to avoid because of pre-existing licenses for the production of Converse goods. These contractual arrangements prohibit the parent company from inspecting factories or applying Nike's code of conduct to operations there. Further, monitoring and oversight is problematic because some of the Converse license holders use subcontractors to perform production, so the factories where the goods are manufactured are not accessible to Nike inspectors.

LEADERSHIP: Seventh Generation Takes CSR to the Next Level[7]

Seventh Generation, the sustainability-driven household cleaning product company, is striving to establish "a new brand of ethical and sustainable corporate behavior … whose reach is great enough to materially address those imperatives that an overburdened Earth and a dysfunctional economic system have placed upon us." Promoting a revolutionary sense of corporate responsibility will require the company to create "new ways of thinking and operating that allow us to resolve environmental challenges, enhance the living systems upon which we depend, and improve the circumstances of our staff, stakeholders, and communities, all while producing the financial rewards that allow this work to continue."

GLOBAL INSIGHT: Home Depot Regains Social License to Operate

Home Depot was once the world's largest retailer of old growth wood products sourced from endangered forests in tropical parts of the world. From 2000 until 2002, environmental groups fought Home Depot expansion plans at local city council meetings, coordinated a hard-hitting national ad campaign, and organized demonstrations at several hundred Home Depot stores across the United States, Canada, and Chile. After suffering the brunt of a two-year grass-roots campaign, one of the leading do-it-yourself supply retailers announced that the company would end sales of wood from endangered areas by the end of 2002. By doing so they ended the reason for protests and earned the license to operate in communities where opposition to unsustainable environmental sourcing decisions was strong. Now Home Depot incorporates social and environmental responsibility into supplier guidelines.[8]

Human Rights The inherent dignity of all human beings deserving respect, enshrined in international treaties.

2.2.3 **Human Rights**

One major theme in sustainability is the newfound sense of social responsibility that companies have for human rights. This norm means that companies must respect the dignity of consumers of their products and services, the health of populations affected by their operations and supply chains, and the physical safety and individuality of their employees. Where a company's impacts are not readily subject to mitigation, some may opt for philanthropic efforts aimed at remedying poverty. One motivation behind these efforts is that poverty is an underlying cause of other social maladies such as disease and crime—so solving economic woes can promote a variety of social goals. Helping families escape from the vicious cycle of debt and need ultimately promotes the health of the overall society by enabling more individuals to thrive and achieve their creative potential. Respecting human rights, and helping people achieve their human potential as rational, creative, caring beings is a goal of social sustainability.

CROSS-LINKAGE

For more on human rights protections, see Chapter 8: Supply Chain Management.

The United Nations publishes Millennium Development Goals that tie sustainability to human rights. The UN calls for sustainable development, defined as development that meets the needs of the present without compromising the ability of future generations to meet their own needs. The UN's funding for social impact investments in developing nations is an attempt to achieve sustainability by releasing millions of people from poverty while simultaneously preserving precious natural resources for future populations. The key here is to increase per capita income to satisfy the basic needs of the present population without at the same time creating the scale effect that leads to increased rates of environmental degradation at the expense of future generations.

2.2.4 **Laws and Regulations**

The laws with which businesses must comply vary from nation to nation. In general, there are two kinds of laws relevant to sustainability: laws governing how people are treated and laws governing how the environment is treated. The first kind controls labor practices that go on inside a factory, or employee discrimination within an office. The second kind regulates how much and what kind of pollutants a company is allowed to emit into the air, water, and soil, and what kind of land uses are permissible in which locations. Usually, laws and regulations set a minimum floor for corporate performance, below which transgressors are subject to punishment by fine or license revocation. Other legal regimes govern the process of corporate decision-making to ensure accountability between control of the company and ownership of the company. Other legal regimes govern how the business impacts complete strangers, as is the case with tort law for accidents leading to harm.

Legal requirements often differ from country to country, as explained in the following section on regulatory arbitrage. Further, large companies and trade organizations representing SMEs within a given industry can exert pressures through lobbying of government officials in order to promote legal regimes that are more comfortable for the company while coming at the expense of consumer safety or environmental protection.

CROSS-LINKAGE

For an extended discussion of the role of law in sustainable business, see Chapter 4: Legal Frameworks.

2.2.5 Ethics and Environmental Justice

Sources of Ethical Conflict In addition to differences in the legal regimes that prevail from nation to nation, there are also distinct ethical guidelines at play when a company crosses borders. Specifically, there are at least three forms of ethical conflict: conflicts of relative development, conflicts of cultural tradition, and cross-country ethical dilemmas.

Conflicts of Relative Development. Conflicts of relative development arise when there are major differences between the legal standards of the host country and the standards of a corporation. Because the host nation may have less economic development and less mature legal institutions than the domiciliary country of the multinational, conflicts may arise between international codes of conduct set in more developed nations and the actual conditions on the ground in the less developed host nation. These include issues such as investment, wages, working hours, health care, and conformity with government regulations.

Conflicts of relative development can compromise the health of communities and employees in less developed nations.

Conflicts of Relative Development Conflicts arising from differences in legal standards of the host country and the standards of the foreign corporation caused by differences in economic development.

Conflicts of Cultural Tradition. These ethical conflicts arise when a company moves into a new territory where local customs are well-established and behaviors that are linked closely with the local setting come as a surprise to the newly-arrived corporation. What is acceptable within the locality may be unacceptable to the culture of the corporation and vice versa.

Cross-Country Ethical Dilemmas. These conflicts occur when practices that are categorized in one country as ethical (such as bribing a government official) are unequivocally unethical in another country where the same company does business. In these situations, the decision-maker is backed into a moral quandary: is it acceptable to provide gifts to government officials in order to convince them to give the business a permit to operate? In one country the answer may be no, in another, yes.

Conflicts of Cultural Tradition Where local customs conflict with the attitudes and expectations of a newly arriving corporation.

Cross-Country Ethical Dilemmas Where a company does business in two countries with conflicting ethical standards.

Anthropocentrism Perspective in environmental ethics holding that only human beings are morally significant.

Biocentrism Perspective in environmental ethics holding that protecting nature is necessary because all forms of life have intrinsic value; they are valuable in and of themselves.

Environmental Ethics There are several varieties of environmental ethics that take different assumptions for granted and are motivated by distinct philosophical rationales for preserving the environment. All schools of thought see humans and the environment as part of an interconnected system. The tension in environmental ethics lies with the axiomatic difference between **anthropocentrism** and **biocentrism**.

Anthropocentrism is the belief that protecting nature is necessary only because other forms of life are valuable to humans, not because they possess some inherent value. Since the environment is crucial for human well-being and survival, humans have merely an indirect duty toward the environment, that is, a duty derived from the self-interest of present and future generations. This is the most common foundation for environmental ethics: we must treat nature with respect because human welfare depends upon continued access to ecosystem services.

The classic definition of sustainable development is inherently anthropocentric: development that meets the needs of the present without compromising the ability of future generations to meet their own needs. Sustainable development demands intergenerational justice, i.e., the appraisal of contemporary human actions according to how they impact future peoples' ability to meet basic needs. Under this view, at no point is social responsibility driven by the welfare of plants, nonetheless, plants are protected because they are useful to people.

In contrast to anthropocentrism, *biocentrism* is the tenet that every being exists with intrinsic moral value in a unified, interdependent living system. The ethical obligation for humans is to protect the right of living creatures to survive and mature.

Views within the biocentrism camp include deep ecology, systems view, and moderate biocentrism.[9] *Deep ecology* is based in biological similarities between life forms, and that a "kinship" exists between all living beings. *Systems view* is the belief that all life depends upon sufficient inputs of resources and sufficiently limited amounts of outputs in terms of waste. *Moderate biocentricism* is the belief that nature is valuable not based on sciences such as biology (as with deep ecology), but on phenomenology considered everyday experiences, such as aesthetic perceptions and creative communication about sustainable ways of living. Moderate biocentrism promotes the protection of a biologically richer natural system, not only for its intrinsic or instrumental value, but for its cultural and communicative content.

Sustainable development can also be expressed in terms of biocentrism: all economic activity and all cultural norms are subsumed and embedded in a global ecosphere that places boundaries and limitations on both. According to this biocentric view, social and economic systems are ancillary to the environmental systems upon which both depend. This view is more popular among environmental activists and non-profit organizations that play a corrective role in policy-making by giving voice to environmental stakeholders such as ecosystems and endangered species.

Environmental Justice
Providing meaningful involvement in the environmental decision-making affecting low-income and minority communities, and addressing disproportionate burdens of environmental harm.

Environmental Justice Often the adverse consequences of industrial and commercial activity accumulate where low-income and minority communities call home. **Environmental justice** communities are those who bear a disproportionate burden of environmental harms and lack of meaningful involvement in the environmental decision-making affecting where they live, work, and play. For instance, the local government's decision to grant a permit to a company seeking to construct a landfill might not have included an assessment of the foreseeable effects on the neighboring low-income community, such as increased heavy truck traffic, noxious odors, and rodents that would be attracted to the area, generally degrading the quality of life for nearby residents.

In order to protect communities from environmental injustice, government agencies and private developers should collaborate with public-interest organizations in order to remain vigilant of the cumulative impacts associated with land use changes and permits to operate or construct new facilities. To the extent feasible, local communities should be given a voice in the environmental decision-making that affects them, even if they have no financial stake in the transaction. Environmental justice will be achieved only when everyone enjoys the same degree of protection from environmental and health hazards regardless of income, race, national origin, or color, as well as equal access to the development, implementation, and enforcement of environmental laws, regulations, and policies that ensure a healthy environment in which to live, learn, and work.[10]

2.3 Economic Perspectives

Topics of this section include opportunities and challenges posed by economic globalization; the economic model known as the Environmental Kuznets Curve and criticism of this model; the role of natural capital accounting in sustainable land use; and perspectives in sustainable engineering, such as industrial ecology.

2.3.1 Globalization and its Discontents

Globalization The term **globalization** originated in the 1980's and has different connotations depending on usage and context. The term is often used as a synonym for either the growing dominance of Western forms of political, economic, and cultural life (westernization); the spread of new information technologies (Internet Revolution); or the idea that humanity stands on the brink of becoming a unified community where major causes of national or cultural conflicts have been addressed (global integration).[11]

> **Globalization** The spread of "Western" political, economic, and cultural norms as the world's national and regional economies become integrated through information technology.

According to economic theorists, globalization typically has a distinctly positive connotation. According to the International Monetary Fund, globalization is an historical process driven by human innovation and technological progress that brings about the integration of previously separate economies through the accelerated movement of goods, services, and other forms of capital (such as labor or knowledge) across borders.[12] This acceleration is caused by the reduction of international transaction costs that facilitates the flow of trade, finance, and information. That said, globalization has its own downsides, specifically, globalization can cause significant adverse environmental and social impacts.

According to social theorists, globalization tends to be portrayed as a disruptive change: it has brought about fundamental changes in the spatial and temporal contours of social existence. Globalization has affected village markets, urban industries, and financial centers that for the last several centuries have defined economic structures, leading to profound implications for almost every aspect of human life.[13]

The globalization trend also carries with it opportunities for large companies to consolidate control over global markets.

Several decades of corporate mergers have created a league of multinationals that must deal with these challenges. As one company merges with another, it absorbs its physical capital, employees, and customers, eliminating competition and increasing the reach of the resulting company. These mergers also offer the competitive advantage of **economies of scale**, where marginal costs reduction is achieved by producing and marketing products that have identical ingredients, packaging and logos in large quantities. These economies of scale make it harder for SMEs to compete with large companies.

Economies of Scale Where marginal costs reduction is achieved by producing en masse.

Within the commodities, automobile, telecom, and food industries, several multibillion-dollar mergers have wiped competitors off the map and resulted in a few staggering giants of industry, where there were previously several companies that competed with one another on service, price, quality, and corporate ethos. The two trends—globalization of commerce and consolidation of assets—present challenges to small businesses attempting to compete on sustainable performance.

Challenges of Globalization What does it mean for a company to exercise corporate social responsibility in the era of globalization—where offices are opened in far reaches of the world; where advertising is done in multiple languages; where materials procurement, production processes, and waste disposal involve compliance with a wide variety of laws and customs? These questions are primarily relevant to companies operating in an international context, where the relevant community of stakeholders has expanded dramatically.

Multinational corporations operate in more than one country, and often take the business ethics, values, and strategies from the nation where the company was formed into their offices abroad. This can create problems on the ground in international outposts when the values, management styles, or strategies of the home country conflict with those of the new host country.

The consolidation of major companies and the resulting mega-multinationals pose three unique regulatory problems that have previously not been at issue in the context of corporate social responsibility: (1) the irrelevancy of the nation state where the identity of the host nation no longer matters; (2) regulatory arbitrage where multinationals move operations from nation to nation in a quest for the least stringent regulatory environment; and (3) the plantation production problem where far-flung suppliers employ laborers in harsh working conditions.[14]

Although these problems benefit the largest of companies, when combined with advantages from economies of scale, they undermine competition over sustainable performance that would otherwise take place on a level regulatory playing field. Therefore, this section is relevant not only to the ecosystems and communities put at risk from under-regulated corporate conduct, but they also present economic challenges for SMEs striving for sustainability.

Irrelevance of the Nation State. Since scholarship began addressing the regulatory problems in the corporate context, caused by the separation of ownership and control, the common assumption has been that companies operated within a sovereign nation that had the legal power and authority to exercise regulatory control over corporate conduct if necessary.[15] Because of the growth of multinational corporations, this assumption may no longer be true. Some companies yield annual profits in the multiple billion dollar range and have leagues of attorneys, experts, lobbyists, and informal connections at high levels in government (including ex-government officials sitting as active board members) that dissuade the domiciliary country from exerting regulatory pressure when it might be appropriate to do so.

When a large company incorporates in a foreign country, regulation may not be forthcoming out of fear that the business will move elsewhere, taking jobs and tax revenue offshore. Indeed, countries may very well reduce regulatory compliance requirements in order to attract countries to incorporate in their jurisdiction. This is called a **race to the bottom** where states compete to have the most lax regulations. While it promotes the tax base in that country, it does so at the expense of public health and environmental integrity by failing to subject companies to adequate regulatory oversight. At a certain point when a company becomes so powerful, the country in which it does business has little relevancy to how that company does business.

> **Race to the Bottom** When governments compete with one another for economic activity by deregulating a business environment, resulting in fewer environmental or worker protections.

Regulatory Arbitrage. As economic conditions improve in a developing host nation, standard of living and customer expectations for socially responsible corporate conduct may increase (according to the Environmental Kuznets Curve, discussed later). The increasingly stringent standards conditioned on social license to operate may lead multinational corporations to shift corporate activities elsewhere. Multinational companies are defined in part by their possession of operations in a wide variety of nations across the globe. This provides flexibility to shift operations from one jurisdiction to another in order to take advantage of lax regulatory requirements, lower labor costs due to no minimum wage laws, less burdensome tax laws, and less stringent environmental laws.[16]

> **Regulatory Arbitrage** When a company shifts operations from one jurisdiction to another in order to dodge regulatory intervention as well as increased social license requirements.

> **CROSS-LINKAGE**
>
> For more on the role of corporate lobbying and national regulatory policy, see Chapter 4: Legal Frameworks.

Plantation Production Problem. Where differences in the regulatory context of business attract a multinational to the country in which production costs the least, this is usually because working conditions may not be safeguarded by regulation, and employee pay need not amount to a living wage. The race to the bottom between nations competing to host multinationals means that even extreme forms of corporate misconduct may be ignored, for fear of competitive disadvantage.[17] This collective action problem can lead to plantation production problems, where labor conditions pose the risk of slavery or human trafficking.

> **Plantation Production Problem** Where under-regulated labor markets pose the risk of harsh labor conditions or human trafficking.

Understanding the market and regulatory dynamics brought about by globalization is important for SMEs to succeed as a sustainable enterprise. Smaller companies are able to make plays in niche markets as the "local" alternative to products from multinational companies. Smaller enterprises may also have an easier time branding themselves as sustainable enterprises in contrast to multinational competitors. For multinational companies, corporate social responsibility and sustainability policies should act as a preventative safeguard against the temptations of under-regulated market opportunities.

> **CROSS-LINKAGE**
>
> For more on the risk of human trafficking in global supply chains, see Chapter 8: Supply Chain Management.

2.3.2 Environmental Kuznets Curve and its Criticism

**Environmental Kuznets
Curve** Economic theory
predicting that environmental
degradation rises then falls in
an inverted U-shaped function
of income per capita.

Environmental Kuznets Curve The **Environmental Kuznets Curve** (EKC) is based on the hypothesis of Kuznets (1955) that the income inequality within a given population rises to an apex and then falls, corresponding to the timeline of economic development. As development begins, inequality increases until a certain maximum is reached, after which further economic growth also drives a more equitable distribution of income. In the EKC, the concept of environmental degradation replaces the concept of economic inequality from the traditional Kuznets curve; the EKC predicts that environmental degradation rises then falls in an inverted U-shaped function of income per capita.[18] The modified hypothesis suggests that in early stages of economic growth, degradation and pollution increase, until a specified level of income per capita (based on several proximate factors) is achieved and the trend thereby reverses, indicating that with high-income levels economic growth leads to environmental improvement.

The Environmental Kuznets Curve is a hypothesized relationship between various indicators of environmental degradation and income per capita, called proximate factors. They include output mix, input mix, state of technology, and scale of production.[19]

Output mix. Different industries have different pollution intensities. Output mix changes depending on the course of economic development.

Input mix. Input mix accounts for substitutions of environmentally damaging inputs into the economic system with less damaging alternatives, and vice versa.

State of technology. The state of the art in relevant technological areas affects the efficiency and emissions levels of production processes. *Production efficiency* is measured in terms of using less, all things being equal, of the polluting inputs per unit of output. *Emissions specific changes in process* result in less pollutant being emitted per unit of input.

Scale of production. Scale of production refers to expanding production at given factor-input ratios, output mix, and state of technology to achieve economies of scale.

According to this hypothesis, these factors are influenced by environmental regulations and public education. See Figure 2.2.

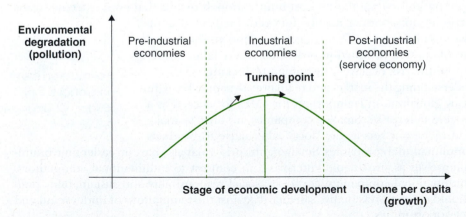

FIGURE 2.2 Environmental
Kuznets Curve
Source: Panayotou (1993).

EKC hypothesis is influential even if tacit in major sustainability publications. The idea that economic growth is necessary in order for environmental quality to be maintained or improved is an essential part of the sustainable development argument promulgated by the World Commission on Environment and Development (1987) in *Our Common Future,* and the World Bank's *World Development Report 1992* (IBRD, 1992). According to the EKC, economic development in low-income regions is the pathway to global environmental improvements. Environmental degradation involving local externalities (like indoor air pollution) is reduced by the first small rise in income levels, whereas environmental degradation involving dispersed externalities (such as greenhouse gas emissions) appears to increase steadily with rising income until the highest levels of wealth are attained.[20]

> **CROSS-LINKAGE**
>
> For more on externalities, see Chapter 1: Introduction to Sustainable Business.

Criticism of the Environmental Kuznets Curve In the last few decades, the EKC would have predicted that global pollution levels would decrease as economic development has increased. Instead of bearing out the EKC hypothesis, empirical trends indicate (1) a like-in-kind substitution in the *form* of aggregate waste rather than a reduction in *volume* of aggregate waste; (2) a change in the types of *impacts* associated with waste (from acid rain to climate change) rather than an abatement of environmental impacts in general; and (3) the relative stability of per capita solid waste levels regardless of increased economic growth.[21]

Another flawed assumption of the EKC is that it assumes that increases in environmental damage do not impede economic production. However, there are feedback loops connecting ecological losses to economic productivity. The EKC assumes that incremental increases in environmental damage do not stop the economic growth process; however, that is precisely what happens when growth significantly impairs resources or causes severe irreversible impacts to the natural resource base.

A simplifying assumption of the EKC is that all environmental sacrifices of the present are acceptable because they would not reduce future population's income level. The solution, according to advocates of the EKC, is simply to promote wealth in developing countries to advance them along the curve toward reduced adverse environmental impacts. However, promoting wealth-maximization in developing countries at the current state of technology does not necessarily compute into sustainable development. The goal of sustainable development should, perhaps, be to improve how wealth and resources are *managed* rather than simply how they are *distributed*.

From the chart in Figure 2.3 it is clear that, contrary to the prediction of the EKC, developed countries have the largest ecological footprint. Notice that North American Human Development Index is not significantly larger than the average European Union or Asia-Pacific member state, yet EU and Asia-Pacific countries are responsible for substantially less than the ecological footprint of the US. Accordingly, increasing resource consumption beyond Earth's biocapacity appears to provide diminishing marginal returns in terms of increases in human welfare near the upper levels of development. Notice that virtually none of the nations in the world currently meet UN Human Development's minimum criteria for sustainability, which consists of sufficiently high human development *within* Earth's biocapacity.

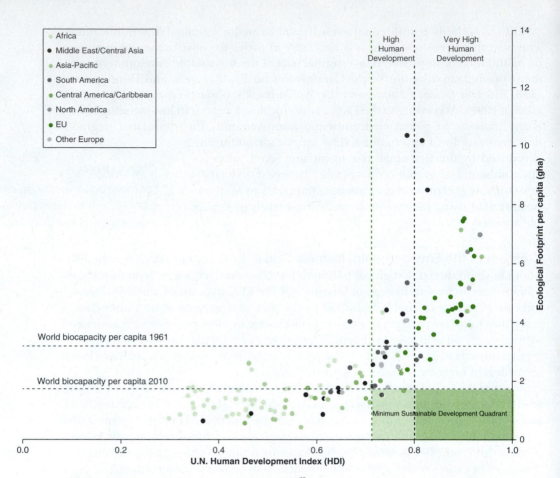

FIGURE 2.3 Comparing Development with Impacts[22]

Source: Global Footprint Network, 2012. National Footprint Accounts, 2012 Edition. Available online at http://www.footprintnetwork.org.

2.3.3 Natural Capital Accounting and Sustainable Land Use

Natural Capital In order to incorporate the value of nature and ecosystem services into business decision-making, it is necessary to provide an accounting of sorts for these values. The concept of natural capital is used to price the stock of natural resources and the services they provide to humanity (see the Chapter Opener on ecosystem services). Just as one would ideally not spend money from a corporate account faster than the account is replenished, one should not deplete natural resources faster than they can be renewed. The concept of natural capital can help stabilize nature's balance sheets, so to speak.

The **Natural Capital Project** aims to provide tools to corporate, government, and NGOs for incorporating natural capital into decision. This is done primarily through quantifying the values of ecosystem services in clear, credible, and practical ways so

> **Natural Capital Project** Aims to provide tools to corporate, government, and NGOs to facilitate incorporating natural capital into decision-making.

the social return on environmental investment can be quantified and forecasted in reliable, objective ways.

The Natural Capital Project is developing InVEST, which stands for a software-based tool that provides Integrated Valuation of Environmental Services and Trade-offs. InVEST enables decision-makers to quantify the value of natural resources, to demonstrate the benefits that accrue in the present as well as projections into the future, to identify and weigh the trade-offs associated with different resource allocation decisions, and to integrate conservation into human development projects.

Applying accounting principles to value ecosystem services allows natural values to be translated into monetary values. This facilitates incorporating ecosystem services into business decisions, and it also enables government actors to design policies that utilize market dynamics (price, incentives, ROI) in order to promote environmental protection and conservation objectives. By applying accounting-based perspectives to ecosystem services, incentives for conservation measures quickly reach into the billions of dollars and millions of acres of land are subject to protective measures. What is not measured or incentivized can hardly be effectively protected.

CROSS-LINKAGE
For an example of the use of natural capital accounting, see the example of Puma's Environmental Profit & Loss sheet in the Case 2 of Chapter 5: Metrics, Tools, and Reporting: The Role of Finance and Accounting.

The concept of natural capital can help align business incentives with sustainable outcomes by showing businesses the monetary value of conservation and preservation. Conservation and preservation both aim to minimize pollution and habitat loss, but with differing degrees of strictness in terms of what kinds of land uses are allowed where.

Investing in Sustainable Land Use This section explores three land use control methods that can be applied to protecting natural resources.

Conservation. Conservation is a process by which natural resources are managed to allow for exploitation of those resources by individuals, communities, or commercial entities in ways that do not jeopardize the long-term viability of natural asset bases and without inflicting excessive environmental damage—that is, degradation from which an ecosystem cannot recover. In order to accomplish conservation of an ecosystem or resource base, decision-makers must find a long-term balance between three factors: (a) human needs that are met by exploiting the resource; (b) the needs of wildlife species that depends on those resources for habitat; and (c) the ability of environmental, social, and economic stakeholders to adapt to modifications in the rate and extent of exploitation of those resources.

Conservation A process by which natural resources are managed to allow for exploitation of those resources in ways that do not jeopardize their long-term viability.

Conservation fits within the sustainability paradigm in that it allows for a balanced and long-term approach to natural resource management, but it can and should be supplemented with preservation, a distinct approach. Conservation efforts can be championed based on the fact that local businesses, not just nature, benefit from environmental integrity.

Preservation. Preservation is a policy of maintaining nature in its pristine state, or at least in its condition prior to human intervention. Under the preservationist paradigm, certain special places such as sensitive ecosystems or historical and aesthetic landscapes should be delineated on official maps and preserved from industrial,

Preservation A policy of maintaining nature in its pristine state, or at least in its condition prior to human intervention.

commercial, agricultural, and even residential development for long periods of time, if not indefinitely.

Preservation initiatives protect the planet's natural resource base from depletion by creating public parks at the exclusion of virtually any other land uses aside from recreational visits such as hiking or eco-tourism.

Whereas conservation of a forest would allow selective harvesting, preservation of a forest would mean not cutting down a single branch from a single tree. For example, the highest court of New York determined that cutting even a small ski line through the trees of the Adirondack Park for the 1980 Lake Placid Winter Olympics would violate the New York State Constitution's guarantee that parcels within the park boundaries would remain "forever wild." By contrast, conservation allows mixed uses: private enterprise that promotes local economic welfare such as organic farming can be nestled nearby scenic public access parks so that natural resources of a region can be appreciated, sustainably used, and conserved for the long run.

Conservation Easements
A form of property right that enables the holder of that right to limit the kinds of uses that are allowed on a specific parcel.

Offset A means of compensating for environmental impacts of land use by purchasing a commensurate amount of land in a sensitive ecosystem to be set aside for preservation purposes.

Conservation Easements and "Offsets." Conservation easements are a form of property right that enables the holder of that right to limit the kinds of uses that are allowed on a specific parcel. An example of a typical conservation easement would be one that applies to a residential area surrounded by forests and a watershed that prohibits a laundry list of industrial activity such as mineral extraction or hazardous waste disposal.

Some non-profit environmental organizations partner with private property owners and environmental agencies of the government to purchase conservation easements over large swaths of territory. For example, the Open Space Institute acquired several hundred acres bordering Catskill Park from the Woodstock Guild of Artists and Craftsman to create the Overlook Mountain Wild Forest.[23] This purchase created a wild corridor around a famous hiking trail and extended the reach of special protections to the lands visible from areas within the park's previous borders. The final process in this conservation initiative will involve the conveyance of the entire bundle of acquired properties to the Department of Environmental Conservation, which will then be under a constitutional duty to manage the land as "Forever Wild" Catskill Park Forest Preserve.

When it is not feasible to preserve natural resources in geographic proximity to where a business operates, there is always the option of purchasing "offsets," where parcels are purchased by the company for preservation purposes in sensitive ecosystems of other parts of the world, as a means of compensating for any destruction caused nearby.

Environmental offsets are used to preserve tropical rainforests, to establish wildlife sanctuaries, and for other purposes related to sustainability such as to create carbon sinks or to promote afforestation.

2.3.4 Sustainable Engineering

The U.S. National Science Foundation sponsors an Environmental Sustainability Program that provides support for research into sustainability, particularly from an engineering-based perspective, including industrial ecology, green engineering, ecological engineering, and earth systems engineering.[24]

Industrial Ecology Industrial ecology designs industrial infrastructures to function as inter-connected artificial ecosystems that sustainably interface with natural ecosystems.[25] An industrial ecologist would design industrial processes to mimic natural systems as much as possible, to preserve order and equilibrium, to maintain cyclic materials flow, and to reduce energy consumption to that human institutions do not disrupt the environment in which they are embedded.

The goal of industrial ecology is to design industrial processes to benefit society as much—and damage the environment as little—as possible. Industrial ecology provides a systems-based methodology to promote advancements in modeling such as life cycle assessment, materials flow analysis, input/output economic models, and novel metrics for measuring sustainable systems.[26]

Green Engineering. Green engineering research seeks to advance the sustainability of manufacturing processes, green building design, and public infrastructure by taking a systems or holistic approach. This field includes improvements in distribution and collection systems that advance smart growth strategies and ameliorate effects of growth.

Improvements in green engineering also lead to innovations in prevention and management of storm water overflows, projects to recycle and reuse drinking water supplies, and techniques to support sustainable construction projects.

Ecological Engineering. Ecological engineering focuses on the engineering aspects of restoring ecological functions and service capabilities to natural systems. Ecological engineering research can enhance natural capital to foster sustainable development, such as projects in stream restoration, revitalization of urban rivers, and the rehabilitation of wetlands that require engineering input. These projects improve the ability of natural systems to generate ecosystem services.

Earth Systems Engineering. Earth Systems Engineering considers aspects of large-scale engineering research into function and stability of the major natural systems of the planet and the infrastructure that sustains civilization. For instance, earth systems engineering research addresses projects to mitigate global greenhouse gas emissions, to adapt coastal urban areas to sea level rise, and other global scale concerns such as adequate provision of water supplies in an era of drought.

> **Industrial Ecology** The design of industrial infrastructures to function as inter-connected artificial ecosystems that sustainably interface with natural ecosystems.

> **Green Engineering** Seeks to advance the sustainability of manufacturing processes, green building design, and public infrastructure by taking a systems or holistic approach.

> **Ecological Engineering** Focuses on restoring ecological functions and service capabilities to natural systems.

> **Earth Systems Engineering** Large-scale engineering research into the function and stability of major natural systems of the planet and infrastructure that sustains civilization.

2.4 Environmental Perspectives

This section provides perspectives on sustainable business that are based on principles derived from natural systems or that are oriented toward the impact of business activities on environmental integrity.

2.4.1 Regenerative Capacity

Regenerative capacity refers to the amount of useful biological material an ecosystem can produce, as well as the amount of human and industrial waste an ecosystem can absorb, given prevailing exploitation and management practices. We look at regenerative capacity to understand how many Earths it would take (at a

> **Regenerative Capacity** The amount of useful biological material and industrial waste that an ecosystem can produce and absorb, respectively, given prevailing uses.

CROSS-LINKAGE

For more information about the Living Planet Index, see Chapter 1: Introduction to Sustainable Business.

constant amount of ecosystem services provision) to support a given population at a given rate of consumption and waste output.

By aggregating up from an average individual's consumption and waste levels to a specified population, and comparing this number to the Earth's regenerative capacity, we get a direct glimpse into the sustainability of a particular population's lifestyle. Experts estimate that the human population has an ecological footprint of 1.5 planet Earths, which means we consume and waste more than 1.5 the rate of the Earth's regenerative capacity.

Sustainability aims to reduce the human impact on the environment until there is a 1 to 1 match with the Earth's regenerative capacity and the demand placed upon it by human activity.

Biocapacity Deficit When the human footprint exceeds the productivity and services that natural resources can provide.

We currently suffer a **biocapacity deficit** because the human footprint exceeds the productivity and services that available land and sea provide. In regional terms, biocapacity deficit can be avoided by importing ecological assets, or liquidating current stocks of natural capital. In global terms, however, our biocapacity deficit cannot be compensated by trading resources (absent interplanetary trade) or liquidating assets (absent infinite resources).

Biocapacity Remainder When the biocapacity of a given area exceeds the dependent population's ecological demand.

A **biocapacity remainder** occurs when the biocapacity of a given area exceeds the dependent population's ecological footprint. While there are certain regions of the world that exhibit biocapacity remainder, the human average is unsustainable.

2.4.2 Biomimicry

Biomimicry Finding practical commercial and industrial applications of biological features of plants and animals.

Over the last few billion years, nature has subjected living organisms, systems, and materials to a sort of trial and error process, where inefficient designs become extinct and efficient designs propagate. **Biomimicry**, or the field of biomimetics, is based on learning from and mirroring the features of living things that have survived the test of natural selection, and finding practical applications of these features.

CROSS-LINKAGE

For more on biomimicry in product and process design, see Chapter 9: Operations Management.

Why is mimicking nature a good idea? Natural selection has solved, at the macro- and nano-scale, many of the problems that humanity struggles to address today: adequate food supply, efficient energy use, non-toxic chemical reactions, transportation systems, self-assembly, wind resistance, climate regulation, and then some. There are nine principles of biomimicry:[27]

1. Nature runs on sunlight.
2. Nature uses only the energy it needs.
3. Nature fits form to function.
4. Nature recycles everything.
5. Nature rewards cooperation.
6. Nature banks on diversity.
7. Nature demands local expertise.
8. Nature curbs excesses from within.
9. Nature taps the power of limits.

2.4.3 Cradle-to-Cradle

Traditionally, we understood the life cycle of a product as extending from **cradle to grave**, which means from the point of origin for raw materials through the production process and on to the point of disposal at a landfill. This understanding of the product life cycle fits the "take-make-waste" paradigm of industrial and commercial activity, which extracts resources from the environment (take), processes these resources for use in manufacturing (make), and then disposes of these resources in the form of a consumed product (waste).

The **cradle-to-cradle**[28] metaphor bypasses the "grave" of consumed products by incorporating materials back as inputs into the production process rather than disposing them as waste products. The materials used and created by humans must be able to circulate through ecosystems and industrial processes in perpetuity and in a healthy manner, that is cost-effective, efficient, and waste-free.[29] The interconnected social, environmental, and economic systems are conceived as a metabolic system that must be able to digest the materials passing through it. Once products end their useful life, they should be used as biological nutrients that return to the environment in a benign, if not useful, form (think fertilizer), or they should be used as technical nutrients which remain contained in closed-loop industrial cycles of production.[30]

Cradle-to-cradle can also be used in conjunction with other concepts, such as biomimicry (discussed earlier) and life-cycle assessment.

Cradle to Grave From the point of origin for raw materials through the production process and on to the point of disposal at a landfill.

Cradle-to-Cradle Extends the cradle to grave metaphor by incorporating materials back as inputs into the production process rather than diverting them as waste products.

CROSS-LINKAGE

For more on life cycle assessment, see Chapter 5: Metrics, Tools, and Reporting: The Role of Finance and Accounting, as well as Chapter 8: Supply Chain Management.

2.4.4 Human Ecology

Human ecology is an interdisciplinary approach to understanding human-environmental systems.[31] Human ecology combines the biophysical realities of human existence (such as dependence on natural resources and exposure to environmental contaminants) with the social and psychological dimensions of human health and well-being (such as culture and social progress).

Human ecology focuses on understanding humans and their environments as parts of a whole. This approach recognizes the limitations of the planet's biocapacity and the ethical implications of resource distribution. The methodology of human ecology is to focus on underlying ultimate causes (rather than superficial, immediate causes) of problems arising in human-environmental systems.

For instance, one could argue that the cause of increased cancer incidents on the part of low-income communities is their proximity to freeway interchanges where exposure to air pollutants is disproportionately high. Human ecology would look instead at the regulatory program which allowed a dangerous chemical composition of fuel to be combusted in vehicles, the underlying social factors that attract low-income communities to environmentally degraded areas, and the lack of proper medical resources on the part of these communities.

Human ecology tends to isolate the sources of sustainability problems in aspects of the dominant culture, its attendant values, and resulting human behavior.

Human Ecology Interdisciplinary approach to understanding human-environmental systems that combines biophysical realities of human existence with social and psychological dimensions of human health and well-being.

By taking a holistic perspective on the environment in which human societies are embedded, human ecology encourages a long time-horizon when it comes to identifying and addressing problems. Human ecology's response to sustainability problems is to propose interventions that improve environmental outcomes in ways that are fair to the humans affected.

To continue with the example, a human ecologist might propose means of reducing vehicle pollution emissions rather than suggesting that affected communities reduce exposure by relocating to less degraded (and likely more expensive) areas. Improving the conditions of human-environmental systems may require attitude and behavioral changes as well as technological innovation. Human ecology aims to promote a healthy interdependence between humans and the environment by considering them as parts of a holistic system. When technology fails to provide a quick fix, behavioral changes and attitude adjustments on the part of the culture may be necessary.

The key to human ecology is that technology is not a cure-all. While technology can promote efficiency in terms of cost or pollution per unit produced, increases in the efficiency of supply are not always enough to keep up with increasing total demand. Just because engines burn fuel more efficiently, if there are more engines on the road, those efficiency gains can be washed out by increased fuel consumption in general.

CONCLUSION

Recall the parable of the three blind men in the desert, each reaching out a hand to touch an elephant for the first time. One man has his hand upon the elephant's tusk, another upon the elephant's leg, and a third upon the elephant's trunk. Each of the blind men describes a completely different reality, but in fact, they are all touching the same creature. This parable applies to the subject of sustainability. For many business students, this chapter may have introduced a bewildering array of new concepts from the fields of sociology, economics, and environmental policy. At first blush, these perspectives are radically distinct, but in reality, they all describe the common underlying challenge of bringing about a sustainable world.

Key Terms

ecosystem services 33
stakeholder theory 35
corporate social
 responsibility 36
CSR and human
 resources 37
CSR and risk
 management 37
CSR and brand
 differentiation 38
CSR and social license to
 operate 38
human rights 40

Conflicts of Relative
 Development 41
conflicts of cultural
 tradition 41
cross-country ethical
 dilemmas 41
anthropocentrism 42
biocentrism 42
environmental justice 42
globalization 43
economies of scale 44
race to the bottom 45
regulatory arbitrage 45

plantation production
 problem 45
Environmental Kuznets
 Curve 46
Natural Capital
 Project 48
conservation 49
preservation 49
conservation
 easements 50
offset 50
industrial ecology 51
green engineering 51

ecological engineering 51
earth systems
 engineering 51
regenerative capacity 51
biocapacity deficit 52
biocapacity remainder 52
biomimicry 52
cradle-to-grave 53
cradle-to-cradle 53
human ecology 53

Discussion Questions

1. Have you ever worked for a company that had a corporate social responsibility policy? Did it make a difference?

2. How have you been personally affected by globalization?

3. How do multinational and transnational companies differ with regards to corporate culture than a small- or mid-sized business?

4. Have you encountered an ethical conflict in the workplace?

CASE 1   ## Emerging Drinking Water Contaminants[32]

Sylvia Platworth studied public health as an undergrad and recently completed her Ph.D. in biomechanical engineering before being recruited by one of the world's leading pharmaceutical companies to work in product design. She was interested in whether drugs are biodegradable, since most of unused drugs are flushed down the toilet or simply thrown in the trash. In her research she came across an alarming news story about the occurrence of pharmaceutical chemicals in drinking water supplies. Unsure of the materiality of this risk, and in order to decide whether to raise this issue with her manager, Sylvia ultimately contacted one of her Ph.D. advisors for additional information about the risks of pharmaceutical contamination of drinking water. He wrote a lengthy response, excerpted here:

> *Dear Sylvia (or, I suppose I should now call you "Dr. Platworth"):*
>
> *Thank you for your letter. I am pleased to see that you are utilizing your superior education in the workplace. As it turns out, this is a subject of some concern to me. I have been investigating endocrine disrupting compounds in the environment for the last several years, including pharmaceuticals (which you wrote to me about), but also a wide range of industrial and commercial chemicals that are used in personal care products as well as consumer products. Because all of these chemicals have a common risk, I have clustered them as a single set of environmental contaminants, known as endocrine disrupting compounds (EDCs). Exposure to EDCs can cause a wide range of adverse health impacts to humans, including birth defects, obesity, and cancer.*
>
> *EDCs include synthetic hormones such as those manufactured for birth control pills, as well as industrial and commercial compounds that can have some hormonal function, such as alkylphenols, pesticides, pharmaceuticals, and phthalates. "Alkylphenols" are the "surfactant" found in dish and clothing soap, paint, cosmetics, and household cleaners and can serve a variety of purposes in manufacturing products such as detergents in household cleaners, emulsifiers in lotions, foaming agents and dispersants in dish soap. "Phthalates" are industrial chemicals that increase the fluidity, flexibility, and resilience of other substances, the "plasticizer" used in toys, food packaging, hoses, raincoats, shower curtains, vinyl flooring, wall coverings, lubricants, adhesives, detergents, nail polish, hair spray and shampoo. Pesticides and pharmaceuticals such as antibiotics are biologically active by design, and exposure to these substances can lead to death of insects and microorganisms, and can concentrate in the food chain, possibly impacting human health. As you may gather from this list, chemicals with endocrine disrupting potential have extensive applications in industrial processes and commercial products.*
>
> *As the news story you cited conveys, these substances have been found in relatively small amounts in drinking water supplies throughout the country. Don't be fooled by the smallness—they are probably in drinking water supplies all over the world, wherever these chemicals are used. EDC contamination is anthropogenic or "man-made." While industry generates the substance that ultimately contaminates watersheds, those who generate the pollution range from the agriculture industry to the mother applying sunscreen to her children at the beach. So, there are diverse pathways of exposure, and this is not an easy environmental problem to fix.*

(continues)

> CASE 1 **(Continued)**

> *Clearly there are a bewildering variety of benefits from the use of chemicals with endocrine disrupting potential in industrial, agricultural, commercial, pharmaceutical, and personal care product applications. That said, are the risks that these substances pose when released into the environment worth the benefit? Perhaps. Are they avoidable? This depends upon the feasibility of making sustainable improvements to product design, product use, and product disposal. It seems to me that the best party to take responsibility for this problem is the producer of the chemicals, because the users of the chemicals have little to no alternative.*
>
> *Please let me know if you have any other questions about my research. Best of luck addressing this issue on behalf of your company. I would be very pleased to see you taking the lead on this growing public health concern.*
>
> *Sincerely,*
> *Dr. Northrup Carlyle (since you are no longer a student*
> *I suppose you can now call me "North")*

After reading the letter from her mentor, Sylvia felt compelled to do something about the issue of EDCs in the water supply resulting from pharmaceuticals manufactured by her company. She plans to write a memorandum to her manager explaining the risks and outlining a variety of proposals for addressing them.

Questions for Case 1

1. Who are the **stakeholders** of concern in the context of contaminated watersheds and drinking water supplies, and what do they have at stake?

2. Is there a justification for extending **corporate social responsibility** to pollution that occurs the end of a product's life cycle? Is your answer different for household disposal of personal drugs versus agricultural uses of antibiotics?

3. How do the principles of **human ecology** and **biomimicry** apply to this situation?

4. What does the **Environmental Kuznets Curve** predict about society's tolerance of endocrine disrupting compounds in drinking water supplies? Do you think this is an accurate prediction?

5. Develop a proposal for addressing this contamination issue that Sylvia could present and defend to her manager as a sustainability initiative. Be sure to make a business case for the proposal.

Additional Material

For a discussion about socially responsible value-creation in the era of globalization, see "Profit's Not Always the Point," a TED-Talk by Harish Manwani, Chief Operating Officer at Unilever.

For a discussion of sustainable design, see the TED-Talk "Cradle to Cradle Design," by William McDonough.

For more information on social dimensions of sustainability in the global context, see the United Nations Research Institute for Social Development website.

For an in depth exploration of corporate social responsibility, see David Crowther & Lez Rayman-Bacchus (Eds.), *Perspectives on Corporate Social Responsibility* (Ashgate 2004).

Harvard Business Review Chapter: Paul Torelli, International Economics, *Chapter 1: A Brief History of Modern Economic Globalization*, Prod #: BEP229-PDF-ENG (November 01, 2013).

Harvard Business Review Case: Elliot N. Weiss, *A Brief Note on the Theory of Constraints*, Prod. #: UV3532-PDF-ENG (February 20, 2004).

Endnotes

1   Living Beyond Our Means: Natural Assets and Human Well-Being, Statement of the Millennium Assessment Board, page 3 (2005), *last accessed May 5, 2014, available at* http://www.millennium assessment.org/documents/document.429.aspx.pdf.

2   Living Beyond Our Means: Natural Assets and Human Well-Being, Statement of the Millennium Assessment Board, page 22–23 (2005), *last accessed May 5, 2014.*

3   *Corporate Social Responsibility Report*, Timberland (2013).

4   *Timberland Responsibility: Worker Engagement and Empowerment*, Timberland, last accessed May 6, 2014, available at http://responsibility.timberland.com/factories/worker-engagement/.

5   *ibid.*

6   "Nike Workers 'Kicked, Slapped and Verbally Abused' at Factories Making Converse," *Daily Mail Reporter* (July 13, 2011).

7   *In Search of Revolutionary Responsibility: A Letter from Co-Founder Jeffry Hollender*, Seventh Generation Corporate Consciousness Report 2.0, last accessed May 6, 2014, available at http://www.7genreport.com/introduction/.

8   The Home Depot, *Import Supplier Handbook: Section 6 Social and Environmental Responsibility Standards*, page 23 (2011).

9   Environmental Ethics, Stanford Encyclopedia of Philosophy (First published Mon Jun 3, 2002; substantive revision Thu Jan 3, 2008), last access May 3, 2014, available at http://plato.stanford.edu/entries/ethics-environmental/.

10 *Environmental Justice*, United States Environmental Protection Agency, last accessed May 6, 2014, available at http://www.epa.gov/environmentaljustice/.

11 William Scheuerman, "Globalization," *The Stanford Encyclopedia of Philosophy (Summer 2010 Edition)*, Edward N. Zalta (ed.), *last accessed May 5, 2014* http://plato.stanford.edu/archives/sum2010/entries/globalization/.

12 IMF Staff, "Globalization: A Brief Overview," *International Monetary Fund*, 08/02 - May 2008, last accessed May 5, 2014, available at http://www.imf.org/external/np/exr/ib/2008/053008.htm.

13 William Scheuerman, "Globalization," *The Stanford Encyclopedia of Philosophy (Summer 2010 Edition)*, Edward N. Zalta (ed.), last accessed May 5, 2014, available at http://plato.stanford.edu/archives/sum2010/entries/globalization/.

14 Douglas M. Branson, "The Social Responsibility of Large Multinational Corporations," 33 *Transnational Law* 121 (2002).

15 *ibid.*

16 *ibid.*

17 *ibid.*

18 Arik Levinson, "Definition of the Environmental Kuznets Curve," *New Palgrave Dictionary of Economics* (2nd ed.).

19 David I. Stern, "The Rise and Fall of the Environmental Kuznets Curve," 32:8 *World Development* pp. 1419–1439 (2004).

20 Arik Levinson, *"Definition of the Environmental Kuznets Curve," New Palgrave Dictionary of Economics* (2nd ed.).

21 David I. Stern, "The Rise and Fall of the Environmental Kuznets Curve," 32:8 *World Development*, pp. 1419–1439 (2004).

22 According to this figure, the twin goals of global sustainable development should be to (1) increase human welfare in Africa, Asia-Pacific, Middle East and Central Asia, and Latin America and the Caribbean, without increasing ecological footprints of these regions; and (2) decrease ecological footprints of North America and Europe without decreasing human welfare.

23 Press Release, *DEC Commissioner Announces State Purchase of 330 Acres in the Catskill Park: Acquisitions Protect Resources and Enhance Recreation on Overlook Mountain*, Open Space Institute (June 2008).

24 Science Foundation, *Environmental Sustainability Program*, last accessed May 5, 2014, available at http://www.nsf.gov/funding/pgm_summ.jsp?pims_id=501027.

25 R. Lifset & T. E. Graedel, "Industrial Ecology: Goals and Definitions," in *Handbook for Industrial Ecology*, edited by R. U. Ayres and L. Ayres (2001).

26 R. Lifset & F. Boons, "Industrial Ecology: Business Management in a Material World," in *The Oxford Handbook of Business and the Natural Environment*, edited by P. Bansal and A. Hoffman (Oxford UP, 2012).

27 Janine Benyus, *Biomimicry: Innovation Inspired by Nature* (2002).

28 Originally coined by Walter Stahel in the 1970s, the term *cradle to cradle* was trademarked by the consultancy McDonough Braungart Design Chemistry, who elaborated the concept and developed a certification system for it. Cradle-to-cradle certification is provided by the non-profit Cradle to Cradle Products Innovation Institute.

29 Michael Braungart & William McDonough, *Cradle-to-Cradle: Remaking the Way We Make Things* (North Point Press, 2002).

30 *ibid.*

31 Robert Dyball, *Human Ecology*, last accessed May 5, 2014, available at http://www.berkshirepublishing.com/assets/pdf/Human Ecology_Dyball.pdf.

32 *See* Jeff Donn, Martha Mendoza & Justin Pritchard, *AP Probe Finds Drugs in Drinking Water*, The Associated Press, March 9, 2008.

Leadership, Change Management, and Corporate Governance

SUSTAINABLE LEADERSHIP, CORPORATE GOVERNANCE, AND INNOVATION AT UNILEVER[1]

In 2008, the year of the global financial crisis, consumer products company Unilever—owner of Ben & Jerry's and Dove—was faltering. Despite cost cutting, restructuring, asset sales, and acquisitions, revenues had been flat at best for the past 10, years. Paul Polman became Chief Executive Officer of Unilever in 2009, and practically hit the reset button. By focusing on sustainability, the company would reconnect with consumers by proving they could help solve real-life problems, not just sell stuff. The **sustainable solutions** approach to designing personal care products and household cleaning supplies was useful in penetrating emerging markets in Asia and Africa where consumers' income and water supplies are limited.

In 2010, Unilever unveiled its Sustainable Living Plan, a manifesto that repositioned the company relative to its main competitor, Procter & Gamble. Unilever vowed to double sales, halve its environmental footprint, and sustainably source all of its agricultural products by the year 2020. By 2012, the company had already increased the percentage of sustainably sourced agricultural raw materials to 36%. Because Unilever procures 6% of the world's tomatoes and 5% of the world's onions, the farming practices of its suppliers literally make a big difference on the ground. According to Unilever's Chief Sustainability Officer Gail Klintworth, by reducing soil depletion, water use, and biodiversity loss in the regions from which its materials are sourced, Unilever is "future-proofing the business."

According to the World Health Organization, approximately 1.8 million people die annually because of waterborne diseases.

> *"This is like the quality revolution that we had in the eighties. What happened was companies either died or they got quality. One day this is going to be the same for sustainability."*
>
> —*Neil Carson (2010)*, **CEO OF JOHNSON MATTHEY**

LEARNING OBJECTIVES

After reading this chapter, you should be able to:

1. Articulate the role of private sector leadership in global collective action problems, as well as leadership for organizational change.
2. Distinguish sustainable from traditional leadership capabilities, and describe the role of the Chief Sustainability Officer.
3. Explain organizational leadership through innovation, strategy, and change management.
4. Explain the governance mechanisms that ensure sustainable corporate conduct.
5. Reconcile the debate between shareholder and stakeholder perspectives on corporate responsibility, and explain the B-Corporation.

Sustainable Solutions Providing goods and services that help solve real-life problems, especially in emerging markets where consumer income and resources are limited.

In order to provide safe drinking water for those in poverty, Unilever launched Pureit, an affordable at-home water purifier that removes bacteria, parasites, viruses, and other water pollutants. Unilever has sold 10 million units of Pureit at $40 each, mostly in India. Nonetheless, Pureit is not profitable, and the company does not expect to break even, despite future growth projections in Asia, Africa, and Latin America. Although CEO Polman claims, "We want to make it a billion-euro business," he is not focused on Pureit's profit margins. "I don't look at it as a P&L. I look at it as creating societies that function. As long as my total business works, I'm not accountable for every SKU."

In addition to sourcing, sustainability also drives product innovation at Unilever. In areas where domestic water supplies are scarce, doing the laundry may mean having less water to drink. Unilever is researching a laundry detergent that can be used at any water temperature with very little water while effectively cleaning clothes. Even in the markets of developed countries such as the United States, product innovation can help consumers live healthier lives. Brands such as Dove beauty products, Lipton iced tea, Hellman's mayonnaise and Ben & Jerry's ice cream (all owned by Unilever) have launched product lines offering healthier product attributes and more sustainable product life cycles. According to CEO Polman, sustainable innovation "drives our top line, it drives costs out, it motivates our employees, it links us with retailers."

3.1 Introduction: Leadership as Antidote to Collective Action Problems

The problems posed by population growth, near-term resource scarcity, long-term climate change impacts, and the struggle for economic development cannot go unanswered by business leaders if they hope to remain relevant. The capacity of communities, individuals, or governments to address these challenges is severely limited when compared to the wealth, influence, long-term strategy, and global reach of corporations. As members of the highest earning and most powerful echelon of professionals worldwide, the C-Suite has a unique role to play in achieving sustainability.

Leadership and corporate governance are distinct, yet share the commonality of being responsible in large part for the control of corporate activities. The general theme of sustainable leadership and corporate governance is to think about and address the needs of stakeholders in corporate decision-making. See Figure 3.1. The social, economic, and environmental landscape of business is constantly changing, making outward-focused leadership and corporate governance increasingly important.

CROSS-LINKAGE

For more on stakeholder theory, see Chapter 2: Perspectives.

Going beyond stakeholders, what needs additional explanation is the role that corporate decision-makers have in addressing the most challenging problems faced by society, when all corporate decisions take place in a competitive market, where success is measured not by trees

FIGURE 3.1 Stakeholders of Corporate Conduct

saved but rather money earned. Competitive markets for natural resources, such as the raw materials of production, can create unsustainable consumption dynamics characterized by demand in excess of supply. The following two sections will describe some of the economic barriers to be overcome by sustainable leadership.

3.1.1 What Is a Collective Action Problem?

Collective action problem is a term from the field of economics which describes a form of market failure in which everyone in a given group has a choice between two alternatives—one apparently good for the individual and the other good for the group—and they tend to make the suboptimal choice.

In a collective action problem scenario in which most agents choose to cooperate, those individuals unwilling to cooperate are described as **freeriders**, because they benefit from the cooperation of others, but are unwilling to reciprocate cooperation. Behind Rawls' veil of ignorance, in a collective action problem, a reasonable person would not choose to freeride on the benevolence of others even if she could get away with it, but rather, would be willing to contribute a fair share to the cooperative arrangement.

Climate change is the quintessential global-scale collective action problem. The number of parties responsible for creating the risk of climate change is so vast that transaction costs and information imperfections render it difficult to organize the responsible parties to agree on greenhouse gas reduction plans. Even if the collective action problem could be overcome, such as via intergovernmental collaboration and effective industry commitments to risk reduction strategies, there is always the possibility of a freerider scenario.

For instance, even if a substantial number of responsible parties agreed to take collective action to reduce the global risk of climate change by curbing greenhouse gas emissions, other nations that are not bound by the same priorities could attract

Collective Action Problem Situation in which everyone in a given group has a choice between two alternatives—to maximize individual expected return or to cooperate with others to maximize aggregate return—and where, if everyone chooses to act individualistically self-serving, the outcome will be worse for everyone involved, in their own estimation, than it would be if they were all to choose a path of cooperation.

Freerider In a collective action scenario, when one party benefits from the cooperation of others, but is unwilling to reciprocate cooperation.

industry from more regulated nations to operate within a more lenient regulatory environment. Acting as a freerider on the effort of others, the un-bound nation could benefit from reduced risk of climate change at the expense of other nations. The effect would be an industry migration, causing **carbon leakage**, where a source of greenhouse gas emissions leaks from a regulated environment into an unregulated one, thereby frustrating the collective response. Because of collective action and freerider problems, global risks like climate change can be intractable and difficult to manage.

The threat of climate change puts the role of corporate leadership in context. The greenhouse-gas effect induced sea level rise, changes in rainfall patterns, and increased intensity of hurricanes (among other risks) cannot be successfully addressed by any single national government acting on its own, by governmental action at a limited geographic scale, nor by individual consumer or community behavioral changes.[2] Intergovernmental bodies such as the United Nations seem like the logical source of policies to address challenges of international scope. However, international momentum on climate change has remained stuck in second gear, with "climate talks" taking place for two decades without producing a binding treaty. By the process of elimination, the only remaining agents of change to address climate challenges are located in the private sector. Business leadership is necessary to combat collective action problems to solve sustainability challenges.

By self-regulation, businesses can curb greenhouse gas emissions without necessarily being mandated to do so by government. We discuss this business leadership option in the section on self-regulation next.

3.1.2 What Is a Tragedy of the Commons?

Tragedy of the commons describes a scenario where people compete with one another for use of a resource, yet there is no way to limit competitors' access to the resource.

The world's oceans, atmosphere, groundwater, and forests resemble what economists term **public goods**. Public goods are non-rival, meaning one person's use does not decrease another person's access to that good. However, public goods are only non-rival up to a certain threshold congestion point of aggregate over-use, at which time the good becomes rival. In addition to beginning as non-rival resources, public goods are also non-excludable, meaning that it is impractical or impossible to limit the enjoyment of the good to those who are willing and able to pay for it.

Natural resources such as forests share these characteristics in common with built resources such as civil infrastructure. The market tends to under-provide and over-exploit public goods because if everyone must pay or no one pays for the good, then no one has an incentive to conserve that good. In a tragedy of the commons, individuals have an incentive to exploit the resource to the maximum of their ability, often leading to inefficient resource use.

As discussed in the chapter opener for Chapter 2: Perspectives, global ecosystem services are being over-burdened by today's levels of resource consumption. The fairest way to ensure that public goods are not depleted is to require some form of user-fee financing. Only if users are required to internalize the costs caused

Carbon Leakage Where a source of greenhouse gas emissions migrates from a regulated environment into an unregulated one in order to avoid compliance with emissions limits.

Tragedy of the Commons A scenario when a public good becomes rival but not excludable.

Public Goods Resources which are non-rival and non-excludable, such as air.

by over-exploiting a resource can incentives for efficient use and conservation be established. As discussed in Chapter 1: Introduction to Sustainable Business, sustainable businesses internalize the externalities created by their operations and supply chains. Additionally, sustainable businesses innovate to reduce reliance on resources in the first place.

In a collective action problem where public goods threaten to be over-exploited, businesses can take initiative in the absence of government involvement through leadership, innovation, and corporate governance mechanisms that effectively reduce the organization's reliance on resources, to help prevent a tragedy of the commons from occurring. Leadership, innovation, and corporate governance will be dealt with in turn in the subsequent sections of this chapter.

3.1.3 Sustainability through Self-Regulation

When government solutions are projected to be expensive, ineffective, or absent, self-regulation appears to be a promising alternative to sustainability problem solving in part because it can be flexible and cost-effective. Self-regulation describes the situation when a business or industry takes the initiative to solve an environmental or a public health problem in the absence of government regulation requiring them to do so. **Self-regulation** is voluntary adherence to a firm- or an industry-specific code of conduct. In practice, self-regulation is usually insufficient to achieve sustainable performance without some form of third-party verification of compliance.

A popular form of self-regulation in the context of sustainable management is the **Environmental Management System** (EMS), which can bring about organizational change through the adoption of voluntary regulatory structures that promote environmental policies and strategies, with the goal of reducing the environmental impacts of industrial activity. Voluntary commitments to greenhouse gas reductions or water conservation are examples of corporate self-regulation.

The American Chemistry Council developed the **Responsible Care Management System** (RCMS), an integrated, structured approach to improve company performance in emergency response, employee health and safety, pollution prevention, and process and product safety.[3]

> **Self-Regulation** Voluntary adherence to a firm- or industry-specific code of conduct.
>
> **Environmental Management System** A voluntary regulatory structure that promotes internal environmental policies and strategies, with the goal of reducing the environmental impacts of industrial activity.
>
> **Responsible Care Management System** An integrated, structured approach to improve company performance in emergency response, employee health and safety, pollution prevention, and process and product safety developed by The American Chemistry Council.

LEADERSHIP: Chemical Manufacturers Association and 'Responsible Care'

Bringing about the Responsible Care program was not without challenges. It began in the late 1980s when the Chemical Manufacturer's Association (CMA) sought support from the chemical industry for a uniform Environmental Health & Safety code of conduct. A classic Harvard Business Review case, "Responsible Care," provides details about the implementation issues surrounding the program, which "makes implementation of the codes a condition of membership in CMA[, and] raises issues of due process, fairness, legitimacy, relations with [Environmental Protection Agency], and fears of small companies."[4]

The first test of the effectiveness of self-regulation programs on the actual reduction of industrial accidents took place in 2012. Researchers studied the effects of firm participation in the Responsible Care program from its inception to 2001, and found that RCMS reduced the likelihood of accidents by 2.99 accidents per 100 plants in a given year (a 69.3% reduction).[5] However, reducing accidents is not the same as reducing pollution. The same research found that "on average, plants owned by RC participating firms raise their toxicity-weighted pollution by 15.9% relative to statistically equivalent plants owned by non-RC[MS] participating firms."[6] The increase in toxic pollution levels at Responsible Care participating firms was not caused by general increases in pollution volumes across industry because, during the same time period, there was a "yearly 4% reduction in pollution among all plants in our sample."[7] In addition to an increase in toxics, participation in Responsible Care appeared to increase "plant-level pollution intensity by 15.1%."[8] Why would firm self-regulation in the chemical sector lead to a decrease in accidents but an increase in toxicity and overall pollution levels?

One explanation is that accidents cause internal operational disruption whereas pollution can be more readily externalized to outside parties; therefore accident prevention will receive more attention than pollution reduction under a self-regulation program. Alternatively, companies may have sought out participation in Responsible Care precisely because they had plans to deal increasingly with chemicals that have toxic characteristics. Importantly, the companies in the study used the pre-2002 version of the Responsible Care program, which did not require independent third-party certification. Today, the American Chemistry Council requirements for RCMS compliance include mandatory certification by an independent, accredited auditor at both company headquarters and facilities to ensure proper implementation.[9]

CROSS-LINKAGE

For more on measuring sustainable performance, see Chapter 5: Metrics, Tools, and Reporting: The Role of Finance and Accounting.

As discussed in Chapter 7: Marketing, a critical ingredient in sustainable certification program design and implementation is independent third-party verification. Some of the weaknesses of self-regulation programs are the temptation to set vague or unambitious performance goals, or to use participation in the program for cover because it lacks external oversight. That said, leaders have a variety of avenues to promote sustainability through self-regulation. For instance, in this chapter we discuss leadership and corporate governance as mechanisms for sustainable management.

3.1.4 The Sustainable Leadership Gap

Sustainability Leadership Gap The disconnect between where companies need to be and where they actually are in terms of sustainable performance.

A perennial **sustainability leadership gap**—the disconnect between good intentions of business leaders and actual sustainable performance—stems from lack of accountability to external stakeholders. As discussed earlier, some evidence would suggest that self-regulation is helpful, but not in itself sufficient, to promote sustainability.

There remain gaps between the talk and action, largely due to the traditional inward focus of leadership and governance policies, as well as the lack of sustainability

> **ETHICAL DECISIONS:** The Sustainability Leadership Gap[11]
>
> Business for Social Responsibility (BSR) is a non-profit that works with its network of 250 of the world's leading companies to integrate sustainability into business strategy and operations through research, collaboration, and advising. According to BSR, "Most large companies acknowledge the need to be more responsive to shifting societal expectations, to be better able to establish trusting relationships with stakeholders, and to become more open and accountable. And yet those same companies often struggle to translate good intentions into good practice." BSR concludes that the reason for the disconnect is "the lack of any serious, practical guidance addressing the outmoded way in which leaders tend to be selected and developed. We refer to this as the 'sustainability leadership gap.'"

literacy among business students. "While a growing number of business schools teach some ethics and corporate social responsibility, the management and organizational development skills and perspectives required to run a sustainable business are rarely taught."[10]

There are two systemic hurdles to sustainable leadership in the private sector: the traditional education of future business leaders has historically lacked sustainability perspectives and skills, and the promotion process for leadership positions has traditionally not been tied to sustainable corporate performance. Both of these hurdles are eroding with the advent of sustainable business curriculum and sustainability-linked compensation (discussed next), clearing the path for sustainable business leadership.

3.2 Leadership

3.2.1 What Is Sustainable Business Leadership?

In the context of corporate activities, **leadership** is the ability to make sound decisions on behalf of the company and to inspire the workforce to perform at their fullest potential. Beyond prudent operations, leadership also requires goal-setting, decisive action in the face of complex and difficult situations, and calculated risk-taking. Although leadership is difficult to quantify, its importance to the success of any business cannot be overstated.

When we think of a business leader, we might conjure an image of someone who is intelligent, tough, determined, and has a vision; however, truly effective leaders also have "soft" characteristics including self-awareness, self-regulation, motivation, empathy, and social tact.[12]

Sustainable business leadership is the effective use of one's skill, knowledge, management style, and personality traits (Figure 3.2) given the internal and external context of one's business (Figure 3.3) to promote the sustainability mission of the company through certain activities (Figure 3.4).[13]

Leadership The ability to make sound decisions on behalf of the company and to inspire the workforce to perform at their fullest potential.

Sustainable Business Leadership The effective use of one's skill, knowledge, management style, and personality trait, given the internal and external context of one's business, to promote the sustainability mission of the company through certain activities.

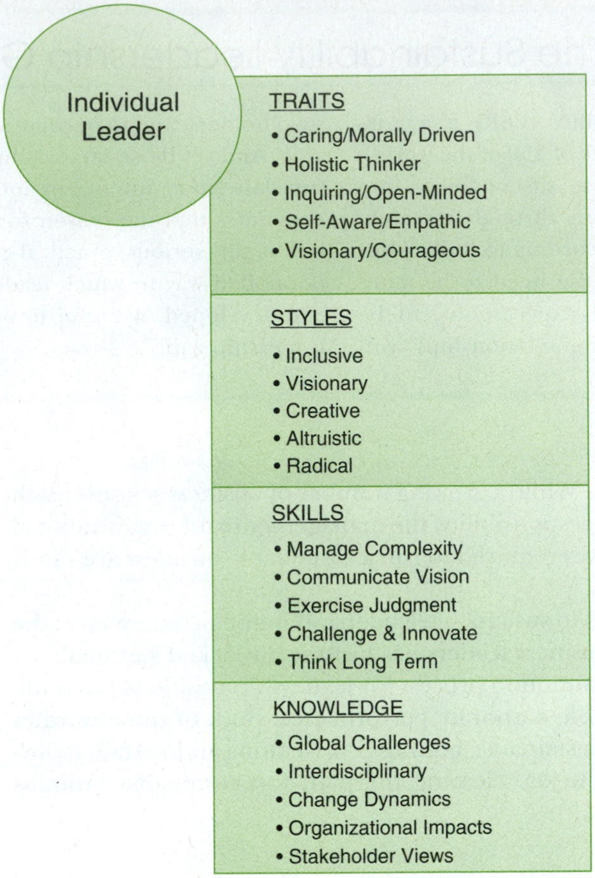

Individual Leader

TRAITS
- Caring/Morally Driven
- Holistic Thinker
- Inquiring/Open-Minded
- Self-Aware/Empathic
- Visionary/Courageous

STYLES
- Inclusive
- Visionary
- Creative
- Altruistic
- Radical

SKILLS
- Manage Complexity
- Communicate Vision
- Exercise Judgment
- Challenge & Innovate
- Think Long Term

KNOWLEDGE
- Global Challenges
- Interdisciplinary
- Change Dynamics
- Organizational Impacts
- Stakeholder Views

FIGURE 3.2 Profile of a Sustainable Leader

Source: Adapted from Wayne Visser & Polly Courtice, *Sustainability Leadership: Linking Theory and Practice,* University of Cambridge Programme for Sustainability Leadership (CPSL) Working Paper (October 21, 2011).

Leadership Context

EXTERNAL
- Ecological
- Economic
- Political
- Cultural
- Community

INTERNAL
- Sector/Industry
- Organizational Reach
- Organizational Culture
- Governance Structure
- Leadership Role

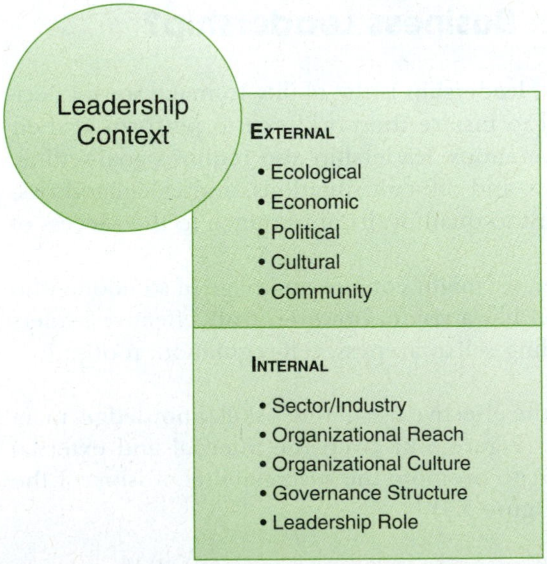

FIGURE 3.3 The Context of Business Leadership

Source: Adapted from Wayne Visser & Polly Courtice, *Sustainability Leadership: Linking Theory and Practice,* University of Cambridge Programme for Sustainability Leadership (CPSL) Working Paper (October 21, 2011).

Leadership Actions

INTERNAL
- Informed Decisions
- Strategic Direction
- Management Incentives
- Performance Accountability
- People Empowerment
- Learning & Innovation

EXTERNAL
- Cross-Sector Partnerships
- Sustainable Products/Services
- Sustainability Awareness
- Context Transformation
- Stakeholder Transparency

FIGURE 3.4 Actions Taken by Sustainable Leadership

Source: Adapted from Wayne Visser & Polly Courtice, *Sustainability Leadership: Linking Theory and Practice,* University of Cambridge Programme for Sustainability Leadership (CPSL) Working Paper (October 21, 2011).

3.2.2 New Competencies of Sustainable Business Leaders

Understanding what it takes to successfully operate and market a company are obvious prerequisites to taking on a leadership position in any company of any size. However, sustainability leadership requires skills that are beyond the scope of those traditionally vetted for promotion and succession. Experience, knowledge of the company, and success in increasing profits are necessary but not sufficient to achieve sustainable leadership. The top competencies overall for sustainable leadership in particular are:[14]

1. External awareness and appreciation of trends
2. Visioning and strategy formulation
3. Risk awareness, assessment, and management
4. Stakeholder engagement
5. Flexibility and adaptability to change
6. Ethics and integrity

According to BSR, "It is startling that five of the six competencies identified as the most important [(all aside from ethics and integrity)] are either new or [require] significant modification from the classic definitions if companies are to select, develop, and promote those able to lead in an increasingly economically connected, ecologically interdependent, and socially accountable world."[15] Clearly, the same old approaches to leading a company will not suffice to lead a sustainable business. In general, traditional leadership is characterized by internal focus, short-term financial performance goals, and basic operational improvement, whereas sustainable leadership is characterized by external focus on social and environmental performance metrics, long-term growth, and innovation that keeps up with the needs of consumers and supply chain partners in a changing world.

The people and positions vested with power and control over corporate activities obviously have a large role to play in sustainability because of the influence they wield over corporate decision-making. The influence of a leader can be used to

> **MANAGERIAL INSIGHT:** Kevin Kruse, We: How to Increase Performance and Profits through Full Engagement (2011)[16]
>
> "Leadership has nothing to do with … position in the hierarchy of a company. Leadership has nothing to do with titles. Leadership has nothing to do with personal attributes. […] Leadership is a process of social influence, which maximizes the efforts of others, towards the achievement of a goal."

ensure decisions are made transparently, accountably, and consistent with ethics at the level of corporate-wide policy. Leaders can also bring out the best in the human resources of the company. We now turn to the methods for formal business leaders to activate the leadership potential of all the company's employees in pursuit of the company's sustainability strategy.

3.2.3 Sustainable Leadership Strategy

Other chapters in this textbook will underscore the importance of metrics, legal compliance, supply chain management, operations, marketing, and risk management in creating a sustainable enterprise. For all of their importance, excellence in these areas depends upon leadership. If leadership lacks values and a vision consistent with sustainable principles, innovation to reduce the environmental footprint of products may not receive adequate funding or support. At the same time, top-down strategy is only important to sustainability if full organizational engagement is the result.

Which approaches, strategies, and characteristics make for a leader that can maximize employee productivity while respecting employee dignity and achieving company goals? Research from *MIT Sloan Management Review* breaks it down into virtues and vices of four different leadership strategies: forceful, enabling, strategic, and operational.[17] See Table 3.1.

> **LEADERSHIP:** LJ Building Maintenance, LLC, SME Leader[18]
>
> Lonnie Williams is the owner of LJ Building Maintenance, a small cleaning company employing 50 people and serving customers in Kansas, Missouri, Nebraska, and North Carolina. Williams, now in his 60s, is an African-American service-disabled Vietnam War veteran who won the Small Business Administration (SBA) Minority Small Businessperson of the Year award in 2007. Williams has the reputation of an effective leader owing to his caring yet no-nonsense style of management. According to Williams, "[When] I expect you to do something, [] I follow up on those expectations," and at the same time, he doesn't expect his employees to be flawless. Williams makes an effort to understand his employees on a personal level: "When they have hardships, I try to be a part of that." While growing his company into an award-winning outfit delivering high quality customer service, Williams still remains down to earth. "I've worked beside just about anybody in any building, just to let them know that I still know the business inside and out."

> **TABLE 3.1**
>
> ## Virtues and Vices of Main Leadership Strategies
>
> | FORCEFUL LEADERSHIP | | ENABLING LEADERSHIP | |
> |---|---|---|---|
> | **Vice** | **Virtue** | **Virtue** | **Vice** |
> | *Eclipses subordinates* | *Takes charge* | *Delegates* | *Lacks oversight* |
> | *Ignores others' ideas* | *Expresses clearly* | *Listens well* | *No spine* |
> | *Insensitive* | *Makes tough call* | *Compassionate* | *Accommodating* |
> | *Rigid* | *Accountability* | *Understanding* | *No accountability* |
> | STRATEGIC LEADERSHIP | | OPERATIONAL LEADERSHIP | |
> | **Vice** | **Virtue** | **Virtue** | **Vice** |
> | *Head in the clouds* | *Long-term focus* | *Gets results* | *Tunnel vision* |
> | *Too conceptual* | *Big picture* | *Knows how* | *Caught up in detail* |
> | *Too ambitious* | *Aggressive* | *Respects limits* | *Too conservative* |
>
> *Source:* On leadership styles. Robert E. Kaplan and Robert B. Kaiser, Developing Versatile Leadership, MIT Sloan Management Review (July 15, 2003). © 2003 from MIT Sloan Management Review/Massachusetts Institute of Technology. All rights reserved. Distributed by Tribune Content Agency, LLC.

Although no one is perfect, the ideal leader would employ the virtues of each management strategy, while indulging the vices of none. The leader of a sustainable enterprise should be able to take charge and make tough calls during complex situations, while also empowering subordinates and effectively delegating; a sustainable leader has a holistic vision for the company and establishes long-term strategy, while also promoting near-term efficiency gains based on a detailed operational knowledge of how the business actually works.

Although leaders of sustainable companies come from various backgrounds, they tend to "exhibit a predictable, five-stage pattern in their efforts to incorporate sustainability practices and policies."[19] See Table 3.2. By expanding awareness, engaging

> **TABLE 3.2**
>
> ## Becoming a Sustainable Leader: The Five-Fold Path
>
> | Stage | Instill Values | Take Action | Deepen Understanding | Sustain Commitment | Learn & Advocate |
> |---|---|---|---|---|---|
> | **Must Have** | Awareness | Experimentation | Systems Thinking | Resource Allocation | Influence |
> | **Steps** | Express desire to change course. | Start small with a pilot project. | Explore implications of sustainability on all aspects of performance. | Commit managerial and financial resources to a complete plan that is monitored and reported. | Continuous learning also drives advocacy within industry. |
>
> *Source:* Pat Hughes & Kathleen Hosfeld, *The Leadership of Sustainability: A Study of Characteristics and Experiences of Leaders Bringing the "Triple-Bottom Line" to Business,* Center for Ethical Leadership, page 10 (2005). Used by permission of Center for Ethical Leadership.

in experimentation, establishing broad systems thinking, ensuring resource commitment, and inspiring businesses within the supply chain to do the same, leaders can integrate sustainability into their company and beyond, regardless of industry or size.

As shareholder and stakeholder expectations shift toward greater accountability and transparency, new leadership competencies for sustainable performance are emerging. Decision-making procedures for promotion to leadership positions should vet candidates for these newly defined capabilities. In addition to leadership succession, sustainability also presents unique opportunities and challenges when it comes to hiring new employees. We discuss this in 3.3.4.

3.3 Change Management

Because sustainable business is a relatively new phenomenon, most organizations have yet to internalize social and environmental responsibility into organizational behavior. In order to integrate sustainability policies throughout an organization's activities, employees and decision-makers throughout all of the divisions and ranks of the company must take on leadership responsibilities to some degree. Change is hard. This section will explain the process of transforming a company from a traditional enterprise to a sustainable enterprise through change management.

We will first explain the entrepreneurial attitude that motivates change in the first place, specifically changes that align the organization's mission with social and environmental challenges and drive innovation. We then explain how sustainability can be incorporated into business strategy for competitive advantage. Once the change management process is underway, leaders must maintain organizational culture of sustainability through hiring strategies and employee engagement.

The dominant constraint for SMEs striving for sustainability is the shortage of resources in terms of time, money, and personnel; as a result, they must optimize what kinds of management changes they are willing to make to leverage the most out of their commitment to sustainability.[20] One of the most important reasons why SMEs invest in environmental benefit measures is to improve the working conditions of employees, with the effect of improving their motivation and performance.[21] As a result, sustainability and employee engagement go hand in hand.

3.3.1 Entrepreneurialism and Innovation

Entrepreneurialism The activation of opportunities to combine limited resources in order to create value and secure returns in new ways, brought about by problem-solving practices under resource constraint and decision-making flexibility.

Eco-entrepreneurialism Innovation that involves enhancements in resource efficiency, environmental impacts, meeting unmet needs of society, and transforming waste into a valuable asset.

Entrepreneurialism is the activation of opportunities to combine limited resources in order to create value and secure returns in new ways, brought about by problem-solving practices under resource constraint and decision-making flexibility.[22]

Entrepreneurs are usually motivated by the pursuit of opportunity, the application of new means-end frameworks for action, the origination of new business ideas, the translation of new ideas into business models that are attractive to investors, and the diffusion of innovation.

Eco-entrepreneurialism characterizes innovation that involves enhancements in resource efficiency, environmental impacts, meeting unmet needs of society, and transforming waste into a valuable asset. Eco-entrepreneurs forge solutions to environmental and social challenges by using creative perspectives to develop new products and services.

Innovation is the investment of resources by a company into research and development (R&D) resulting in improvements upon current activities. Change for change's sake does no good for anyone. The kind of change that leaders are looking for is innovation—that is, modifications to the way things are done that generate greater benefits, and avoid costs generated by, the old way of doing things.

There are four types of innovation: product, process, marketing, and organizational innovation.[23]

Product innovation is the development of new or significantly improved goods or services through improved technical specifications, materials, software, use-friendliness, or other functional characteristic.

Process innovation is a new or significantly improved method of production or delivery, including modified production techniques or manufacturing equipment.

Marketing innovation is development of a new marketing practice based on significant improvements to product design, packaging, product placement, promotional material, or price.

Organizational innovation is the implementation of a new method of business practice, workplace structure, or external relations. Sustainability initiatives can stimulate progress along all four dimensions of innovation.

According to the Organization for Economic Cooperation and Development, **eco-innovation** is the incremental or radical change of a firm's processes and responsibilities, which reduces environmental impact and supports organization learning, and goes beyond products, processes, marketing, and organizational innovation to include social and institutional structures.[27]

Eco-entrepreneurialism and eco-innovation are driven by reducing costs, capturing new markets, attracting investors, and remaining competitive. However, there are many other independent drivers of sustainable innovation. These include meeting the demands of cause-motivated consumers, satisfying ethical obligations, improving relationships

Innovation The investment of resources by a company into research and development (R&D) resulting in improvements upon current activities.

Product Innovation The development of new or significantly improved goods or services through improved technical specifications, materials, software, use-friendliness, or other functional characteristic.

Process Innovation A new or significantly improved method of production or delivery, including modified production techniques or manufacturing equipment.

Marketing Innovation The development of a new marketing practice based on significant improvements to product design, packaging, product placement, promotional material, or price.

CROSS-LINKAGE

For more on product and process innovation, see Chapter 9: Operations Management.

LEADERSHIP: CLIF Bar Founded on Product and Organizational Innovation[24]

The founder of CLIF Bar, Gary Erickson, was inspired to create a nutritious and tasty energy bar after attempting to sustain himself on a 175-mile bike ride on six indigestible energy bars. The CLIF Bar product line offers a variety of flavors (think dessert) that provide the nutrition needed to sustain an active lifestyle, and yet they don't taste like something that would be considered health food! In 1991, Erickson named the company after his father, Clif, and launched his first product in a single bike shop. Within months the CLIF Bar was being sold in 700 bike shops; within a year the company recorded $700,000 in revenue; in two years, revenue reached $1.2 million; for several years successively after that, revenue grew by 50 to 100 percent; ultimately Erikson was presented with the opportunity to sell CLIF Bar to Quaker Oats for $120 million. Instead of selling, Erikson put the future of the company in the hands of his staff, asking them to help him shape the company into a sustainable enterprise. Employee feedback and Erikson's personal values led to a corporate-wide commitment to the long-term health of the company itself as well as the surrounding environment and communities.[25] CLIF Bar became dedicated to five aspirational principles: sustaining our brands, business, people, community, and the planet.[26]

between buyers and suppliers, and establishing legitimacy and license to operate with key stakeholders such as NGOs and government offices.

Innovation requires change. Change must be managed to avoid business losses and project failures resulting from the disruptions caused by that change. We discuss developing a sustainable business strategy to guide change, next.

3.3.2 Developing a Sustainable Business Strategy

There are basically four traditional business strategies for competitive advantage: (1) cost leadership, (2) differentiation, (3) focus, and (4) the combination of differentiation and cost leadership.[28] This section will demonstrate how these strategies can be deployed in pursuit of sustainability to bring about competitive advantages. We will also explain two additional strategies—(5) minimizer and (6) transformer—which are unique to sustainable organizations.

The strategy of **cost leadership** involves increasing profit margins by maintaining financial costs at levels lower than competitors' costs while maintaining comparable levels of price and quality.[29]

Lower financial costs can be achieved through efficiency gains in production, distribution, and a variety of other avenues. If these savings are passed on to consumers through lower prices, cost leaders can increase market share and gain even greater operating cost reductions through increased economies of scale. Companies can use cost leadership strategy to benefit from sustainability by innovating operations to reduce waste, increase production process resource efficiency, and designing products that use less material inputs.

The strategy of **differentiation** involves offering a special product or service for which buyers are willing to pay price premiums.[30] The features that make a sustainable product or service unique can be high quality, creative design, augmented technical ability, the social impacts of production, environmental friendliness, increased durability, product longevity, and so forth.

Some consumer segments are willing to pay a premium for sustainable products and services. Companies like Method Products are able to command price premiums for eco-chic household cleaners and personal care products because they offer the unique feature of being toxic-free and high quality.

The strategy of **focus** involves selecting a small niche in geographic area, consumer segment, or specialty product or service.[31] Focus is an especially useful strategy for small- and medium-sized enterprises (SMEs) because, for these companies, it is easier to target a local audience than to compete in the international or national marketplace. For example, a variety of small businesses in the states of California, Oregon, and Washington focus on the robust yet niche markets of consumers in those areas who prefer organic, locally sourced food.

The strategy of **cost leadership and differentiation** means offering a general portfolio of products that is lower in cost on average than competitors, while also offering a distinct product line that commands a price premium.[32] For example, Kia can offer a fleet of vehicles that compete on price with other automobile makers by keeping their operating costs low (cost leadership), while also offering a hybrid version of the

Kia Optima that is several thousand dollars more expensive than the regular Optima because of its advanced fuel efficiency rating (differentiation).[33]

The **minimizer** strategy provides goods or services in a method that reduces costs across the triple-bottom-line of financial, environmental, and social accounts. By reducing internal financial as well as external social and environmental costs, a minimizing strategy is to increase profit margins without increasing prices, while also fostering goodwill within the community in which it does business and benefiting the environment.

For example, in 2013 the Mountain Equipment Co-op, a Canadian-based consumer cooperative that sells outdoor recreation gear and clothing to its 4.1 million members, measurably reduced greenhouse gas emissions from operations and diverted 92% of its waste from landfills, thereby minimizing its environmental impacts and increasing its operational efficiency while maintaining competitive pricing for members.[34]

The **transformer** strategy takes advantage of a discarded or undervalued resource (waste, pollution) by redeeming it into desirable goods through recycling, refurbishing, or repurposing.[35] Office Max, Samsung, Epson, Brother, Hewlett-Packard, and Staples all promote recycling and take-back programs for printer ink and toner cartridges, which take a waste product that is unsafe for domestic disposal and redeem it into a new product. Further, companies can make transformation of waste central to their business model. For example, some companies recycle discarded rubber tires into mats, hoses, office supplies, and rubberized asphalt concrete for road surfaces.[36]

Business leaders have a variety of models from which to choose when developing a sustainability strategy. These strategies for sustainable competitive advantages are not mutually exclusive—they can be combined and modified as necessary to suit the company's goals, needs, and circumstances.

Now that we have explained the role of entrepreneurship, innovation, and strategy in creating a sustainable business model, we take on the topic of change management, next.

> **Minimizer** Providing goods or services in a method that reduces costs across the triple-bottom-line of financial, environmental, and social accounts, in order to increase profit margins without increasing prices.

> **Transformer** Taking advantage of a discarded or undervalued resource (waste, pollution) by redeeming it into desirable goods through recycling, refurbishing, or repurposing.

> **CROSS-LINKAGE**
>
> For more on product take-back, see Chapter 8: Supply Chain Management. For more on recycling, see Chapter 9: Operations Management.

3.3.3 Change Management

Change does not take place *tabula rasa*, from a blank slate. Change presupposes a prior state and an end state, and describes the transition from the former to the latter. In our case, we mean the transition from a traditional company to a sustainable company. **Change management** means altering corporate behavior and processes in response to environmental influences in order to achieve a goal.[37] According to early research by John Kotter, there are a variety of obstacles to leading organizational change, including the feeling of being personally threatened on the part of employees, uncertainty and mistrust created by the change, doubt about the ability of the company to endure the change, and conflicting perspectives over what the change should entail.[38] Especially during the process of change, according to management author and consultant Peter Drucker, managers should nurture the development of individual and group competencies in order to promote the new organizational culture, strategy, and behavior.[39]

> **Change Management** Altering corporate behavior and processes in response to environmental influences in order to achieve a goal.

Leaders should strive to inspire employees at all levels of the company to embrace a leadership role within their unique sphere of influence in order to usher the company through the change process. This can be accomplished through human resource management in the form of training and education about the company's sustainability mission and strategy, environmental issues affecting (and affected by) the company, as well as corporate citizenship programs that connect the company with the local community while addressing social needs.[40] Although the goals and stakeholders are different, leading organizational change to promote sustainability follows a path similar to the company-wide change initiatives that took place during the total quality management (TQM) movement.

The **organizational development** approach to change management uses a planned change process that draws on behavioral sciences to systematically improve individual, interpersonal, and structural aspects of organizations.[41] Allowing employees to actively participate through open dialogue is a critical ingredient for success in any organizational change process.[42]

The classic framework for change management comes from the work of Kurt Lewin, and consists of a three-step process of unfreezing, changing, and refreezing, that secures buy-in from everyone in the organization.[43] See Figure 3.5.

Change management guides the transformation of a traditional for-profit company into a sustainable enterprise. In order for this change to endure, however, new employees must be on-board with the agenda. Sustainability needs to be a part of ongoing hiring strategy to ensure new employees are engaged in the company's strategy and committed to seeing it through. We discuss hiring strategy and employee engagement, next.

Organizational Development Change management approach using a planned change process that draws on behavioral sciences to systematically improve individual, interpersonal, and structural aspects of organizations.

Unfreezing Step 1 in the classic change management process when managers inform employees that the status quo is no longer sustainable and that change is needed.

Changing Step 2 in the classic change management process involving communication over various media within the organization—employee training, town hall meetings, and the like—to reinforce the new sustainability strategy.

Refreezing Step 3 in the classic change management process where new behaviors and attitudes are adopted on the part of the organization's people toward the organization's sustainability strategy.

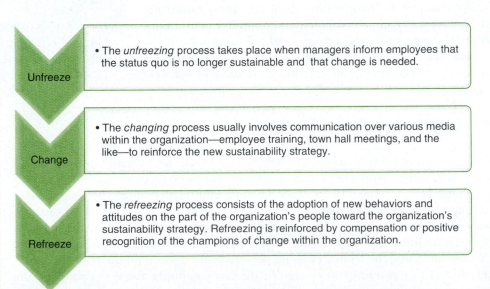

- The *unfreezing* process takes place when managers inform employees that the status quo is no longer sustainable and that change is needed.

- The *changing* process usually involves communication over various media within the organization—employee training, town hall meetings, and the like—to reinforce the new sustainability strategy.

- The *refreezing* process consists of the adoption of new behaviors and attitudes on the part of the organization's people toward the organization's sustainability strategy. Refreezing is reinforced by compensation or positive recognition of the champions of change within the organization.

FIGURE 3.5 Three Processes of Change Management

Source: Bernard Burnes, *Kurt Lewin and the Planned Approach to Change: A Re-appraisal*, Vol. 41 No. 6 Journal of Management Studies 977–1002 (September 2004).

3.3.4 **Hiring Strategy and Employee Engagement**

In this section we draw from the Center for Advanced Human Resource Studies qualitative survey data from potential new employees assessing attitudes toward the sustainability initiatives of their potential employer. Companies leading in sustainability, such as Timberland, use charitable gift matching and employee volunteer programs to recruit socially responsible employees (who tend to be better employees) while contributing to the communities in which the company does business.[44] The benefits of engaging employees in the company's sustainability strategy include competitive advantages at the hiring stage, employee loyalty and retention, enhanced worker productivity and efficiency, and improved work product quality.[45]

"About 90% of respondents said they would be more likely to join or stay with a company with strong reputation for CSR that supports charitable initiatives and promotes sustainability efforts. However, only 65% of respondents said they would take a pay cut to work for such a company."[46] While "CSR is one important factor in an employee engagement strategy, … it should be paired with other factors to create a balanced, total rewards strategy."[47]

Potential employee attitudes toward employer sustainability efforts are nuanced. Some would rather work for a values-oriented company than a traditional company that simply required volunteer hours. "I can do [charity] on my own time… If I'm spending 40+ hours/week striving for excellence in a company, I only want to do so if the mission, vision, and values of said company represent what I believe in."[48] The general theme is that potential employees are not "willing to take a pay cut to simply work for a company with green initiatives/charitable affiliations," but they would take a pay cut "if the company's actual product/service/line of business itself were mission-driven."[49]

Although sustainability ranks high in relevance to business students and potential employees, a strong trend among younger entrants into the labor market is a marked regard for self-determination. Some would "prefer a higher income that allows me to support social issues I believe in than have my company make that decision for me" by donating profits that might otherwise be employee pay.[50]

The lesson here is that potential future employees are concerned with sustainability but want to express this concern authentically. That means they would rather work for competitive wages at a traditional company and promote sustainability on their own prerogative than take a pay-cut to work for a company with ancillary sustainability programs. At the same time, they would be willing to take a pay cut to work for an organization with a mission aligned with their personal values.

Indeed, there is some skepticism toward stand-alone corporate sustainability initiatives such as mandatory employee volunteer hours. One respondent noted, "They are useful insomuch as they signal something interesting about corporate culture, but in my experiences, they are often mere smokescreen, and are of little functional utility."[51]

What does this mean for hiring strategy from the latest generation of talent? Because of the willingness to sacrifice higher pay for meaningful work, businesses that have integrated sustainability throughout their organization are in a position to recruit the best and brightest from Gen-Y at relatively low wages. Alternatively, recruiters should expect to offer competitive wages to attract talent from this generation if sustainability is merely ancillary to the company's main mission.

In addition to employee volunteer hours, Timberland has integrated sustainability into their product design, manufacturing, and supply chain activities.[52] For sustainability leaders, employee engagement is not window-dressing, but a means of including the employees of a company in the company's expression of its core values.

3.4 Strategic Alignment for Sustainability Through Corporate Governance

The extent to which leaders may pursue sustainable strategy depends in part on the corporate governance structures that circumscribe the actions of business leaders. One of these is the **Articles of Incorporation**, which are the legal agreements between shareholders and management that spell out the fiduciary duties owed by management personnel to the organization and which must be borne out in how the company is managed.

> **Articles of Incorporation**
> Legal agreements between shareholders and management that spell out the fiduciary duties owed by management personnel to the organization and which must be borne out in how the company is managed.

Traditional companies usually make it optional for leadership to consider the interests of stakeholders that are external to the corporation. However, sustainable enterprises can use governance mechanisms to prioritize, if not mandate, sustainable conduct.

We start by looking at the corporate strategy itself, specifically how to align the corporate mission with sustainability. We then look at corporate governance structures that can ensure sustainable performance. Then we show how specific mechanisms of corporate governance, including Independent Directors, special committees, and shareholder resolutions can promote sustainable business performance in unique ways. Next, we help resolve the tension between what the company should do for shareholders versus what it should be doing for external stakeholders, introducing the concept of the B-Corp along the way. Finally, we conclude this part with a discussion of executive compensation as an incentive for sustainable performance.

3.4.1 Strategic Alignment: Integrating Sustainability into Corporate Strategy

> **Strategic Alignment** When a company has attained a fit between its core strategy, its organizational structure, and its competitive landscape through the performance of its employees and the consequences of its activities.

Strategic alignment is what happens when a company has attained a fit between its core strategy, its organizational structure, and its competitive landscape through the performance of its employees and the consequences of its activities.

There are three aspects of successful strategic alignment for sustainable performance:[53] (1) developing a corporate identity through the mission statement, and aligning this mission with customer needs; (2) communicating the mission throughout the organization, and aligning the mission of each division of the company with the overall corporate mission; and (3) executing the corporate mission by aligning division activities with sustainable performance goals. How is a company's sustainability mission integrated throughout all levels of an organization? The answer is through corporate governance.

3.4.2 Sustainable Corporate Governance

Corporate governance is the system of rules, practices and processes by which a company is directed and controlled. This system can be used to ensure all business units are working together to fulfill the corporate mission. Corporate governance is also necessary to achieve ethical, transparent, and sustainable corporate conduct. The use of corporate governance mechanisms depends upon the values and goals of corporate leaders.

Corporate governance should balance the interests of relevant company stakeholders (shareholders, employees, customers, suppliers, financiers, government, and community) to create value.

Sustainable corporate governance uses the mechanisms of corporate control to create long-term value that benefits internal and external stakeholders, contrasted with traditional corporate governance used to create short-term profits solely for the company's direct economic beneficiaries.

Sustainability is not merely a marketing, operational, or supply chain issue, because energy, carbon emissions, water, and waste have become financial assets in terms of reduced cost, risk mitigation and new lines of revenue, putting environmental performance under the auspices of Finance and Accounting, Risk Management, as well as Corporate Governance. This section will focus on the latter.

Integrating sustainability into corporate governance, for instance by creating the position of Chief Sustainability Officer, or by establishing standing committees on sustainability,

> **Corporate Governance** The system of rules, practices and processes by which a company is directed and controlled, used to ensure all business units are working together to fulfill the corporate mission.
>
> **Sustainable Corporate Governance** Using the mechanisms of corporate control to create long-term value that benefits internal and external stakeholders.

> **CROSS-LINKAGE**
>
> For more on stakeholder theory, see Chapter 2: Perspectives.

> **CROSS-LINKAGE**
>
> For more on the role of finance and accounting in monitoring sustainable performance, see Chapter 5: Metrics, Tools, and Reporting: The Role of Finance and Accounting. For more on the role of risk management in promoting a resilient, sustainable enterprise, see Chapter 6: Risk Management.

GLOBAL INSIGHT: Corporate Governance and Stakeholder Theory at Unilever[54]

In order to eliminate the tendency toward short-term thinking that tends to dominate the C-suite, Paul Polman announced on the day he became CEO that Unilever would no longer publish earnings guidance or quarterly profit reports. Instead, under Polman's leadership, the company integrated the need to deal with sustainability challenges such as climate change and poverty into its mission. Polman boldly addressed investors with this new vision of the company's business model: "If you buy into this long-term value model, which is equitable, which is shared, which is sustainable, then come and invest with us. If you don't buy into this, I respect you as a human being, but don't put your money in our company." By changing the measures of success by departing from a traditional corporate governance protocol, Polman changed Unilever.

provides a unified framework for attaining a company's financial and sustainability-related objectives.

The basic **corporate governance framework** brings together the company's mission, strategy, objectives, culture, and leadership. In general, a company's corporate governance structure will have some form of the following six elements:

1. Board of Directors and Committees
2. Legal and Regulatory Compliance
3. Organizational Hierarchy (i.e., CEO, managers, employees)
4. Monitoring and Internal Control
5. Transparency and Accountability
6. Policies and Procedures

These elements ensure alignment of the company's activities with the company's mission. Although the Board of Directors is technically a separate entity from any particular business division, not all of the elements of corporate governance are so. For instance, monitoring and accountability may be supported by a single entity within the company, or it may be represented as separate working groups within the various business units of the company. What is important for corporate governance to be effective is for each of these six elements to be present.

Consider the corporate governance framework of Fujitsu Global, a leading provider of Information Technology products and services.[55] Fujitsu Global uses a Corporate Governance Framework that includes all six elements of corporate governance:

1. The Board of Directors and Executive Nomination and Compensation Committees
2. FUJITSU Way Internal Control Division
3. Corporate Executive Officers
4. Corporate Internal Audit Division
5. Annual Shareholders' Meeting
6. President and Representative Director, Management Council

LEADERSHIP: Eli Lilly Promotes Sustainability through Corporate Governance[56]

The pharmaceutical company Eli Lilly's sustainability report explains the cross-organizational role of corporate governance. Eli Lilly corporate governance has set clear goals for sustainability performance. *Global Policy on Health, Safety, and the Environment* sets environmental expectations related to compliance and environmental protection, and Lilly's *Environmental Standard* establishes the core governance requirements to manage significant environmental and energy-related aspects of operations. Lilly's governance structure ensures that environmental, health and safety issues are managed company-wide. "Our global HSE committee—which includes senior executives from key areas of the business—ensures proper oversight and plays a central role in monitoring corporate performance and ensuring continuous improvement."

Furthermore, the various corporate governance entities have a variety of relations between them, including advising, reporting, supervising, and coordinating. The FUJITSU Way Internal Control Division, located in the heart of the company's corporate governance structure, ensures that environmental, legal, and risk management issues are included in all corporate decision-making. Arranging a company's governance structures in this way is essential to aligning business performance with the mission and strategy of the company.

3.4.3 Corporate Governance Mechanisms

Independent directors, sustainability executive committees, and shareholder resolutions all play a role in sustainable corporate governance. Ideally, these separate governance structures keep the company on the right path by acting as a check-and-balance. Executives, directors, and shareholders are accountable to, and in some respects monitor the behavior of, one another. However, corporate governance does not always work out as planned. See End-of-Chapter Cases.

Independent Directors Under New York Stock Exchange (NYSE) Listed Company rules, businesses are required to populate their Board of Directors with a majority of **Independent Directors**.[57] A director is independent only if the Board affirmatively determines that the director has no material relationship with the listed company. The Independent Director requirement is a corporate responsibility safeguard that ensures corporate governance decisions benefit from objectivity and impartiality, and are not motivated by conflicts of interest between the Board of Directors and the company's shareholders.

> **Independent Directors** An outside director determined by the Board of Directors to have no material relationship with the listed company prior to appointment.

Executive Committees Similar to many other companies, Ford's Board of Directors addresses the most significant business issues facing the company both as a full group, and through specific **executive committees** upon which the directors serve.

At Ford, these executive committees are Audit, Compensation, Finance, Nominating and Governance, and Sustainability. "The Sustainability Committee was formed in 2008 from the former Environment and Public Policy Committee, reflecting the evolution of its responsibilities and the Company's challenges and opportunities. During 2012, nine Directors served on the Sustainability Committee, which is chaired by … an independent director."[58]

> **Executive Committees** Task-oriented subgroups consisting of Directors and Executives appointed to address specific themes or issues within the company.

While leadership and corporate governance are distinct, so too is corporate governance and management. Ford divides its sustainability initiatives between Board-Level Governance and Sustainability Management. At the board level, the President and CEO serves on the Sustainability Committee, which is chaired by an Independent Director, and policy is advanced through Corporate Governance Principles and a Code of Ethics for the Board of Directors. Additionally, the Sustainability Committee has its own Committee Charter, providing more specific policy for handling the company's sustainability affairs. At the managerial level, Ford has a Vice President for Sustainability, Environment, and Safety Engineering, and policy is advanced through a Code of Conduct Handbook, and a Code of Ethics for Senior

Financial Personnel. In addition to sustainability at the corporate governance and managerial levels, Ford also employs a senior level team called Sustainable Mobility Governance that defines the company's climate change strategy and delivers this message to the marketplace.

Sustainable corporate governance can be promoted at the Board of Director level through special committees, provided such a committee has ample jurisdiction over corporate activity. Consider the following responsibilities and duties for the Sustainability Committee at Ford.[59]

> ➤ Assist management in the formulation and implementation of policies, principles and practices to foster the sustainable growth of the Company on a worldwide basis. *Sustainable Growth* means the ability to meet the needs of present motor vehicle customers while taking into account the needs of future generations. Sustainable Growth shall also encompass a business model that creates value consistent with the long-term preservation and enhancement of financial, environmental, and social capital.
> ➤ Assist management in the formulation and implementation of policies, principles and practices to permit the Company to respond to evolving public sentiment and government regulation in the area of motor vehicle and stationary source emissions, especially in the area of greenhouse gas emissions and fuel economy and CO_2 regulation.
> ➤ Assist management in setting strategy, establishing goals and integrating sustainability into the daily business activities across the Company.
> ➤ Review on a continuing basis new and innovative technologies that will permit the Company to achieve sustainable growth and Company actions to protect those technologies.
> ➤ Review on a continuing basis partnerships and relationships, both current and proposed, with customers and others that support the Company's sustainable growth.
> ➤ Review on a continuing basis the Company's communication and marketing strategies relating to sustainable growth.
> ➤ Review the Company's annual sustainability report prior to its issuance.

The Sustainability Committee at Ford is responsible for setting sustainability strategy, ensuring responsiveness to external stakeholders, integrating sustainability principle into practice, fostering technological innovation, reviewing "green" marketing efforts, and overseeing transparency. The purview of any Sustainability Committee should transect finance, marketing, operations, supply chains, and legal compliance in order to ensure consistency across the company. By virtue of an appropriately structured Sustainability Committee, the left hand knows what the right hand is doing.

Shareholder Resolutions The Board of Directors is guided not only by committee deliberations, but also by **shareholder resolutions**. Shareholders are the owners of a traded company, whereas Directors enjoy control of the company. Shareholder resolutions are an accountability mechanism between those holding ownership and those holding control. In recent years, the number of shareholder resolutions addressing sustainability issues has increased across virtually all sectors. See Table 3.3.

Shareholder Resolutions
An accountability measure available to owners of voting stock in a publicly traded company that can influence corporate behavior.

> **TABLE 3.3**
>
> ## 2012 Shareholder Resolutions on Sustainability Issues
>
> | Sector | Issue | Resolution |
> |---|---|---|
> | *Oil and Gas* | Water pollution, worker safety | Accident risk mitigation protocols |
> | *Retail* | Climate change, greenhouse gas emissions, and energy efficient products | Climate risk disclosure requirements |
> | *Electric Utility* | Local community impacts of coal-powered electric plant | Closure of the plant |
> | *Food and Beverage* | Deforestation | Comprehensive sustainable palm oil policy |
> | *Communications* | Energy efficiency | Product innovation |
> | *Consumer Goods* | Human rights violations in the supply chain | Suppliers to issue sustainability reports |
>
> *Source:* See CERES database on shareholder resolutions, available at http://www.ceres.org/investor-network/resolutions#.

Investors are waking up to a wide range of global trends such as water scarcity and human rights, and are calling on business leaders and Boards of Directors to do something about it.

3.4.4 Resolving Conflicts Between Shareholders and Stakeholders: Rise of the B-Corp

In the ongoing debate about the extent and justifications for corporate responsibility, three distinct views have emerged. Disagreement centers around the issue of who is the proper beneficiary of corporate leadership, and what time-horizons are relevant for assessing business performance.

The **shareholder view of corporate responsibility**, put simply, states that the sole objective of business is to maximize shareholder value.[60] In 1962, Nobel laureate Milton Friedman expressed this idea with appropriate nuance. "[T]here is one and only one social responsibility of business—to use its resources and engage in activities designed to increase its profits so long as it stays within the rules of the game, which is to say, engages in open and free competition without deception or fraud."[61] The only legitimate reason to promote sustainability, under this view, is if doing so would increase shareholder profit.

The **stakeholder view of corporate responsibility** emerged over time as an alternative view on the social responsibility of management. Stakeholder theory aims to include in its decision-making calculus not just shareholders but also any group or individual that can affect or be affected by corporate conduct.[62] In 1984, Edward Freemen argued that the pursuit of profit must be put in service of creating "as much value as possible for multiple stakeholders, without resorting to trade-offs."[63]

Shareholder View of Corporate Responsibility Theory that the sole objective of business leadership is to maximize shareholder value.

Stakeholder View of Corporate Responsibility Theory that business leadership decision-making should include not just shareholder interests, but also any group or individual that can affect or be affected by corporate conduct.

Under the stakeholder view, communities and employees should be benefited as much as possible by corporate conduct, but not to the extent that doing so would interfere with profitability for shareholders.[64] Under a short-term perspective, such as quarterly reporting, there may appear to be differences between what is good for shareholders and what it good for stakeholders.

Enlightened Value Maximization View of Corporate Responsibility Theory that business leaders should use social, economic, and environmental resources in the most efficient ways, while striving to maximize total value creation for all stakeholders.

The **enlightened value maximization view of corporate responsibility** reconciles the dilemma between shareholder and stakeholder perspectives.[65] The tension between the shareholder and the stakeholder views of corporate responsibility is dissolved if we take the long-term perspective on business performance. According to business and finance expert Michael Jensen, "it is obvious that we cannot maximize the long-term market value of an organization if we ignore or mistreat any important constituency."[66] The enlightened value maximization perspective on corporate responsibility is consistent with the sustainability imperative. Business should use social, economic, and environmental resources in the most efficient ways, that is, limiting waste and over-consumption, while striving to maximize total value creation for all stakeholders, not just benefiting stakeholders when it's convenient.

Far from creating a conflict between the executive's duty to shareholders and the duty to the public at large, sustainability means balancing social, economic, and environmental considerations to promote enduring prosperity. The days of tragic trade-offs, where executives putatively had to choose between doing what is right by people and the planet versus doing what is right by those with a direct financial interest in the firm, are long gone. Businesses operate in markets that are increasingly well-informed and responsive to social, economic, and environmental issues. Enlightened business leaders are recognizing that the profitability of a company and its social and environmental responsibility are inter-connected.

Despite these insights, in practice there may be times when shareholder and stakeholder interests appear to be in conflict. One way to resolve this conflict is to change the legal structure of the organization to reflect its commitment to sustainability. Companies now have the option of amending their Articles of Incorporation to become a **B-Corporation** (rather than C-Corporation). A B-Corporation is "designed to deliver benefits beyond profits (the 'B' stands for 'beneficial')."[67] Examples of successful B-Corporations include Method Products, PBC, which provides non-toxic personal care products and home cleaners, and Freelancers Insurance Company, which provides health insurance options to independent workers.

B-Corporation A corporate form designed to deliver social, economic, and environmental benefits beyond shareholder profits (the 'B' stands for 'beneficial').

Businesses can make this legal change to reflect their dedication to stakeholders only through a certification process undertaken by B Lab, a non-profit certifier of socially responsible companies. "Certified B-Corporations are a new type of corporation which uses the power of business to solve social and environmental problems."[68] The certification process involves setting a benchmark for social and environmental impacts; once passed, the company can amend their legal structure to require (rather than merely permit) management to consider the interests of stakeholders, not just shareholders.[69]

There are currently over 900 certified B-Corporations in 29 countries, serving 60 industries, including agriculture, construction, business products and services, consumer products and services, education and training services, energy and environmental services, financial services, health and human services, legal services, media, restaurants, hospitality, travel, retail, transportation, and logistics.[70]

3.4.5 Executive Compensation

Aligning the incentives of business leaders with the mission of an organization is the purpose of **executive compensation** structures, which are critical to achieve the company's strategic goals as well as sustainable growth. Executive compensation is a matter of corporate governance. Often, committees are put into place simply to determine who gets a promotion, who gets a raise, and by how much. These corporate governance decisions create incentives for business leaders that influence behavior for better or worse. If CEOs are rewarded exclusively for increasing quarterly earnings, that will be the primary focus of current and future leaders. Alternatively, CEOs can be rewarded for tangible reductions in the environmental footprint of the company, creating incentives for leadership to prioritize natural resource stewardship and pollution reduction.

CEO earnings have increased substantially over the last several decades. "[A]fter adjusting for inflation, CEO pay in 2009 more than doubled the CEO pay average for the decade of the 1990s, more than quadrupled the CEO pay average for the 1980s, and ran approximately eight times the CEO average for all the decades of the mid-20th century."[71] Estimates of the income distribution that qualifies as top 1% of earners in the United States ranges from $500,000 to $1.3 million, with the average CEO salary around $3.9 million. CEOs for companies listed on Standard & Poor's 500 have an average salary of $10.6 million, and CEOs at companies in the Dow Jones Industrial Average earn on average $19.8 million. This means corporate leaders enjoy majority status in the elite, powerful, and perhaps unjustly vilified "1%."

The Occupy Wall Street Movement's rallying-cry, "We are the 99%," (discussed in Case 1, later) was based on the fact that in the United States, one percent of the country's population has dramatic wealth and income inequality when compared to the rest of the country. Of course, **wealth inequality** is not unique to the United States: the global 1% holds 39% of the world's wealth.

According to Congressional Budget Office analysis, between 1979 and 2007 (before the Great Recession), the top 1% of U.S. earners saw after-tax-and-benefit incomes grow by an average of 275%, compared to around 40%–60% for the bottom 99%. During the 2000s, in the United States, CEO pay rose dramatically, and many companies avoided taxes through shifting assets overseas, and others outsourced manufacturing jobs to lower production costs. Meanwhile, the middle class shrank. By 2007, the top 20% of Americans owned 85% of the country's wealth. These trends were compounded by the 2008 global economic recession, which caused relatively fewer losses and relatively quicker recovery for the top 1%. Media reports that Verizon laid off 1,700 employees after the CEO gave himself a $22 million bonus highlighted the disparity of wealth and power between the average person and the corporate leader amidst troubling economic times.

In order to align CEO incentives with natural resource stewardship, long-term growth, and corporate social responsibility, compensation packages can include sustainability performance metrics such as environmental impacts per units of production; CEO compensation per average employee wage; or locally hired employees per total employees, respectively. The Corporate Knights ranking methodology for the Global 100 Clean Capital list includes as selection criteria whether leadership incentives are aligned with sustainability through executive compensation. Many of the businesses on the list have done so. Across the globe and across industry sectors,

Executive Compensation The incentive package decided by executive committee and offered to business leaders to align behavior with the organizational mission and to compensate for excellent performance.

Wealth Inequality Where a small percentage of people capture a disproportionate amount of a population's total wealth.

ETHICAL DECISIONS: Unilever CEO Weighs in on Corporate Governance[72]

The tradition of quarterly financial reporting is one of the standard measures of modern business performance. However, quarterly P&L statements are inherently short-term indicators, and fail to capture many aspects of corporate performance that can influence stock price, and therefore shareholder value. What is measured becomes what is prioritized. Quarterly reporting prioritizes short-term financial payoff, possibly at the expense of external stakeholders and the longevity of the business itself.

According to Unilever CEO Paul Polman, "I saw a recent survey in the U.S. that 75 percent of the CEOs were willing to postpone the right decisions if it would affect their quarterly reporting, and that cannot be healthy for the long-term of the business." By focusing on long-term sustainability performance, Polman has successfully grown Unilever and remained at the helm for four and a half years and counting, longer than his short-lived peers at comparable companies.

companies such as Intel, Xcel Energy, and ING have tied executive compensation to the sustainability performance of the company's business units.

In addition to defining the overall mission, policies, and incentives of a company, corporate governance can also be used to define the roles and responsibilities of various leadership positions. Some companies have integrated sustainability into corporate governance by creating the position of Chief Sustainability Officer, discussed next.

3.4.6 Rise of the Chief Sustainability Officer

C-Suite The collection of "Chief" officers near the top of an organizational hierarchy that exercise control over the various divisions of the company.

The **C-Suite** is the hypothetical row of offices dedicated to the various "Chief" officers within a company that exercise control over the divisions of the company. These professionals are near the top of the organizational hierarchy, just below the Board of Directors. New C-Suite positions are emerging as companies respond to the call for sustainable leadership. At the same time, traditional roles within the C-Suite are

MANAGERIAL INSIGHT: View from the Top: Executive Opinions on Sustainability[73]

According to an international survey of C-suite decision-makers, the majority of businesses that have pursued sustainability initiatives report that benefits from these programs have exceeded expectations, especially when it comes to brand attributes and cost-savings. Of the 247 executives from the United States, United Kingdom, and China, the majority of respondents (1) view sustainability as an integral part of their business,

(2) believe sustainability initiatives are an investment for a business, not just a cost, and (3) plan to invest more in sustainability initiatives next year. Despite the rosy view from the top, about a third of business leaders surveyed are not convinced of the value of sustainability, believe it is peripheral to their business, and think their company already invests too much into such practices.

being modified to integrate sustainability into how these professionals lead. This section addresses the emergence of the Chief Sustainability Officer.

More than a fourth of Fortune 500 companies have created a formal corporate sustainability leadership function via a new C-level position titled **Chief Sustainability Officer** (CSO), primarily driven by customer demand for corporate sustainability.[74] The background qualities that define a successful CSO include extensive operational experience, broad management background, the ability to manage virtual teams dispersed throughout an organization's various business units, the ability to cultivate relationships with constituencies inside and outside the organization, and to translate lofty goals into concrete plans of action.[75]

A background in environmental policy is not necessary for success as a CSO. The diversity of acceptable experience is demonstrated by the fact that Alcoa's CSO transitioned from a role at the International Council on Mining and Metals, DuPont's transitioned from the Environmental Protection Agency, and 3M's came in from an executive position within the company. Some companies have gone further than appointing a CSO. Mitsubishi International Corporation hired the same person to the position of CSO *and* CEO of its North America operations in a move that, according to a company spokesperson, "signals the rise in the importance of environmental and social considerations to management."[76]

The accompanying diagram illustrates the position of Chief Sustainability Officer (CSO) within a generic corporate structure. See Figure 3.6.

Two takeaways are especially important from this model. First, for sustainability initiatives to be effective, someone with access to senior leadership policy-making and decision-making must champion it. Sustainability with no leadership is just

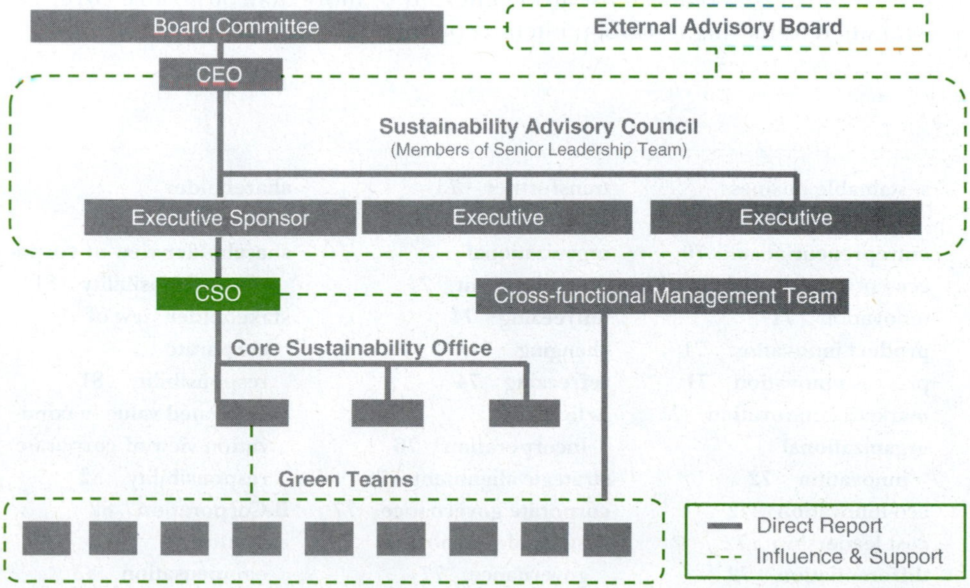

> **Chief Sustainability Officer**
> A formal corporate leadership function positioned in the C-Suite, responsible for overseeing sustainability performance.

FIGURE 3.6 Chief Sustainability Officer (CSO)

Source: Amy Longsworth, Hannah Doran, & Jennifer Webber, *The Sustainability Executive: Profile and Progress*, page 11, PWC (2012).[77]

MANAGERIAL INSIGHT: Chief Sustainability Officers Weigh In

According to Verizon CSO James Gowen, "We don't want to go green for the sake of going green. [Our] sustainability initiatives [must] make sense for our business and the environment. We are at the cusp of an innovation revolution similar to the days of Henry Ford."[79]

For a slightly different view on the role of the private sector in sustainability, consider the perspective of Peter Graf, CSO of SAP, a leader in enterprise management software and related services. "Sustainability is [not] about sacrificing the present for the sake of the future[.] It's about finding the right balance between short and long-term considerations. Once businesses embrace this perspective, they start using business arguments to understand and maximize their long-term success, while having the short term under tight control."[80]

---

another weak PR move and will be treated by investors, customers, and external stakeholders as such.

Second, sustainability initiatives must be cross-functional and integrated across the various business units of a company. Sustainability without cross-functional integration is just an add-on to standard business operations with little to offer by way of innovation, supply chain relationship management, or corporate strategy.

Verizon is a leading provider of internet, television, and phone services. The company's main sustainability performance metric is its "carbon intensity," measured in terms of the amount of energy used to transmit one terabyte of data over its network (carbon intensity can be defined specifically for any industry or business model in terms of carbon per unit sold). Since James Gowen became Chief Sustainability Officer, the company has reduced its carbon intensity by more than 30% since 2010, and is committed to halving its carbon intensity by 2020.[78]

Key Terms

Discussion Questions

1. How can individual employees, who lack formal leadership positions, nonetheless make a contribution to their company's sustainability agenda?

2. Has your employer undergone a company-wide change? What was the process like? Was it successful?

3. Are you convinced that the tension between corporate social responsibility to shareholders and stakeholders can be resolved?

| CASE 1 | **Corporate Leadership Amidst Turbulent Times**[81] |

The 2008 global economic recession, or the "Great Recession," was triggered in part by the U.S. stock market collapse. The costs were so staggering, the U.S. government intervened by providing billions of dollars in a financial "bail-out" to banks presumed "too big to fail."

In 2010, the U.S. Congress passed the Dodd-Frank Wall Street Reform and Consumer Protection Act to regulate large banks. Among other requirements, the Dodd-Frank Act requires an annual supervisory "stress test" to determine whether these financial institutions could withstand future system shocks.

The Federal Reserve developed the "stress tests" in order to ensure institutions have sufficient capital to absorb losses and support operations during adverse economic conditions so that they do not pose risks to their communities, other institutions, or the broader economy. The stress-tests are administered by the banks.

In August 2013, the Federal Reserve Board opined that the banks were failing to apply the "stress test" rigorously enough to their own entity's risk profile. By using general risk estimates, instead of using risks that were particular to their actual assets and operations, banks were ignoring evidence relevant to their "idiosyncratic vulnerabilities."

As if the 2008 housing crisis was out of sight and out of mind, the Federal Reserve noted that some banks were not recognizing the possibility that housing prices might fall again when they were valuing mortgage-backed assets. Some banks were assuming in their risk calculations that, in times of crisis, they could always take business away from their competitors. Five years after the onset of the Great Recession, the financial institutions at the heart of the collapse were still underrepresenting their risk.

In 2011, the Occupy Wall Street movement began as a sit-in protest near the financial district of lower Manhattan. Banners and chants raised awareness of wealth inequality and criticized the "big banks" for wrecking the economy and then accepting hundreds of billions of dollars in a taxpayer-funded bailout. After weeks of protests, and once news vans, police barricades, and protester arrests became the daily news-feed online, the Occupy Movement became a global phenomenon, with activists uniting in sit-in protests in major cities throughout the world.

The Occupy Movement did not emerge from nothing. Since the Great Recession started, civil unrest had been directed against what was perceived to be the root of social, economic, and environmental problems: centralized power and wealth. This growing discontent with the distribution of wealth and power found an outlet in the Occupy Movement. According to this view, wealth inequality enables large companies with squadrons of lobbyists and attorneys to tailor regulations to their preferences, while individuals are incarcerated for minor victimless crimes; wealth inequality enables the highest earning individuals to make record profits and enjoy tax loopholes while the rest of the country languishes in underemployment and unemployment; wealth inequality enables companies to continue the destruction of natural resources and contribute to increased climate change impacts while public access to ecosystem services becomes limited, and so on.

The controversies raised by the Occupy Movement were ignored by many large business leaders, criticized by a few others, and embraced by one large outlier: Ben & Jerry's. The famous ice cream and frozen yogurt company publicly supported the movement on its website and even donated its delicious ice cream to protesters in Zuccotti

(continues)

Park. Ben & Jerry's is owned by Unilever, one of the largest companies in the world. Because Ben & Jerry's has an independent board of directors, it has the freedom to act on its leaders' convictions about social justice. A Unilever representative wrote, "Unilever respects the unique social mission of Ben & Jerry's and the independence of its board in speaking out on social issues."

Witold Henisz, an associate professor of management at The Wharton School of the University of Pennsylvania, studied the public reaction to the financial crisis, and opined that the banking sector response to anti-Wall Street sentiment had been "woefully inadequate." According to Henisz, the response has been "in terms of, 'You can't tell me what to pay my workers, you can't regulate me, that's not the role of government[.]' Leadership from the heads of some of these banks would be a powerful signal and it's just not there."

The Occupy Movement earned at most a passing recognition from the industry giants that these protesters sought to challenge. The protestors were united by the common sense of discontent with the status quo, but the Occupy Movement had no alternative action plan. The Occupy Movement slogan, "We are the 99%," basically advocates for the redistribution of wealth. Would the leader of a sustainable company embrace this message?

Although sustainability encourages the inter-generational stewardship of natural resources, it does not necessarily require the redistribution of wealth. This point sharply distinguishes sustainability from political ideologies such as communism, socialism, or progressive social movements such as the Occupy Movement. Rather than call into question the current *distribution* of wealth and natural resources *per se*, sustainability calls upon leaders to improve the *management* of resources to ensure long-term availability.

Questions for Case 1

Consider collective action problems from Section 3.1 and leadership strategy from Section 3.2 of this Chapter.

1. How should business leaders respond to consumer activism?

2. Does your answer to the first question change if the caused-based activism is consistent with, or antithetical to, your company's business model?

3. Does your answer to the second question change if the caused-based activism concerns social, economic, or environmental issues?

Consider concepts from Section 3.4 of this Chapter.

4. What practices and policies could the Board of Directors of a large financial institution use to promote sustainable wealth management?

CASE 2 Drilling Down on Corporate Governance[82]

Geologists working for the natural gas company Luminate, LLC, are exploring the possibility of tapping into the Bakken shale formation, an unconventional shale play under Wyoming. The company's competitors have already entered into contracts with landowners near Pavillion, Wyoming, and drilling is underway across the Wind River Indian Reservation.

Under treaty between the U.S. government and the Native American tribes, the land, water, and minerals of the Wind River Indian Reservation are held in trust for the tribes by the U.S. government, which must consult with the tribes before taking actions that affect their interests. In recent years, controversy erupted from Pavillion when gas-drilling operations in the area were linked to groundwater contamination by a draft U.S. Environmental Protection Agency study. Tribes expressed concern that neither the U.S. government nor the drilling companies were respecting their interests in the land.

Under pressure from the gas industry, the U.S. EPA recently backed off the Pavillion investigation, and ceded authority over the matter to the State of Wyoming. According to Darrell O'Neal, Sr., co-chairman of the Northern Arapaho Business Council, "EPA's recent action violates clear federal policy requiring agencies to engage in meaningful consultation with Tribes before taking action affecting tribal property or other interests." Doubts about the contamination lingered on the part of environmental advocates and community members. In other news, headlines ran about questionable leasing practices and conflicts of interest amongst some of the wildcatting gas companies.

The CEO of Luminate, LLC, owns ten acres of land in the Pavillion area. When she proposed that the company lease her land to drill for gas, the matter was put to the Board of Directors for a vote.

Questions for Case 2

Consider corporate governance mechanisms introduced from Section 3.4 of this Chapter.

1. How can the Board of Directors ensure that the transaction between Luminate, LLC, and the CEO, including the decision to purchase and the negotiated purchase price, is free from conflicts of interest?

2. How can Luminate, LLC, ensure that drilling operations conducted on the Wind River Indian Reservation are responsive to stakeholders? Distinguish between social, economic, and environmental considerations.

Further Research

Michael Porter, University Professor at Harvard Business School and influential author in competitive business strategy, argues that the private sector should take a leadership role in addressing sustainability challenges. See his TED-Talk, "Why Business Can Be Good at Solving Social Problems."

Harvard Business Review Case: Lena G. Goldberg & David Kiron, *Family Corporate Governance: A Brief Literature Review*, Prod. #: 311055-PDF-ENG (October 04, 2010).

Harvard Business Review Case: Robert G. Eccles, George Serafeim, & Shelley Xin Li, *Dow Chemical: Innovating for Sustainability*, Prod. #: 112064-PDF-ENG (January 25, 2012).

Harvard Business Review Case: Robert G. Eccles, Kathleen Miller Perkins & George Serafeim, *How to Become a Sustainable Company*, Prod. #: SMR425-PDF-ENG (July 1, 2012).

Endnotes

1 Marc Gunther, *Unilever's CEO has a Green Thumb: Paul Polman Embraces Sustainability, and the Consumer Products Colossus Grows Like Crazy*, Fortune, page 126 (June 10, 2013).

2 Daniel Esty & Anthony Moffa, *Why Climate Change Collective Action Has Failed and What Needs to be Done Within and Without the Trade Regime*, 15(3) Journal of International Economic Law 777–791 (2012); *see also* Maria Ivanova, *UNEP in Global Environmental Governance: Design, Leadership, Location*, 8(1) Global Environmental Politics 35–59 (2010).

3 Guiding Principles of the Responsible Care, American Chemistry Council, last accessed May 7, 2014, available at http://responsiblecare.americanchemistry.com/Responsible-Care-Program-Elements/Guiding-Principles.

4 For more on the history of this initiative, see the Harvard Business Review Case by George C. Lodge & Jeffrey F. Rayport,

"Responsible Care," Prod. #: 391135-PDF-ENG (January 15, 1991), last accessed May 7, 2014, available at http://hbr.org/product/responsible-care/an/391135-PDF-ENG.

5 S. Finger and S. Gamper-Rabindran, *Testing the Effects of Self-Regulation on Industrial Accidents*, 43(2) Journal of Regulatory Economics 115–146 (2013).

6 *ibid.*

7 *ibid.*

8 *ibid.*

9 Responsible Care Program Elements, American Chemistry Council, last accessed May 7, 2014, available at http://responsiblecare.americanchemistry.com/Responsible-Care-Program-Elements/Management-System-and-Certification.

10 Pat Hughes & Kathleen Hosfeld, *The Leadership of Sustainability: A Study of Characteristics and Experiences of Leaders Bringing the*

"Triple-Bottom Line" to Business, Center for Ethical Leadership, page 4 (2005).

[11] BSR, *Sustainability and Leadership Competencies for Business Leaders*, pages 5–6 (2012).

[12] Daniel Goleman, *What Makes a Leader?*, Harvard Business Review (January 2004).

[13] Researchers at the University of Cambridge Programme for Sustainability Leadership have developed a model that puts the traits of a leader and the forms of governance and accountability mechanisms into a global context, connecting leadership with external stakeholders and internal operations. *See* Wayne Visser and Polly Courtice, *Sustainability Leadership: Linking Theory and Practice*, University of Cambridge Programme for Sustainability Leadership (CPSL) Working Paper (October 21, 2011).

[14] BSR, *Sustainability and Leadership Competencies for Business Leaders*, page 20 (2012). Used by permission of BSR.

[15] *ibid.*

[16] Kevin Kruse, *What Is Leadership?*, Forbes (4/09/2013).

[17] Robert E. Kaplan and Robert B. Kaiser, *Developing Versatile Leadership*, MIT Sloan Management Review (July 15, 2003).

[18] L. Ridgely, *Executive Interview: Lonnie J. Williams*, Contracting Profits (November 2008), last accessed May 7, 2014, available at http://www.cleanlink.com/cp/article/Executive-Interview-Lonnie-J-Williams–10141.

[19] Pat Hughes & Kathleen Hosfeld, *The Leadership of Sustainability: A Study of Characteristics and Experiences of Leaders Bringing the "Triple-Bottom Line" to Business*, Center for Ethical Leadership, page 4 (2005).

[20] Wen-Hsien Tsai, Wen-Chin Chou, *Selecting Management Systems for Sustainable Development in SMEs: A Novel Hybrid Model Based on DEMATEL, ANP, and ZOGP*, Vol. 36 Issue 2(1) Expert Systems with Applications 1444–1458 (March 2009).

[21] Enno Masurel, Why SMEs Invest in Environmental Measures: Sustainability Evidence from Small and Medium Sized Printing Firms, Vol. 16 Issue 3 Business Strategy and the Environment, pages 190–201 (2007).

[22] Elizabeth Garnsey, Nicola Dee, and Simon Ford, *Clean Technology Ventures and Innovation*, Center for Technology Management Working Paper No. 2 (2006).

[23] *Oslo Manual: Guidelines for Collecting and Interpreting Innovation Data*, OECD (3rd ed.).

[24] C. Neck, C. Lattimer & J. Houghton, *Management: Think. Decide. Act.*, 154–55 (Wiley, 2014).

[25] J. B. McGuire, A. Sundgren & T. Schneeweis, *Corporate Social Responsibility and Firm Financial Performance*, 31. 4 Academy of Management Journal 854–872 (1998).

[26] D. Bornstein, *How to Change the World: Social Entrepreneurs and the Power of New Ideas* (New York: Oxford University Press, 2004);

R. J. Bies, J. M. Bartunek, T. L. Fort & M. N. Zaid, *Corporations as Social Change Agents: Individual, Interpersonal, Institutional, and Environmental Dynamics*, 32.3 Academy of Management Review 788–793 (July 2007).

[27] *Sustainable Manufacturing and Eco-Innovation: Framework, Practices and Measurement*, OECD Synthesis Report, pages 13–14 (2009).

[28] M. E. Porter, *Competitive Strategy: Techniques for Analyzing Industries and Competitors* (Free Press, 1980); M. E. Porter, *Competitive Advantage: Creating and Sustaining Superior Performance* (Free Press, 1985).

[29] Mitchell J. Neubert & Bruno Dyck, *Organizational Behavior: Conventional + Sustainable Approaches*, page 303 (Wiley 2014).

[30] *ibid.*

[31] *ibid.*

[32] ibid at page 304.

[33] 2013 Optima Hybrid, Kia, last accessed May 7, 2014, available at http://www.kia.com/us/en/vehicle/optima-hybrid/2013/experience.

[34] Mountain Equipment Co-op, *Collaborate: 2012 Accountability Report Summary*, last accessed May 7, 2014, available at http://www.mec.ca/media/Images/pdf/accountability/accountability-2012-summaryreport_v2_m56577569831501421.pdf.

[35] Mitchell J. Neubert & Bruno Dyck, Organizational Behavior: Conventional + Sustainable Approaches, page 304 (Wiley 2014).

[36] CalRecycle: Recycled Tires, State of California, last accessed May 7, 2014, available at http://www.calrecycle.ca.gov/Tires/Products/.

[37] Phil Merrell, *Effective Change Management: The Simple Truth*, Vol. 56 No. 2 Management Services, 20–23 (Summer 2012).

[38] John P. Kotter & Leonard A. Schlesinger, *Choosing Strategies for Change*, Vol. 57 No. 2 Harvard Business Review pages 106–114 (March 1979).

[39] Peter Drucker, *They're Not Employees, They're People*, Harvard Business Review (February 2002).

[40] Dexter C. Dunphy, Andrew Griffiths & Suzanne Benn, *Organizational Change for Corporate Sustainability* (Routledge, 2003).

[41] C. G. Worley & A. E. Feyerherm, *Reflections on the Future of Organization Development*, 39(1) Journal of Applied Behavioral Science 97–115 (2003).

[42] B. Michael, M. J. Neubert & R. Michael, *Three Alternatives to Organizational Value Change and Formation: Top Down, Spontaneous Decentralized, and Interactive Dialogue*, 48(3) Journal of Applied Behavioral Science 380–409 (2012).

[43] Kurt Lewin, *Frontiers in Group Dynamics : Concept, Method and Reality in Social Science; Social Equilibria and Social Change*, 1 Human Relations 5–41 (1947).

44 *Timberland Service: Engaging Communities*, Timberland, last accessed May 7, 2014, available at http://responsibility.timberland.com/service/?story=1.

45 Jenny Davis-Peccoud, James Allen & Melissa Artabane, *Honing Talent Through Sustainability: Three Things Companies can do to Improve their Sustainability Agenda to Attract Talent and Improve Employee Productivity*, Stanford Social Innovation Review (Aug. 13, 2013).

46 Winnie Kwan and Emily Tuuk, *Corporate Social Responsibility: Implications for Human Resources and Talent Engagement*, Center for Advanced Human Resource Studies (May 2012).

47 *ibid.*

48 *ibid.*

49 *ibid.*

50 *ibid.*

51 *ibid.*

52 *Timberland Responsibility*, Timberland, last accessed May 7, 2014, available at http://responsibility.timberland.com/.

53 Larry Myler, *Strategy 101: It's All About Alignment*, Forbes (October 16, 2012).

54 Marc Gunther, *Unilever's CEO has a Green Thumb: Paul Polman Embraces Sustainability, and the Consumer Products Colossus Grows Like Crazy*, Fortune, page 125 (June 10, 2013).

55 FUJITSU Global Corporate Governance System, last accessed May 6, 2014, available at http://www.fujitsu.com/global/about/responsibility/management/governance/

56 2011–2012 Corporate Responsibility Update, Eli Lilly, page 47 (2012).

57 New York Stock Exchange Manual, Section 3: Corporate Responsibility, § 303A.01.

58 Corporate Governance – Sustainability 2012/13, Ford Motor Company, last accessed May 7, 2014, available at http://corporate.ford.com/microsites/sustainability-report-2012-13/blueprint-governance-sustainability-board.

59 Charter of the Sustainability Committee of the Board of Directors, Ford Motor Company, IV (1)-(7).

60 Deloitte, *Drivers of Long-Term Business Value: Stakeholders, Stats, and Strategies*, pages 2–3 (2012).

61 Milton Friedman, Capitalism and Freedom (University of Chicago Press, 1962); Milton Friedman, "The Social Responsibility of Business Is to Increase its Profits," New York Times Magazine Sept. 13, 1970.

62 R. Edward Freeman, Strategic Management: A Stakeholder Approach (Boston: Pitman, 1984).

63 *ibid.*

64 Deloitte, *Drivers of Long-Term Business Value: Stakeholders, Stats, and Strategies*, pages 2–3 (2012).

65 *ibid.*

66 Michael C. Jensen, *Value Maximization, Stakeholder Theory, and the Corporate Objective Function*, No. 2 Business Ethics Quarterly 12 (2002).

67 Mitchell J. Neubert & Bruno Dyck, ORGANIZATIONAL BEHAVIOR: CONVENTIONAL + SUSTAINABLE APPROACHES, page 304, Wiley (2014).

68 *About Certified B-Corps*, B-Corporation, last accessed May 7, 2014, available at http://www.bcorporation.net/about.

69 *ibid.*

70 Find a B-Corp, B-Corporation, last accessed May 7, 2014, available at http://www.bcorporation.net/community/find-a-b-corp.

71 Sarah Anderson, Chuck Collins, Sam Pizzigati, Kevin Shih, *Executive Excess 2010: CEO Pay and the Great Recession*, Institute for Policy Studies (2011).

72 *Unilever CEO: For Sustainable Business, Go Against 'Mindless Consumption,'* Marketplace (June 23, 2013).

73 Accenture, *Decision Maker Attitudes and Approaches towards Sustainability in Business* (2011).

74 Lisa Walker & Ronald Wintzéus, *Why, and How, Companies Create Sustainability Programs and Appoint Chief Sustainability Officers*, page 2, The Korn/Ferry Institute (2008).

75 *ibid.*

76 Eric Krell, *Sustainability So Far: Why and How Companies Launch Sustainability Programs*, Baylor Business Review (2013).

77 Amy Longsworth, Hannah Doran, & Jennifer Webber, *The Sustainability Executive: Profile and Progress*, page 11, PWC (2012).

78 Philip Fava, *Verizon's CSO James Gowen: Sustainability Matters for Our Children's Future*, Forbes (7/20/2012).

79 *ibid.*

80 The Sustainable Organization: The Chief Executive Officer's Perspective, Accenture (2012).

81 Lauren Tara LaCapra, *How Wall Street Is Responding, Or Not, to Protests*, Reuters (October 11, 2011); Andrew Sorkin, *Banks Not Tough Enough on Themselves in Stress Tests, Fed Says*, The New York Times Dealbook (August 19, 2013); Congressional Budget Office, *Trends in the Distribution of Household Income Between 1979 and 2007*, Report (October 25, 2011), last accessed May 7, 2014, available at http://www.cbo.gov/publication/42729).

82 Abrahm Lustgarten, *EPA's Abandoned Wyoming Fracking Study One Retreat of Many*, ProPublica (July 3, 2013); Ron Feemster & Dustin Bleizeffer, *Tribes, Residents Say EPA Deserted them In Pavillion*, WyoFile (June 25, 2013).

PART II

Accountability

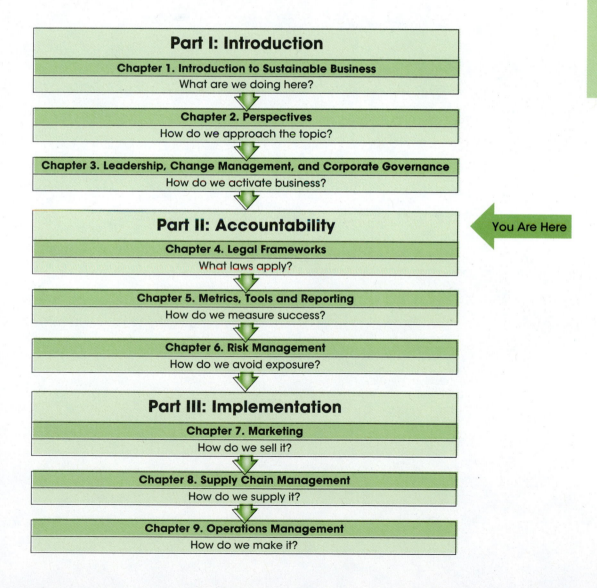

Part I: Introduction

Chapter 1. Introduction to Sustainable Business

What are we doing here?

Chapter 2. Perspectives

How do we approach the topic?

Chapter 3. Leadership, Change Management, and Corporate Governance

How do we activate business?

Part II: Accountability

You Are Here

Chapter 4. Legal Frameworks

What laws apply?

Chapter 5. Metrics, Tools and Reporting

How do we measure success?

Chapter 6. Risk Management

How do we avoid exposure?

Part III: Implementation

Chapter 7. Marketing

How do we sell it?

Chapter 8. Supply Chain Management

How do we supply it?

Chapter 9. Operations Management

How do we make it?

Legal Frameworks for Sustainability

CLIMATE CHANGE DIVIDES CORPORATE LOBBYING EFFORTS

For a long time, the response to climate change science from carbon-intensive industries has been a strategy of denial, whereby the science is called into question, similar to the strategy of the tobacco industry in denying the adverse health effects of cigarette smoke. After the last two decades of research findings by the global scientific community, the strategy of denying the science behind climate change theory is no longer viable. Today the carbon-intensive lobbying strategy has shifted to issuing doom-and-gloom warnings to lawmakers, with predictions of economic hemorrhage and job losses that will follow regulation of greenhouse gases.

Industries responsible for heavy pollution loads are no longer able to deny that these pollutants pose a risk to the environment and public health. The argument now runs that pollution is necessary to industrial productivity, and laws regulating such pollution inevitably destroy business. Within the United States highly capitalized companies have pumped millions of dollars into Congress to stall action on climate change, with the pro-pollution lobby outnumbering the anti-pollution lobby by a ratio of five to one.[2]

However, not all businesses oppose environmental and public health regulations. In fact, many businesses have a view that is very different. In what is perhaps a surprising move for

DISCLAIMER: This chapter discusses general principles of law for the benefit of the public through education only, and does not undertake to give individual legal advice. Nothing in this chapter should be interpreted as creating an attorney-client relationship with the author(s). The discussion of legal frameworks in this chapter is not intended to persuade readers to adopt general solutions to general problems, but rather to inform readers about a variety of laws that apply to various aspects of sustainable business. Readers should not rely on this chapter as a substitute for legal counsel. For specific advice about legal issues, see a licensed attorney.

> *"Law and regulation have an extremely important role to play in the transition to more sustainable business practices. Law can provide structure for firms that pull transition by enabling sustainability leadership and competitive advantage[.] Additionally, law can work to push transition by compelling firms to act[.]"*
>
> **Penn State Smeal College of Business: The Impact of Law and Regulation on Transitioning to Business Sustainability (October 2013)[1]**

LEARNING OBJECTIVES

After completing this chapter, you should be able to:

1. Understand the role of legal compliance in corporate sustainability.
2. Identify laws applicable to design, production, and pollution.
3. Identify rules for supply chain, marketing, and consumer protection.
4. Identify requirements for packaging, waste disposal, and land use.
5. Distinguish between sustainable performance and legal compliance.

those accustomed to thinking that the business community as one united in opposition to environmental regulation, a coalition of 33 major U.S.-based companies has announced support for progressive climate legislation. The coalition, Business for Innovative Climate and Energy Policy (BICEP), is flexing its muscles side-by-side with nonprofit environmental organizations in calling for action on climate change.

In economic terms, BICEP is calling for a carbon-limited economy where prices are attached to greenhouse gas emissions, creating a deterrent to atmospheric pollution and creating incentives for energy efficiency and pollution reduction. This would be a departure from the status quo, which currently allows businesses to externalize the risk of greenhouse gas pollution.

The BICEP Declaration has been endorsed by (among others): Adidas Group, Ben & Jerry's, Ebay, GM, Ikea, intel, KB Home, L'Oreal, Levi Strauss & Co., Method, Nestle, Nike, Patagonia, Seventh Generation, Starbucks, Swiss Re, Symantec, The North Face, Timberland, and Unilever.[3] These companies see major economic opportunities from addressing the risks of climate change.

This chapter will address both sides of the "law & business" coin: the role of law in establishing sustainable business frameworks, as well as the role of business in lobbying to influence the scope of legal protections.

4.1 The Role of Law in Corporate Sustainability

Sustainable business involves collaboration with stakeholders, such as businesses in the supply chain, governments, and NGOs. When asked which organizations are easiest to collaborate with, virtually all business professionals working on sustainability issues said that it is *not* government.[4] We can infer that in practice it is not easy for businesses to collaborate with regulatory agencies in pursuit of sustainability. So we should ask, what is the role of law in corporate sustainability?

One potentially effective method for promoting sustainability is for government to enact laws to require or incentivize sustainable conduct. Most of the legislation that is widely regarded as pertaining to sustainability is known as **environmental law.**[5] These are the laws discussed in this chapter, which define the legal boundaries for pollution and risk-creation. Examples of legal frameworks are drawn from a variety of jurisdictions and do not apply to every business nor every circumstance.

Environmental Law The subset of laws that define legal boundaries for pollution and risk-creation across all environmental media, protecting ecological integrity, and public health.

However, sustainability has become embedded in the foundational laws of developed and developing nations, calling for a balance of social, economic, and environmental factors, as well as intergenerational equity. For instance, in France, the Constitutional Charter for the Environment explicitly endorses sustainability via the mandate to "reconcile the protection and enhancement of the environment with economic development and social progress."[6] Law has the power to force the balancing of social, environmental, and economic goals, when an otherwise under-regulated market may trade off diffuse social and environmental values for concentrated economic advantages.

Law, in its various forms, requires the commitment of substantial corporate resources and plays a large role in the external operating environment of any business.[7] Therefore, legal frameworks are a crucial area of study for those interested in developing a sustainable business. Furthermore, businesses can use their relationship with the law as a source of sustainable competitive advantage.[8] Business managers who are "legally astute" understand and proactively address legal issues, heading off risks before they become liabilities, and can thereby increase the value created and captured by their organization.[9]

Businesses that adhere to environmental, social, and economic rules and regulations are less likely to compromise the environment, public health, or consumer welfare. On the other hand, reckless risk taking and unlawful, unethical or deceptive business practices can cause reputational harm and economic loss for culpable businesses.

This chapter explains some of the more prominent legal frameworks applicable to the environmental impacts of business. What this chapter does not focus on are international treaties and programs aimed at sustainable economic development, which are predominantly investment projects to promote social outcomes at the state level. Rather, here the focus is on laws that pertain to business activities relevant to environmental sustainability, such as operations or product design. Worker safety law as well as human trafficking law is also included to round out the social aspect of sustainability in the law.

Business owners should be knowledgeable of the laws that apply to their industry and profession because they can establish enforceable standards for corporate conduct, product attributes, and business operations. Businesses must find ways to grow and survive under increasing government regulation of markets, increased shareholder demand for legal compliance programs, and the growing use of litigation by advocacy groups and class action lawsuits from consumers as a means for accomplishing social and environmental-themed business reform. Law is both a deterrent for bad conduct, and an incentive for good conduct.

> **CROSS-LINKAGE**
>
> For legal frameworks on sustainable corporate governance, including the B-Corporation, see Chapter 3: Leadership, Change Management, and Corporate Governance. For laws related to public disclosures, including the Sarbanes-Oxley Act, see Chapter 5: Metrics, Tools, and Reporting: The Role of Finance and Accounting.

The business case for sustainability includes profitability, which can certainly be negatively impacted by legal compliance challenges. However, profitability can also be positively impacted by the relationship of the business to applicable laws. If businesses leverage legal resources to advance strategic goals, they can unlock value-creating and value-claiming potential.

Not all business leaders share the same attitude toward the law, as we have seen in the Chapter Opener, and some attitudes limit the value of legal resources to the firm. Some business leaders might avoid legal compliance issues altogether, while others are sticklers for compliance. Some use law for competitive advantage, while others go beyond all the rest by using law to create value for external stakeholders.

Companies typically go through a series of evolutionary stages in their relationship toward legal environmental compliance, from mere compliance to their ability to leverage it for their own competitive advantage. These evolutionary stages are shown in Figure 4.1, with detailed characteristics of each of these offered in Table 4.1.

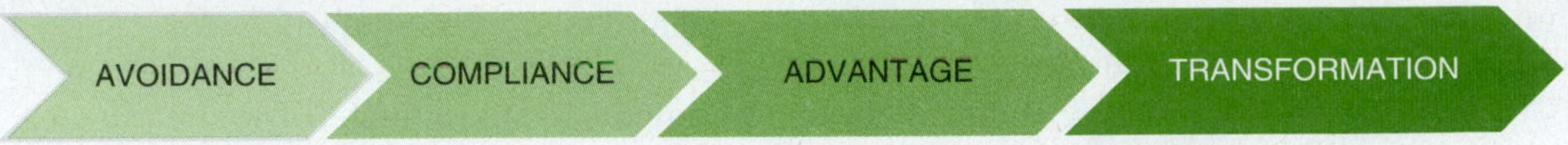

AVOIDANCE → COMPLIANCE → ADVANTAGE → TRANSFORMATION

FIGURE 4.1 Evolutionary Stages of Business Attitudes Toward Legal Resources

Source: Robert C. Bird, *Law as a Source of Competitive Advantage* (2007), available at http://ssrn.com/abstract-964329. Robert C. Bird, *Law, Strategy, and Competitive Advantage*, 44 CONNECTICUT LAW REVIEW 61, 96 (2011). Used by permission of Robert C. Bird.

Avoidance Attitude that sees law as a barrier to economic growth and impediment to strategic planning.

Compliance Attitude that sees law as a source of unavoidable costs and obligations.

Advantage Attitude that sees law as a source of enforceable rights that can be leveraged to create value.

Transformation Attitude that sees law as an opportunity to transform the business and its value chain.

TABLE 4.1

Characteristics of Evolutionary Stages of Business Attitudes

Evolutionary Stage	Attitude	Legal Resources Used	Response
1. Avoidance	"Law is a barrier to economic growth and impedes our strategic planning."	*Lawyers handle adversarial and adjudicatory issues.*	Avoid legal restrictions (incorporate in a different jurisdiction), regulatory arbitrage, find loopholes.
2. Compliance	"Law creates costs and obligations with which we must comply."	*Internal controls, audits, codes of conduct, internal sanction.*	Measure performance by conformity to rules.
3. Advantage	"Law provides us with enforceable rights that can be leveraged to create value."	*Lawyers and business leaders collaborate to maximize the value of business assets.*	Find the right fit between law and business assets. Capture value by ownership of innovation.
4. Transformation	"Law transforms our business and our value chain."	*Legal resources are used to improve all functional aspects of a business and even positively impact its supply chain.*	Use law to create strategic advantages throughout supply chain, with ancillary benefits for external stakeholders.

Notice that at the highest stage in the evolution of business attitudes toward law, organizations can be transformed while having a transformative influence on their supply chain and market. Businesses in the first through third stages of evolution should consider rethinking the benefits of legal resources to their organization, as they might be creating less than their full potential value, or claiming less value than they might otherwise be entitled to. Leading companies are going beyond mere compliance with the law and innovating to transform products and supply chains without the need of government enforcement.

Before diving into specific business issues impacted by laws, such as marketing and product manufacture, we discuss the difference between hard law and soft law, as well as the complex layers of law in the legal hierarchy. Then we explain the difference between the legal environment

CROSS-LINKAGE

For more on industry self-regulation and sustainability leadership, see Chapter 3: Leadership, Change Management, and Corporate Governance.

MANAGERIAL INSIGHT: *Stephen Meyer: Does Environmental Regulation "Kill Jobs"?*[10]

Environmental regulation can actually be good for the economy by fueling innovation and increasing efficiency. Consider the following expert insights from Stephen Meyer, former Professor in Political Science at Massachusetts Institute of Technology and Conservation Commissioner of Massachusetts.

Compliance costs for environmental regulations are not funneled into a government agency's discretionary budget. Rather, "a very large portion of the expense of environmental compliance (upwards of 90%) is plowed back into the private economy [in the form of] sales and income to environmental product/service providers, who are private businesses."

"Environmental regulations simply force environmental impacts into the competitiveness equation, thereby producing a form of environmental-economic Darwinism." Companies that are capable of internalizing social and environmental costs thrive and survive, while those companies whose profitability depends upon externalizing costs will not. For more on externalities, see **Chapter 1: Introduction to Sustainable Business**.

"Regulatory incentives to avoid the expected high costs of waste disposal and pollution abatement can fuel process and product innovation that improve productivity, increase input-output efficiencies, and provide substantial cost savings." Regulations that put a price on waste and pollution create incentives to innovate operations and production processes. 3M, DuPont, and Raytheon have all innovated in step with regulatory pressure.

---

of business and legal frameworks for sustainable business. The former provides the rights, incentives, protections, and preconditions for economic activity that businesses require to thrive. The latter governs the social, economic, and environmental impacts of business, which are the primary focus of this textbook. The heart of the chapter is the discussion of legal frameworks applicable to product design, production, marketing, and waste disposal. We conclude with reasons for going beyond mere compliance with the law by looking at the effects of corporate lobbying.

4.1.1 Hard Law, Soft Law, Legal Hierarchy, International Law

Law is the system of rules that a particular community recognizes as regulating the actions of its members, and which government institutions can enforce.

Hard laws, such as the environmental laws of the United States, are enforceable and carry stiff fines and penalties for noncompliance. Companies that violate environmental laws can be held accountable through civil or criminal charges.

Soft law, on the other hand, consists of rules created by non-governmental entities or "law-making bodies that do not comply with procedural formalities necessary to give the rules legal status yet nonetheless may influence the behavior of other law-making bodies and of the public."[11]

Other sources of policy, such as declarations of aspirational goals with which businesses agree in principle, are also soft law. Soft laws may influence corporate conduct, but they are not enforced through government coercion. The consequences for deviating from soft law, if any, are more or less limited to possible bad

> **Law** System of rules that a particular community recognizes as regulating the actions of its members, and which government institutions can enforce.
>
> **Hard Law** Civil and criminal laws that are enforceable and carry fines and penalties for non-compliance.
>
> **Soft Law** Informal rules that lack legal status but still influence the behavior of other law-making bodies and the public.

LEADERSHIP: Soft Laws Impact Corporate Actions

An excellent example of a soft law that has had a large impact on corporate actions is the United Nations Global Compact CEO Water Mandate. This is a soft law public-private initiative geared to promote sustainable policies. The mandate is designed to assist companies in the development, implementation and disclosure of water sustainability policies and practices.[12] Although the mandate is a non-binding soft law, it has garnered substantial attention and support and has translated into real world financial and natural resource savings. Numerous companies have endorsed it including PepsiCo, Nike, Merck & Co, Unilever, GlaxoSmithKline, and others.

publicity and fallout from concerned customers. On the other hand, compliance with soft laws applicable to one's business can establish credibility and proactively address public relations concerns that might otherwise plague a similarly situated business. International laws, such as United Nation's treaties on human rights, are soft laws, and do not carry the force of law. Nonetheless, soft law is important because it organizes stakeholders for meaningful collective action addressing issues of sustainability.

A business can encounter hard and soft laws from many sources of government authority. The **legal hierarchy** is the nested jurisdiction of government institutions that can regulate conduct at the international, regional, national, and local levels. The legal systems that make up the legal hierarchy differ from location to location, but in general, they include global nongovernmental bodies such as the United Nations, regional governments such as the European Union, national governments such as the People's Republic of China, state governments such as the California legislature, and local government agencies such as the New York City Department of City Planning. At each level in the hierarchy from global to local, there can be multiple forms of government authority, generally in the legislative, executive, and judicial roles.

At the global level, the United Nations serves as a soft law making institution, and various tribunals and arbitrators serve a quasi-judicial role in arbitrating international commercial and criminal disputes. Within the United States alone, businesses are subject to hard law from multiple sources of overlapping governmental authority. At the national level, three branches of the federal government have legal authority to restrict what kinds of business practices, processes, and products are allowed. Running a business in the United States requires compliance with state and local law as well.

The three branches of legal authority, legislative, executive, and judicial, are duplicated at the state level, where state laws, programs, and environmental regulations create an added layer of compliance. Further, major metropolitan areas usually have environmental and land use-planning protocols in place when it comes to breaking ground or expanding in a new facility or obtaining a permit to operate a factory.

The U.S. Constitution empowers the legislative branch to create law, the executive branch to enforce law, and the judicial branch to interpret law. The **legislative branch** may continue to pass laws giving the U.S. Environmental Protection Agency

Legal Hierarchy The nested jurisdiction of government institutions that can regulate conduct at the international, regional, national, and local levels.

Legislative Branch The law making institution within government.

authority to regulate additional pollutants or pollutants from additional sources. For instance, legislation has been introduced in the House of Representatives and the Senate to set a price per ton of greenhouse gas emissions, to create a marketable permit-trading program for greenhouse gas reductions, and to provide funding for renewable energy programs. These would all be new developments flowing from legislative action.

The **executive branch**, through the U.S. Environmental Protection Agency, may enforce environmental regulations when business facilities or activities meet the criterion for major sources of pollution. For instance, several businesses each year are subject to substantial fines and are required to fund environmental remediation projects in order to bring facilities into compliance and to reduce the adverse impacts of their violation.

> **Executive Branch** The enforcement arm of government.

The **judicial branch** may entertain litigation under common law theories of tort liability when product defects lead to frustrated consumer expectations. For instance, pharmaceutical companies can be subject to class-action lawsuits in federal court for undisclosed medical side effects. In short, legal norms can flow from legislative, judicial, and executive government institutions.

> **Judicial Branch** The final arbiter of legal questions and common law claims within a government.

There is no binding international regulatory framework for corporate sustainability. The first ever government-sanctioned international gathering devoted to environmental protection was the 1972 Stockholm Conference, which resulted in non-binding principles that essentially suggested that nations should not exploit natural resources in such a way as to cause damage to those natural resources of other nations. This conference eventually lead to the creation of the United Nations Environmental Program, followed by the World Commission on Environment and Development, which resulted in the famous articulation of the triple-bottom-line and intergenerational equity principles of sustainable development in the Brundtland Report (discussed in Chapter 1).

Much international law that has arisen since the Brundtland Report related to sustainability is soft, meaning it results in unenforceable Multilateral Environmental Agreements, such as the **1997 Kyoto Protocol on Climate Change**. The Kyoto Protocol was signed and ratified by almost 200 nations, signaling a global commitment to reduce greenhouse gas emissions below specified baseline emissions rates. However, the unenforceable agreement failed to earn the ratification of the United States, it set inadequate emissions reduction goals for developed nations, and it failed to set any goals for developing nations such as China, India, and Brazil—all of which were projected to dramatically increase emissions rates in the near term. Indeed, global greenhouse gas emissions rates have actually increased since the Kyoto Protocol came into effect. That said, international agreements can and have successfully promoted sustainability.

> **1997 Kyoto Protocol on Climate Change** Unenforceable international agreement ratified by almost 200 nations, signaling a global commitment to reduce greenhouse gas emissions below specified baseline emissions rates.

The best examples of successful international cooperation to bring about sustainable business are the Basel Convention and the Montreal Protocol.

While soft law may lack enforcement mechanisms, it can successfully set the agenda for governments to follow and provide normative guidelines for businesses to take into account.

Legal standards for corporate conduct, product attributes, and operations management originate from a variety of legal institutions at a variety of levels. These will be discussed in Section 4.2: Law and Sustainability by Business Area.

GLOBAL INSIGHT: The Basel Convention and Montreal Protocol

In 1992, 175 nations agreed to the Basel Convention on the Control of Trans-boundary Movements of Hazardous Waste and their Disposal. The **Basel Convention** curbed the dumping of hazardous waste generated by developed nations into developing nations. The convention also required giving notice, obtaining consent, and tracking the movement of wastes across national boundaries. Another successful international soft law related to sustainability is the **Montreal Protocol**, a measure to protect the Earth's ozone layer from destructive chlorofluorocarbons (CFCs). The 1989 Montreal Protocol established a system for monitoring and phasing out the production and use of ozone depleting substances in industrial processes in order to protect the Earth's surface from harmful ultraviolet solar radiation. Since then, it has garnered the reputation as the most successful environmental treaty, and possibly the most successful international agreement of all time.

Basel Convention Successful international agreement to curb dumping of hazardous waste generated by developed nations into developing nations, requiring notice, consent, and tracking hazardous wastes across national boundaries.

Montreal Protocol Successful measure to protect the Earth's ozone layer from destructive chlorofluorocarbons by establishing a system for monitoring and phasing out the production and use of ozone depleting substances in industrial processes.

Legal Environment of Business The context of legal frameworks that provide the economic preconditions for efficient economic activity in the form of property, contract, and business law.

Legal Framework for Sustainable Business Protective laws primarily designed to reduce the risk of adverse social, economic, environmental, and public health impacts resulting from economic activity.

4.1.2 The Legal Environment of Business

Businesses are legal entities that exist in a web of laws from formation to dissolution, sale, or bankruptcy, and laws govern all the operations and transactions in between. For instance, law governs what can be sold and under what conditions sales are valid, which ingredients products can contain, how much pollution is allowed in the production process, and how much profit a business is allowed to keep free from taxation. Law influences business decision-making from resource extraction to boardroom negotiations, and law follows products from the marketplace to the dump. The **legal environment of business** offers a number of benefits such as providing for skilled labor markets, efficient trade, protection of intellectual property, access to capital markets, and incentives for innovation. These are shown in Figure 4.2. A stable legal environment with such features provides the economic preconditions for sustainable business.

Stability within a legal system provides the certainty and predictability that businesses need to make investments into sustainability. This chapter defers a comprehensive discussion of the legal environment of business in order to focus on a subset of laws that address the adverse environmental and social impacts of business. Protective laws provide a **legal framework for sustainable business** because they are primarily designed to reduce the risk of adverse social, economic, environmental, and public health impacts. These will be discussed in Section 4.2: Law and Sustainability by Business Area.

4.1.3 Incentives for Legal Compliance

Compliance simply means conformity to the requirements of a law. Incentives for legal compliance range from the publicity that comes with strong sustainability ratings to decreased operating costs from avoided fines and penalties. Companies with stellar track records for legal compliance not only benefit from well-earned public trust, but also open up recognition and opportunities for showcasing their brand by being featured on prestigious indices and rankings. The Dow Jones

FIGURE 4.2 Benefits of Legal Environment of Business

Source: Adapted from Robert Bird, *Law, Strategy, and Competitive Advantage*, page 30 (2011).

Sustainability Indexes provide some of the most comprehensive and credible sustainable ratings, and legal compliance problems can present hurdles to making the cut. Being featured, or being dropped from, DJSI and other corporate sustainability rankings, can influence perceptions of NGO groups, company employees, journalists and other stakeholders.

Launched in 2005, the Global 100 is the most extensive data-driven corporate sustainability assessment in existence, and inclusion is limited to a select group of the top 100 large-cap companies in the world. The annual Global 100 is announced each year during the World Economic Forum in Davos. The methodology for evaluating companies' sustainability or clean capitalism performance is having a leading global practice (by SustainAbility in their Rate the Raters research program, Phase 4).[13] One of the screening criteria for the Global 100 list is the amount a business paid on a trailing 1-year basis for legal violations. Only those companies with relatively few if any legal violations remain eligible for this prestigious sustainability ranking.

Legal violations are one criterion for eliminating a company from consideration in the Global 100 Short List of Clean Capital companies. The legal compliance screen is designed to eliminate all companies that are bottom quartile performers for financial sanctions, a screen which measures the amount of money that companies have paid out in fines, penalties or settlements related to legal repercussions from environmental accidents, generalized environmental pollution, infringement of labor standards, human rights-related abuses, child exploitation, or violation of collective bargaining arrangements.[14] Complying with the legal frameworks may help ensure corporate conduct is on the straight and narrow path that avoids enforcement actions by government agencies or reputational scandal from environmental or consumer-advocacy watchdogs. In the United States, the U.S. EPA will waive or significantly reduce penalties for small businesses that voluntarily discover violations of environmental law and promptly disclose and correct them.[15]

MANAGERIAL INSIGHT: Compliance Challenges at Legacy Facilities[16]

Compliance to environmental laws can sometimes take firms by surprise. Consider the situation of New Cingular Wireless which found itself responsible for lack of compliance as the new owners of 332 legacy AT&T Wireless sites. As the new owners, the company suddenly found itself in violation of laws that range from hazardous materials to health & safety. The result was a major settlement between the U.S. Environmental Protection Agency (EPA) and New Cingular Wireless for violations of environmental laws at hundreds of legacy sites throughout the country. On January 7th, 2013, the EPA and New Cingular Wireless reached a settlement requiring the company to pay a civil penalty of $750,000 and spend $625,000 on environmental projects to resolve alleged reporting, planning, and permitting violations.

The violations of federal environmental law occurred at AT&T Wireless sites in 43 states, such as cellular towers, transmitter sites, switching stations and warehouses. The violations included (1) failure to comply with Emergency Planning and Community Right-to-Know Act reporting requirements related to the presence of sulfuric acid and diesel fuel; (2) inadequate or no Clean Water Act spill prevention plans; and (3) failure to obtain permits for air pollution under the Clean Air Act. These requirements help communities plan for emergencies involving hazardous substances, prevent oil discharges into water bodies, and ensure air emissions are within legal limits, respectively. As the new owners, New Cingular Wireless is responsible for the AT&T legacy sites, and as a result of the settlement, must provide certification of compliance for 1,356 sites, including audits and site inspections. Additionally, New Cingular Wireless has agreed to provide hazardous materials awareness and health & safety training to building inspectors and fire fighters in the home district of their sites, as well as emergency response equipment for fire fighters and police departments across the United States

This settlement is one of the latest in the U.S. EPA's efforts to improve environmental law compliance. Violating laws should never be a routine part of doing business. Accidents do happen, but effective risk management, the use of environmental management systems, and prudent operations management should reduce the likelihood of environmental incidents and allow businesses to keep operating costs and compliance costs low. Legal compliance is therefore an important aspect of the business case for sustainability.

4.2 Law and Sustainability by Business Area

We are now at the heart of this Chapter, where we introduce the legal frameworks that address the environmental and human health impacts of core functional areas of business. In order to guide this sweeping tour, we provide a table of contents for this section here.

4.2.1 Design, Production, and Pollution

1. Standards for Sustainable Product Design
2. Standards for Production Processes
   a. Chemical Use
   b. Workplace Safety

3. Regulation of Pollution
   a. Clean Water
   b. Clean Air

4.2.2 Supply Chain, Marketing, and Consumer Protection

1. Supply Chain
   a. Conflict Minerals
   b. Slavery and Human Trafficking
2. Marketing
3. Consumer Product Safety
   a. Pre-Sale Product Restrictions
   b. Post-Sale Liability

4.2.3 Packaging, Waste, and Disposal

1. Packaging Materials
2. Product Take-Back
3. Disposal of Dangerous Waste Products

4.2.4 Land Use Planning

4.2.1 Design, Production, and Pollution

1. Standards for Sustainable Product Design **Design** is the process of transforming legal, technical, safety, functional, market, or other requirements into the technical specification for a product.

Sustainable product design or eco-design means improving the environmental performance of a product's life cycle by integrating environmental aspects into product design.

Performance standards can stipulate at the design stage how a product performs, or they can prohibit certain ingredients from being used in the manufacturing process. Standards for eco-design differ across product categories, but generally cover the following matters:

- Use of raw materials and natural resources.
- Contribution toward climate change via greenhouse gas emissions.
- Energy consumed during the extraction of raw materials, transportation, production, sale, use, and disposal of the product.
- Waste generated by the manufacturing process and the product.
- Release of hazardous substances.
- Use of renewable fuels.
- Fuel efficiency.

Many countries have introduced legislation to prohibit the use of certain chemicals in products, specifically global ozone depleting substances, polychlorinated

Design The process of transforming legal, technical, safety, functional, market, or other requirements into the technical specification for a product.

Sustainable Product Design Improving the environmental performance of a product's life cycle by integrating environmental aspects into product design.

biphenyls (PCBs), and restrictions of hazardous substances. Many such laws apply to electronics-related products which are the most likely to involve dangerous heavy metals and synthetic chemicals in the manufacturing process, and which pose environmental risks during product use as well as disposal.

Although the United States does not have comprehensive legislation on sustainable product design, individual states within the United States do have such legislation, such as California's Electronic Waste Recycling Act. The EU has regulated hazardous substances affecting the supply chain of electronic parts manufacturers, with legislation prohibiting six chemicals, including lead and mercury, from electrical and electronic equipment. China has also regulated the use of hazardous substances in electronics through the Management Methods for Controlling Pollution by Electronic Information Products, prohibiting the same chemicals as the EU and requiring manufacturers, importers, and distributors to obtain testing from a Chinese laboratory to certify compliance.

Any company doing business within member states of the European Union should be aware of EU Directives that apply to their operations. In the EU, product manufacturers are subject to the **Eco-Design of Energy-Using Products (EuP)** Directive.[17]

> **Eco-Design of Energy-Using Products (EuP)** EU Directive requiring manufacturers of "energy-using products," to design with the goal of reducing the energy consumption and negative environmental impacts attending the product life cycle.

Manufacturers of energy-using product, which are products dependent on energy input (electricity, fossil fuels and renewable energy sources),[18] must comply with the directive at the design stage, by reducing the energy consumption and negative environmental impacts attending the product life cycle. According to the directive, "[a]ction should be taken during the design phase of EuPs, since it appears that the pollution caused during a product's life cycle is determined at that stage, and most of the costs involved are committed then."[19]

The EU issued this directive to create consistent environmental standards for products across the international borders of member states and to reduce the natural resources, energy, and pollution of consumer products in the affected markets. Interestingly, the Directive itself expresses a preference for firm self-regulation, which would curtail the need for bureaucracy and outside regulation. Specifically, the directive places priority on self-regulation by the industry in situations where that is "likely to reach policy objectives faster or in a less costly manner than mandatory requirements."[20] The directive suggests legislative measures for sustainable product design only "where market forces fail to evolve in the right direction or at an acceptable speed," otherwise industry self-regulation is preferred, such as voluntary agreements and unilateral commitments to sustainable product design, since these "can provide quick progress due to rapid and cost-effective implementation, and allow for flexible and appropriate adaptation to technological options and market sensitivities."[21]

> **CROSS-LINKAGE**
>
> For more information about life-cycle assessment for product design, see Chapter 5: Metrics, Tools, and Reporting: The Role of Finance and Accounting.

2. *Standards for Production Processes* **Production** – or **Operations Management** – is the process of transforming a design into a material object. Various laws apply to the production process, from the chemicals and substances used, to the safety of employees, to the emissions of pollutants during the manufacturing process. These laws address registering substances and chemicals used in the production process, workplace health and safety, and pollution control legislation.

> **Production/Operations Management** Overseeing all stages of the process for transforming a design into a material object.

Sustainable production involves reducing as much as feasible the use of harsh chemicals and toxic substances in products, ensuring the safety of employees, and reducing the emissions of pollution during the manufacture process.

a. Chemical Use Within the United States, the **Emergency Planning and Community Right-to-Know Act**[22] requires the U.S. EPA to publish a list of extremely hazardous substances based on toxicity, reactivity, combustibility, or flammability.[23] The owner or operator of every facility where these listed substances are present must notify the state emergency planning commission of their presence at certain threshold quantities[24] as well as any incident of their release into the environment.[25]

Under the **Pollution Prevention Act**,[26] companies filing annual toxic chemical release forms must also report the quantity of the chemicals entering the waste stream prior to recycling, treatment, or disposal; the amount of each chemical treated and recycled; the source reduction practices used; and the amount of toxic chemicals released into the environment as a result of a catastrophic event.[27]

The European Union has a more comprehensive and arguably more effective approach than the United States for the registration and control of chemicals used in business. The EU's **Registration, Evaluation, Authorization, and Restriction of Chemical Substances** (REACH) program creates a registration system for the nearly 30,000 substances manufactured or imported into the EU each year, providing superior transparency and accountability for the public to easily access information on the chemicals used by businesses.

The REACH program reverses the burden of proof found in many other nation's legal systems: under the REACH program, manufacturers and importers of substances are required to demonstrate that those substances are safe in advance, instead of requiring victims of pollution or exposure to demonstrate that it was the substance that did the harm after the impact is done. The REACH program also improves supply chain communication between upstream manufacturers and downstream users regarding information about substance usage and risk management measures.

b. Workplace Safety The **Occupational Safety and Health Act** (OSHA) empowered an administration to establish standards to prevent employees from being killed or seriously harmed at work; to require employers to provide their employees with working conditions that are free of known dangers; and to provide information, training and assistance to workers and employers.[28]

OSHA standards provide for safe working conditions (such as ventilation to get rid of harmful fumes to promote indoor air quality) and safety equipment such as earplugs, gloves, non-slip walking surfaces, and goggles. Workers are empowered to file a complaint about unsafe working conditions, without risk of retaliation from their employer. Worker complaints will lead to an OSHA inspection of their workplace to check for safety violations or the existence of hazards.

3. *Regulation of Pollution* Many industrial processes emit pollutants. Adverse environmental and public health impacts from these pollutants depends upon several factors, including volume and toxicity of emissions, as well as the proximity of pollution-emitting facility relative to exposed ecosystems and populations. Many environmental laws apply to sources of pollution based on the volume of emissions

CROSS-LINKAGE

For more information about sustainable production, see Chapter 9: Operations Management.

Sustainable Production/ Operations Reducing as much as feasible the use of harsh chemicals and toxic substances in products, ensuring the safety of employees, and reducing the emissions of pollution during the manufacture process.

Emergency Planning and Community Right-to-Know Act Requires the U.S. EPA to publish a list of extremely hazardous substances, and the owner or operator of every facility where these listed substances are present must notify the state emergency planning commission of their presence at certain threshold quantities as well as any incident of their release into the environment.

Pollution Prevention Act Requires companies with annual toxic releases to report the quantity of the chemicals entering the waste stream prior to recycling, treatment, or disposal; the amount of each chemical treated and recycled; the source reduction practices used; and the amount of toxic chemicals released into the environment as a result of a catastrophic event.

Registration, Evaluation, Authorization, and Restriction of Chemical Substances Creates an open-access registration system for substances manufactured or imported into the EU.

Occupational Safety and Health Act Enables standards to prevent workplace injury; require employers to provide employees with working conditions that are free of known dangers; and provide information, training and assistance to workers and employers.

in order to protect and maintain the air and water quality of the regions in which the polluting company operates.

a. Clean Water The mission of the Office of Water within the U.S. Environmental Protection Agency is to ensure safe drinking water; restore and maintain oceans, watersheds, and aquatic ecosystems to protect human health and support economic and recreational activities; and to provide healthy habitat to protect fish, plants and wildlife populations. The **Clean Water Act** made illegal any unpermitted point source discharges of any pollutant into the navigable waters of the United States.

Point sources of effluent water pollution are pipes or culverts that discharge pollutants from industrial, municipal, or other facilities into nearby surface water.

The U.S. Environmental Protection Agency has implemented the **National Pollutant Discharge Elimination System** (NPDES) to regulate water pollution, and has crafted pollution control programs in the form of nation-wide water quality standards for industry as well as watershed-specific water quality standards for contaminants in surface waters.

All point sources of waste, such as a pipeline channeling pollution into a nearby river, must apply the **best practicable control technology** to limit water pollution.[29] This technology standard forces effluent to be filtered or treated before it is released into the environment.

b. Clean Air The **Clean Air Act** (CAA) is the comprehensive federal law that regulates air emissions from **stationary sources** (such as a power plant) and **mobile sources** (such as tractors) of air pollutants.

Among other things, this law authorizes the U.S. EPA to establish **National Ambient Air Quality Standards** (NAAQS) to protect public health and public welfare and to regulate emissions of hazardous air pollutants.

The law divides the country into three areas, with different rules for each: (1) areas that have pristine air quality, such as national parks; (2) areas that are currently in compliance with the national standards but which may fall below those standards if additional pollution occurs (called Prevention of Significant Deterioration regions); and (3) areas that are currently not in compliance with the air quality standards (called nonattainment regions).[30]

Before a new major stationary source of air pollution (like a factory) can be constructed in a nonattainment area, the owner must obtain offsetting emission reductions in that area.[31] This ensures that when a new source of pollution is added to an area that is already failing to meet applicable air quality standards, the total volume of air pollution does not increase. For instance, if a business wanted to build a new cement refinery in a nonattainment area, that business would have to obtain emission reductions from another source in the area to compensate for, or **offset**, the new source of air pollution.

Before construction of a major emitting facility begins in a Prevention of Significant Deterioration region, the owner must obtain a preconstruction permit that requires the use of the best available control technology for regulated air pollutants.[32]

For categories of stationary sources (such as factories, refineries, or coal-powered electricity generating units), the U.S. EPA applies regulations for New Source Performance Standards that reflect the emission limits achievable through application of the **best system of emissions reduction**. These standards are based on the cost of achieving the reduction, health impacts, environmental impacts, and the energy required to achieve the reductions.[33]

Clean Water Act Prohibits unpermitted point source discharges of any pollutant into the navigable waters of the United States.

Point Sources Effluent water pollution from pipes or culverts that discharge pollutants from industrial, municipal, or other facilities into nearby surface water.

National Pollutant Discharge Elimination System A pollution control program for point sources, based on water quality standards.

Best Practicable Control Technology Regulatory standard applied to mitigate water pollution through filtration or treatment before discharge.

Clean Air Act Regulates air pollution emissions from stationary and mobile sources.

Stationary Source Air pollution from a fixed location, such as from a coal-fired power plant or factory.

Mobile Source Air pollution from a moving vehicle, such as a diesel powered heavy truck, tractor, or automobile.

National Ambient Air Quality Standards Standards for protecting public health and welfare from a wide range of air pollutants, including hazardous air pollutants and ozone.

Offset Pollution emission reductions achieved in order to compensate for increased emissions from another source.

Best System of Emissions Reduction Standards that reflect the emission limits achievable considering cost, health impacts, environmental impacts, and the energy required to achieve the reductions.

4.2.2 Supply Chain, Marketing, and Consumer Protection

Once a product has been designed and manufactured, it is transported across geographic boundaries from the supplier to the customer before the ultimate business puts the product on the market for sale to end-use consumers. Laws apply to suppliers to ensure goods are not produced using labor practices that violate human rights. Once the product is ready to be sold to consumers, laws apply to the methods used to market products to prevent deception and greenwashing. Additionally, laws apply to protect reasonable consumer expectations of product safety and quality.

1. *Supply Chain* The social impact of business is beginning to be addressed by legal frameworks at an international level, specifically rules that apply to suppliers whose conduct might very well be omitted from regulation by traditional state laws. One method for improving accountability and corporate social responsibility internationally is to require transparency in the form of disclosures that apply across supply chains. Voluntary social and environmental reporting has been inadequate to date—specifically, "only a minority of the reports use internationally accepted standards and principles, cover the company's full supply chain or involve independent monitoring and verification."[34] Therefore, the European Parliament passed a resolution in 2007 to ensure "that social and environmental reporting is included alongside financial reporting requirements."[35] Transparency is the cornerstone of corporate responsibility when it comes to reducing the adverse impacts of business through a company's supply chain.

a. Conflict Minerals **Title XV of the Dodd-Frank Wall Street Reform and Consumer Protection Act** requires companies to disclose dealings in conflict minerals as well as labor problems at mining operations.[36]

Conflict minerals are resources that are looted from a nation during times of armed conflict and human rights violations. The five most common so-called conflict minerals are coltan (used for high performance capacitors), cassiterite (used to produce tin and circuit board soldering), wolframite (used to make tungsten for golf club heads and ammunition), gold (used for jewelry and dental products), and diamonds (used for jewelry).

Section 1502 of the law requires companies to disclose annually whether any conflict minerals are necessary for functionality or production of a product, and if so, the extent of due diligence on the source and chain of custody of those minerals. The due diligence also requires an independent private sector audit of the report. Section 1503 of the law requires mine operators to disclose health and safety violations and imminent dangers at the mines.

b. Slavery and Human Trafficking Slavery or **human trafficking** is a serious crime and violation of human rights, as it generally involves kidnapping, physical abuse, and deprivation of basic rights such as autonomy and fair compensation for labor.

There are about 27 million people trapped in modern-day slave labor, all over the world, with women and girls accounting for approximately 80% of transnational victims of human trafficking.[37] Of these, 70% of females end up in the commercial sex industry and the remaining 30% of females end up as victims of forced labor.[38] Over $30 billion in annual profits are made through the human trafficking and

Title XV of the Dodd-Frank Wall Street Reform and Consumer Protection Act Requires companies to disclose dealings in conflict minerals as well as labor problems at mining operations.

Conflict Minerals Resources looted from a nation during times of armed conflict and human rights violations.

Human Trafficking A criminal violation of human rights, generally involving kidnapping, physical abuse, slavery, and deprivation of basic needs.

slavery industry,[39] which affects almost every nation on the planet as a source for export, transit, or destination of the victims.[40]

Article 3 of the United Nations' Trafficking in Persons Protocol defines human trafficking according to the following rubric. A person is guilty of human trafficking if they perform one of the following acts, using one of the listed methods, for any one of the enumerated purposes. See Table 4.2.

Article 5 of the United Nations' Trafficking in Persons Protocol calls upon UN member states to pass national legislation that criminalizes human trafficking according to this rubric.

The state of California passed **SB 657: California Transparency in Supply Chains Act**[41] to eradicate slavery and human trafficking from businesses operating within their state, and to address criminal labor practices on the part of manufacturers and suppliers around the world.

The state of California is the 8th largest economy in the world, and many goods shipped to the United States find their port of call in California. Therefore, this law has sweeping implications for business. SB 657 requires retailers and manufacturers with $100 million in gross worldwide receipts doing business in California to publicly disclose their efforts to eradicate slavery and human trafficking in their supply chains.

Specifically, the California law requires regulated entities to make publicly available five distinct disclosures—namely, the extent to which the following initiatives to expose and eliminate human trafficking have been undertaken:

1. the organization's slavery and human trafficking risk levels are verified by a 3rd party;
2. supply chain audits are independent and unannounced, where standards are set and suppliers are audited against those standards;
3. direct suppliers are contractually obligated to certify compliance with human trafficking laws;
4. existing internal accountability mechanisms ensure adherence to laws and self-imposed standards; and
5. employee training to identify, mitigate, and report risks of human trafficking in the organization's supply chain.

Article 3 of the United Nations' Trafficking in Persons Protocol Defines human trafficking according to a rubric of illicit acts, methods, and purposes.

Article 5 of the United Nations' Trafficking in Persons Protocol Calls upon UN member states to pass national legislation that criminalizes human trafficking.

SB 657: California Transparency in Supply Chains Act Law requiring certain companies to disclose efforts taken to combat human trafficking in their supply chain.

TABLE **4.2**		
Operative Definition of Human Trafficking		
An Act such as:	**+ By any of these Methods:**	**+ For any of these Purposes:**
Recruiting	Threat or use of force	Exploitation
Transporting	Coercion	Prostitution
Transferring	Abduction	Sexual Exploitation
Harboring	Fraud	Forced Labor
Receipt of Persons	Abuse of Power or Vulnerability	Slavery
	Giving Payments or Benefits	Removal of Organs

Source: Article 3 of the United Nations' Trafficking in Persons Protocol.

> ## ETHICAL DECISIONS: Safeway Takes on Human Trafficking[42]
>
> To understand the far-reaching impact of California's anti-human trafficking law on business, consider the following disclosure from Safeway groceries. Safeway is in the process of "surveying its merchandise supply chains in order to evaluate and to address risks of slavery and human trafficking inherent in those activities. This survey will form the basis for additional anti-slavery, anti-human trafficking efforts by Safeway, including targeted supplier requirements and third-party audits."
>
> Safeway uses contractual provisions in supplier contracts to prohibit child and involuntary labor while protecting workers that supply the store's merchandise. Safeway's Code of Conduct is mandatory for suppliers, and requires them "to allow factory inspections for contractual compliance, as well as for compliance with laws and regulations dealing with child or forced labor and unsafe working conditions."

Notice that the California human trafficking law does not *require* businesses to *actually inspect* their supply chains for signs of human trafficking violations. Rather, the law merely requires regulated businesses to *disclose* to their consumers whether - and to what extent - the business has taken the five steps discussed earlier.

Note that **transparency** laws are information forcing, in that they require the production and disclosure of information so that consumers can make informed decisions, thereby patronizing those companies based on an informed ethical judgment about the entire life cycle of the products sold, rather than simply based on product price.

Carl Graziani, Senior Vice President of Supply Chain for Safeway, has publicly encouraged retailers and consumer products manufacturers to begin mapping their own global supply chains in order to pinpoint suppliers with the highest risk of suspect labor practices.[43] Supply chain information-sharing initiatives and the development of industry-wide standards for supplier labor practices can make the effort to combat human trafficking more realistic and feasible.

Unlike transparency laws, many other laws discussed in this chapter are **command-and-control** laws, which involve direct regulation of business by a government agency that determines what conduct is required and what conduct is illegal.

2. *Marketing* In Chapter 7: Marketing, we learn that marketers are not to make general environmental benefit claims without some evidence or qualification in support of the claim. This and other specific guidelines for marketing sustainability come from the U.S. Federal Trade Commission's **Green Marketing Guidelines** as well as truth-in-advertising laws.[44]

Instead of merely describing a product as eco-friendly, and leaving it at that, marketers should include specific environmental benefits that are appropriately understood by the consumer to be significant and which effectively distinguish a sustainably-made product from its traditional competitors.

Acceptable environmental benefit claims are usually based on life-cycle analysis to analyze the overall environmental profile of a product to ensure the benefits of a particular product feature are not outweighed by the pollution or waste generated in bringing that product to market. For example, claiming a product is sustainable because it is made with recycled content may be deceptive if the environmental costs

Transparency When by law companies must produce and disclose information about social, economic, environmental, and governance issues affecting the company.

Command-and-Control Direct regulation of business by a government agency that determines what conduct is required and what conduct is illegal.

Green Marketing Guidelines Require marketers using environmental claims to substantiate and specify these claims to prevent misleading consumers.

Greenwashing Spending more on marketing environmental attributes than actually mitigating environmental impacts.

of using recycled content outweigh the environmental benefits of using it. Marketers must be careful to avoid **greenwashing**, which is essentially deceptive advertising based on false or misleading claims about the sustainable nature of the product or service being offered.

The Federal Trade Commission's Green Marketing Guidelines highlight the main marketing strategies for sustainable products and the difference between what is acceptable and what regulators may view as inappropriate greenwashing.[45] These marketing guidelines help companies ethically take credit for sustainability initiatives only to the extent that evidence is available to prove products actually have the environmental attributes claimed. These guidelines for marketing sustainable products apply to the marketing stage of business activity, however they should be borne in mind at the product design stage, when the environmental attributes of the product are chosen.

3. *Consumer Product Safety* There are two primary legal frameworks related to consumer product safety: regulation and litigation. Regulation includes pre-market safe and effective approval, and litigation includes post-sale liability for harms resulting from consumer products. Most of these legal frameworks apply to food and drugs, but also to imports such as children's toys.

a. Pre-Sale Product Restrictions Various government programs restrict which products are acceptable to markets within their borders in order to protect the unwitting consumer from exposure to unreasonable risks. Canada's **Hazardous Products Act** sorts consumer products into lists of items that are (1) banned from import, sale, and advertisement; (2) subject to regulations as a prerequisite to import, sale, or advertisement; (3) subject to industry-government negotiated voluntary standards for certain products; and (4) unregulated products that should be reviewed internally by industry. Existing legislative proposals such as the Consumer Product Safety Act would add teeth to these protocols by flatly banning the import or sale of any product that is dangerous to human health or safety.

Hazardous Products Act Sorts consumer products into lists of items that are banned, subject to regulation, subject to voluntary standards, or unregulated.

The European Union **General Products Safety Directive** (GPSD) seeks to ensure that the only products sold in the EU are safe ones. In the EU, legislation for product safety is usually sector-specific, so the GPSD applies in a complimentary way to residual product safety risks.

General Products Safety Directive Seeks to ensure that products sold in the EU are only safe ones.

The **U.S. Food and Drug Administration** ensures the safety and effectiveness of pharmaceuticals, animal and veterinary drugs, food additives, and cosmetics sold in the United States.[46]

U.S. Food and Drug Administration Oversees the safety and effectiveness of pharmaceuticals, animal and veterinary drugs, food additives, and cosmetics sold in the United States.

Safety testing by the U.S. FDA is done with respect to clinical endpoints of drugs (such as the dosage-response of prescription quantities). This practice generates information about the risk profile of the substances in consumer products before they are marketed and informs prospective purchasers of possible adverse side effects, allergic reactions, and other risks of consumption. The chemicals commonly used in pharmaceutical and personal care products including household cleaning products may be safe for users on an individual basis, but ultimately unsafe once released into the environment and combined with other such substances.[47] That means, simply because a product has been approved as safe and effective by the U.S. FDA, this does not actually mean the product is safe in all circumstances, or that the product is sustainable. The limited assurance that FDA approval provides to consumer products reinforces the theme of this chapter, namely, that legal standards often set the minimum floor for acceptable conduct, and mere compliance with law is not the same as ethical or sustainable conduct.

b. Post-Sale Liability Consumer products are also regulated in the United States by tort law that provides compensation to victims of product defects. Specifically, there are three kinds of product defects that can be remedied under four different theories of liability. In the United States, when an unreasonably unsafe product injures a consumer, the injured party has a cause of action in court against the product designer, manufacturer, or seller. There are three types of product defects: manufacturing defect, design defect, and warning defects.[48] Product defect litigation typically proceeds under one of four theories: the responsible party was negligent, the seller breached a warranty made to the buyer, the seller misrepresented product attributes to the buyer, or the seller is just strictly liable for injuries resulting from the product even in the absence of fault. These various kinds of product defects and theories of product liability combine to provide injured consumers with alternative paths to getting a remedy in the form of money judgment from the party profiting from the sale of risk-creating products.

Manufacturing defects are where the product departs from its intended design, even if the manufacturer exercised all possible care for product quality and safety. The glass Coke bottle that explodes because it was manufactured with a hairline crack is an example of this type of defect. Between the manufacturer who did the best they could to design a safe product, and the innocent consumer injured by the departure of that product from its intended design, product liability law shifts the cost of manufacturing defects onto the manufacturer in order to protect consumer safety. If a customer was unreasonably misusing the product in such a way as to cause the injury (such as using the Coke bottle as a drum-stick), they might fail in their claim for compensation, even if they can prove the product was defective.

> **Manufacturing Defects** Where the product departs from its intended design, even if the manufacturer exercised all possible care for product quality and safety.

Design defects are the foreseeable risks of harm created by a product that renders it unreasonably safe, which risks could have been avoided by adopting some reasonable alternative design. A child's crib designed to be collapsible by pressing a button accessible from inside the crib is an example of this kind of defect. The risk of harm to a child trapped inside a collapsed crib are foreseeable, and the risk could have been avoided by adopting an alternative design that wouldn't be prohibitively expensive or frustrate the purpose of the product. Alternatively, a kitchen knife may injure a consumer if it cuts their hand, however, the risk of being cut by the knife does not render the product defective because there is no reasonable alternative design of a cutting utensil that completely avoids the risk of cutting the user.

> **Design Defects** Foreseeable risks of harm created by a product that renders it unreasonably safe, which risks could have been avoided by adopting some reasonable alternative design.

Warning defects, or inadequate user instructions, can create product liability when the foreseeable risks of harm posed by a product could have been reduced by providing reasonable instructions or warnings, the omission of which renders the product unreasonably risky. Failing to warn a consumer that a hair blow-dryer can cause electric shock if used in the bath-tub could create liability for a defective warning because it is foreseeable that some consumers might attempt to multi-task in the bathroom, or may have the blow-dryer perched close to the bath-tub when plugged in. Adequate warning labels function as an "I told you so!" that product manufacturers can use to avoid liability when a consumer is injured by the warned-against product use.

> **Warning Defects** Inadequate user instructions that create product liability when the foreseeable risks of harm posed by a product could have been reduced by providing reasonable instructions or warnings, the omission of which renders the product unreasonably risky.

Negligence When a ompany breaches their legal duty to exercise ordinary care, resulting in physical injury to a foreseeable victim.

Negligence in this context means a company breaches their legal duty to exercise ordinary care, resulting in physical injury to a foreseeable victim. An example could be failing to inspect products off the assembly line before selling them, failing to adequately train employees to properly care for a customer, or failure to prepare and enforce appropriate operating procedures, resulting in injury to a consumer. If a nursing home hires a caretaker with a criminal record for violence, without conducting a proper background check, and that person intentionally injures a client, then the nursing home may be liable for negligent hire.

Breach of Warranty The seller's failure to fulfill the terms of a representation made regarding the quality of the product sold.

Breach of warranty means the seller's failure to fulfill the terms of a representation made regarding the quality of the product sold. Even in the absence of a written contract, the law implies the warranty on the part of the seller that the goods sold are fit for the ordinary purposes for which they are to be used.[49] The law assumes that sellers of goods provide to buyers the generic warranty that the sold items are of similar quality and value as similar items sold under similar circumstances. When the breaks on a car fail, leading to the injury of the driver, the car manufacturer may be liable for breach of warranty, even if the driver was never told explicitly that the breaks would function properly, because the law implies such a warranty in the transaction.

Misrepresentation When the seller gives consumers false security regarding product safety, for instance by intentionally concealing potential hazards with statements that were relied upon by the consumer.

Misrepresentation can be a source of liability when the seller gave consumers false security regarding product safety, for instance by intentionally concealing potential hazards with statements that were relied upon by the consumer. For instance, if the salesperson tells the consumer that a plastic container is microwave safe or microwaveable, and then the consumer is injured when the container explodes in the microwave, the seller may be liable for misrepresentation.

Strict Liability Allows anyone injured by a product to sue the manufacturer if they can prove the product was defective, which defect caused the injury, and which rendered the product unreasonably dangerous according to reasonable consumer expectations.

Strict liability allows anyone injured by a product to sue the manufacturer if they can prove the product was defective, which defect caused the injury, and which rendered the product unreasonably dangerous according to reasonable consumer expectations. This cause of action does not require any fault on the part of the manufacturer. For example, if a company is engaged in hazardous activities, such as the use of explosives, or the keeping of wild animals, and someone is injured as a result of the explosion, or because of the escaped tiger, then the company is strictly liable for those injuries, even if they did everything possible to prevent the injuries.

4.2.3 Packaging, Waste, and Disposal

The sheer volume of consumer goods being shipped internationally due to increased Internet sales and the internationalization of consumer demand has led to an unsustainable rate of waste generation, meaning obsolete products and discarded product packaging exceeds waste disposal capacity. Per-capita consumption of packaging is increasing in all developed countries, and single-serving packages (when compared to bulk purchases more common to large families) are on the rise, leading to dramatic increases in the amount of paper and plastic waste being generated.[50] The short life span of consumer electronics such as cellular phones and personal computers also lead to a boom in electronic waste. **Extended producer responsibility** (EPR) requires manufacturers to take responsibility for the disposal of waste from their products, which creates the incentives necessary to encourage producers to reduce the volume of packaging and to substitute the material used.

Extended Producer Responsibility Requires manufacturers to take responsibility for the disposal of waste from their products.

1. *Packaging Materials* Although the United States does not have comprehensive legislation regarding product packaging material or quantity, various states and local governments have taken leadership on this front. The state of California introduced a plastic bag law to require retail stores of certain sizes to provide customers with bins to collect plastic bags. The store is required to collect, transport, and recycle the bags in order to reduce the overall volume of plastic bag waste littering streets, filling up garbage dumps, and contaminating California's famous shorelines. Other cities are considering or have imposed plastic bag taxes that apply to the customer at the point of sale to encourage consumers to bring their own shopping bags, with fees going to local environmental cleanup efforts.

Two provinces in Canada have taken measures to reduce product waste and to compensate municipal governments for the expense of recycling. Printing companies, publishers, and the packaging industry abide by a cost recovery fee structure to ensure the recovery of 50% of their products.

The European Union has long maintained a product packaging waste directive to prevent barriers to trade that might arise with a variety of different requirements between member states. The packaging waste directive sets the priorities of reducing the amount of packaging used and increasing the reuse of packaging through better recovery and recycling.

2. *Product Take-Back* The European Union and Japan were among the first governments to introduce requirements for manufacturers to plan financially and physically to ensure that obsolete products and their containers are collected and processed, rather than simply sent to landfills. Although recycling of cans and bottles is common, the growing concern with extended producer responsibility is in the electronics sector because of the expanding volume of product offerings, the short life-cycle of these products (sometimes called planned obsolescence), and the variety of waste streams generated by their use—for instance, it is not just the cell phone box, but also the battery, the plastic case, the charge cord, and the headset that accompany the cell phone. DVD players, cell phones, portable music devices, cameras, GPS systems, and the like are top sellers, and each year they are replaced with newer models, leading to the discard of millions of tons of electronic waste each year. Landfills and incinerators are commonly filled with these waste items, leading to practical capacity issues among governments.[51]

The United States has yet to pass legislation requiring extended producer responsibility for electronic waste, however over a dozen states have passed laws to create electronic waste recycling programs at the state level, either through **producer responsibility** or through **recovery fees**.

The European Union has enacted the **Waste Electrical and Electronic Equipment** (WEEE) directive to reduce waste from this sector, increase recovery and recycling rates, improve environmental performance throughout the life cycle of these products, and to extend producer responsibility over their disposal.

3. *Disposal of Dangerous Waste Products* The **Resource Conservation and Recovery Act**[52] governs the generation, transportation, treatment, storage, and disposal of hazardous waste, which is solid waste that is potentially dangerous to human health or the environment.[53] This law bans the disposal of hazardous wastes in landfills or in deep underground injection wells unless the waste has been pre-treated to

Producer Responsibility Electronic waste recycling programs where the manufacturer pays.

Recovery Fees Electronic waste recycling programs where the consumer pays.

Waste Electrical and Electronic Equipment Directive to reduce waste from the electronics sector, increase recovery and recycling rates, improve environmental performance throughout the life cycle of these products, and to extend producer responsibility over their disposal.

Resource Conservation and Recovery Act Governs the generation, transportation, treatment, storage, and disposal of solid waste, in particular hazardous waste.

remove its hazardous characteristics.[54] The Resource Conservation and Recovery Act also creates a cause of action in federal court for citizens to enforce the law when it has been violated in such a way as to pose an imminent and substantial endangerment to public health or the environment.[55]

Similarly, the **Oil Pollution Act**[56] creates liability for parties responsible for an oil spill. Each responsible party for a vessel or facility from which oil is discharged into navigable waters or shorelines is liable for the cost of removal of the oil as well as resulting damages.[57] Damages recoverable under this law include natural resource damages, damages to real and personal property, loss of subsistence uses of natural resources, loss of tax and other revenue, increased costs of public services, and loss of profits or earning capacity.[58] When British Petroleum was charged under the Oil Pollution Act for the 2010 Deepwater Horizon explosion and oil spill in the Gulf of Mexico, the company paid $4.5 billion in criminal penalties, and created a $20 billion compensation fund for fishing companies, coastal hotels, and restaurants impacted by the spill. See the Harvard Business Review case for more on this subject, in **Further Research**.

4.2.4 Land Use Planning

In the United States, land is subject to a variety of controls to facilitate the rational layout of industrial, commercial, and residential uses. Local governments typically have land use plans in the form of zoning districts that may require land developers to obtain a permit for new construction projects before they break ground. Furthermore, some state governments as well as major metropolitan areas such as New York City have **environmental impact statement** (EIS) requirements. EIS programs require the leading government agency to publish a record of the social, economic, and environmental impacts, both positive and negative, of a proposed change in land use.

Failure to prepare an adequate environmental impact statement can lead to costly delays. In New York State, the gas industry has waited for several years as the New York State Department of Environmental Conservation has published inadequate draft after draft of the environmental impacts associated with developing the Marcellus Shale through the use of the controversial gas extraction technique known as hydraulic fracturing. The leading agency consults with scientists and public policy experts as well as the regulated industry to develop the EIS. One could say that the environmental law is the cause of the delay, but it may be more appropriate to say that the industry's reluctance to provide complete information to the regulatory body is the reason for the delay.

When the first EIS draft was published, environmental activists pounced on the deficiencies and oversights of the study, challenging its adequacy under the state law. This led to a reset, where the EIS process began all over again. If all of the major impacts had been disclosed in the first draft, the drilling may have already begun. However, New York State is yet to tap its shale formation, in large part because of the ongoing environmental review process. Currently, the health impacts of the proposed shale development are being studied. Activists wonder why it has taken so many years for the lead agency to finally require health impacts to be considered—indeed, if they had been addressed from the get go, drilling might already be underway.

EIS requirements at the state and local level reflect the requirements placed on the federal government by the **National Environmental Policy Act**, or NEPA.[59] For all major federal actions significantly affecting the quality of the human environment, federal agencies must prepare a detailed statement on the environmental impacts of the proposed action.[60] For example, the company TransCanada has planned since 2008 to build a pipeline, known as the Keystone XL, connecting the tar sands of Alberta, Canada, to a refinery and export terminal in the Gulf of Mexico along the coast of Texas. In order to do so, the company needed the approval of the United States Department of State, because it is a project crossing U.S. borders. Therefore, the proposal implicated the National Environmental Policy Act, because the approval of the Keystone XL pipeline would constitute a "major federal action significantly affecting the quality of the human environment."

The entire project was put on hold for several years as the Department of State prepared an Environmental Impact Statement describing the social, economic, and environmental impacts the project would create. In the mean time, protesters rallied in Washington, D.C. against the project and lobbyists sought its approval, making it one of the most high-profile environmental controversies of the decade.

NEPA states that the federal government, in cooperation with state and local governments and other concerned public and private organizations, shall use all practicable means to foster and promote the general welfare; develop conditions for the harmonious coexistence of people and nature; and fulfill the social, economic, and other requirements of present and future generations.[61] Despite this lofty language, the law is actually procedural only, meaning it provides for a process to be followed, but does not require any particular substantive outcomes. In order words, once the environmental impacts have been published, even if they are tremendous, the federal agency can still approve the project. All that NEPA requires is that the impacts be identified ahead of time. Sometimes, however, delay is all that environmental activists need: if the project is delayed for several years, financing may fall through, and the project proposal may be withdrawn despite the fact that the leading agency was poised to approve it.

> **National Environmental Policy Act** For all major federal actions significantly affecting the quality of the human environment, federal agencies must prepare a detailed statement on the environmental impacts of the proposed action.

4.3 Limits of the Law

4.3.1 Legal Compliance vs. Sustainable Performance

Mere compliance with the law should not be mistaken as ethical or **sustainable performance**.

The law may prohibit dumping toxic waste into the neighborhood rain gutter, but it will not require a business to reform production processes to eliminate the generation of toxic waste in the first place. The law may prohibit deceiving consumers about the attributes of products, but it does not require that marketing agencies educate consumers about healthy lifestyles. It is not morally praiseworthy for a grocer to provide correct change to a customer—that much is simply required by law. However, it would be morally praiseworthy for that grocer to donate a portion of her groceries to low-income families with unmet nutritional needs, though no laws exist that would require such a thing. Compliance with the law is an important part of the

> **Mere Compliance** When a company seeks to comply with minimum standards for legal performance without going beyond these standards.
>
> **Sustainable Performance** When a company goes beyond mere compliance with the law to satisfy social, economic, and environmental objectives.

business case for sustainability because it reduces the risk of liabilities. Businesses should consider ways of going above and beyond legal requirements to create value for stakeholders.

Refer to Table 4.1. Complying with the law is superior to merely avoiding the law altogether, yet businesses stand to gain by using law as a source of competitive advantage. Indeed, a company that has superior pollution controls would benefit from increased stringency of environmental laws because it would provide a competitive advantage vis-à-vis businesses lacking in sophisticated pollution controls.

Businesses with sustainable operations and supply chains stand to gain from efforts to lobby government entities to improve the legal system for a more sustainable marketplace, causing the tide to rise and lift all boats. Transformation through legal rules is possible when businesses see the benefits of sustainability and want to ensure that industry competition leads to a race to the top rather than a race to the bottom. The opposite phenomenon, lobbying for weaker laws, is a barrier to sustainability and will be explored in the next section.

4.3.2 Lobbying for Lax Laws

Lobbyist Professional hired to influence public policy on a particular issue in favor of the client, especially through personal contact with legislators and staff members.

Businesses or industry trade groups employ **lobbyists** to influence public policy on a particular issue in their favor.[62] Although a variety of tools exist for lobbying, such as mobilizing citizens to write letters, testifying at hearings, and submitting written comments to regulators, the most important tool is personal contact with legislators and staff members by a lobbying specialist.[63]

Corporate lobbying generally has a bad reputation. The global economic recession beginning with the 2008 collapse of Wall Street was arguably due to inadequate regulatory oversight of the finance industry. In the years leading up to the mortgage-backed securities meltdown, the finance industry had nearly 3,000 lobbyists in the United States capitol, and that decade, banks had spent $5 billion in lobbying fees and political campaign contributions to ensure continually lax regulations.[64] Unduly weak regulations, apparent conflicts of interest that would allow money managers to profit even when investors lost money, the ability to externalize risk, and a culture of reckless risk taking arguably contributed to the financial collapse of Wall Street.

According to a report by the non-profit environmental organization Natural Resources Defense Council,[65] during the period of 2011 to 2012, eight leading U.S. electric utility companies spent millions of dollars lobbying and litigating to block, weaken or delay major Clean Air Act environmental and public health safeguards, at the same time as their coal-fired power plants emitted enough pollution to contribute to nearly 10,400 deaths, 65,000 asthma attacks, 6,600 hospital and emergency room visits, 3.4 million lost workdays, and as much as $78 billion in health care costs.

Revolving Door Where a leader in industry takes over as the chief regulator responsible for overseeing her prior industry, and vice versa—the chief regulator takes over as a director of the previously regulated industry.

The corrupting influence of money in politics can lead to laws that are written predominantly with the interests of the regulated community in mind, rather than the proper role of protective law, which is to protect public welfare from unethical or unreasonable business practices. Further, lobbying can lead to under-enforcement of laws as well as partisanship and favoritism amongst lawmakers and regulators. The concept of the **revolving door** refers to the scenario where a leader in industry takes over as the chief regulator responsible for overseeing her prior industry, and vice versa—the chief regulator takes over as a director of the previously regulated industry. These situations can cause apparent and real conflicts of interest. Lobbying and revolving door employment between business and government posts can degrade the protective force of law.

Given that many laws already set bare minimum standards of care, it may be surprising to learn that some industry and trade groups actively lobby government to reduce the consumer health, safety, and environmental protections of existing laws, and to prevent the passage of new, protective laws that would curb corporate pollution or other forms of harmful conduct. As discussed in Case 1 in Chapter 7: Marketing, the plastics industry lobbied to prevent the state of California from banning the chemical BPA from use in sippy cups for infants, even though the health impacts of the chemical had been established. It would be fair to ask whether intentionally exposing infants to harmful chemicals is unethical, but lobbying for the continued right to do so is clearly legal. The Supreme Court of the United States, in the landmark ruling **Citizens United** *v.* **Federal Election Commission**, ruled that political expenditures constitute free speech, and restrictions on such expenditures would be an unconstitutional violation of corporations' right to free speech. As a result, unrestricted corporate lobbying continues.

> **Citizens United v. Federal Election Commission** Landmark ruling by the U.S. Supreme Court allowing unlimited political campaign contributions by corporations.

Between 2008 and 2010, environmental groups including The Nature Conservancy, the Natural Resources Defense Council, the Sierra Club, World Wildlife Fund, and others lobbied Congress to encourage the passage of legislation that would limit the amount of greenhouse gasses emitted by industries within the United States. Although environmental groups spent a record $22.4 million with high hopes of combating climate change, their lobbying effort paled when compared to the $175 million spent by the oil and gas industry during the same time period, which were in opposition to any limits on greenhouse gas pollution.[66] Just one company, ExxonMobil, spent more than the entire sum of environmental organizations, with $27.4 million on political contributions to fight climate change legislation. The industry prevailed, and still no greenhouse gas legislation exists in the United States.

"The large sums of money spent lobbying and litigating to block or otherwise water down environmental regulations … might be more productively spent reengineering business accounting systems to accurately track environment-related costs (and returns)[.] Gutting environmental statutes merely prolongs public subsidization of inefficient uncompetitive businesses."[67]

4.3.3 Under-Enforcement of Good Laws

Laws are meaningless words unless they are obeyed. When it comes to environmental protection, public health, and workplace safety, enforcement is often necessary to ensure compliance with laws. The Natural Resources Defense Council conducted a study in the state of California to determine whether protective laws were actually being enforced, and found that virtually every protective law, whether governing air, water, hazardous waste, or workplace safety, had been violated a substantial number of times

> **CROSS-LINKAGE**
>
> For more on the how globalization affects regulatory compliance, see Chapter 2: Perspectives.

in the studied years, and that "enforcement authorities may not consistently and firmly sanction businesses and other regulated entities that break environmental, health, or workplace safety laws."[68]

Because of the pervasive influence of corporate moneys on the setting of public policy to reduce the public protection of laws, and because of the **under-enforcement** of those protective laws that do exist, it hardly needs to be said that compliance with prevailing legal standards may not be sufficient to bring about a sustainable world.

Despite the shortcomings of existing legal frameworks, bringing a company into compliance with applicable environmental, public health, and workplace safety laws is the best place to start, and a variety of intelligently drafted and justly executed laws and legal frameworks do exist to guide companies on the path to sustainable supply chains, sustainable operations, and sustainable marketing. Obtaining compliance, then going beyond compliance to sustainable performance, is the gateway to profitability, public protection, and environmental integrity.

Under-Enforcement Failure to take adequate legal actions to mandate compliance with laws such as fines, penalties, permit revocation, or prison for noncompliance.

Key Terms

environmental law 96
avoidance 98
compliance 98
advantage 98
transformation 98
law 99
hard law 99
soft law 99
legal hierarchy 100
legislative branch 100
executive branch 101
judicial branch 101
1997 Kyoto Protocol on
   Climate Change 101
Basel Convention 102
Montreal Protocol 102
legal environment of
   business 102
legal framework for
   sustainable business 102
design 105
sustainable product
   design 105
Eco-Design of Energy-
   Using Products
   (EuP) 106
Production/Operations
   Management 106

Sustainable Production/
   Operations 107
Emergency Planning and
   Community Right-to-
   Know Act 107
Pollution Prevention
   Act 107
Registration, Evaluation,
   Authorization, and
   Restriction of Chemical
   Substances 107
Occupational Safety and
   Health Act 107
Clean Water Act 108
Point Sources 108
National Pollutant
   Discharge Elimination
   System 108
Best Practicable Control
   Technology 108
Clean Air Act 108
Stationary Source 108
Mobile Source 108
National Ambient Air
   Quality Standards 108
Offset 108
Best System of Emissions
   Reduction 108

Title XV of the Dodd-Frank
   Wall Street Reform and
   Consumer Protection
   Act 109
conflict minerals 109
human trafficking 109
Article 3 of the United
   Nations' Trafficking in
   Persons Protocol 110
Article 5 of the United
   Nations' Trafficking in
   Persons Protocol 110
SB 657: California
   Transparency in Supply
   Chains Act 110
transparency 111
command-and-control 111
Green Marketing
   Guidelines 111
greenwashing 112
Hazardous Products
   Act 112
General Products Safety
   Directive 112
U.S. Food and Drug
   Administration 112
Manufacturing defects 113
Design defects 113

Warning defects 113
Negligence 114
Breach of warranty 114
Misrepresentation 114
Strict liability 114
extended producer
   responsibility 114
producer responsibility 115
recovery fees 115
Waste Electrical and
   Electronic Equipment
   Directive 115
Resource Conservation
   and Recovery Act 115
Oil Pollution Act 116
Environmental Impact
   Statement 116
National Environmental
   Policy Act 117
Mere compliance 117
Sustainable
   performance 117
lobbyist 118
revolving door 118
Citizens United v.
   Federal Election
   Commission 119
under-enforcement 120

Discussion Questions

1. What role does legal compliance play in the business case for sustainability?

2. Has your company been involved in litigation or regulatory compliance problems related to sustainability? How was the matter resolved?

3. How can law help inform sustainable product design, manufacturing, supply chain, and marketing?

4. What is the difference between legal compliance and sustainable performance? Why might mere compliance be insufficient to promote sustainability?

5. What are some ethical concerns associated with lobbying for favorable laws?

CASE 1

Can Litigation Set Public Policy on the Use of Drugs in Industrial Agriculture?

After the famous actress Julia Roberts starred in the Hollywood movie *Eric Brockovich*, most of us have heard of the pro-bono legal assistant who in the 1990's began researching Pacific Gas & Electric's contamination of a small town's water supply. Her research ultimately revealed 30 years of toxic dumping that had poisoned countless families in Hinkley, California. The lawsuit based on her research led to a $333 million settlement, the largest toxic tort settlement in U.S. history. Most of us also know of the lawsuit arising from the Exxon Valdez oil spill off the coast of Alaska that went all the way to the U.S. Supreme Court and resulted in a $500 million settlement. More recently, BP's Deepwater Horizon oil spill in the Gulf of Mexico resulted in $4.5 billion in criminal and civil penalties. With jaw-dropping money damages and elite star power raising awareness, it is hard to ignore such epic lawsuits.

Perhaps, less of us are aware of behind the scenes litigation that takes place between non-profit environmental organizations and the regulatory agencies responsible for protecting the environment and public health. Nonetheless, these lawsuits can have major repercussions for business and public safety.

The U.S. Food and Drug Administration is responsible for assuring the public that foods, drugs, cosmetics, medical products, and other consumer products are safe, effective, and properly labeled for consumption. However, sometimes government agencies can fail to properly enforce laws, or can fail to base their safety regulations on adequate scientific evidence. In these scenarios, public-interest organizations can petition the agency to revisit regulatory decisions based on new and substantial evidence,

and if the petition is denied arbitrarily, they can appeal the denial in court to obtain independent review.

The U.S. Food and Drug Administration has approved the use of antibiotic drugs in livestock feed for pigs, cows, chickens, and turkeys in order to stimulate faster growth and to compensate for unsanitary living conditions at Confined Animal Feeding Operations (CAFOs) at industrial-scale farms. According to the non-profit Union of Concerned Scientists, about 70% of all antibiotics consumed in the United States are not used to treat human illnesses, but rather, are actually fed at low-doses to meat-producing farm animals.[69] The use of pharmaceuticals such as penicillin and tetracyclines at low-dose levels results in the survival of superbugs, highly resistant to medical treatment, such as salmonella and e-coli, which can escape from the farm and contaminate food and water supplies, threatening the health and safety of consumers.

When the Natural Resources Defense Council and a coalition of public-health organizations sued the U.S. Food and Drug Administration in the most recent battle over this use of drugs in livestock, the agency was met with a stinging reprimand from the federal court. According to the presiding judge, "For over thirty years, the Agency has been confronted with evidence of the human health risks associated with the widespread subtherapeutic use of antibiotics in food-producing animals, and, despite a statutory mandate to ensure the safety of animal drugs, the Agency has done shockingly little to address these risks." Despite the court's order to revisit their approval of antibiotics in animal feedstock, as regulations currently stand, the use of antibiotics in animal feed remains legal, despite substantial evidence

(continues)

that the practice poses environmental and human health risks, and despite the feasibility of smaller scale organic farming that avoids these risks. Recently, the FDA did ask pharmaceutical companies to voluntarily implement a program to ensure the judicious use of antibiotics in food animals by phasing them out.[70]

Sasha Millbrand works in the Office of Regulatory Compliance for a large dairy farm in the U.S. that uses antibiotics in its cattle feed. She was asked to answer questions about antibiotics in feedstock so the Vice President for Public Relations has some talking points ready for an upcoming conference hosted at a local university. These are the questions she needs to research:

1. What is the state of research in support of and against the conclusion that our use of antibiotics in feedstock actually poses a threat to the environment or consumer health?
2. Is the U.S. Food and Drug Administration nearing a point where they might change their policy of approving these uses of antibiotics? What seems to be the Agency's position?
3. If the Agency changes its policy on the use of antibiotics in feedstock, how long do we have to get our operations into compliance? If the Agency issues "recommendations" instead of "rules," should we change our operations, or can we continue along with business as usual?

CASE 2 The American Legislative Exchange Council and So-Called Ag Gag Rules.[71]

The American Legislative Exchange Council (ALEC) is a non-profit think-tank on public policy issues that "develops model bills and resolutions on economic issues" and "provides a forum for the private sector to provide practical input on how state public policy decisions can impact jobs and the local economy."[72] Although its spokespeople claim that "ALEC is run by and for state legislators," it turns out that 98% of funding of ALEC's activities come from *industry sponsors* rather than legislator membership dues.[73] So, an alternative description of ALEC is that it is a forum for industry representatives to tell state lawmakers what kinds of laws they would like to apply to themselves.

Perhaps not surprisingly, the laws promoted by ALEC generally aim to limit the government's regulatory oversight of commercial activity, and even to eliminate existing consumer protection measures altogether. For example, model legislation produced by ALEC includes the Resolution Opposing EPA's Regulatory Trainwreck, State Withdrawal from Regional Climate Initiatives, and Resolution Opposing State and Local Mandates Requiring Warning Labels on Wireless Devices and Packaging.[74]

The latest ALEC model legislation to garner attention from the public-interest community is known as the Animal and Ecological Terrorism Act, which "creates penalties for persons encouraging, financing, assisting or engaged in acts of animal and ecological terrorism." Ecological terrorism, which sounds horrifying, is actually defined as "entering an animal or research facility to take pictures by photograph, video camera, or other means with the intent to commit criminal activities or defame the facility or its owner."[75] Anyone convicted under this law would also be placed on a terrorist registry. Under ALEC's proposed legislation, anyone taking pictures of a slaughterhouse with the intent to defame the owner would be guilty of animal terrorism. Someone who walked into a logging zone to photograph the effects of clear-cutting would be guilty of ecological terrorism.

This law would criminalize citizen journalists as well as conscientious employees who use their cell-phone camera to film animal cruelty, unsanitary conditions, or other illegal practices at farms and other agricultural facilities. Versions of this legal proposal have cropped up in various states throughout the United States, and have earned the epithet Ag Gag by critics, because they appear to restrict citizen rights to free speech about the dangers of industrial farming.

The major fast-food retailer McDonald's, in part of its sustainability initiatives, actually cancelled contracts with its largest egg supplier, Sparboe Farms, after undercover video revealed incidents of animal cruelty. Although animal cruelty is a crime in many states, this ALEC model rule would actually make it a crime to *report* those crimes.

Sasha Millbrand works in the Office of Regulatory Compliance for a diary farm in the U.S. (see Case 1). The state where her company is located recently enacted a so-called Ag Gag law. One of their employees turns out to be an undercover volunteer for the activist group People for the Ethical Treatment of Animals (PETA), and he was caught filming allegedly unsanitary conditions and animal

cruelty in their slaughterhouse. Sasha's boss has asked her a few questions about how they can handle the incident.

1. Should we prosecute the PETA activist? If we do, are there any publicity risks for initiating public litigation about this issue?

2. Will any of the businesses to which we supply dairy products find out about the conditions in our slaughterhouse? Is it better to restrict access to the slaughterhouse to all but the most loyal employees, or should we modify our practices so there is nothing to report on?

3. After the most recent wave of political elections, it looks like the state legislature might repeal the Ag Gag law. Should the company lobby to keep the law in place?

Further Research

For information on the ongoing developments in environmental law, consider publications by the Environmental Law Institute, such as the *Environmental Law Reporter*, available at http://elr.info.

For a discussion of the role of law in shaping private sector behavior, for better and worse, watch the TED-Talk by the founder of Common Good, Philip K. Howard, "Four Ways to Fix a Broken Legal System."

Although this textbook argues for private sector leadership in addressing sustainability, there is a robust role for national governments in positively shaping market

innovation. For more on the role of government in private sector innovation, see the TED-Talk, "Government: Investor, Risk-Taker, Innovator," by economist Mariana Mazzucato.

Harvard Business Review Case: Adam Fremeth, *Profiting from Environmental Regulatory Uncertainty: Integrated Strategies for Competitive Advantage*, Prod. #: CMR498-PDF-ENG (November 11, 2011).

Harvard Business Review Case: Julio J. Rotemberg, *BP's Macondo: Spill and Response*, Prod. #: 711021-PDF-ENG (September 16, 2010).

Endnotes

1. See the PennState Smeal College of Business web page for the Law and Business Conference description, last accessed May 7, 2014, available at http://www.smeal.psu.edu/rm/law-and-business-conference.

2. International Consortium of Investigative Journalists, The Global Climate Change Lobby, last accessed May 7, 2014, available at http://www.icij.org/project/global-climate-change-lobby.

3. Bill Baue, US Companies Issue Declaration Urging Government to Act on Climate Change, *The Guardian* (April 12, 2013).

4. State of Sustainable Business Survey 2013, BSR/GlobeScan, page 7, last accessed May 7, 2014, available at https://www.bsr.org/reports/BSR_GlobeScan_Survey_2013.pdf.

5. Leslie Paul Thiele, SUSTAINABILITY, 128 (Polity, 2013).

6. Thiele, SUSTAINABILITY, 130.

7. Robert C. Bird, *Can Law be a Source of Sustainable Competitive Advantage?*, Page 2 (2007).

8. *ibid.*

9. See Constance E. Bagley, *Winning Legally: The Value of Legal Astuteness*, 33 Acad. Mgmt. Rev. 378 (2008).

10. See Stephen M. Meyer, *The Economic Impact of Environmental Regulation*, last accessed May 7, 2014, available at http://web.mit.edu/polsci/mpepp/Reports/Econ%20Impact%20Enviro%20Reg.pdf.

11. Jacob Gersen and Eric Posner, *Soft Law: Lessons from Congressional Practice*, 61 Stanford Law Review 573 (2008).

12. See CEO Water Mandate, United Nations Global Compact, last accessed May 7, 2014, available at http://www.unglobalcompact.org/Issues/Environment/CEO_Water_Mandate/index.html.

[13] See Global 100, Corporate Knights, last accessed May 7, 2014, available at http://www.global100.org/.

[14] See Methodology, Corporate Knights, last accessed May 7, 2014, available at http://www.global100.org/methodology/criteria-a-weights.html.

[15] See Notice, Federal Register, Vol. 65, No. 70, page 19632 (April 2000).

[16] See AT&T Wireless Settlement, U.S. Environmental Protection Agency, last accessed May 7, 2014, available at http://www2.epa.gov/enforcement/att-wireless-settlement.

[17] Directive 2005/32/EC of the European Parliament and of the Council of 6 July 2005 establishing a framework for the setting of ecodesign requirements for energy-using products and amending Council Directive 92/42/EEC and Directives 96/57/EC and 2000/55/EC of the European Parliament and of the Council.

[18] Directive 2005/32/EC, Article 2, Definition (1).

[19] Directive 2005/32/EC, Preamble, Whereas (5).

[20] Directive 2005/32/EC, Preamble, Whereas (16).

[21] Directive 2005/32/EC, Preamble, Whereas (17).

[22] 42 U.S.C. § 11001.

[23] 42 U.S.C. § 11002(a).

[24] 42 U.S.C. § 11002(c).

[25] 42 U.S.C. § 11004(a).

[26] 42 U.S.C. § 13101.

[27] 42 U.S.C. § 13106(b).

[28] Title 29 Code of Federal Regulations Part 1900–1999.

[29] 33 U.S.C. § 1311(b)(1)(A).

[30] 42 U.S.C. § 7472.

[31] 42 U.S.C. § 7503(c).

[32] 42 U.S.C. § 7475(a)(4).

[33] 42 U.S.C. § 7411(a)(1).

[34] European Parliament Resolution of 13 March 2007 on Corporate Social Responsibility: A New Partnership.

[35] European Parliament Resolution of 13 March 2007 on Corporate Social Responsibility: A New Partnership.

[36] Title XV of the Dodd-Frank Wall Street Reform and Consumer Protection Act, U.S. Securities Exchange Commission, last accessed May 7, 2014, available at http://www.sec.gov/spotlight/dodd-frank/speccorpdisclosure.shtml.

[37] U.S. Department of State, *Trafficking in Persons Report* (2007).

[38] U.S. Department of Justice, *Assessment of U.S. Government Activities to Combat Trafficking in Persons* (2004).

[39] International Labor Organization, *A global alliance against forced labor* (2005).

[40] UN Office on Drugs and Crime, *Trafficking in Persons: Global Patterns* (April 2006).

[41] SB 657: California Transparency in Supply Chains Act.

[42] Safeway, *Disclosure: California Transparency in Supply Chains Act of 2010* (2012), last accessed May 7, 2014, available at http://shop.safeway.com/corporate/safeway/documents/Safeway-SB657.pdf.

[43] Michael Garry, Safeway Executive Calls for Industry Effort to Combat Human Trafficking, Supermarket News (February 15, 2013).

[44] See 15 U.S.C. §§ 41–58 and 16 Code of Federal Regulations Part 260: Guides for the Use of Environmental Marketing Claims.

[45] This table is a summary only. For detailed guidelines, see the Federal Trade Commission's *Green Guide*.

[46] Authorized by the Food, Drug, and Cosmetic Act (21 U.S.C. § 301).

[47] Gabriel Eckstein & George William Sherk, Tex. Tech Univ. Ctr. for Water Law & Policy, Alternative Strategies for Managing Pharmaceutical and Personal Care Products in Water Resources 5–8 (2011).

[48] The American Law Institute, *Restatement of the Law Third, Torts: Product Liability*.

[49] See the Uniform Commercial Code, § 2-314.

[50] Department of Environmental Quality, *International Packaging Regulations*, 2005.

[51] Christine Murner, *Plastics, Electronics & the Environment: How New Global Regulations Affect Material Choices*, Plastics Technology (October 2006).

[52] 42 U.S.C. § 6901

[53] 42 U.S.C. § 6903(5).

[54] 42 U.S.C. § 6924(g).

[55] 42 U.S.C. § 6972(a)(1)(B).

[56] 33 U.S.C. § 2701.

[57] 33 U.S.C. § 2702(a).

[58] 33 U.S.C. § 2702(b)(2).

[59] 42 U.S.C. § 4321.

[60] 42 U.S.C. § 4332(2)(C).

[61] 42 U.S.C. § 4332(2)(A).

[62] Richard Hasen, *Lobbying, Rent-Seeking, and the Constitution*, 64 STAN. L. REV. 191, 219–221 (2012).

[63] *See* Frank R. Baumgartner et al., LOBBYING AND PUBLIC POLICY CHANGE: WHO WINS, WHO LOSES, AND WHY, 151 tbl.8.1 (2009).

[64] Susan George, *Whose Crisis, Whose Future: Towards a Greener, Fairer, Richer World*, 57 (Cambridge 2010).

[65] Pete Altman, *The Price of Pollution Politics: Eight Companies Attacking Clean Air Standards... and the Toll on America's Health*, NRDC Issue Brief 12-06-A (June 2012).

[66] Evan Mackinder, *Pro-Environment Groups Outmatched, Outspent in Battle Over Climate Change Legislation*, Center for Responsive Politics (August 23, 2010).

[67] Excerpt from *The Economic Impact of Environmental Regulation*, by Stephen M. Meyer, Professor in Political Science at Massachusetts Institute of Technology, Director of the Project on Environmental Politics & Policy, and Conservation Commissioner of Massachusetts.

[68] Natural Resources Defense Council Report, *An Uneven Shield: The Record of Enforcement and Violations Under California's Environmental Health and Workplace Safety Laws*, 11 (2008).

[69] Doug Gurian-Sherman, *CAFOs Uncovered: The Untold Costs of Confined Animal Feeding Operations*, Union of Concerned Scientists (2008).

[70] See Phasing Out Certain Antibiotic Use in Farm Animals, U.S. Food and Drug Administration, last accessed May 7, 2014, available at http://www.fda.gov/ForConsumers/ConsumerUpdates/ucm378100.htm.

[71] Richard A. Oppel, Jr., *Taping of Farm Cruelty Is Becoming the Crime*, The New York Times (2013); Cynthia Galli, Angela Hill and Rym Momtaz, *McDonald's, Target Dump Egg Supplier After Investigation*, ABC 20/20 (2011); Mike McIntire, *Conservative Nonprofit Acts as a Stealth Business Lobbyist*, The New York Times (2012).

[72] See Frequently Asked Questions, American Legislative Exchange Council, last accessed May 7, 2014, available at http://www.alec.org/about-alec/frequently-asked-questions/.

[73] Lisa Graves, *Special Report on ALEC's Funding and Spending*, Center for Media Democracy (2011).

[74] See Model Legislation, American Legislative Exchange Council, last accessed May 7, 2014, available at http://www.alec.org/model-legislation/.

[75] ALEC Model Legislation: Animal and Ecological Terrorism Act, Section 3(2)(e).

Metrics, Tools, and Reporting: The Role of Finance and Accounting

NATURE'S INVOICE[1]

One reason most companies have not fully integrated sustainability into their business model is because they lack reliable metrics for understanding the impacts of their business on communities and the environment. As a result, many businesses have a limited focus on their own short-term financial bottom-line. Breaking from tradition, PUMA, one of the world's leading sports-lifestyle companies that designs and develops footwear, apparel and accessories, teamed up with Trucost, PLC, a company that provides data, metrics, and insight, in order to measure the environmental cost of PUMA's products.

PUMA developed the **Environmental Profit & Loss (EP&L)** analysis in order to demonstrate the greenhouse gas emissions, waste, air pollution, water use, and land use impacts of the entire value chain of a PUMA product, from raw material extraction, production processes, and even consumer uses including washing, drying, and disposing of PUMA products. Often environmental costs and liabilities are hidden within a company's value chain and are not reflected in the price of the goods or services provided. Indeed, these costs are usually externalized to the environment, the public, or future generations.

The EP&L is an analytical tool for promoting sustainability. By tallying environmental metrics into a financial indicator, the EP&L analysis provides business managers with information about resource dependency and impacts, which are easy to understand because they translate environmental issues into business terms. Environmental metrics provide information that can be valuable across business functions, including government

> *"If you can't measure something, you can't understand it. If you can't understand it, you can't control it. If you can't control it, you can't improve it."*

—*H. James Harrington CEO,* **HARRINGTON INSTITUTE**

> *"Not everything that counts can be counted, and not everything that can be counted counts."*

—*Albert Einstein*

LEARNING OBJECTIVES

After completing this chapter, you should be able to:

1. Understand the uses of metrics and tools in managing performance.
2. Understand the role of reporting in achieving transparency.
3. Explain the drivers of monitoring and reporting sustainable performance.
4. Explain ISO sustainability standards, the Global Reporting Initiative, the Greenhouse Gas Protocol, and varieties of environmental footprint assessment.

Environmental Profit & Loss (EP&L) Metric developed by PUMA used to put environmental performance into financial terms.

relations, finance, product design, and marketing. Additionally, environmental metrics, if applied with the right tools, can be used at the product design stage to project the life-cycle environmental impacts of specific products before they are even produced. These metrics can be used to make supplier selection decisions and serve as "a proxy for nature's invoice," according to Steven Bullock, head of supply chain research at Trucost.

According to PUMA's Chairman Jochen Zeitz, "Just as the calorie and nutrition information table on your cereal box helps you compare the dietary impacts of one breakfast choice to another, our new PUMA Product EP&L helps you to judge whether one shoe or shirt is more environmentally-friendly than another."

5.1 Introduction: Why Measure and Report?

Measuring sustainability performance is necessary for assessing performance, explaining outcomes, and managing them. As Peter Drucker famously said, "You can't manage what you don't measure." Reporting corporate sustainability performance improves transparency by increasing visibility along the supply chain. Where measuring increases accountability for performance within an organization, reporting that performance increases accountability between the organization and external stakeholders, such as the government and customers. Information gained by the company from external feedback on reporting disclosures can assist with risk management, strategic planning, and leadership.

When measuring and reporting sustainability performance is done properly, businesses can improve customer access, company reputation, and marketing credibility. In these ways, finance and accounting practices can have implications for sustainability performance across legal compliance, supply chain, operations, marketing, risk management, business strategy, and leadership functions.

5.1.1 The Role of Finance & Accounting

Resource availability and reliance on raw materials such as forest products, water resources, and rare earth metals and minerals, pose such significant business risks that including these issues is becoming a *de facto* requirement for investor disclosure and reporting.[2] Even though traditionally these disclosures have been treated as discretionary, there are a number of financial reporting and accounting standards that arguably require disclosure of the business's reliance on ecosystem services or natural resources through the use of natural capital accounting.[3]

When the impacts of environmental issues are measurable in financial terms, they can and should be included as quantitative elements in business accounts by financial and accounting professionals. Some of the existing financial disclosure and reporting standards contained in the International Financial Reporting Standards (IFRS) and the International Accounting Standards (IAS) can be interpreted and applied to require the measurement and disclosure of the company's dependence on natural capital, biodiversity, and ecosystem services.[4] However, if significant risks and opportunities associated with environmental issues are not quantified and not assigned monetary value, in practice they will be excluded from accounts.

Measuring sustainable performance uses **key performance indicators** (KPIs), custom metrics, as well as qualitative and quantitative analytical tools. The function of applying metrics and analytical tools to corporate performance and disclosing these findings to investors is rooted in finance and accounting business functions. These methods have been adapted to help business leaders monitor, benchmark, and disclose corporate sustainability performance.

According to Harvard Business School professor Karthik Ramanna: "If we were to put an accounting lens on corporate accountability reporting, there is potential for innovation both for practice and for academic research to advance practice."[5]

According to a report published by KPMG, Fauna & Flora International, and ACCA, externalities related to biodiversity impacts and reliance on ecosystem services are material issues, which poses a challenge to Chief Financial Officers and accountants to ensure that environmental costs "are incorporated into risk and materiality assessments, financial accounts and reporting cycles."[6]

The Association of Chartered Certified Accountants, the global body for professional accountants, surveyed its members about the relevance of natural capital to the accounting profession. Sixty percent of respondents agreed that the natural world was important to their business, more than half said they had included natural capital issues in their company's business risk evaluations at some point, and 49% identified natural capital as a material operational, regulatory, reputational, and financial risk to their business.[7]

According to the International Federation of Accountants, businesses should develop an organizational reporting strategy, include sustainability impacts in corporate financial statements, provide narrative instead of numerical reporting on sustainability issues to increase transparency with investors, provide a materiality assessment, and obtain external review and quality assurance of their sustainability disclosures.[8]

Sustainable performance can be promoted through accountancy by integrating environmental and social values into the economic structure of the firm. The International Federation of Accountants provides an integrated approach in the **Sustainability Framework 2.0**.[9] This framework is divided into Business Strategy, Operational Perspectives, and Reporting Methods, with the latter providing a template table of contents for annual corporate disclosures to investors and the public.

Financial and accounting professionals have a unique role to play in the sustainable enterprise. See Tables 5.1 and 5.2.

The concepts in this chapter apply broadly, not just to the finance and accounting profession, by enabling leaders to set objective goals and performance targets, while benchmarking progress with key performance indicators. These frameworks also enable business leaders to integrate accounting functions with risk management functions to measure, manage, and possibly disclose material social and environmental risks that could affect the viability of the company.

Key Performance Indicator Measures progress based upon data relating to the mission, stakeholders, and goals of an organization.

CROSS-LINKAGE

For more on natural capital accounting and externalities, see Chapter 1: Introduction to Sustainable Business.

Sustainability Framework 2.0 The International Federation of Accountants' framework for measuring sustainable performance through accountancy by integrating environmental and social values into the economic structure of a firm.

CROSS-LINKAGE

For more on the connection between monitoring, reporting, and risk management, see Chapter 6: Risk Management.

TABLE 5.1

The Role of Finance Officers

➤ Monetize the extent of natural capital dependency in terms of revenues, costs, and going concern status.

➤ Include natural capital in risk and materiality assessments.

➤ Work with finance teams to build analytic skills for accurate assessment of organizational impacts, and dependence on natural resources.

➤ Disclose material environmental issues using a data quality assurance system.

➤ Incorporate natural capital into financial accounts using existing finance and accounting methods.

➤ Collaborate with others to develop new tools for measuring and reporting natural resource concerns.

Source: KPMG, Fauna & Flora International & ACCA, *Is Natural Capital a Material Issue? An Evaluation of the Relevance of Biodiversity and Ecosystem Services to Accountancy Professionals and the Private Sector,* page 35 (September 2013).

TABLE 5.2

The Role of Accounting Professionals

➤ Develop methodologies to quantify environmental externalities using unique accountancy skills and expertise.

➤ Address natural capital issues in annual reports and accounts.

➤ Adhere to guidelines for natural capital accounting as they emerge.

➤ Promote pilot programs to test accounting methodologies with clients.

➤ Work with regulatory bodies on disclosure guidance and assurance practices.

Source: KPMG, Fauna & Flora International & ACCA, *Is Natural Capital a Material Issue? An Evaluation of the Relevance of Biodiversity and Ecosystem Services to Accountancy Professionals and the Private Sector,* page 35 (September 2013).

Although the appropriate scope and expected benefits of disclosure may be uncertain, what is clear is that companies interested in sustainable performance are in fact disclosing a substantial amount of information about all aspects of corporate activities impacting sustainability. Over the last few years it became increasingly common for companies to have a tab on their home website detailing the sustainability initiatives of the company and providing access to sustainability reports.[10] See Section 5.1.3: (Almost) Everyone is Doing It.

5.1.2 Information-Driven Sustainable Business Model

How do metrics and reporting fit within the overall effort to promote sustainable business? When integrated into an information feedback loop, metrics and reporting are necessary for improving sustainable performance across all functional areas of business, including legal, supply chain, operations, marketing, risk management, business strategy, and leadership.

The **information-driven sustainable business model** uses a continual process of information gathering and disclosure that enables a company to be responsive to stakeholder concerns and environmental considerations while meeting its own performance goals. See Figure 5.1.

Information drives sustainable business conduct in a variety of ways. The external environment of a business, including global issues, market trends, and environmental factors, is a constantly shifting stage for business performance. **External data** gathering enables a business to establish situational awareness and assess external pressures. Conducting an **internal analysis** is where metrics play a central role. You cannot report what is not measured, and without data on past and present performance there is no reliable way to benchmark progress or regress. During the **public disclosure** process, the information gathered during internal analysis is put into context of relevant external data and published in an annual report. **Stakeholder feedback** on these public disclosures becomes part of the universe of relevant external data.

Information-Driven Sustainable Business Model A continual process of information gathering and disclosure that enables a company to be responsive to stakeholder concerns and environmental considerations while meeting its own performance goals.

External Data Enables a business to establish situational awareness and assess external pressures.

Internal Analysis Benchmarking progress and regress based on past and present performance data.

Public Disclosure When the information gathered during internal analysis is put into context of relevant external data and published in an annual report.

Stakeholder Feedback The response to public disclosures from the various external stakeholders of an organization.

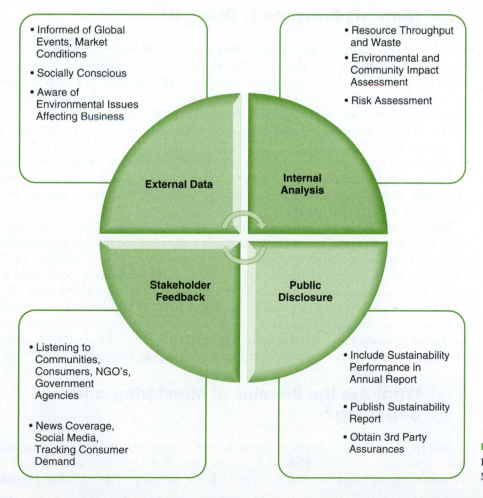

FIGURE 5.1 Information-Driven Sustainable Business Model

This process of gathering, monitoring, and reporting information, and listening to feedback, enables business decision-makers to strategically address sustainable performance problems, to identify strengths, and to constructively engage with consumers and others affected by corporate conduct.

Independent, third-party verification is essential to the success of public disclosures in the information-driven sustainable business model. The same is true for industry self-regulation (discussed in Chapter 3: Leadership, Change Management, and Corporate Governance).

> **Independent, Third-Party Verification** Objective assessment and validation of sustainability reporting and marketing claims by an outside impartial entity.

The information-driven model builds on corporate sustainability reporting by internalizing the results of stakeholder engagement, leading to a continual refinement of products and services, greater resource conservation, and limited impacts on human health or the environment. When equipped with a continuous "live feed" of relevant environmental and operational information, corporate decisions can proactively address stakeholder concerns and ongoing management strategy can be adapted and modified to remain on the cutting-edge.

> **CROSS-LINKAGE**
>
> For more on independent, third-party certification of sustainable performance, see Chapter 7: Marketing.

5.1.3 (Almost) Everyone Is Doing It

A key driver of corporate social responsibility and the shift to the sustainable business paradigm is the demand on the part of consumers for transparency with respect to corporate conduct. Today, the majority of S&P500 Index® companies measure, manage, and disclose their strategies and performance on environmental, social, and corporate governance dimensions. Yes, almost everyone is doing it.

The trend of transparency and disclosure of sustainable performance is rapidly increasing, from 19% in 2010 to 53% in 2012.[11] Indeed, among large companies, non-reporting is now in the minority, and market expectations seem to require either reporting or a good explanation as to why reporting is not done. When it comes to sustainability reporting among large companies, the GRI framework appears to be the primary means for doing so.

The playing field looks slightly different when broken down by sector rather than size.[12] Industries with the most instances of non-GRI reporting include energy, financial services, and technology hardware, where in-house reporting guidelines are followed. For the most part, companies either use the GRI framework, or they did not report using any framework. Sectors where non-reporting is more common than reporting include automotive, retail, technology hardware, real estate, media, health care products, financial services, and energy. Sectors where reporting is more common than non-reporting include food & beverage, utilities, computers, chemicals, mining, agriculture, forest & paper products, and tourism & leisure.

5.1.4 What Are the Benefits of Monitoring and Reporting?

Before diving into the details of sustainability measurements, we should address two preliminary concerns. First, does monitoring and reporting on sustainability influence capital markets, and if so, what is the investor response? Sustainability

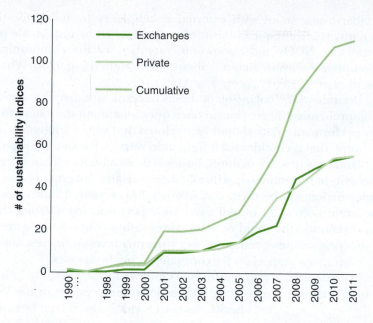

FIGURE 5.2 Growth in Sustainability Indices

Source: This figure is not exhaustive. Deloitte, Drivers of Long-Term Business Value: Stakeholders, Stats, and Strategies, page 7 (2012). Source: World Federation of Exchanges, Deloitte analysis. Copyright © 2013 Deloitte Development LLC. All rights reserved.

performance is a growing concern among investors, as evidenced by the growth of sustainability indices for private and public exchanges. See Figure 5.2.

Disclosure of environmental and social impacts may be necessary to satisfy investors; to become eligible for sustainability certifications from third-party providers; and to attain listing on certain indices, such as the Dow Jones Sustainability indices.

Second, is it worthwhile to share internal performance information about waste, resource consumption, workplace safety, supply chain risks, and other potentially

ETHICAL DECISIONS: Should all Information Requests Be Treated Equally?

The National Association for Environmental Management (NAEM) is the largest professional community for environmental, health, and safety (EHS) and sustainability decision-makers. Their mission is to empower corporate leaders to advance environmental stewardship, create safe and healthy workplaces, and promote global sustainability. Many of the members of NAEM are responsible for responding to requests for information relevant to corporate EHS performance.

The challenge with transparency is that responding to information requests requires the investment of substantial time and resources—some companies must dedicate up to two full time staff members exclusively to responding to information requests. For some period of time, information requests were phrased in such a way as to engender "a general feeling among corporate leaders that many of the questions external entities pose [we] re not necessarily appropriate or sufficient for illuminating actual EHS or sustainability performance."[13] These concerns are being addressed as voluntary reporting standards mature through a multi-stakeholder process that focuses information requests on material issues and bottom-line results. Practical realities, public relations, and risk management determine which survey questions garner a response. "[T]here is a need to balance the reasonable expectation for corporate transparency with our members' professional responsibility to carefully manage legal, reputational and business risks."[14]

embarrassing items with external stakeholders (non-investors)? Companies frequently receive requests for information related to sustainable performance from reporters, NGOs and non-profits, members of the community, and academics. Complete disclosure may not always be the right thing to do. Where should the line be drawn?

Because of the balancing of these concerns, sustainability reporting is not always comprehensive. There remain open questions about the extent to which sustainability performance data should be disclosed and who is ultimately in charge of determining what is confidential information versus what should be publicly available.

Until this practice matures, business professionals remain uncertain over the full benefits of reporting—specifically, there remains uncertainty over how the disclosed information will be used, and whether the requested information will provide an accurate portrait of overall sustainable performance. Despite these concerns and uncertainties, the trend of external reporting continues to grow, driven largely by "satisfying customer requirements, attracting investor interest and creating competitive advantage, especially for consumer-facing businesses."[15]

For companies with few investors and that deal primarily in business-to-business rather than consumer-facing transactions, the pressure to disclose environmental, health, and safety risk is also driven by supply chain masters, maintenance of business relationships, and the desire to maintain preferred supplier status. There remain open questions about the extent to which sustainability performance data should be disclosed and who is ultimately in charge of determining what is confidential information versus what should be publicly available.

> **CROSS-LINKAGE**
>
> For more on the role of supply chain masters, see Chapter 8: Supply Chain Management.

5.1.5 Drivers of Sustainability Reporting

In the field of finance, sustainability performance can be described in terms of environmental, social, and governance (ESG) issues as well as environmental, health, and safety (EHS) issues, that affect corporate financial value. There are a variety of reasons why companies disclose their performance along these lines either by providing responses to information requests or through formal reports. Drivers of disclosure include risk management, legal compliance, and stakeholder relations. However, virtually all (97%) of sustainability professionals deem "responding to customer request/inquiry" as the driving factor in disclosing sustainable performance. See Figure 5.3.

Reporting can also attract investors by improving the chances of being recognized by credible third parties such as ranking providers and equity index managers.[16] Additionally, companies that report on sustainable performance projects and progress can enjoy long-term success in capital markets and a premium from investors, relative to non-reporting peers.[17] After the global economic recession of 2008, companies that reported on sustainability tended to recover faster from financial troubles, perhaps because of a "flight to safety" pattern on the part of investors.[18] Even if sustainability reports indicate that a company is responsible for substantial amounts of resource consumption or pollution, the act of disclosure signals a commitment to transparency, and thereby increases the credibility of other company publications such as progress reports.

Ultimately, there are several possible business benefits of external reporting. Of course, these benefits are not guaranteed. They include improved customer access, public image, stakeholder relations, competitive positioning, preferred supplier status, market dynamics, employee morale, investor interest, and access to capital.[19] However, as the trend in sustainability reporting is a relatively new development, the majority of companies believe it is too early to tell whether the effort pays off. See Figure 5.4.

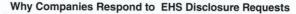

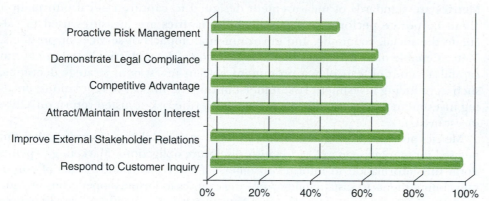

FIGURE 5.3 Drivers of Sustainability Reporting

Source: Adapted from National Association for Environmental Management, *Green Metrics that Matter: Identifying Corporate EHS and Sustainability Metrics: What Companies are Tracking and Why,* 20 (2011).

FIGURE 5.4 Mixed Results on the Benefits of Reporting

Source: National Association for Environmental Management, *Green Metrics that Matter: Identifying Corporate EHS and Sustainability Metrics: What Companies are Tracking and Why,* 21 (2011).

Reporting, at least yet, does not always capture all of the associated benefits one would expect. That said, some companies have been fully successful at capturing all of the benefits from reporting, and on average there is more success than failure in capturing the benefits of reporting.

5.2 Metrics

5.2.1 What Are Metrics?

Metrics Standards of measurement designed to capture critical information about corporate performance in the form of objective data.

Sustainability Metrics Measures used to calculate the social, economic, and environmental impacts of services or products.

Metrics are standards of measurement designed to capture critical information about corporate performance. **Sustainability metrics** are measures used to calculate the social, economic, and environmental impacts of services or products. Metrics enable objective decision-making based on data. Metrics based in natural capital accounting can play a prominent role in investment strategy decisions, such as reducing investment risk, understanding the impact of regulations, creating investment products, and generating alpha (the risk-adjusted return on active investments).

Metrics provide information about corporate sustainability performance that can be used for marketing as well as to satisfy disclosure obligations. Marketing depends upon this information to inform consumers of the context and results of corporate commitments to sustainability. Applying metrics to business operations provide marketers with the objective, empirical data they need to comply with sustainable marketing guidelines.

In order to manage sustainability efforts, sustainability metrics are used to gauge the incremental social, economic, and environmental improvements or shortcomings over time. Therefore, companies that apply metrics to and disclose sustainability performance are able to more effectively market themselves and manage this performance.

Although businesses have long internally collected data about environmental, health and safety performance, reporting standards for these metrics is still in its infancy. There may be no universal set sustainability indicators relevant to all businesses in all places, and there may be no set formula for the appropriate scope and content of disclosures in corporate reporting. The possibilities featured in this chapter are merely examples of existing standards and are not one-and-for-all exemplars of how to measure and disclose sustainable performance.

CROSS-LINKAGE

For more on marketing strategy, see Chapter 7: Marketing.

However, most businesses can draw from general frameworks discussed herein to develop custom-metrics that are appropriate and insightful given a specific operating environment and business model. Quantifying natural capital dependency across industry sectors enables investors, regulators, and thought leaders to understand the risk of environmental impacts (pollution, raw material use, extraction, processing, and distribution) in business terms.

Metrics enable companies to measure progress toward goals as well as to determine the business value of sustainability investments. In the context of sustainability,

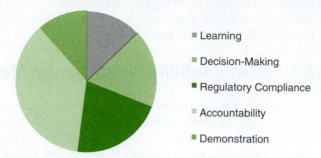

Purpose of Internal Metrics Collection

- Learning
- Decision-Making
- Regulatory Compliance
- Accountability
- Demonstration

FIGURE 5.5 Why Do Companies Analyze Sustainability Metrics?

Source: National Association for Environmental Management, *Green Metrics that Matter: Identifying Corporate EHS and Sustainability Metrics: What Companies are Tracking and Why,* 12 (2011).

businesses can use social, economic, and environmental metrics in order to measure the benefits and costs flowing from nearly all aspects of organizational and supply chain activities. There are several reasons for companies to internally monitor sustainability metrics. See Figure 5.5.

According to a study, "Finding Common Ground on the Metrics that Matter," commissioned and funded by the Investor Responsibility Research Center (IRRC) Institute: 1) There is agreement on key corporate sustainability issues, but not on which metrics should be used to measure them; 2) Although environmental, safety, and governance metrics are reported routinely by a substantial percentage of companies, few companies actually report all of the information they gather internally; and 3) researchers, investors, and corporate representatives approach sustainability metrics from a risk mitigation perspective, rather than a value creation perspective.[20]

Clearly, there is room for improvement in the methods of gathering and disclosing data about sustainability performance. Some well-established metrics provide a form of standardization; however, there is room for innovation to promote more efficient, complete, and less time consuming measuring and reporting.

5.2.2 The Triple Bottom Line

Recall that thematically sustainable business involves three separate domains of accounting for costs—economic, social, and environmental. The twin goals of business leaders under the **triple bottom line** approach is (1) to avoid social and environmental costs while reducing operating costs and (2) to create financial value while benefiting communities and the environment. The triple bottom line approach to sustainability applies in a wide range of management contexts, whether in the private or public sector.[21]

Although environmental and social impact indicators can supplement traditional financial indicators of business performance, keep in mind that the science of sustainable performance monitoring is still developing, and we should not expect there to be a single, comprehensive, integrated, ultimate metric for sustainable business. The triple bottom line approach is a helpful organizing framework for gathering

Triple Bottom Line Accounting for social, economic, and environmental performance of an organization.

CROSS-LINKAGE

For more on the triple bottom line approach to sustainable business, see Chapter 1: Introduction to Sustainable Business.

together data from a variety of metrics to provide a more complete picture of the health and impacts of an organization. Using the triple bottom line framework helps analysts identify the non-monetary costs of business, an initial step in the process of reducing the externalities of business activities.

5.2.3 Sustainability Performance Metrics

New metrics, beyond traditional finance and accounting metrics, provide insight into the sustainability performance of an organization.[22] Like traditional financial indicators, some of these metrics are actually ratios of two or more separate data points. Keep in mind that the following metrics are not exclusive—many other metrics exist or may be developed in the future. This section samples just a few interesting new metrics that can be employed to measure sustainable performance, especially focusing on environmental impacts. For additional factors applicable to social and governance concerns, see Section 5.4.5 on Global Reporting Initiative.

Greenhouse Gas Emissions Indicate the company's contribution to climate change.

Greenhouse Gas Emissions Greenhouse gas emissions indicate the company's contribution to climate change. Companies can assess how many tons of carbon dioxide or methane emissions result from their operations—the amount coming out of factory smokestacks, of vehicle exhaust from transportation fuel, and from electricity consumption to power, heat, cool, and illuminate facilities. Firms track carbon emissions to reveal hidden fossil fuel risks and to reduce potential liabilities from carbon taxes. Companies monitoring carbon emissions have shown greater financial performance than the average for Global 500 businesses.[23]

CROSS-LINKAGE

For more on carbon emissions and facilities management see Chapter 9: Operations Management.

Revenue Share from Sustainable Products The share of annual revenue derived from investments into sustainable products or services.

Revenue Share from Sustainable Products By measuring the share of annual revenue derived from sustainable products or services, companies get a better understanding of the return on investment (ROI) for sustainability initiatives. Sometimes the benefits of a sustainable product spill over into other aspects of business by virtue of the halo effect. Companies like Campbell's (the soup company) that sell "better for you" products with data to back up these betterment claims report revenue growth and strong operating profits.[24]

CROSS-LINKAGE

For more on the halo effect, see Chapter 7: Marketing.

Real-Estate Efficiency Ratio Measures the amount of energy, water, and resources consumed per square foot of corporate-owned real estate.

Real-Estate Efficiency Ratio Measuring the amount of energy, water, and resources consumed per square foot of corporate-owned real estate can assist with cost reductions. Trane realized average energy savings of 25% in reduced operational costs as a result of tracking this ratio.[25]

Balanced Scorecard Integrating financial and operational information in a single dashboard allows managers to identify the real-time relationship between market dynamics, sustainability initiatives, operation efficiency, and profit improvement. Better information makes for better management.

Human Capital Value People are usually categorized as an expense on balance sheets, but it turns out that intangibles such as the "power of people" contribute more to market value than book value. New metrics for human capital value, such as those developed by Infosys, ensure the proper evaluation of people as productive assets.[26] Properly accounting for the value of human capital enables optimal utilization of human resources.

Percent of Nature Mimicked The use of ecosystem services to accomplish environmental remediation that would otherwise require major capital expenditure should be understood as an avoided expense. Dow partnered with The Nature Conservancy to design a wetland treatment area that mimicked nature's biological processes to absorb pollutants. Mimicking nature allowed Dow to avoid a proposed $40 million water treatment plant and instead build a facility that cost only $1.4 million and utilized natural processes to achieve the same results.

Water Intensity Per Product Unit This metric tracks water use through the entire supply chain and production process for a given time period and divides that total volume of water by units of production. Isolating a single resource input can focus analysts on the most critical environmental issues. By 2012, Coca-Cola reduced the water intensity of their bottled beverages by 20% measured against the 2004 baseline.[27] This effort reduces the risk of water shortages from depleting aquifers.

For more examples of the use of ratios to develop sustainability performance metrics, see the discussion in Section 5.4.5 concerning the Corporate Knights' use of the Global Reporting Initiative disclosures to rank companies by clean capital leadership.

> **Balanced Scorecard** Financial and operational information integrated in a single dashboard that allows managers to identify the real-time relationship between market dynamics, sustainability initiatives, operation efficiency, and profit improvement.
>
> **Human Capital Value** Attributing capital value to intangible benefits derived from effective human resources management, instead of merely categorizing personnel as an expense on the balance sheet.
>
> **Percent of Nature Mimicked** The use of ecosystem services to accomplish environmental remediation that would otherwise require major capital expenditure.
>
> **Water Intensity Per Product Unit** Tracks water use through the entire supply chain and production process for a given time period and divides that total volume of water by units of production.

5.2.4 What to Look for in a Metric

The way business impacts are measured and analyzed depends upon the nature of the activity in question. Different metrics and tools are appropriate for specific issues in sustainable business. The challenge is to choose the right key performance indicators to serve as metrics. Metrics should be objective (so they are not biased), quantifiable (so they are empirically measurable), standardized (so they are the same regardless of who applies them), and insightful (so they provide novel information).

> **CROSS-LINKAGE**
>
> For more information on biomimicry in product design, see Chapter 2: Perspectives and Chapter 9: Operations Management.

Whether a performance metric is even applicable to one's company depends upon the company's value proposition, business model, sector, size, material inputs, and outputs. For example, tracking water intensity per unit of production does not make sense for a Public Relations firm that sells online social media services. However, that same company may find it useful to measure human capital value to ensure employees are being properly utilized and adequately appreciated.

The guiding principles established in the Greenhouse Gas Protocol (discussed in Section 5.3.3) for measuring greenhouse gases are equally applicable to choosing the right metrics for traditional pollutants, water impacts, and human rights. Metrics are worthwhile insofar as they are relevant (with boundaries defining impacts from your business), complete (accounting for all impacts within those boundaries), consistent (allowing for meaningful comparisons of performance over time), transparent (based on a clear audit trail with explicit assumptions and methodologies), and accurate (precise with reasonable data quality assurance).[28]

Once useful metrics are developed, it is also necessary to determine whether performance in terms of these metrics should be reported to shareholders. If the metrics could be indicative of business risks, such as pollution emissions, water dependency, or human trafficking, they might be material, and therefore should be disclosed to shareholders. Refer to Section 5.4.2.

5.3 Tools

Analytical Tools Methods and devices that enable analysis and interpretation of information.

Sustainability Tools Analytical frameworks for applying metrics to the social and environmental dimension of business performance.

Sustainable performance management requires selecting the appropriate metrics and applying the appropriate analytical tools to company data. **Analytical tools** are methods and devices that enable analyzing and interpreting information. **Sustainability tools** are analytical frameworks for applying metrics to the environmental dimension of business performance.

This chapter will discuss a variety of these analytical tools available for sustainable performance management. For example, environmental footprint analysis reveals the impacts that business operations, including production and transportation, have in terms of toxic pollutants and greenhouse gases emitted, and water resources consumed or impaired. Environmental footprint analysis is a tool, while toxic pollutants, greenhouse gas emissions, and water consumption are all metrics. Whereas "carbon emissions" is a metric, "carbon footprinting" is a tool. The following list is intended to provide examples of presently available tools and should not be treated as exhaustive.

5.3.1 Natural Capital Accounting

Natural Capital Accounting Measuring, managing, and reporting the environmental externalities of business in order to inform business decision-making with proper valuation of environmental assets.

Natural capital accounting involves measuring, managing, and reporting the environmental externalities of business in order to inform business decision-making. In order to manage the risks of natural resource dependency, volatile commodity prices, investor-prompted calls for transparency, and increasingly stringent government regulations, companies must have some objective, empirical basis for measuring the extent to which they impact natural and human resources, as well as accurate pricing for those impacts.

The business case for natural capital accounting flows from the dependency of businesses on environmental resources. Trucost, as discussed in the Chapter Opener, conducts economic valuations of environmental factors in a company's entire value chain by providing natural capital data in financial terms using environmental cost analysis. The purpose is to enable clients to understand potential financial impacts of environmental dependency and to integrate natural capital risk into traditional financial metrics.

Natural capital accounting can come to bear on the preparation of financial statements,[29] including Profit and Loss Statements (See Table 5.3) and corporate balance sheets.[30]

TABLE 5.3

Applying Natural Capital to a P&L Statement

Example of Profit and Loss Statement

	2013 ($ million)	2012 ($ million)
Revenue	89	75
Cost of Goods Sold	−65	−52
Operating Profit	24	23
Operating Expenses	−12	−10
Depreciation	−3	−2.5
Earnings Before Income & Tax	9	10.5
Interest	2	2
Tax	2	2.3
Profit After Tax	5	5.9

P&L Considerations of Natural Capital Accounting

P&L Element	Reporting Considerations
Revenue	Dependence on natural capital means revenue may decrease with degraded environment.
Cost of Goods Sold	Higher input costs for production (e.g., water costs) and liabilities for environmental damage may increase cost of goods sold.
Operating Expenses	Pollution from operations, impairment of written-down assets, and environmental remediation add up to increased operating expenses.
Depreciation	Natural capital loss can alter the useful economic life of assets, which may need to be re-valued to reflect depreciation.
Interest	A bad track record of environmental performance may increase the cost of capital if lenders associate this with higher risk.
Tax	Taxes levied on greenhouse gas emissions may increase tax liability.

Source: KPMG, Fauna & Flora International & ACCA, *Is Natural Capital a Material Issue? An Evaluation of the Relevance of Biodiversity and Ecosystem Services to Accountancy Professionals and the Private Sector*, Appendix 2, Table A2.1 (September 2013).

5.3.2 Life Cycle Assessment

Life cycle assessment discloses the full environmental and human health impacts of a product or service. According to the United Nations Environment Program/ Society of Environmental Toxicology and Chemistry (UNEP/SETAC), which developed a Social Life Cycle Assessment for products, a product's life cycle

Life Cycle Assessment Disclosure of the sum total of adverse impacts of all stages of a product system, from raw material acquisition or natural resource production to the disposal of the product at the end of its life, including extracting and processing of raw materials, manufacturing, distribution, use, re-use, maintenance, recycling and final disposal (i.e., cradle-to-grave).

> **MANAGERIAL INSIGHT:** Natural Capital Accounting from Alcoa to Xerox[31]
>
> At the 2012 Rio + 20 Earth Summit, twenty-four companies worth half a trillion dollars in combined revenues agreed to incorporate the value of ecosystems and biodiversity into their business strategies through the use of natural capital accounting. "The companies featured in our report are united in the view that immediate leadership to safeguard well-functioning ecosystems is a business imperative, not a matter of philanthropy," said MR Rangaswami, Founder of the Corporate Eco Forum. "Rio+20 is an extraordinary opportunity to help a critical mass of global influencers grasp the true economic value of our planet's natural assets and infrastructure." Companies that made the commitment to natural capital accounting include Alcoa, the Clorox Company, the Coca-Cola Company, Dell, Disney, Dow, Duke Energy, Enterprise, GM, Lockheed Martin, Marriott, TD Bank, and Xerox.

includes "all stages of a product system, from raw material acquisition or natural resource production to the disposal of the product at the end of its life, including extracting and processing of raw materials, manufacturing, distribution, use, re-use, maintenance, recycling and final disposal (i.e., cradle-to-grave)."[32] LCA involves the following steps:

1. *Define the Goal and Scope*: An LCA starts with an explicit statement of the goal and scope of the study, which sets out the context of the study and explains how and to whom the results are to be communicated, including ISO standard requirements for environmental communications (discussed in Chapter 5: Marketing Sustainability).

2. *Life-Cycle Inventory Analysis* (LCI): Create an inventory of flows for a product system using a flow chart. The chart includes inputs of water, energy, and raw materials, and pollution releases to air, land, and water.

3. *Impact Assessment*: This phase of LCA is aimed at evaluating the significance of potential environmental impacts based on the LCI flow results.

4. *Interpretation*: Identify, quantify, check, and evaluate information from the results of the life cycle inventory and/or the life cycle impact assessment. The outcome of the interpretation is a set of conclusions and recommendations that are tailored for the appropriate audience (supply chain partners, manufacturers, customers, etc.).

Life cycle analysis does not limit itself to the performance of a product retailer, but rather, its aperture includes the performance of all nodes in a product's supply chain, from product and packaging design, to sourcing, manufacturing, transportation, sale, product use, and disposal. "Managing the full product lifecycle... designing products with an eye to environmental efficiency—and cost savings and product innovation—is crucial. To do so first requires alignment within the company, including involvement from the merchandising, sourcing, and product design teams and then partnerships with suppliers."[33]

Certain tools for sustainable business, such as life-cycle analysis, require some degree of shared intentions and shared information through a company's supply chain in order to accurately assess (and reduce) the adverse impacts of products.

For example, the pharmaceutical company Eli Lilly takes a life-cycle approach to managing the environmental impacts of their pharmaceutical products.[34] The company has distinct strategies for managing the impacts of research and development, materials and natural resources, manufacturing, sales and marketing, product transport and packaging, product use, and product end-of-life. Life cycle assessment is used by GoodGuide to assess consumer products, discussed in Section 5.4: Reporting.

CROSS-LINKAGE
For more on the role of life cycle assessment, see Chapter 8: Supply Chain Management.

5.3.3 Environmental Footprinting

Environmental footprint analysis can be used to determine aggregate or individualized impacts on climate change, air quality, water resources, forests, fisheries, and soil quality, among other environmental mediums. Environmental footprinting comes in a variety of forms. This section will discuss greenhouse gas and water resource footprinting, with emphasis on the latter.

Greenhouse gas footprinting is a tool for businesses to determine aggregate climate change impacts from air pollution associated with a supply chain, a single facility, or a single product or service. Greenhouse gas footprinting can be used to identify the most cost-effective investment in emissions reductions within a single firm, as well as to determine proportional accountability for emissions amongst firms in a supply chain. Greenhouse gases are largely emitted by energy-consuming operational and supply chain activities, as well as by transportation.

The **Greenhouse Gas Protocol**, a partnership between the World Resources Institute and the World Business Council for Sustainable Development, is an accounting tool used to understand, quantify, and manage greenhouse gas emissions.[35] The Greenhouse Gas Protocol provides guidance, frameworks, and calculation tools for virtually every greenhouse gas standard in the world, including ISO. Some of the tools available are cross-sector measures (i.e., for energy, transport, refrigeration, and combustion), sector-specific tools (i.e., for paper mills, cement factories, and steel production), and custom tools.[36] A version of the Greenhouse Gas Protocol is available for office-based small and medium sized companies.[37]

Water footprint tools measure water use, polluted water discharge, and water-related business risks across a variety of geographic contexts and industry sectors.[38]

The **CEO Water Mandate**, launched by the Secretary-General of the United Nations in 2007, is a public-private initiative designed to assist companies in developing, implementing, and disclosing sustainable water policies and practices.[39] There are several water footprint assessment tools available. These will be discussed in turn.

The Water Footprint Network developed the **WFN Water Footprint** methodology to measure the total volume of freshwater used to produce the goods and services consumed by any well-defined group of consumers, including a family, municipality, province, state, nation, or business/organization. The consumer-based Water Footprint provides insight into aggregate impacts on water resources as well as comparisons between the water demand of different market segments.

World Business Council for Sustainable Development developed the online **Global Water Tool** to integrate corporate water use, discharge, and facility operational

Environmental Footprint Analysis Used to determine aggregate or individualized impacts on climate change, air quality, water resources, forests, fisheries, and soil quality among other environmental mediums.

Greenhouse Gas Footprinting A tool to determine aggregate climate change impacts from air pollution associated with a supply chain, a single facility, or a single product or service.

Greenhouse Gas Protocol An accounting tool used to understand, quantify, and manage greenhouse gas emissions, including guidance, frameworks, and calculation tools for virtually every greenhouse gas standard in the world.

Water Footprint Tools Measures water use, polluted water discharge, and water-related business risks across a variety of geographic contexts and industry sectors.

CEO Water Mandate A public-private initiative designed to assist companies develop, implement, and disclose sustainable water policies and practices.

WFN Water Footprint Methodology to measure the total volume of freshwater used to produce the goods and services consumed by any well-defined group of consumers, including a family, municipality, province, state, nation, or business/organization.

Global Water Tool Used to integrate corporate water use, discharge, and facility operational information with specific watershed and country-level data about water resources.

Water Sustainability Tools Used to enable companies to build a corporate water strategy.

information with specific watershed and country-level data about water resources. The Global Water Tool allows companies to assess and communicate water risks within the context of their geographic water resource availability. Twenty million gallons of freshwater means one thing near Lake Michigan, and quite another in North Africa, where water resources are generally scarce. The Global Water Tool is useful for companies in planning their operation's and supply chain's water use to fit within regional availability.

The Global Environmental Management Initiative developed online **Water Sustainability Tools** in order to enable companies to build a corporate water strategy. Doing so requires an understanding of the relationship between business facilities and water access, risk identification, and developing a business case for action based on water conservation opportunities.

Aqueduct An online global database of local and global water risk indicator metrics and reporting standards.

The World Resources Institute developed **Aqueduct**, an online global database of local and global water risk indicator metrics and reporting standards. Aqueduct water risk assessment is based on information about water supply, water quality, government regulations, climate change impacts, socioeconomic factors affecting water, and other factors. Companies including Dow Chemical, Talisman Energy, GE, and United Technologies have formed an alliance to provide companies with an unprecedented level of detail on global water risks using the World Resources Institute water-mapping project, a sort of water risk management atlas.

Water footprint tools enable sustainable businesses to answer important questions with ramifications across all aspects of the company. These tools focus the discussion on material issues by identifying the facilities, products, supply chain activities, product life cycle, and operations with the most significant adverse impacts to watersheds, human health, and business risk.

Groundwater Footprint The area required to sustain groundwater use and groundwater dependent ecosystem services.

Many of the available water resource metrics and tools are limited to surface water supplies. However, unsustainable groundwater withdrawal is taking place all around the world. Groundwater supplies, such as freshwater aquifers, replenish surface waters, such as rivers. Excessive groundwater withdrawals, such as by pumping wells, can be just as impactful to supply as excessive surface water withdrawals.

In a 2012 publication of the influential science journal *Nature*, researchers introduced a tool they dubbed groundwater footprint that provides insight into the extent of groundwater impacts globally.[40]

GLOBAL INSIGHT: Water Footprints Go Beneath the Planet's Surface[41]

A team of scientists recently developed the first analytical tool to assess the impacts of groundwater withdraws. They named it **groundwater footprint**, defined as "the area required to sustain groundwater use and groundwater dependent ecosystem services."

The scientists determined that (1) humans are overexploiting aquifers in Asia and North America that are critical to agriculture; (2) the global groundwater footprint is 3.5 times the area of the planet's actual aquifers; and (3) approximately 1.7 billion people currently live in geographic regions where groundwater resources and dependent ecosystems are threatened.

Metrics and tools are instrumental in determining what human and natural resources are at stake, and providing objective data about corporate sustainability performance. This large variety of metrics and tools inform corporate sustainability reporting initiatives, which we will discuss next.

5.4 Reporting

Using sustainable metrics and tools, companies can achieve transparency by reporting on their sustainable performance. **Transparency** means that those affected by corporate conduct, whether investors, regulators, customers, or communities impacted by business activities, are able to access information about such conduct.

Reporting is the forthright disclosure of relevant information regarding corporate conduct to affected stakeholders. Reporting allows companies to share progress demonstrated by metrics with investors and other stakeholders to achieve transparency and to document success. Using transparency for sustainability involves measuring then reporting social, economic, and environmental performance of one's business. As discussed in Chapter 1: Introduction to Sustainable Business, there is growing demand on the part of various external stakeholders for data about corporate sustainability performance. Metrics, tools, and reporting allow this growing demand for sustainability-related information to be satisfied.

Sustainability reports can take a variety of forms. What is important is that material risks are disclosed and the scope and content of these disclosures are tailored to appropriate audiences. Reporting sustainability issues from the **horizontal view** focuses on the behavior and impacts of a single entity or organization, such as the end producer or the brand under which a product is sold. Reporting sustainability issues from the **vertical view** focuses on the impacts associated with a product life cycle, as measured through its entire value chain.

The **Carbon Disclosure Project** is a non-profit that collects climate change information from voluntary business disclosures, including emissions amounts and associated risks, on behalf of 475 institutional investors.[42] These disclosures are often pursuant to the United Nations' Greenhouse Gas Protocol, discussed earlier.

Companies can report different boundaries of emissions, as defined by the Greenhouse Gas Protocol: **Scope 1 emissions** (direct emissions from internal operations), **Scope 2 emissions** (indirect emissions from other companies over which the reporting company has control, such as consumption of electricity), and **Scope 3 emissions** (indirect emissions caused by entities in the company's supply chain over which it has no control).[43] Scope 1 and 2 emissions would be contained in a horizontal report; from a vertical point of view, Scope 3 emissions are reported.

Collaborative reporting between industry and non-profit sustainability advocacy groups, as well as between nodes in a supply chain, have produced environmental measurement tools tailored to the informational needs of specific industries and geographic regions.

For instance, PepsiCo's collaboration with other bottlers and NGOs to develop the Global Water Mapping tool helps the company to protect its most valuable ingredient: clean water. Collaboration between entities in a supply chain is also important to prepare a proper life-cycle assessment.

Transparency When those affected by corporate conduct - whether investors, regulators, customers, or communities impacted by business activities - are able to access information about such conduct.

Reporting The forthright disclosure of relevant information regarding corporate conduct to affected stakeholders.

Horizontal View Reporting focused on the behavior and impacts of a single entity or organization, such as the end producer or the brand under which a product is sold.

Vertical View Reporting focused on the impacts associated with a product life cycle, as measured through its entire value chain.

Carbon Disclosure Project A non-profit that collects climate change information from voluntary business disclosures, including emissions amounts and associated risks, on behalf of 475 institutional investors.

Scope 1 Emissions Greenhouse gas metric bounded by direct emissions from internal operations.

Scope 2 Emissions Greenhouse gas metric bounded by indirect emissions from other companies over which the reporting company has control, such as emissions generated by energy suppliers resulting from the reporting company's electricity consumption.

Scope 3 Emissions Greenhouse gas metric bounded by indirect emissions caused by entities in the company's supply chain over which it has no control, such as second or third tier suppliers.

Collaborative Reporting Reporting process between industry and non-profit sustainability advocacy groups, as well as between nodes in a supply chain.

5.4.1 **Leadership and Reporting**

Excellence in reporting on sustainability performance is distinct from excellent sustainability performance. Companies can do a good job with respect to transparency and reporting, even if they are not the most sustainable companies with respect to pollution or social issues.

There are many reasons why a company would want to analyze metrics and report upon these performance indicators, even if only internally and confidentially. Organizational learning, strategic planning, and risk management are benefitted by internal assessment of metrics and internal reporting throughout the organizational hierarchy. Notice the trend among business leaders to remain informed on key sustainability performance indicators. See Figure 5.6.

In addition to internal information sharing, the data and insights gleaned from the application of sustainability metrics and tools can also be shared. However, not all companies publish sustainability reports. Nonetheless, mandatory annual financial disclosures may require an explanation of risks from environmental impacts and natural resource dependency. In the Section 5.4.2 we discuss when certain information related to environmental performance *must* be shared by publicly traded companies.

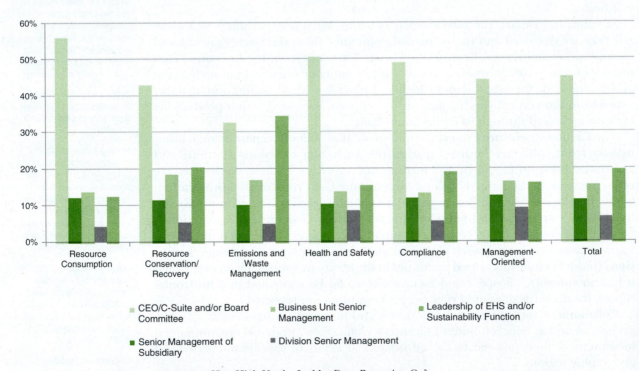

FIGURE 5.6 How High Up the Ladder Does Reporting Go?

Source: National Association of Environmental Management, *Green Metrics that Matter: Identifying Corporate EHS and Sustainability Metrics: What Companies are Tracking and Why,* 12 (2011).

5.4.2 Threshold for Reporting: Materiality

After applying metrics and tools to understand corporate sustainability performance and related risks, company leaders must determine which issues to disclose to investors and the public. The **Sarbanes-Oxley Act** of 2002 was enacted to protect investors by improving the accuracy and reliability of corporate disclosures.[44]

The law requires senior management to certify the accuracy of financial information and carries severe penalties for fraudulent activity. The law empowered the Securities and Exchange Commission (SEC) to develop and enforce rules.

One of the purposes of these mandatory disclosures is to provide a narrative explanation of the financial statement that allows investors to see the company through the eyes of management. If managers know of a risk to the profitability of the enterprise, so should the investors. This is beginning to hold true even when the risks have traditionally not been monetized, such as the value of ecosystem services upon which the company depends.

The SEC requires companies to disclose material risks in annual financial reports, and has issued guidance regarding the duty to provide early warning disclosures of risk factors that are "reasonably likely to cause reported financial information not to be necessarily indicative of future operating performance or future financial condition."[45] The SEC's **Commission Guidance Regarding Disclosure Related to Climate Change** advises managers to provide future-oriented disclosures about known trends and uncertainties associated with climate change that are reasonably likely to have a material impact on a company's liquidity, capital resources, or operations.[46] Consider the oil and gas industry for example. Existing and planned refineries, ports, offshore drilling rigs, and related infrastructure are exposed to extreme weather events, and therefore vulnerable to climate change.[47]

SEC risk disclosure obligations require a company to follow a process known as **Management's Discussion and Analysis of Financial Condition and Results of Operations (MD&A)**.[48] The MD&A process presumes that risks should be disclosed unless one of two possible conditions is met. Once management is aware of a trend or uncertainty, it must assess whether the risk is likely to occur. Disclosure is required unless it can be determined that no risk is likely. If it is impossible to tell the likelihood of a risky event, disclosure is still required unless the consequences of the risk would not be material.

Information is **material** if there is a substantial likelihood that a reasonable investor would consider it important to an investment decision.[49] In order to determine whether a complex and uncertain risk (such as climate change impacts) is material, managers must balance the probability that the event will occur with the magnitude of the risk to the company's total activities.[50]

In the context of financial reporting and accounting audits, an item is material if shareholders, investors, or lenders would be influenced by its omission or misstatement; environmental externalities created by the reporting company may be material issues.[51]

For a detailed visual example of materiality assessment, refer to Mountain Equipment Co-op's Materiality Analysis, in the form of the 2013 Materiality Matrix.[52]

Sarbanes-Oxley Act Enacted to protect investors by improving the accuracy and reliability of corporate disclosures, requiring senior management to certify the accuracy of financial information, and carrying severe penalties for fraudulent activity.

Commission Guidance Regarding Disclosure Related to Climate Change Advises managers to provide future-oriented disclosures about known trends and uncertainties associated with climate change that are reasonably likely to have a material impact on a company's liquidity, capital resources, or operations.

MD&A SEC disclosure obligations that require a company to follow a specific process of management-level discussion and analysis of risks.

Material Information bearing a substantial likelihood that a reasonable investor would consider it important to an investment decision.

CROSS-LINKAGE

For more on materiality assessment, see Chapter 6: Risk Management.

This assessment is available to the public and illustrates the material sustainability issues on a two-dimensional matrix, where plotting is done according to influence on business success (x-axis) and importance to stakeholders (y-axis). The size of the plotted points describes the significance of the issues on a global scale.

5.4.3 Sharing Sustainability Information With End Consumers

CROSS-LINKAGE

For more on marketing sustainable products, see Chapter 7: Marketing.

The business case for sustainability depends in part on informed consumers expressing demand for products and services that carry less impact on the environment and human resources than those offered by competitors. Because customers can transform the marketplace, consumers can in fact drive corporate sustainability, but only if they are informed about the true costs associated with the products and services they aim to purchase. Sustainability disclosures can provide this critical information to consumer advocacy organizations and consumers alike.

As more consumers buy sustainable products, retailers and manufacturers face compelling incentives to make products that are safe, environmentally sustainable, and produced using ethical sourcing of raw materials and labor. However, without full transparency and disclosure of objective, science-based health, social, and environmental metrics, there persists a large information gap between conscientious consumers and the products and services they might purchase. Often enough, performance information is unavailable to consumers, too complex for non-experts to understand, or unsubstantiated by evidence.[53]

GoodGuide A source of authoritative information for consumers about the health, environmental, and social performance of products and companies.

To fill this gap, **GoodGuide** was formed to provide authoritative information about the health, environmental, and social performance of products and companies, in order to help consumers make purchasing decisions that better reflect their preferences and values.[54]

GoodGuide was founded in 2007 by Dara O'Rourke, an expert on global supply chains and a professor of environmental and labor policy at the University of California at Berkeley. GoodGuide employs about 20 people, including environmental scientists, chemists, toxicologists, and nutritionists, who rate thousands of products across product categories. Each product gets a numerical rating from 1 to 10 for health, environment, and social impacts depending on the life cycle analysis for that product.

5.4.4 ISO Standards For Sustainability Reporting

The International Organization for Standardization (ISO) now offers managerial and organizational guidance in the form of frameworks that organizations of any size and industry can use to promote social responsibility and continuously improve environmental management.

ISO 26000 A set of standards emphasizing a process to ensure business decisions affecting society or the environment are made ethically and transparently.

ISO 26000 series Guidance on Social Responsibility emphasizes a process to ensure business decisions affecting society or the environment are made ethically and transparently.[55] See Table 5.4.

TABLE **5.4**	
ISO 26000 Guidance on Social Responsibility	
Topic	**Issues Covered**
Human Rights	due diligence, risk situations, avoiding complicity in human rights abuse, resolving grievances, avoiding discrimination of vulnerable groups, and respecting civil and political rights
Labor Practices	employment relationships, conditions of work, social dialogue, workplace health and safety, as well as workplace development and training
Environment	pollution prevention, sustainable resource use, climate change mitigation and adaptation, and ecosystem conservation
Fair Operating Practices	anti-corruption, responsible political involvement, fair competition, socially responsible value chain, respecting property rights
Consumer Issues	fair marketing, consumer health and safety, sustainable consumption, customer support, data protection and privacy, access to essential services
Community Involvement	education and culture, skill development, access to technology, shared wealth creation, community health, infrastructure investment

The **ISO 14000** series provides tools to identify and report on the adverse impacts of business, including environmental management systems that track energy use and water consumption at specific facilities; life cycle impact analysis of products in development; methods of communicating about sustainability; and auditing protocols.[56] Businesses use these standards to reduce waste management costs, reduce material and resource consumption, reduce the costs of distribution, and improve reputation among government officials and their clients.

ISO 14000 A set of tools to identify and report on the adverse impacts of business, including environmental management systems that track energy use and water consumption at specific facilities; life cycle impact analysis of products in development; methods of communicating about sustainability; and auditing protocols.

ISO even publishes sustainability checklists for small- and mid-sized enterprises. These standards can guide the selection of new technology, identify opportunities to reduce cost, waste, and pollution, and ensure operations are socially responsible through transparency. ISO standards can be introduced voluntarily or a company's supplier may request compliance.

5.4.5 Global Reporting Initiative

Metrics enable managers to develop performance indicators, without which objective-setting and performance management are impossible. Several sustainability performance indicators become available once a company begins to track its performance using metrics, such as those offered in the Global Reporting Initiative. The **Global Reporting Initiative (GRI)** provides comprehensive sustainability reporting frameworks for organizations to promote economic, environmental, and social sustainability.

Global Reporting Initiative A framework providing comprehensive sustainability reporting metrics for organizations to promote economic, environmental, and social sustainability.

According to a Governance and Accountability Institute analysis, in 2012 the majority of companies that report in the S&P 500 use the Global Reporting Initiative

Framework.[57] Although the GRI framework is common among highly capitalized companies, the metrics provided can also be usefully applied to develop sustainability performance indicators for small- and mid-sized enterprises. The GRI framework is widely used across industries and geographic regions. The purpose is to provide a transparent and trustworthy account of corporate sustainability performance.

The GRI is the most widely used sustainability reporting framework in the world. The framework is continually being improved to add greater value to the reporting company and to provide new tools and concepts. GRI offers sector-specific supplements for airport operators, construction and real estate professionals, event organizers, electric utilities, financial services, food processing, media, mining and metals, NGOs, and oil and gas industries, to enable deeper reporting and topical guidance. There are over 13,000 reports using the GRI framework available on GRI's searchable online database.[58]

The primary performance indicators from the most recent Sustainability Reporting Guideline apply to all sectors, and address economic impacts, environmental impacts, labor standards, human rights, impacts on society, and product responsibility. See Figure 5.7.

GRI offers a generic reporting framework accompanied by sector guidance and a technical protocol. Companies prepare, grade, and publish their own sustainability reports in accordance with the GRI disclosure guidelines, which enable companies to demonstrate their commitment to sustainability through benchmarking performance against laws, social norms, voluntary initiatives, industry codes, and objective performance standards. The report is graded not by how well the company relates to the environment or local communities per se, but rather, according to the completeness and objectivity of their disclosures. Reports that are responsive to all sections of the GRI reporting framework and which receive third-party verification earn the highest score.

Energy Productivity Reveals how much energy per dollar of revenue the company is responsible for consuming.

Greenhouse Gas Productivity How much greenhouse gas emissions per dollar of revenue the company is responsible for generating.

Water Productivity How much water per dollar of revenue the company is responsible for consuming.

Waste Productivity How much waste per dollar of revenue the company is responsible for generating.

Safety Performance An employee injury rate per hours of work time.

LEADERSHIP: Using the GRI to Rank the World's Clean Capital Giants[59]

The Global Reporting Initiative is tied-in to other measures of sustainability, such as the Corporate Knights' Global 100 List of leading companies in clean capitalism. The research model used to select the world's leading clean capital companies is based on 12 key performance indicators (KPIs) that are prioritized for each sector. Each KPI is linked to a specific Global Reporting Initiative Code. The Corporate Knights rank clean capital firms based on impact-to-benefit ratios. To determine a company's **energy productivity** using the Global Reporting Initiative, add the response to EN3 (Direct energy consumption by primary energy source) to EN4 (Indirect energy consumption by primary source). Divide annual revenue by the sum total of EN3 and EN4. This reveals how much energy per dollar the company is responsible for consuming. The same method can be used to determine company's **greenhouse gas productivity** (divide total revenue by EN16: Total direct and indirect greenhouse gas emissions by weight), **water productivity** (divide total revenue by EN8: total water use), and **waste productivity** (revenue/EN22: total waste generated). This approach to measuring sustainable performance is similar to that used to determine **safety performance**, which divides "Lost Time Injuries" by 50,000 employee hours.

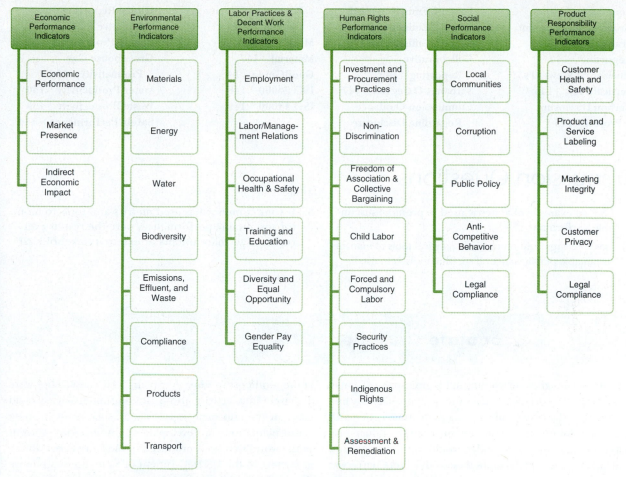

FIGURE 5.7 Global Reporting Initiative Sustainability Performance Aspects, G3.1.[60]

Source: Global Reporting Initiative Sustainability Performance Indicators. Http://www.globalreporting.org. Used by permission.

Key Terms

Discussion Questions

1. Give an example of a metric used to promote sustainable performance.

2. Has your organization utilized analytical tools to manage sustainable performance? If so, what tools were used?

3. If your company has used metrics and tools to monitor sustainable performance, were the results ever reported to shareholders or external stakeholders?

CASE 1   ## Chocolate Crusaders

Charlie Delano grew up working at his grandparents' chocolate shop. He worked at the register every weekend, while leaving the artistry of candy making to the time-honed skill of his grandmother and grandfather. The two of them prepared the ingredients, Grandpa would fill the chocolates, and Grandma would decorate them with icing. Charlie was allowed to clean the mixing bowls.

During high school, Charlie was "too cool" to work at the register of the old candy store. When he went away for college, he never thought he would work there again. It wasn't until he began his MBA program that he realized his family may be sitting on a gold mine in the form of a candy store. Using his hard-earned knowledge, the store's low operating costs and high profit margins could be scaled up for exponential growth. By the time Charlie finished his program, his grandparents were looking to retire and he was preparing to take over the chocolate company. After three years of sustained growth, Charlie opened new stores across the region and was looking to take the company public.

It was about this time that a human rights organization called the Chocolate Crusaders visited Charlie's office at the mother-ship store to explain their cause. They were a shareholder activist group drawing attention to child labor in the chocolate supply chain, specifically at some cacao plantations in developing countries. Forty percent of the world's cocao is produced in the Ivory Coast where, according to the US Department of State, there are more than 109,000 children working under the worst forms of child labor, including 10,000 victims of human trafficking and slavery.[61] Charlie listened attentively but denied any knowledge of the issue within his company. However, he knew that some of his cacao suppliers were from the same regions of concern to the Chocolate Crusaders, and that once his company was public, issues like this could create fallout with investors and customers.

Questions for Case 1

1. Why is the issue of child labor in the supply chain material, warranting disclosure to shareholders?

2. Develop sustainability metrics for Charlie's chocolate company using concepts from this chapter. What kinds of issues should be included in the first sustainability report of Charlie's chocolate company?

CASE 2   **Suede Shoe Blues**[62]

In conjunction with the release of a new line of biodegradable and recyclable shoes and sports apparel, PUMA has applied their Environmental Profit & Loss process (discussed in the Chapter Opener) at the product level, specifically focusing on the life-cycle environmental impacts of their signature shoe. PUMA is "planning an industry coalition to broaden adoption of the sustainability accounting method" embodied by the EP&L. In the EP&L for shoes, PUMA applies certain metrics to a shoe's entire supply chain, from activities associated with direct company operations through that of 4th tier suppliers. See Table 5.C1.

TABLE 5.C1

Source of Impacts and Associated Activities

Source	Activities
PUMA Operations	• Office buildings • Retail outlets
1st Tier Suppliers	• Shoe manufacturing company • Apparel manufacturing company
2nd Tier Suppliers	• Textile work (cutting, embroidery) • Insole and outsole production
3rd Tier Suppliers	• Leather, petroleum, and cotton processing • Cotton weaving and dyeing
4th Tier Suppliers	• Cattle, cotton, and rubber farming • Petroleum production

For each of these activities, PUMA applies the metrics of water use, greenhouse gas emissions, land use conversion, air pollution, and waste. This provides a complete picture of the aggregate environmental impacts, both "profits" and "losses," associated with the entire product life-cycle.

Questions for Case 2

1. What kinds of metrics (units of measurement) were used in PUMA's Environmental Profit & Loss Account? How do these compare to metrics used in traditional P&L statements?

2. Using PUMA's EP&L Account as a template, develop sustainability metrics for an existing consumer product of your choice. Which metrics did you choose and why?

Further Research

For a comprehensive summary of sustainability metrics, see William R. Blackburn, *Appendix 7.1: Examples of Sustainability Metrics for Companies*, The Sustainability Handbook: The Complete Management Guide to Achieving Social, Economic, and Environmental Responsibility, 725–735 (Environmental Law Institute (2008).

For an approach to sustainable business that fuses the perspectives of Environmental Health and Safety (EHS) management with that of an investor and analyst, see Peter A. Soyka, *Creating a Sustainable Organization: Approaches for Enhancing Corporate Value Through Sustainability* (Financial Times Press 2012). This book explores the linkages between sustainability and value creation and methods for

measuring sustainability performance from the point of view of both investors and internal management.

In her TED-Talk "The Trade-Offs of Building Green," Catherine Mohr explains how choosing the right metrics is essential to achieving sustainable performance.

Harvard Business Review Case: Denise Akason, Bill Bennett & Louis Merlini, *Financial and Environmental Impact Analysis of Sustainable Retrofitting*, Prod. #: KEL430-PDF-ENG (February 19, 2010).

Harvard Business Review Case: Sandra J. Suchar, Daniela Beyersdorfer & Ian McKown Cornell, *A Note on Socially Responsible Investing*, Prod. #: 609060-PDF-ENG (February 19, 2009).

Endnotes

[1] PUMA, *New PUMA Shoe and T-Shirt Impact the Environment by a Third Less Than Conventional Products*, Press Release, October 8, 2012.

[2] *Six Growing Trends in Corporate Sustainability*, An Ernst & Young survey in cooperation with GreenBiz Group, page 22 (2011).

[3] Table A2.3 points out a number of accounting and financial reporting standards that concern natural capital reliance. See KPMG, Fauna & Flora International & ACCA, *Is Natural Capital a Material Issue? An Evaluation of the Relevance of Biodiversity and Ecosystem Services to Accountancy Professionals and the Private Sector*, Table 2A.3 (September 2013).

[4] KPMG, Fauna & Flora International & ACCA, *Is Natural Capital a Material Issue? An Evaluation of the Relevance of Biodiversity and Ecosystem Services to Accountancy Professionals and the Private Sector*, page 34 (September 2013).

[5] Lagace, Martha, "New Agenda for Corporate Accountability Reporting," *Harvard Business School Working Knowledge*, November 14, 2012.

[6] Quoting Helen Brand, Chief Executive of ACCA. See KPMG, Fauna & Flora International & ACCA, *Is Natural Capital a Material Issue? An Evaluation of the Relevance of Biodiversity and Ecosystem Services to Accountancy Professionals and the Private Sector*, page 10 (September 2013).

[7] KPMG, Fauna & Flora International & ACCA, *Is Natural Capital a Material Issue? An Evaluation of the Relevance of Biodiversity and Ecosystem Services to Accountancy Professionals and the Private Sector*, page 8 (September 2013).

[8] Adapted from *Sustainability Framework 2.0: Professional Accountants As Integrators*, AccountAbility, International Federation

of Accountants, last accessed My 7, 2014, available at http://www.accountability.org/images/content/4/3/435.pdf

[9] *ibid.*

[10] See, for example, the UPS web pages on corporate responsibility and the 2012 Sustainability Report, last accessed May 7, 2014, available at http://www.responsibility.ups.com/Sustainability.

[11] *Corporate ESG/Sustainability/Responsibility Reporting: Does it Matter?*, Governance & Accountability Institute, page 3 (2012).

[12] *ibid.*, page 12.

[13] National Association for Environmental Managers, *Green Metrics that Matter: Identifying Corporate EHS and Sustainability Metrics: What Companies are Tracking and Why*, 9–11 (2011).

[14] *ibid.*

[15] *ibid.*

[16] *Corporate ESG/Sustainability/Responsibility Reporting: Does it Matter?*, Governance & Accountability Institute, page 10 (2012).

[17] *ibid.*

[18] *ibid.*

[19] National Association for Environmental Managers, *Green Metrics that Matter: Identifying Corporate EHS and Sustainability Metrics: What Companies are Tracking and Why*, 21 (2011).

[20] Peter A. Soyka, Mark E. Bateman, *Finding Common Ground on the Metrics that Matter*, IRRC Institute (2012), last accessed May 10, 2014, available at http://www.irrcinstitute.org/pdf/IRRC-Metrics-that-Matter-Report_Feb-2012.pdf.

[21] For an example of a triple bottom line approach to natural resource conservation, see Benjamin S. Halpern, et. al, *Achieving the Triple Bottom Line in the Face of Inherent Trade-Offs Among*

Social Equity, Economic Return, and Conservation, Vol. 110 No. 15 Proceedings of the National Academy of Sciences 6229–6234 (2013).

22 Sustainable Brands & HIP Investor, *Surprising Business Value from New Metrics of Sustainability* (2012).

23 *ibid.*

24 *ibid.*

25 *ibid.*

26 *ibid.*

27 See the Performance Highlights on Coca-Cola's 2011/2012 Sustainability Report, last accessed May 10, 2014, available at http://www.coca-colacompany.com/sustainabilityreport/ performance-highlights.html#section-activehealthyliving.

28 See Greenhouse Gas Protocol, Working 9-5 on Climate Change: An Office Guide, page 14 (2002), last accessed May 10, 2014, available at http://www.ghgprotocol.org/files/ghgp/tools/ working9-5.pdf.

29 KPMG, Fauna & Flora International & ACCA, *Is Natural Capital a Material Issue? An Evaluation of the Relevance of Biodiversity and Ecosystem Services to Accountancy Professionals and the Private Sector*, Appendix 2 (September 2013).

30 *ibid.*, Appendix 2, Table A2.2 (September 2013).

31 See the article on corporate commitment to natural capital valuation by Sustainable Brands, last accessed May 10, 2014, available at http://www.sustainablebrands.com/news_and_views/ articles/coke-nike-kimberly-clark-commit-valuing-natural-capital-rio20; as well as the Corporate Eco Forum, last accessed May 10, 2014, available at http://www.corporateecoforum.com/ valuingnaturalcapital/.

32 The Sustainability Consortium, *Social Sustainability Assessment Literature Review*, Measurement Science Working Paper, December 2010, page 4, last accessed May 10, 2014, available at http:// www.sustainabilityconsortium.org/wp-content/themes/sustainability/assets/pdf/whitepapers/Social_Sustainability_Assessment.pdf.

33 *2013 Retail Sustainability Report: Fueling Continuous Development*, Retail Industry Leaders Association, 32 (2013).

34 *2011–2012 Corporate Responsibility Update*, Eli Lilly, page 46 (2012).

35 See the Greenhouse Gas Protocol website, last accessed May 10, 2014, available at http://www.ghgprotocol.org.

36 See the GHG Protocol tools website, last accessed May 10, 2014, available at http://www.ghgprotocol.org/calculation-tools/ all-tools.

37 See Samantha Putt del Pino & Pankaj Bhatia, Working 9 to 5 on Climate Change: An Office Guide, World Resources Institute (2002), last accessed May 10, 2014, available at http://www. ghgprotocol.org/files/ghgp/tools/working9-5.pdf.

38 See the United Nation's Global Compact web page on the CEO Water Mandate, last accessed May 10, 2014, available at http:// ceowatermandate.org/water-assessment-tools-methods/ what-tools-are-available/.

39 See the United Nations web page introducing the CEO Water Mandate, last accessed May 10, 2014, available at http://ceowatermandate.org/about/.

40 Tom Gleeson, Yoshihide Wada, Marc F. P. Bierkens & Ludovicus P. H. van Beek, *Water Balance of Global Aquifers Revealed by Groundwater Footprint*, 488 Nature 197–200 (2012).

41 *ibid.*

42 See the Carbon Disclosure Project website, last accessed May 10, 2014, available at www.cdp.net.

43 See the Greenhouse Gas Protocol, last accessed May 10, 2014, available at http://www.ghgprotocol.org.

44 Sarbanes-Oxley Act, Pub. L. 107–204, 116 Stat. 745 (2002).

45 SEC Rel. No. 33-9106 (Feb. 2, 2010), 75 FR 6290, page 17, last accessed May 10, 2014, available at http://www.sec.gov/rules/ interp/2010/33-9106.pdf.

46 *ibid.*

47 U.S. Department of Energy, U.S. *Energy Sector Vulnerabilities to Climate Change and Extreme Weather* (2013); International Energy Agency *Redrawing the Energy-Climate Map* (2013).

48 Item 303 of Regulation S-K, 17 C.F.R. 229.303.

49 *TSC v. Northway*, 426 U.S. 438 (1976).

50 See, e.g., *Basic v. Levinson*, 485 U.S. 224, 238 (1988).

51 *The Conceptual Framework for Financial Reporting*, International Accounting Standards Board (2010); *Guide to Corporate Ecosystem Valuation: A Framework for Improving Corporate Decision-Making*, WBCSD, ERM, IUCN and PWC (2011).

52 Mountain Equipment Co-op's Materiality Analysis, page 6, last accessed May 10, 2014, available at http://www.mec.ca/ media/Images/pdf/accountability/MEC_2013_materiality_ matrix_v2_m56577569831501444.pdf.

53 Marc Gunther, *Can Consumers Drive Corporate Sustainability?* (April 09, 2012), last accessed May 10, 2014, available at http://www.greenbiz.com/blog/2012/04/09/ can-consumers-drive-corporate-sustainability.

54 See the GoodGuide website, last accessed May 10, 2014, available at http://www.goodguide.com.

55 See Discovering ISO 26000: Social Responsibility, last accessed May 10, 2014, available at http://www.iso.org/iso/discovering_iso_26000.pdf.

56 See the ISO website on ISO 14000: Environmental Management, last accessed May 10, 2014, available at http://www. iso.org/iso/home/standards/management-standards/ iso14000.htm.

57   The Global Reporting Initiative (GRI) promotes the use of sustainability reporting as a way for organizations to become more sustainable and contribute to a sustainable global economy. GRI's mission is to make sustainability reporting standard practice. To enable all companies and organizations to report their economic, environmental, social and governance performance, GRI produces free Sustainability Reporting Guidelines. GRI is a not-for-profit, network-based organization; its activity involves thousands of professionals and organizations from many sectors, constituencies and regions. www.globalreporting.org. Contact: info@globalreporting.org.

58   See the Sustainability Disclosure Database, last accessed May 10, 2014, available at http://database.globalreporting.org/.

59   See the Global 100 website on the methodology behind the selection criteria, last accessed May 10, 2014, available at http://www.global100.org/methodology/selection-criteria.html.

60   See generally the Global Reporting Initiative website, last accessed May 10, 2014, available at www.globalreporting.org.

61   *Oversight of Public and Private Initiatives to Eliminate the Worst Forms of Child Labor in the Cocoa Sector in Cote d'Ivoire and Ghana*, Payson Center for International Development and Technology Transfer at Tulane University (March 31, 2011); see also U.S. Department of State, *Trafficking in Persons Report 2009* (June 16, 2009), last accessed May 10, 2014, available at http://www.state.gov/g/tip/rls/tiprpt/2009/; and U.S. Department of State, *Trafficking in Persons Report 2010* (June 14, 2010), last accessed May 10, 2014, available at http://www.state.gov/documents/organization/142979.pdf.

62   *New PUMA Shoe and T-Shirt Impact the Environment by a Third Less Than Conventional Products*, Press Release, October 8, 2012; *Dozen Companies Join Puma EP&L Coalition; Firm Now Reporting at Product Level*, Environmental Leader (October 9, 2012), available at http://www.environmentalleader.com/2012/10/09/dozen-companies-to-join-puma-ep-firm-now-reporting-at-product-level/; and *PUMA's Environmental Profit and Loss Account for the Year Ended 31 December 2010*, available at http://about.puma.com/wp-content/themes/aboutPUMA_theme/media/pdf/2014/EPL_Report_Final_09062014.pdf.

CHAPTER 6

Risk Management

Happy Meals Dodge Tainted Toys

In the summer of 2004, the Kellogg Company found itself in a scandal over a seemingly routine cross-promotion with the new blockbuster movie *Spider-Man 2*. The maker of Rice Krispies and Pop-Tarts received criticism over the new Spidey Signals toy packaged with their food products. As it turned out, a small battery that contained toxic mercury powered each electronic toy, posing a risk to human health, particularly among children. The company had to remedy the growing publicity problem, and quickly, to maintain its reputation.

The company offered to send a prepaid return envelope to each of the 17 million customers who had received the toy. Further, Kellogg committed to never again use the mercury-based batteries in children's toys. Although the matter was resolved, it proved quite costly to Kellogg.

At about the same time that Kellogg had to manage a crisis, executives at another food giant were breathing a huge sigh of relief. McDonald's is famous for their Happy Meal which contains child-sized portions and a small toy. Although the golden arches of McDonald's are frequently paired with cinematic characters in cross-promotions using plastic toys, the company had dodged this mercury battery bullet, and not by luck.

After years of facing pressure over everything from litter and packaging to mad cow disease, McDonald's decided to get ahead of the curve by taking sustainability seriously. Through a risk management process the company studied environmental and social trends to identify potential dangers to the business. Early on, they identified the issue of mercury in batteries used in children's toys as an emerging threat to consumer safety. Although at the time it was an obscure issue, McDonald's calculated the downside to be high and the corrective cost to be low, and used its market

> *"Some things are so unexpected that no one is prepared for them."*
>
> —*Leo Rosten,* **ROME WASN'T BURNED IN A DAY**

> *"The life expectancy of a Fortune 500 company has declined from 75 years (back at the beginning of the century) to less than 15 years today. [That's] what happens when you're pressuring managers to get that share price up at all costs even if it means taking on enormous risks[.]"*
>
> —*Professor Lynn Stout,* **CORNELL LAW SCHOOL, THE SHAREHOLDER VALUE MYTH: HOW PUTTING SHAREHOLDERS FIRST HARMS INVESTORS, CORPORATIONS, AND THE PUBLIC (2012)**

LEARNING OBJECTIVES

After completing this chapter, you should be able to:

1. Understand the role of risk management in sustainability.
2. Distinguish risk assessment from risk response, and explain the Enterprise Risk Management continuum.
3. Explain the categories of risks to business.
4. Explain the factors that determine risk materiality.
5. Develop a risk management strategy.

clout to pressure suppliers to find different options for their Happy Meal toys. By the time states started regulating mercury in toys that come near food, McDonald's had long solved the problem. Unlike Kellogg that paid a high price to salvage their brand, the problem never became costly for McDonald's because the company systematically identified the risk and then took measures to avoid it before the risk became a crisis.

6.1 Risk Management and Sustainable Business

Typically, the subject of risk management is taught as ancillary to the subject of project management. However, the challenges of sustainable development pose risks with such broad ramifications that they affect entire organizations, supply chains, and even nations, not just the execution of a single project. Therefore, we focus here on risk management in its own right, highlighting the traditional elements of the discipline, while incorporating the themes of water vulnerability and climate change risks.

This chapter ties in to the discussion of risk disclosure obligations and materiality assessment as well as sustainable performance metrics from **Chapter 5**. Sustainable performance metrics for water, natural capital, greenhouse gases, social impacts, and more can find practical applications in the context of risk management, specifically in risk identification and assessment. According to a survey of CEOs from PricewaterhouseCoopers, 93% of CEOs believe that measuring the company's total environmental footprint (instead of financial performance alone) enables better risk management and enhances the firm's reputation with regulators as well as employees and investors.[1]

Risk management has taken on prominence in today's era of consumer activism, product liability lawsuits, and increased regulatory oversight of corporate risks, with implications for financial, marketing, supply chain, and operations management disciplines. In the Chapter opener, McDonald's had followed a systematic risk assessment process that enabled it to identify the risk of button batteries as being high and to decide on measures to address it, whereas Kellogg failed to detect the risk until it had materialized in a costly way. Effectively identifying, assessing, and responding to risks is a necessary ingredient in the continued economic success of any business.

In this chapter, we focus on protecting the continued operation of business from various threats. Reducing risk is consistent with the effort to run a sustainable company because risks resulting from corporate conduct can often harm external as well as internal stakeholders. Adapting to risk-laden conditions is also necessary in order for those businesses already on the path to sustainability to stay alive. Successful enterprises continually monitor risk, choose strategic risks wisely, and build a resilient enterprise that can thrive through unavoidable risky conditions.

GLOBAL INSIGHT: Climate Change Risks are Changing Leadership Mindsets[2]

According to former U.S. Treasury Secretary Henry M. Paulson, Jr., "business leaders are not adequately focused on the economic impact of climate change." For the most part this is true, but there are exceptions. In 2004, major water shortages in India cost Coca-Cola a profitable license to operate. According to Jeffrey Seabright, Coca-Cola's Vice President for Environment and Water Resources, water and other essential ingredients including sugar cane, sugar beets, and citrus are compromised by "increased droughts, more unpredictable variability, 100-year floods every two years," and so forth. The President of the World Bank, Jim Yong Kim believes that global warming is the primary culprit of rising global poverty and falling Gross Domestic Products in developing countries, and accordingly has aligned the bank's mission squarely with addressing the risks of greenhouse gas pollution. The impacts of climate change to industry include increased costs for food products and commodities, supply chain disruptions, and augmented financial risks. Climate change risks from drought and extreme weather events are real and directly impact the financial bottom line. Companies are waking up to this new environmental reality and must implement risk management protocols in order to remain competitive in a changing global climate.

Risk management and sustainability are intertwined. Using sustainability to guide business decisions across functional areas reduces the risk level of business activities, and risk management can protect the economic viability of a company focusing on the triple bottom line of sustainable performance. Consistent with the message throughout this textbook, becoming a sustainable company is not just for the benefit of distant ecosystems and foreign populations—sustainable businesses are more likely to thrive and prosper in a risky, uncertain, and dynamic business environment.

Effective risk management blunts the force of catastrophe, diminishes the likelihood of adverse occurrences, and promotes a more sustainable world by ensuring the organizations that provide goods and services for society are able to continue providing goods and services when catastrophes occur, to minimize economic disturbances, and to respond to global risks.

6.1.1 The Role of Risk Management in Sustainable Business

The challenges of sustainability all involve some degree of risk. **Risk** is exposure to the chance or likelihood of a disaster or hazard. **Risk management** is the process of deciding which risks are worth addressing and the extent to which these risks should be avoided.

Global trends of population growth, dwindling water resources, globalization, widespread poverty, overburdened ecosystems, and supply chain disruptions all present intertwined social, economic, and environmental challenges that can be unforeseeable and costly. Hurricanes, earthquakes, tsunamis, tornadoes, and billowing ash from erupting volcanoes have over the last several years disrupted business operations and global supply chains. Risk is everywhere, and must be managed for a

Risk Exposure to the chance of hazard.

Risk Management The process of deciding which risks are worth addressing and the extent to which these risks should be avoided.

business to survive, much less grow. Effective risk management is an integral part of any organization's efforts to be sustainable.

An important aspect of risk management is evaluating the trade-off between risk aversion and the willingness to accept risk, or what is called a **risk appetite**.

Entrepreneurs are usually high in willingness to accept risk and low in risk aversion. On the other hand, those who are completely risk averse may not be willing to accept any risks. They may choose to never invest in the stock market or fly on an airplane. A common misperception, both in business and at a personal level, is that risky endeavors are always to be avoided. Yet, businesses and people who never take any kind of risk likely will not achieve much by way of success. Risk management does not prevent a company from undertaking risky ventures; indeed, it enables a company to achieve a balanced overall risk profile, with conservative strategies in some functional areas enabling higher-risk higher-reward strategies in others.

In the wake of scandalous crises like the Bhopal gas tragedy, the Exxon Valdez spill, and the Enron collapse, risk management became a requisite management activity. Like other management activities, risk management helps an organization meet its objectives through the allocation of resources to undertake planning, make decisions and carry out other productive activities. Risk management should therefore play a prominent role in a business' sustainability initiatives.

Companies develop strategies to manage risks by utilizing risk management frameworks. **Risk management frameworks** are descriptions of a specific set of functional activities and processes that an organization will use to manage risks. A good risk management framework should enhance and improve risk management by: 1) making risks more transparent and understandable to stakeholders; 2) making organizational processes more efficient; and 3) allowing for sharing of best practice in the implementation of risk identification, risk assessment, and risk treatment. Risk management frameworks are necessary for organizational success because there are limited resources available to minimize an infinite possible set of risks, whether the organization's duty is to protect itself, its customers, or the general public. These frameworks enable decision-makers to prioritize certain risks over others in a way that is consistent and logical.

Effective risk management can be what sets apart a successful business enterprise from the floundering failure of a start-up company. Risk management can also be what sets apart the surviving incumbent from the toppling industry giant. Just consider that every business decision involves risks, such as Facebook deciding to go public, Dell deciding to become a private company once again, and Starbuck's introducing instant coffee. It is important to remember that no company can avoid risks entirely, as controlled risk is part of running a company in an uncertain world, and environmental catastrophes—so-called acts of God—are beyond human control. As with the McDonald's example, it is up to business leaders to determine which risks are worth taking and how to match up strategies, resources, and best practices to the appropriate degree of risk that will allow for profitability. Additionally, business leaders can design their organizations and supply chains to be resilient in order to thrive despite the occurrence of disruptive natural events.

Small- and mid-sized enterprise (SMEs) are especially susceptible to losing business or even failing entirely because of outside risks, such as mistakes made by other members of their supply chain. Even for larger companies, neglecting risk management will only hasten business failure. Effectively and proactively responding to the

Risk Appetite An individual's or firm's preference for risk, lying along a spectrum between risk aversion and willingness to accept risk.

Risk Management Frameworks Descriptions of a specific set of functional activities and processes that an organization will use to manage risks.

LEADERSHIP: Got an Oil Spill? "Dawn" to the Rescue

After catastrophic oil spill in the Gulf of Mexico by BP's Deepwater Horizon offshore drilling rig in 2011, millions of gallons of crude oil spewed from the bottom of the ocean floor where the well failure occurred. As oil rose to the surface of the ocean and drifted toward the coastline, emergency workers tried to mitigate the impact of the oil that could harm wildlife and spoil pristine beaches. Amidst the highly publicized emergency situation, Proctor & Gamble's Dawn showed goodwill by donating their signature grease-fighting bottles of soap to animal rescue teams in order to remove the sheen of crude oil from the fur and feathers of affected marine wildlife. According to Dawn, "Dawn dishwashing liquid has been a vital tool for wildlife conservation organizations, with thousands of donated bottles cleansing and helping more than 75,000 animals in the last 30 years."[3] Dawn's contributions to risk response in the form of cleanup efforts generate goodwill in social media and boost the reputation of the company.

business risks posed by environmental, economic, and social problems provides firm-specific advantages, including low insurance premiums, a lack of business interruption, and increased public appreciation when businesses can step in to assist in a time of crisis—such as the case of Dawn, discussed next.

6.1.2 The Risky Environment of Business

There is a general perception among business decision-makers that risk levels are increasing. There are numerous drivers of this trend. One is the increased reliance on technology that makes companies especially vulnerable to disruptions, including cyber attacks. Another is the increasing business complexity of organizations as they evolve to respond to a global business landscape, geographical distribution of organizations, and the need to update facilities, data centers, and infrastructure. Further, companies are increasing outsourcing capabilities to third parties, which gives them needed flexibility and responsiveness, but high dependence on external entities. Water-related risks and climate change impacts are also a major financial burden to some companies. In a single quarter of fiscal year 2010, heavy rainfall, flooding, and high speed winds in Guatemala caused a significant loss of volume in banana operations for Fresh Del Monte Produce, totaling $4 million in losses.[4] Add to this an increasingly stringent regulatory environment, global financial instability, political and social instability, as well as energy and fuel shortages, and we have a good picture of the risk-laden environment of business.[5]

6.1.3 The Moral Psychology of Risky Business Decisions

It is not enough to ask simply *what* the risk is, and *whether* it is likely to occur. Risk managers must know *who* will be impacted by a risk. The party responsible for generating a risk may not be the party who will bear the risk if it occurs. For example, generators of electronic waste (e-waste) left from outdated or broken computers, televisions, and cell phones create the risk of being poisoned by leaching heavy metals that make up the circuitry of those electronics into the surrounding soil. As long as e-waste is shipped to low-income countries for disposal, the generators of the risk of heavy metal poisoning are not the ones exposed to that risk.

The gap between creating and bearing a risk poses challenging questions about the extent of responsibility that manufacturers and consumers of polluting products have for the risks they generate.

A variety of commercial instruments such as insurance policies and contract provisions enable businesses to efficiently allocate risk amongst one another. In general, the party who stands to benefit from risky activity also sees the downside of that activity (otherwise the situation is a moral hazard) and can hedge against loss by obtaining insurance or contracting with another party.

However, the actor responsible for generating a risk is not always the one who bears the consequences if that risk occurs. For example, Company A owns a factory that emits a certain kind of pollution that increases the risk of cancer in those exposed to it, while Person B happens to be exposed to that pollutant, and no one from Company A is exposed to it. One party's activity generates a risk that another party bears without consent or compensation. In economic terms, the risk of developing cancer in the scenario is an **externality**.

Externality When one party's activity generates a risk that another party bears without consent or compensation.

Internalize Risk When the party responsible for generating risk ultimately pays for the consequences if the risk materializes.

Ideally, the role of law is to **internalize risk**, meaning that the party responsible for generating risk must ultimately pay for the consequences if the risk materializes. In other words, companies must internalize risk in order to see the true cost of the risks they take. This will lead to overall minimization of risk to both the company and outside parties who might have otherwise been exposed to risk.

To continue with the previous example, Company A must internalize the cost of their pollution-generating activity if the prevailing legal system allows Person B to sue Company A for the harm caused by their pollution. Businesses operate within different legal jurisdictions where differing rules of conduct apply. Legal systems tend to establish not a lofty ideal but rather a bare minimum floor for permissible risk-generating conduct. Therefore, accomplishing sustainability often involves reducing risks below the level of risk that prevailing legal systems allow.

CROSS-LINKAGE

For more about the concept of externality, see Chapter 1: Introduction to Sustainable Business.

CROSS-LINKAGE

For more on the role of law in sustainability, see Chapter 4: Legal Frameworks.

Sustainability requires more than mere compliance with existing environmental, contract, tort, property, and constitutional law. Sustainability will require corporate performance above the level of commitment to external social, environmental, and economic considerations that brought us to the brink of global system failure. Because of the globalized nature of the economy and the global nature of risk impacts, businesses must expand the scope of considerations when determining which of their activities generates risks to others, and which scenarios constitute a strategic risk to their own success.

Enterprise Risk Management A process that enables the organization to properly evaluate risks, prepare a response plan that is aligned with the company's objectives, and have a system in place to respond when needed.

6.1.4 The Enterprise Risk Management Continuum

Every organization needs to have a process in place in order to effectively assess and develop a plan to respond to risks, as the ones we just discussed. **Enterprise risk management (ERM)** is a process that enables the organization to properly evaluate risks, prepare a response plan that is aligned with the company's objectives, and have a system in place to respond when needed.

ERM provides a framework for risk management, which involves identifying particular events or circumstances relevant to the organization's objectives, assessing them in terms of likelihood and magnitude of impact, determining a response plan, and monitoring progress. This is a framework that has been used by leading companies, such as SCRM, Cisco, Coca-Cola, Ericsson, Nokia, and Bayer Crop Science.

Risk information is gathered through this process and used to accomplish three primary objectives: help the organization develop a risk strategy across all functional areas; maintain risk levels within the risk appetite of the enterprise; and provide reasonable assurance to investors, customers, and other stakeholders that risks are not compromising the objectives of the enterprise.[6] This process involves the engagement of all stakeholders, including the board of directors, management, and employees in an information-feedback strategy-development loop. This is illustrated in Figure 6.1. There are eight elements to an ERM framework: the internal environment of a business, the process of setting objectives, risk identification, risk assessment, the management of risk response, operational control activities, processing and communicating information, and monitoring risk management performance.[7] These eight elements of ERM form a continuum integrated into the organization's management activities.

We now discuss the eight elements of the risk management continuum in more detail. The remainder of this chapter will focus especially on the critical areas of risk identification, risk assessment, and risk response.

Element 1: Internal Environment For enterprise risk management purposes, the **internal environment** of a company is the organization's culture, the ethical principles and values that define the character of an organization, how the core team of leaders responsible for critical functions view risk, and the extent to which leaders

Internal Environment The organization's culture, the ethical principles and values that define the character of an organization, how the core team of leaders responsible for critical functions view risk, and the extent to which leaders of a company desire risk.

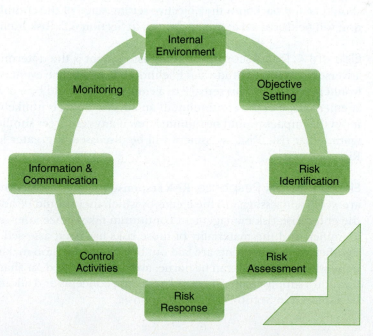

FIGURE 6.1 Enterprise Risk Management Continuum

Source: ERM Framework Committee of Sponsoring Organizations (COSO) of the Treadway Commission, Enterprise Risk Management: Integrated Framework Document (2004). Used by permission of AICPA as agent for COSO.

of a company desire risk. A current state assessment that ascertains the prevailing attitude toward risk within a company can help determine the existing internal environment and the antecedent events in a company's history that fostered the prevailing risk appetite of the organization. How risk averse is the company? What risks is it willing to take? The features of a company that make up its internal environment can change over time, especially given feedback from other elements in the continuum.

Element 2: Objective Setting It is impossible to tell whether a particular event or course of action will constitute a risk to company objectives unless those objectives have already been established. For that reason, **objective setting** must come prior to risk assessment and risk management. What is the company trying to accomplish? What are its goals? Leaders of a company, or managers of a division, should set performance objectives that are in alignment with the company's overall mission and that are within the bounds of the core leadership team's desire for risk. At the objective setting stage, leaders should set as an objective that the enterprise risk management system improves the quality and timing of risk response decisions, addresses cross-enterprise risks (say, between supply chain and operations), taking intelligent risks and capturing opportunities when they are presented, and improving the use of capital expenditures to reduce risk exposure and improve resilience.

> **Objective Setting** The process of determining what a company seeks to accomplish.

> **CROSS-LINKAGE**
>
> For more about leadership in organizational objective setting, see Chapter 3: Leadership, Change Management, and Corporate Governance.

Element 3: Risk Identification The **risk identification** stage of the continuum involves using risk identification tools, such as performing a SWOT analysis (analysis of strengths, weaknesses, opportunities, and threats) to identify critical risks for the company. Risk identification involves a survey of the social, economic, and environmental systems in which the business operates to identify potential risks for further risk assessment, management, and response, as well as to identify opportunities that should be fed back into the objective setting stage of the continuum. Risk identification will be discussed at greater length in Section 6.2: Risk Identification.

> **Risk Identification** Identifying weaknesses of and threats to the company.

Element 4: Risk Assessment **Risk assessment** is the determination of a potential adverse event's magnitude and likelihood. If an adverse event is highly probable and would present a serious setback to a company, it should be a priority in the risk management stage of the continuum. If an adverse event is unlikely to occur and even if it did the impacts would be minimal, few if any resources should be allocated to mitigating that risk. Risk assessment will be discussed at greater length in Section 6.3: Risk Assessment.

> **Risk Assessment** Determination of a potential adverse event's magnitude and likelihood.

Element 5: Risk Response **Risk response** requires a determination of which risks are worth addressing and the means by which they should be addressed. This stage of the enterprise risk management continuum takes place after salient risks have been identified and the materiality of those risks has been assessed. The most likely and significant adverse events are laid out before the decision-making authority to determine whether the risk can be borne, avoided, mitigated, or shared through the organization's supply chain. These risk response concepts and additional frameworks will be explored in Section 6.4: Risk Response.

> **Risk Response** Determination of which risks are worth addressing and the means by which they should be addressed.

Element 6: Control Activities

Control activities are the procedures and protocols that an organization implements to make sure the path chosen in the risk response stage of the enterprise risk management continuum is actually carried out. Control activities are set forth in planning documents that identify next steps, key responsibilities, milestones for project development, the resources dedicated to enterprise risk management, and a timeline for the progression through the continuum.

> **Control Activities** The procedures and protocols that an organization implements to make sure the path chosen in the risk response stage is actually carried out.

Element 7: Information and Communication

Information and communication means the identification of salient information about risks and the transmission of that information to those within a company responsible for managing those risks. Risk information must be communicated across the entire organization so there is transparency of process and agreement. It is impossible to set appropriate objectives or to identify risks without relevant information communicated to all decision-makers.

> **Information and Communication** The identification of salient information about risks and the transmission of that information to those within a company responsible for managing those risks.
>
> **Monitoring** Tracking risk performance through information technology (IT) and risk-related metrics.

Element 8: Monitoring

Monitoring means tracking performance. This is usually accomplished using some type of information technology (IT) system and risk-related metrics. Monitoring allows modifications to be made to control activities when one or more of the activities are not being performed properly. Additionally, monitoring enables a company to substantiate its communications regarding risk management successes. Monitoring is accomplished through ongoing assessment of performance across business functions, separate evaluations for individual departments, or both.

Implementation of an enterprise risk management system within any company ensures that risk management decisions are made based on the best available information, driven by business objectives, and that the overall risk portfolio of a business is sustainable.

> **CROSS-LINKAGE**
>
> For standards for monitoring corporate sustainability performance, see Chapter 5: Metrics, Tools, and Reporting: The Role of Finance and Accounting.

A process rather than a set of rules, the Enterprise Risk Management continuum provides business leaders with a framework for continually assessing and responding to risks before they become a crisis.

MANAGERIAL INSIGHT: Traditional Risk Management Is Not Good Enough[8]

"Despite all the rhetoric and money invested in it, risk management is too often treated as a compliance issue that can be solved by drawing up lots of rules and making sure that all employees follow them." Rules-based risk management is useful in obvious risky situations—for instance, a rule to unplug machines before attempting repairs, or to check with corporate counsel before signing a merger agreement. However, "rules-based risk management will not diminish either the likelihood or the impact of a disaster such as Deepwater Horizon, just as it did not prevent the failure of many financial institutions during the 2007–2008 credit crisis." For risks arising from complex and unpredictable scenarios, risk management must be an ongoing process integrated into the operating strategy of the company.

6.2 Risk Identification

Three crucial stages of the Enterprise Risk Management continuum receive additional discussion in this chapter: risk identification, risk assessment, and risk response. These steps enable a company to identify, analyze, evaluate, and treat risks based on their categorization, classification, probability of occurrence, and relative impact. Risk assessment and risk response will be discussed in Sections 6.3 and 6.4, respectively. In this section we look at ways to categorize and identify risks.

Why is risk categorization important? The reason is that not all risks have equal likelihood of occurrence or an equal impact on business organizations, and different mitigation techniques, tactics, tools, and strategies exist for different categories of risk.

6.2.1 Business Risks Managed by Sustainability

Reputational Risk Impairs a company's brand through negative association.

A common way to categorize business risks that sustainable policies and practices prevent is in terms of reputational, regulatory, operational, strategic, hazard, and financial risk. We now look at these in more detail.

CROSS-LINKAGE

For more on communicating about sustainability, see Chapter 7: Marketing.

CROSS-LINKAGE

For more on government relations, regulatory standards, and product liability, see Chapter 4: Legal Frameworks.

Reputational risk **Reputational risk** impacts customer purchasing decisions by impairing the company's brand through negative association. With greater access to information, industrial accidents can take on the form of high profile news stories that light up social media overnight. Negative stigma associated with environmental and human health impacts can take years to overcome. Responsible risk management and proactive public relations in the event of an accident can go a long way in preserving reputation.

Regulatory risk When a government agency perceives that an industry is creating high risk levels, it may intercede in the market by imposing restrictions on a variety of commercial

---

ETHICAL DECISIONS: Zicam Recalls a Risky Cold Remedy.[9]

Is it ethical to launch a consumer product without disclosing risks of potential side effects? Matrixx Initiatives, manufacturer of the popular cold remedy Zicam, encountered a regulatory and reputational risk when it introduced a nasal gel version of their traditional nasal swab. Complaints came in accusing the product of causing temporary and permanent loss of the smell and taste senses in some users. The U.S. Food and Drug Administration warned patients to quit using the products immediately, Zicam's Cold Remedy Nasal Gel products were recalled, and consumers allegedly injured by the product defect launched a $15.5 million lawsuit. This type of risk has a substantial potential to erode consumer confidence in a company's brand and can be quite costly in the end. The risk of product defect may be reduced by superior quality control. Quality control processes that detect an error before products are dispatched to the market can help ensure against operational risks such as tainted products that lead to product recall or product defect lawsuits.

activities. The volume of resource use may be limited by permits or pricing mecha-nisms, pollution emissions may be subject to a tax or technology standards, licenses to operate may be revoked, and permits for planned expansions may be subject to delays. These challenges are called **regulatory risk**.

Operational risk **Operational risks** are those associated with failing to properly manage operations and supply chain activities. This includes tactical activities tak-ing place in the operation of the organization, or failures on the part of employees, management, equipment, information technology, and other internal processes of a business. Many operational risks are within the control of a company and can be prevented because they arise from internal actions. Routine employee training, quality and safety inspections, management training, proactive equipment main-tenance, state-of-the-art data and premises security systems, and other investments can reduce operational risk.

Operational risks also include supply chain risks, which include poor supplier quality, late deliveries, product or equipment safety issues, high costs, excessive inventory, and other breakdowns in the adequate provision of supplies to a business. Supply chain risks can result from transportation infrastructure problems that prevent deliveries from arriv-ing on time. They can also result from operational problems on the part of suppliers who are unable to deliver goods or services at an acceptable level of quality or within specified time parameters. Consider the range of supply chain risks in Figure 6.2.

Some supply chain risks are impossible to prevent as they are outside of the control of the company, such as natural disasters. These can result in disruptions such as supply

Regulatory Risk When a gov-ernment agency perceives that an industry is creating high risk levels, it may intercede in the market by imposing restrictions on a variety of commercial activities.

Operational Risk Associated with failure to properly manage a company's operation and its supply chain.

CROSS-LINKAGE

For more on managing operational risks see Chapter 9: Operations Management.

CROSS-LINKAGE

For more on reducing supply chain risks, see Chapter 8: Supply Chain Management.

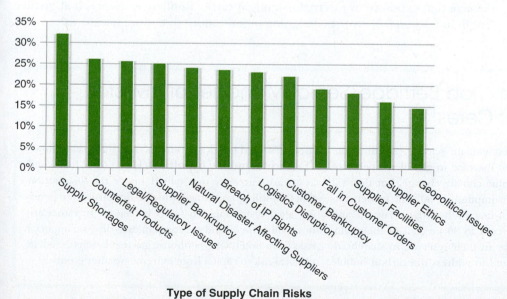

Type of Supply Chain Risks

FIGURE 6.2 Risks that Have Supply Chain Executives "Very Concerned"[10]

Source: SCM World CSCO 2012 Survey, n = 1,312. Used by permission of SCM World.

shortages. The global context of businesses involved in international trade adds additional risks. For example, some actions of suppliers may be legal or ethical in the supplier's region but not in that of the buyers' region. Ethical or legal differences between regions can cause supply chain risks that compromise the reputation of a company.

Strategic Risk Relates to decisions made by executive management that may be high risk but also high reward.

Strategic risk **Strategic risks** are the trade-offs, often made under conditions of uncertainty, which businesses must make to compete in a specific industry at any given time. This risk category relates to decisions made by executive management. Examples include risks associated with mergers and acquisitions, assessment of the competitive environment, social trends and compliance, global currency risk, liquidity, and capital availability. Should the company introduce a new product? Are consumer preferences shifting? Is emerging technology disrupting the market? Should a company acquire its competitor? Companies must remain vigilant of changes in market conditions because emerging risks can undermine the effectiveness of existing business strategies. Strategic risks offer an upside and a downside. The risk may pay off, leading to a competitive advantage, or the risk may cost the company in a variety of ways, depending upon what is at stake and how the risk is managed. The discipline of business strategy offers frameworks that are available to help guide strategic risk decisions.

Hazard Risk Random disruptions from wild card events.

Hazard risk These risks pertain to random disruptions from wild card events. Some hazards could be intentionally malicious—for example, crime, terrorism, or product tampering. Other hazards result from natural forces, such as hurricanes, floods, or wildfires. Excessive wind speeds, severe flooding, widespread power outages, population dislocation, and impaired transportation are all typical results of a hurricane, and each of them would constitute a hazard risk in its own right. These risks must be dealt with through impact mitigation and organizational resilience because avoidance or control is beyond reach. Impact mitigation means reducing the severity of damage that exposure to external risk might cause. Resilience, discussed at greater length in Section 6.5, involves designing organizations to endure hazard risks.

Carbon Bubble Hypothesis Theory that carbon assets are currently over-valued because of the failure to appreciate the risk of legal restrictions on future carbon emissions.

EXPERT INSIGHT: Rob Berridge, Senior Manager of Investor Programs at Ceres[11]

According to the latest climate science, avoiding the 3.6 degrees Fahrenheit increase in global temperature will stave off catastrophic climate change, but this will require foregoing consumption of 80% of proven fossil fuel reserves. According to Berridge, "For oil and gas companies, 50 percent to 80 percent of their valuation is estimated to be in their reserves, so shareholders are now asking them to address the carbon bubble hypothesis and how it may impact their future cash flow." The **carbon bubble hypothesis** is that fossil fuel-based assets are currently over-valued under the assumption that they will be consumed, which is doubtful given pending legal restrictions on GHG emissions. Investors are now calling on oil and gas companies to disclose financial risks from potential greenhouse gas regulations as well as physical risk to capital from extreme weather events.

Financial risk This category relates to internal and external financial challenges. Financial risks arise from the management of company capital, debt, cash flow, and equity. Sustainability impacts financial risk; for instance, if a company is highly dependent upon continued supply of natural resources from resource-stressed area. If legal frameworks were to force companies to internalize the costs of natural capital, company balance sheets would look quite different. The potential for a tax on greenhouse gas emissions, for example, could substantially impact the financial performance of many industries, creating risks for laggards and rewarding sustainable leaders.

> **Financial Risk** Internal and external financial challenges arising from the management of company capital, debt, cash flow, and equity.

6.2.2 Preventable Versus Uncontrollable Risk

> **CROSS-LINKAGE**
>
> For more on mandatory disclosure of sustainability-related financial risks, see Chapter 5: Metrics, Tools, and Reporting: The Role of Finance and Accounting.

An alternative to the traditional categorization of business risks is to prioritize managerial relevance by categorizing risks into preventable and uncontrollable risks. This categorization is important as it allows us to identify those risks we can minimize through planning and operations, and those risks for which we may simply need to prepare to endure.

Preventable risks are those that can be prevented through careful planning and operational excellence. Preventable risks include breakdowns in regular business processes such as employee accidents, machine malfunctions, or poor supplier quality. Managing preventable risks means carefully selecting employees and suppliers, maintaining best practices and codes of conduct, and proactively protecting business continuity. Preventable risks are the low-hanging fruit of risk management because they are foreseeable and within the scope of managerial or employee control.

> **Preventable Risks** Can be prevented through careful planning and operational excellence.

Although many risks to business success stem from within a company—such as a poorly researched investment decision—most businesses already have protocols and best practices in place to manage internal preventable risks. The more challenging types of business risks are those arising from uncontrolled external events. **Uncontrollable risks** are external to the company and outside the scope of the company's control. Sources of external risks include natural disasters, failure of government, or major macroeconomic changes such as a global recession. External risks that are foreseeable can often be mitigated, such as the ongoing misbehavior of a company's supplier. However, unforeseeable external risks simply require endurance through resilience.

> **Uncontrollable Risks** Arise external to the company and outside the scope of the company's control.

Uncontrolled risks are especially challenging as they can have a large impact. Just consider the earthquake that caused the Fukishuma nuclear disaster in Japan, the volcanic eruption in Iceland that spewed a plume of ash across Europe, drought sweeping through the breadbasket of the United States, the global economic recession, and the terrorist attacks of September 11, 2001. Each carried tremendous economic impacts that affected regional if not global travel and trade. Threats to infrastructure such as navigable waterways, highways, bridges, tunnels, and flight patterns are uncontrolled risks. Threats to natural resources such as fresh clean water due to seasonal drought and flood are uncontrolled risks, whereas pollution that threatens fresh water is a controllable risk, meaning it is within the power of the responsible organization to minimize.

Impact mitigation means reducing the severity of damage that exposure to external risk might cause. For example, this may be accomplished through capital investment into high-quality buildings and on-site energy supply, back-up IT support and workaround plans to reduce downtime, as well as through property insurance coverage to recoup the cost of repairs. Risk mitigation also involves reducing exposure in the event of unavoidable risks. Even if external risks are inevitable, a business can fortify its physical presence to withstand impacts, and business owners can take out lines of insurance protection so that after a disaster they are made financially whole again.

6.2.3 Water-Related Business Risks

The water-related risks to business can be categorized in terms of the point of impact to the organization as well as the type of risk. See Table 6.1.

A.1. When water scarcity occurs, water-intensive industries such as energy and food production are directly impacted. Severe droughts can limit energy and agricultural production, which in turn can impact the supply chain of other companies.

A.2. During a water crisis, governments may impose tariffs, quotas, or other limitations on water withdrawals for commercial uses. This can lead to reduced operating capacity, delays, and increased costs.

A.3. If a company's supply chain depends upon impaired water resources in developing countries, there is a risk of reputational damage for frustrated expectations on the part of shareholders and stakeholders. Even if the company is doing its utmost to preserve water access, it may suffer from the mere perception that it is not acting responsibly to steward water resources upon which local communities depend. News outlets and investors will scrutinize water-related risks, even if management does not.

TABLE 6.1

Water-Related Business Risk[12]

Point of Impact / Type of Risk	A. Supply Chain	B. Operations	C. Product Use
1. Hazard	Spikes in commodity prices increase costs	Water supply disruptions can cause business interruption	Scarcity limits sales
2. Regulatory	Water standards impact energy supply	Court settlements that limit operations	Water rights challenged or limited
3. Reputation	Singled out for violating water quality	Inefficient water consumption	Competition for social or environmental uses of water

Source: Adapted from *Treating Water – Sector Report For Engagement: Water Exposure of Food and Beverage Companies,* Robeco Asset Management & World Resources Institute (April 2009).

B.1. Water shortage can interrupt a variety of operations that depend upon abundant suppliers of water as an input for production, irrigation, material processing, cooling, washing, or cleaning. Flooding can interrupt operations by diverting human resources toward disaster response instead of productivity, or by contaminating water supplies necessary for operations.

B.2. Government bodies may impose effluent limitations, water withdrawal limitations, or reallocations of water rights.

B.3. Few issues engender controversy in a local community more than jeopardizing their water supply. Inefficient uses of water or pollution in a population's water supply can lead to a bad reputation.

C.1. Customers who have limited access to clean water will have reduced interest in purchasing water-intensive products.

C.2. Even if a company has solid legal rights to access water, if water resources are poorly managed by government, then infrastructure for commercial and industrial uses may be impaired.

C.3. Corporate water use may compete with the needs of local communities.

If a company's water risk assessment consists in merely measuring water usage and polluted water discharge, they lack a complete picture of their risk profile. That is because water risks are highly dependent on local factors particular to the watershed, ecosystems, communities, and competing uses. Water risk management should go beyond assessing the available amount of water in a region. More nuance is necessary to capture the full risks involved in consuming water in a particular area. For example, of the available water, how much is suitable for human use? How much is necessary to preserve stream flow? How does the local government manage water infrastructure and rights? Do the local communities have sufficient access to water suppliers? All of these factors impact the risk levels associated with water availability and water quality.

6.2.4 Climate Change-Related Business Risks

According to the SEC's *Commission Guidance Regarding Disclosure Related to Climate Change*, "there may be significant physical effects of climate change that have the potential to have a material effect on … personnel, physical assets, supply chain and distribution."[13] These impacts are in addition to sector-specific physical risks.[14] See Table 6.2.

There are concrete benefits from risk identification processes. "The identification of climate risks is a key factor in spurring investment in emissions reductions activities, and in delivering year-on-year emissions reductions." Companies that conduct a comprehensive climate change risk identification process are "six times more likely to make investments [in abatement], and three times more likely to reduce emissions."[15]

6.3 Risk Assessment

Risk assessment is the process used to determine the gravity of harm associated with a potential event, as well as the likelihood that the event will occur. These two variables help determine the risk level associated with a given event, which will be further

TABLE **6.2**	
Physical Risks to Business from Climate Change[16]	
Operations and Facilities	Increased storm intensity, sea-level rise, melting permafrost, temperature extremes, water quality or availability, damaged facilities, impaired efficiency of equipment.
Marketing	Decreased consumer demand for cold-dependent residential and commercial products and services (such as heating fuel, equipment, and services), decreased demand for water- and energy-intensive products or services.
Financial	Credit risks for lenders whose borrowers are located in high-risk areas.
Supply Chain	Risks from dependence on suppliers (especially agricultural products) potentially impacted by extreme weather events.
Regulatory	Risk of increased regulatory compliance costs for greenhouse gas emissions standards.

Source: SEC Rel. No. 33-9106 (Feb. 2, 2010), 75 FR 6290, last accessed May 10, 2014, available at http://www .sec.gov/rules/interp/2010/33-9106.pdf (page 9).

developed in section on materiality, in Section 6.3.2 Risk assessment can be used to determine a wide range of potential adverse events, such as the environmental and human health impacts of pollution from a specific industrial process, or personal injury from product misuse. A risk assessment process is critical to making the best-educated decisions in order to properly prioritize risk responses. The key concepts in risk assessment are measuring risk level, exposure, and vulnerability.[17] An important tool at this stage is scenario planning that can help risk assessment. We conclude this part by identifying a variety of risks to business stemming from water and climate change vulnerability.

6.3.1 Scenario Planning

Companies are constantly faced with making strategic decisions, such as deciding on new products and markets. Just consider the countless business examples: Toyota bet on hybrids; GM bet on fuel cells; Nexen-Opti has bet on coke-to-gas technology. How does a company make such an assessment regarding decisions and their associated risks? One tool is **scenario planning**, "a disciplined method for imagining possible futures" with applications in strategic management, specifically the evaluation strategic options.[18]

Scenario Planning Serves to raise issues and provide context and perspective on the nature of risks and what strategic responses are available.

Scenarios are alternative descriptions of the future. Rather than trying to reduce uncertainty to a single most likely forecast, scenarios try to identify the major forces driving change and the key uncertainties that lead to a wide range of possible future outcomes. Scenarios map out the boundaries of risks for each possible future. Therefore, they provide a context of expectations for generating and evaluating options. Scenario planning begins by identifying critical decisions and driving forces. Next, the organization identifies various risks of each in order to develop possible outcomes or scenarios. Each scenario is then analyzed for threats and opportunities.

Scenario planning serves to raise issues and provide context and perspective on the nature of risks and what strategic responses are available. The scenarios then serve to generate strategic options (e.g., If scenario X occurs, what strategies should we pursue?) and to evaluate their risks and rewards. Once the scenarios have been developed and strategic decisions are made, then the company monitors ongoing change and responds accordingly.

Scenario planning does not remove risks. Rather it allows the organization to make decisions while considering all the risks and rewards associated with the possible options. Scenario planning is a process undertaken by a company to broaden its thinking about the future as a basis for developing and implementing robust strategies. Forecasts using quantitative modeling can be a part of scenario planning used to identifying risks. In order to determine which risks to incorporate into scenario planning, risk managers must first identify which risks are possible, then assess the materiality of these risks to their organization.

6.3.2 Measuring the Materiality of Risk

Material risks should be included in scenario planning and corporate reporting. The use of materiality assessment in probabilistic risk assessment is technically different than the definition of materiality used in the context of financial reporting.

A simple qualitative risk assessment formula can be used order to determine the **materiality** of a risk. This tells us whether the risk posed is high, moderate, or low, significant or insignificant to an organization's objectives.

The two variables of the risk assessment formula are the extent of harm that would happen if the risk were to manifest, and the likelihood that the risk will in fact occur. **Probabilistic risk analysis** uses this formula:

$$\text{Risk Level} = \text{Likelihood of Occurrence (Magnitude of Harm)}$$
$$\text{Risk Level} = L(M)$$

Likelihood of Occurrence (L) depends upon the nature of the risk and the historical frequency of its occurrence. The likelihood of an event's occurrence is somewhere between 0 (for an event with impossible occurrence) and 1 (for actual occurring event). Magnitude of Harm (M) can either be quantitative (measured in monetary or other numerical terms) or qualitative (measured in terms that describe a hierarchy of impact levels).

The key concepts involve determining the magnitude of harm associated with an event, the extent of vulnerability, and the capacity of resilience.[19] **Exposure** is the extent of a system that would be impacted if an event were to occur; **vulnerability** is the capacity of a system to endure shocks to its environmental conditions (discussed at greater length in Section 6.3.3); and **resilience** is the ability of a system to adapt and survive in the event of a disaster.

These elements make up the **magnitude of harm** associated with an event, which is equal to the extent of exposure and vulnerability, less the degree of resilience enjoyed by the impacted system.

CROSS-LINKAGE

For more on reporting material risks to company investors, see Chapter 5: Metrics, Tools, and Reporting: The Role of Finance and Accounting.

Materiality Qualitative assessment of whether a risk is high, medium, or low—in other words, whether it is the kind that needs to be addressed by management.

Probabilistic Risk Analysis Formulaic approach to determining the risk level of a given event.

Exposure The extent of a system that would be impacted if an event was to occur.

Vulnerability The capacity of a system to endure shocks to its environmental conditions.

Resilience The ability of a system to adapt and survive in the event of a disaster.

Magnitude of Harm The extent of exposure and vulnerability, less the degree of resilience enjoyed by the impacted system.

Stated formulaically:

$$\text{Magnitude of Harm} = (\text{Exposure} \times \text{Vulnerability}) - \text{Resilience}$$
$$M = V(E) - R$$

We can see that the lower the exposure and vulnerability, the lower the magnitude of harm. Similarly, magnitude of harm is reduced through higher resilience. This section will explore vulnerability and exposure in greater depth, while the concept of resilience will be discussed in Section 6.5: Risk Management Strategies in Business.

The business risks of natural capital dependency, biodiversity loss, and ecosystem services may very well be material risks, but without adequate tools for applying metrics to natural capital, it is difficult to make this calculation. The majority of companies report little to no information about environmental risks because they perceive them to be immaterial, even though investors are increasingly concerned with these issues.[20] Without measuring environmental performance, it is impossible to properly manage environmental risks.

Companies can develop a materiality matrix in order to put risks in context relevant to stakeholders of the company. See Figure 6.3.

> **CROSS-LINKAGE**
>
> For more on monitoring, materiality, and disclosing environmental risks, see Chapter 5: Metrics, Tools, and Reporting: The Role of Finance and Accounting.

6.3.3 Vulnerability

Vulnerability was originally used in the field of disaster risk management to describe the physical resistance of engineered structures, such as to high winds or earthquakes. The present usage, however, takes a broader application of the term, as it describes the capacity of an organization to withstand adverse effects if faced with a disaster. The extent of an organization's or system's vulnerability depends on its predispositions, susceptibilities, fragilities, weaknesses, deficiencies, and lack of capacities. Cumulative effects of small disasters can lower the overall capacity of a system to deal with future shocks, rendering it more vulnerable over time, similar to the weakening of a human immune system. Adverse effects can be large or small, financial,

FIGURE 6.3 Materiality Matrix of Ford Motor Company[21]

Source: See the Materiality Matrix of Ford Motor Company, Collaborative Action on Climate Risk, Supply Chain Report 2013–14, Accenture & Climate Disclosure Project, page 17 (2014).

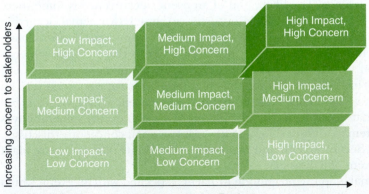

Increasing concern to stakeholders

Low Impact, High Concern | Medium Impact, High Concern | High Impact, High Concern

Low Impact, Medium Concern | Medium Impact, Medium Concern | High Impact, Medium Concern

Low Impact, Low Concern | Medium Impact, Low Concern | High Impact, Low Concern

Increasing current or potential impact on Ford

human, or ecological, and of short or long duration. Economic vulnerabilities result in business interruption from power outage, the inability to access inputs from suppliers, the inability to provide products or services to clients, lost productivity from employees unable to commute to work, and the deferment of planned expenditures as resources are allocated toward recovery efforts.

A system's underlying lack of capacity to deal with extreme scenarios can increase the risk level of activities that depend upon that system functioning.[22] For instance, a water system in a given region may not be capable of withstanding extreme rainfall shortages, and businesses that depend upon that water supply are at risk when those conditions occur. For example, the bottled water company Fiji Water depends upon steady production of pure water from an aquifer in Yaqara Valley. Hypothetically, if the pressure in the aquifer were to drop because of a prolonged drought, artesian wells would fail to produce and bottling activities could be compromised. Risk assessment should include direct risks to impacted systems, such as a failed hydrological system, and also residual risk to other systems that depend upon the primarily impacts system, such as the businesses that depend upon the hydrological system for feedstock into their value chain.

The last 50 years have seen a general increase in the risk and cost of natural disaster, as shown in Figure 6.4. This suggests that global vulnerability and exposure have been increasing.[23]

Over the last five decades, economic losses from extreme weather events (such as hurricane) increased exponentially while economic losses from geological disasters (such as earthquake) increased substantially as well. At the same time, the toll of human life from weather-related disasters fell precipitously while the loss of human life increased from geological disasters.

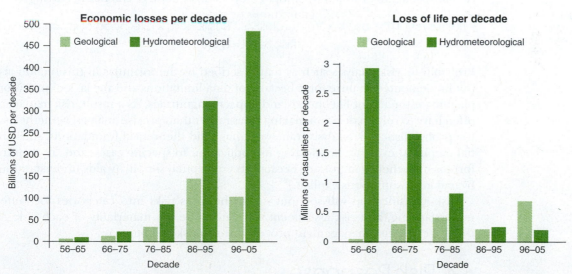

Trends in natural hazard impacts over the five last decades show increasing economic losses and decreasing loss of life associated with hydrometeorological hazards

FIGURE 6.4 The Increasing Cost of Natural Disasters

Source: U.S. System Task Team on the Post-2015 U.N. Development Agenda, Disaster Risk and Resilience, page 6 (2012).

For the most part, high vulnerability and exposure is the result of inappropriate land use and over-development involving environmental mismanagement, poorly planned urbanization, and chronic poverty. Ultimately, vulnerability is a large determinant of overall risk levels. Hazards that spread geographically, such as drought, can reveal vulnerabilities such as inadequate water supply infrastructure in areas that had not previously experienced such extreme rainfall conditions. Social conditions such as poverty or corruption in government can increase vulnerability to all hazards because of potential breakdowns in the provision of public services such as police, fire fighters, environmental regulation, transportation infrastructure, and the like. The vulnerability of communities and businesses is also influenced by false perceptions of risk that lead to lack of motivation to reduce risk, perceived inability to adapt, and unsustainable adaptation to stressors, all of which ultimately increase vulnerability.

Resilience is the opposite of vulnerability. A resilient organization is able to endure and adapt to risks, thriving from changing scenarios at a time when competitors stumble. Resilience is relevant to risk assessment because vulnerability can be reduced through resilient organizational and supply chain design. The topic will be addressed at greater length in Section 6.5: Risk Management Strategies in Business.

6.3.4 Putting It All Together

We now understand the meaning of vulnerability and resilience and can use these concepts in our basic measurement of risk level. Recall that risk assessment is the process of identifying the likelihood and magnitude of harm associated with a given event in order to determine the materiality of that risk to an organization's objectives. Putting it all together, the **risk level formula** of an event is a function of the vulnerability of exposed elements of the affected system, less the extent of resilience of that system, all of which is multiplied by the likelihood of the risk occurring.

Risk Level Formula A function of the vulnerability of exposed elements of the affected system, less the extent of resilience of that system, all of which is multiplied by the likelihood of the risk occurring.

$$\text{Risk Level} = [(\text{Exposure} \times \text{Vulnerability}) - \text{Resilience}] \times \text{Likelihood of Occurrence}$$
$$\text{Risk Level} = L[V(E) - R]$$

Probabilistic risk analysis such as that described by the formulas in this section are not implemented in pure form because of data limitations and the lack of precision plaguing estimates of likelihoods and impact magnitudes. As a result, risk managers often have to rely on decision-making rules rather than precise analysis. Nonetheless, the probabilistic risk analysis framework has solid theoretical foundations, substantial empirical evidence supporting its application to specific cases, and "in its pure form is nonetheless important because its conceptual simplicity aids understanding by making assumptions explicit."[24]

Risk identification will sort out salient business risks into categories for better understanding, and risk assessment will determine the materiality of each risk. At this stage, the risk management process turns to risk response.

6.4 Risk Response

As discussed above, risk response is the determination of the means by which identified, material risks to business should be addressed. The most likely and significant adverse events are laid out before the decision-making authority to determine

GLOBAL INSIGHT: CEO Water Mandate Risk Assessment and Identification[25]

One technique for assessing and identifying water-related risks is hot-spotting. Hot-spotting is a method for identifying reliance on stressed watersheds to enable strategic prioritization of investment into operational efficiency, scenario planning, public relations, and risk management activities at the right locations. Factors that go into a hot-spot assessment are the locations of water stressed regions; the nature of use and effluent in those locations; the percentage of water used by an individual company; allocations of water rights to other parties and for other uses; and ecosystem services that depend on the water resources in that location.

whether the risk can be borne, avoided, mitigated, or shared. There are of course a variety of rubrics for describing risk response alternatives.[26] These four basic risk response alternatives are described in Table 6.3.

Because many risks to business are unavoidable, risk mitigation is a frequently called upon risk response, and therefore will be discussed at greater length.

6.4.1 Bearing Risk

Bearing risk means voluntarily taking on a risk. The most common example of risk bearing we are all familiar with relates to choosing to bear the risk of medical treatment side effects, with the hope that the benefits outweigh the risks. Patients may choose to bear a risk considering the potential benefits versus the likelihood of countervailing adverse consequences of the treatment. If we decide to take the treatment and accept the side effects, this is an example of bearing a risk. For businesses, bearing risk is common to nearly every transaction. Especially in strategic and financial risk situations, bearing risk is often necessary in order to create wealth. Like an individual, an organization should choose to bear risks wisely considering their own risk appetite and situation-specific factors.

Bearing Risk Voluntarily assuming risk.

TABLE **6.3**		

Risk Response Alternatives

Risk Response	Definition	Ideal Scenario
Bearing Risk	Voluntarily assuming risk.	Financial investments and strategic planning, limited unavoidable risks.
Avoiding Risk	Reducing risk likelihood.	Preventable/controllable risks from marketing, operations, and supply chain.
Mitigating Risk	Reducing risk impact.	Unavoidable risks from operations, supply chain, and environmental-social-economic conditions.
Sharing Risk	Spreading risk impact.	When risks could be more efficiently borne by another party.

6.4.2 **Avoiding Risk**

Avoiding risk means reducing the likelihood of risks through behavior change. Unlike bearing, where the organization assumes a risk, here the organization simply changes behavior to avoid the likelihood of a risk occurring. To continue with the medical patient example from above, risk avoidance would involve making behavioral changes to reduce the likelihood of contracting an illness in the first place. There are a number of situations where risk avoidance may be a good strategy. For instance, declining to introduce a product that might harm consumers, instead of merely affixing an ambiguously helpful warning label, is one means of avoiding of risk of product defect liability. After learning that a current supplier may be using child labor, a company can avoid risk of consumer boycott by changing suppliers. A business does not usually stand to gain by exposure to avoidable risks, and avoiding can often be more prudent than bearing risk. Methods for avoiding risks related to sustainability are discussed in other chapters according to business function.

> **CROSS-LINKAGE**
>
> For more on avoiding controllable risks, see Chapters 7–9.

6.4.3 **Mitigating Risk**

Mitigating risk means reducing vulnerability and exposure to unavoidable risk. Mitigation can be accomplished by reducing the amount of assets that are exposed to risks or reducing the severity of damage that exposure to risk might cause. Vulnerability and exposure are discussed above in Section 6.3: Risk Assessment. Reducing vulnerability and exposure of a business can be accomplished through capital investment into high-quality buildings and on-site energy supply, back-up IT support and workaround plans to reduce downtime, as well as property insurance coverage to recoup the cost of repairs. Even if external risks are inevitable, a business can fortify its physical presence to withstand impacts, and business owners can take out lines of insurance protection to expedite and assist financially with the recovery process.

The extent to which a business can mitigate risk depends upon situational factors that provide challenges and opportunities. These include inventory, transportation, outsourcing, environmental conditions, social conditions, and economic conditions. Let's look at these a bit further.

> **CROSS-LINKAGE**
>
> For more on inventory management, see Chapter 9: Operations Management.

Inventory Too much inventory leads to overstock storage costs and possible waste, whereas too little leads to inability to meet consumer demand. Carrying extra inventory to guard against uncertainty is a classic way to mitigate risk. A lean supply chain that minimizes waste and storage overhead may be more vulnerable to disruptions from fluctuations in demand.

> **CROSS-LINKAGE**
>
> For more on transportation, see Chapter 8: Supply Chain Management.

Transportation In order for a company to be responsive to fluctuations in demand, it must have reliable transportation to ship goods to and from warehouses to the sales floor. Transportation costs can fluctuate and availability and space on transport units is limited. Factors such as road congestion, fuel cost, the conditions of road or rail lines impact the degree of risk from transportation.

Outsourcing Globalization has made outsourcing labor and services to foreign countries just another part of doing business. Companies such as Nike and Apple have outsourced their manufacturing, which introduces substantial risk into their supply chain. The further away operations are from the nucleus of control, the harder it is to manage risk. However, outsourcing merely pushes some of the risk onto another entity.

> **CROSS-LINKAGE**
> For more on outsourcing, see Chapter 8: Supply Chain Management.

Environmental Conditions Companies generally need stable environmental conditions in order to succeed. Risks to business from environmental conditions include power outages, flooding, high speed wind events, and other weather patterns that may cause population evacuation or disrupt the normal operation of business. The availability and quality of natural resources can also pose environmental risk. In 2010, 39% of companies had experienced detrimental impacts related to water issues, such as operations disruption from drought, flooding, and declining water quality; expensive on-site pre-treatment; increased water prices; and fines and litigation relating to pollution incidents.[27] Careful land use planning and site-selection for facilities can reduce the risk of operational disruptions, and compliance with environmental laws can reduce the risk of environmental liabilities.

Social Conditions Changes in preferences for working conditions can affect business performance. For example, employee demands for higher wages and benefits can disrupt business operations and impact profitability. Consider the examples of Hostess and Wal-Mart in dealing with the changing social conditions of the labor force. One union protest led Hostess precipitously into bankruptcy. The risk of unionization threatened to disrupt Wal-Mart operations on the most profitable day for retailers of the fiscal year, Black Friday. Sustainable marketing, effective labor relations policies, and organizational ombudsmen can reduce risks from changing social conditions.

Economic Conditions Highly consequential decisions such as where to locate operations can be influenced by economic conditions that can change depending upon government monetary policy and trade barriers such as import and export taxes. Other economic conditions that effect business decisions like how to price products or whether to go through with a merger or acquisition include factors such as consumer confidence, trust between businesses, and the availability of financial support.

6.4.4 Sharing Risk: Insurance

Certain risks, such as extreme weather events, may be unavoidable and subject to partial mitigation only. Businesses can respond to these kinds of risk through **sharing risk**. Businesses can share supply chain risks with suppliers in order to manage inventory surplus or deficit. Operational risks can be shared by outsourcing operations to

> **Sharing Risk** Spreading risk impact through contract.

another party. In these situations, the risk is shifted in terms of who it impacts, but the risk is not reduced in likelihood or in magnitude of impact. However, the risk may be borne by a more efficient risk bearer, meaning that the production of goods and services is impacted less if the risk is borne by the contracting party than if the original party were to bear the risk. A cardinal example of efficient risk sharing is the insurance market. Businesses can allocate the cost of external risks (such as extreme weather events) to an insurance company for a premium; risk is pooled across property owners with varying risk levels who all share the risk with the insurance industry, the relatively efficient risk bearer amongst them. Typically, an insurance company will insure against specified types of risks during a specified time period and will be paid monthly during that interval to step in and compensate the insured in the event of a covered loss. Virtually all industries benefit from insurance coverage, therefore the insurance industry stands in a unique position of influence when it comes to setting standards for risk management.

When disaster hits and a business suffers the loss of a factory or warehouse full of equipment and inventory, the only hope for the owner is that the losses are covered by an insurance policy that provides compensation to the owner up to the replacement cost of what was damaged or destroyed. A good insurance policy will also compensate for lost revenue during the period of business interruption accompanying the loss. For instance, if a hurricane floods a restaurant and interrupts its operations for a month, a good insurance policy will pay to repair and restore the restaurant and will provide cash to compensate for the interval of time where the company was not able to serve customers. Insurance provides a safety net for businesses to shield them from the impacts of risks.

Insurance is the largest industry on the planet, accounting for 7% of the global economy. Insurance has been called the grease that lubricates the global economy. The widespread and extensive scope of business and property insurance coverage that could be triggered by adverse impacts associated with climate change means that climate change will pose a major test to the insurance industry. The insurance industry is intimately involved, from a financial point of view, with virtually every other industry by stepping in when certain kinds of risk manifest.

That is because insurance is the first line of defense for a business or property owner that suffers a weather-related loss. Extreme weather events have tangibly increased in frequency and cost across the globe, with inflation-adjusted insurance claim values more than doubling every decade since the 1980s. Climate change is projected to impose $1.2 trillion of losses in 2013 alone. "We are already vulnerable to the impacts of weather related natural catastrophes. We expect climate change to compound the problems," says Swiss Re Natural Hazards Expert Megan Linkin.[28] Climate change increases the vulnerability of property and business owners, leading to a greater number of loss-events and a greater amount of damage.

In-house insurance industry experts rely on climate science to assist in the quantification of risk and to ensure model accuracy. Climate change risk assessment also helps diversify the exposure of insured assets. Further, climate science enables the insurance industry to put a better price on the risks undertaken by their clients. For instance, in the era of sea-level rise, building a manufacturing plant in a low-lying area near the coast involves a risk of flood that building the plant in an elevated area would not pose, so the cost of insurance premiums for that construction project

"With 40 percent of industrial insurance claims that [our company] now pays out being due to natural catastrophes, climate change represents a threat to our business," according to a leading global insurance company Allianz. High wind events such as tropical storms, hurricanes, and tornadoes, as well as hail damage, wildfires, and floods, all can cause major damage to a business or property, and all are likely to increase in frequency above the historic averages according to climate change forecasts. The insurance industry is poised to make a substantial positive impact on corporate sustainability by encouraging climate change mitigation and adaptation initiatives across agriculture, transportation, manufacturing, residential construction, and other sectors.

should be more expensive to better reflect the potential for incurring loss. Climate science also enables insurers to communicate risks more effectively to the public and clients, promote adaptation measures, and to incorporate loss-prevention measures into new projects. When new buildings are constructed with insurance proceeds after a loss, the time is ripe to renovate the design in ways that both reduce climate change impacts (say, through energy-efficient heating and cooling) and adapt to climate change impacts (say, with grey-water capture and recycling).

Risk identification, risk assessment, and risk response form the heart of the Enterprise Risk Management continuum. We now conclude with two nearly universal business strategies for risk management: continuity planning and resilience.

6.5 Risk Management Strategies in Business

Businesses can take on numerous proactive strategies to address identified risks. For organizational risks faced by the traditional brick-and-mortar company, businesses should conduct business continuity planning. To reduce vulnerability to unavoidable risks, principles of resilience should inform organizational design.

6.5.1 Business Continuity Planning

Risk management involves developing plans to address wide range of risk situations. **Business continuity planning** is the process of addressing possible disruptions in business functions.

There are four stages to business continuity planning: 1) conduct a business impact analysis; 2) identify and implement a process to recover critical business functions; 3) prepare a core team to manage a business disruption; and 4) conduct employee drills and training for a variety of risks in order to evaluate the effectiveness of the business continuity plan.[30] Although employees may consider the random fire drill to be an inconvenience, business continuity preparedness is a critical strength. In 2008, half of surveyed business continuity decision-makers had invoked their business continuity plan at least one time in the last 5 years; just 3 years later in 2011, 61%

Business Continuity Planning
The process of anticipatory preparation for disruptions in business functions to avoid being caught by surprise.

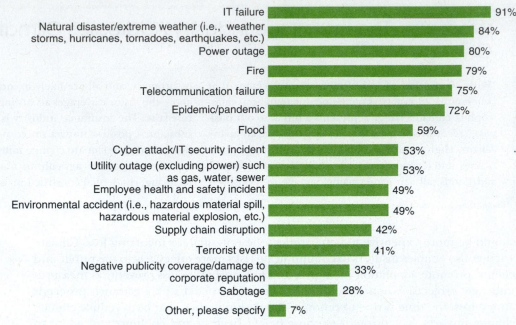

Base: 220 global business continuity decision-makers and influencers that have or are planning scenario specific BCPs (2011)

FIGURE 6.5 Risk Situations Addressed in Business Continuity Plans

Source: Stephanie Balaouras, *The State of Business Continuity Preparedness*, Disaster Recovery Journal, page 22 (Winter 2012). Contacts available here: http://www.drj.com/drj1.html. Used by permission of Disaster Recovery Journal.

of respondents had relied on their business continuity plan in the same time span. The main reasons why emergency responses were needed came down to extreme weather and natural disasters, power outages, information technology failures, and building fires.[31] Figure 6.5 shows the risk situations that are addressed in traditional business continuity plans.

Business continuity planning can address a wide range of risk categories and enable an organization to maintain operations when others might experience disruptions.

6.5.2 Resilience

As described earlier, resilience is the ability of a system to endure, adapt, and even improve when a risk occurs, which can be called maintaining system function in the event of disturbance.[32] Global business risks are systemic in nature, and a system – unlike an object – may show resilience not by returning exactly to its previous state, but instead by finding different ways to carry out essential functions; that is, by adapting. Organizations are less vulnerable when they are designed to be resilient. Resilience, the opposite of vulnerability, is necessary for a system to survive because not all risks are avoidable. Resilient systems will not only survive a disaster; they will have enhanced capabilities or improved competitive position after a disaster. What makes a system resilient? Components of organizational resilience are robustness, redundancy, resourcefulness, and recovery. See Figure 6.6.

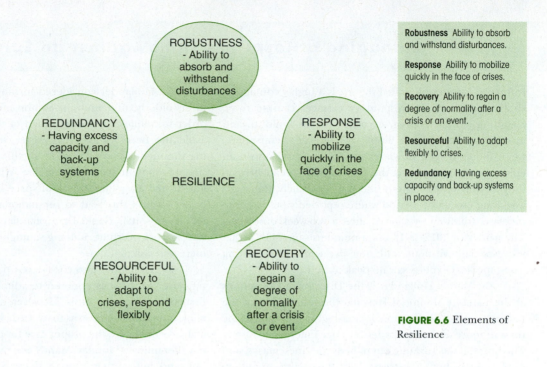

Robustness Ability to absorb and withstand disturbances.

Response Ability to mobilize quickly in the face of crises.

Recovery Ability to regain a degree of normality after a crisis or an event.

Resourceful Ability to adapt flexibly to crises.

Redundancy Having excess capacity and back-up systems in place.

FIGURE 6.6 Elements of Resilience

Key Terms

Discussion Questions

1. Consider the risks covered in Figure 6.5: Business Continuity Planning. Do you believe businesses preparing for the most likely or most impactful risks?

2. Does your business utilize any elements of the enterprise risk management system? Explain.

3. What kinds of risks has your company encountered in the last few years? Answer in terms of the categories and types of risks discussed in this chapter.

| CASE 1 | **Managing a Hospital's Fight Against an Epic Flu[33]** |

Influenza, commonly called the *flu*, is a highly contagious viral infection of the respiratory passages causing fever, coughing, severe aching, excessive mucus buildup, and in extreme cases, death. Every year in every hemisphere, when the cold spell of winter sets in, the flu takes on an epidemic proportion, as the flu is easily spread by sniffling victims venturing out into public. Usually, there is a weeklong escalation period where reported cases begin to increase, followed by a peak, then a two-week downturn. The winter of 2012–2013 saw a unique strain, H3N2, that was especially virulent, and after five weeks of escalating cases, medical experts saw no peak in sight.

Dr. Mandy Hollander is the Director of Operations at the Lamont Memorial Hospital located outside of the nation's capital. She became increasingly concerned as the flu sent more and more patients to her Emergency Room. The hospital was running out of beds, vaccines, masks, and staff. Many of her staff became sick themselves, unable to tend to victims. As the cases increased, her facilities began to be overwhelmed. To complicate matters, the Presidential Inauguration was scheduled to take place in a matter of weeks, which usually brought a million visitors to town to celebrate the most recent national election. Dr. Hollander saw a perfect storm brewing.

Hospitals in other parts of the country had to expand their urgent care centers by propping up tents outside in order to provide additional space for flu victims. These tents provided little comfort during the icy cold of January, but seemed necessary in order to quarantine flu victims from other patients in the hospital who might be especially vulnerable to the virus. What if patients staying in the tents happened to perish because of inclement weather or insufficient attention from overwhelmed medical staff?

Dr. Hollander considered turning away all but children, elderly, and immune-compromised flu victims in order to manage the patient load of the hospital and to avoid the need for tents. However, she feared instructing the medical staff to follow anything but their professional judgment about patient care. What if a patient who was turned away due to lack of space happened to die at home—would this lead to reputational harm or liability for the hospital? Could Dr. Hollander risk requiring her staff to work overtime, if doing so might expose the staff to increased risk of illness?

Dr. Hollander also considered prioritizing local victims over tourists, as opposed to admitting patients on a first-come, first-serve basis. However, she was hesitant to allow operational concerns to override her staff's best medical judgment as to the proper care for patients. With every day seemingly a Monday, Mandy was overworked, stressed out, and not getting enough sleep. She eventually contracted the flu herself and was bed-ridden at home just one week prior to the Presidential Inauguration. She had to make some tough decisions and provide instruction to her diminishing medical staff before another million potential flu victims arrived in the capital.

In addition to the questions raised in this case, answer the following questions.

1. To what risks is the hospital exposed? Qualitatively describe the risk level of the risks you identify.

2. What risk responses are available for the Lamont Memorial Hospital?

3. How can the Enterprise Risk Management continuum improve the hospital's risk response in time for next flu season?

Further Research

For a science and policy-based discussion of global climate change risks by leading climate scientist James Hansen, see the TED Talk "Why I Must Speak Out About Climate Change."

For a comprehensive review of the current global risk landscape, including a graphic for impact and likelihood of economic, environmental, geopolitical, societal, and technological risks, see *Global Risks 2014*, World Economic Forum, page 16, Figure 1.1 (Ninth Edition, 2014).

For a real-life story of supplier responses to a catastrophic flood, see Thomas Fuller, *Thailand Flooding Cripples Hard-Drive Suppliers*, The New York Times (November 6, 2011).

For strategy on managing unpredictable supply chain risks, see David Simchi-Levi, William Schmidt & Yehua Wei, *From Superstorms to Factory Fires: Managing Unpredictable Supply-Chain Disruptions*, Harvard Business Review (January – February 2014).

Harvard Business Review Case: David Robinson, *A Primer on the Management of Risk and Uncertainty* (May 7, 2007), Prod. #: ROT045-PDF-ENG.

Endnotes

1 PricewaterhouseCoopers, *Measuring and Managing Total Impact: A New Language for Business Decisions* (September 2013), last accessed May 10, 2014, available at http://pwc.blogs.com/files/measuring-and-managing-total-impact-230913.pdf.

2 Coral Davenport, *Industry Awakens to Threat of Climate Change*, The New York Times, A1, January 23, 2014.

3 See the website on Saving Wildlife, Dawn, last accessed May 10, 2014, available at http://www.dawn-dish.com/us/dawn/savingwildlife.

4 See Fresh Del Monte Produce Inc., "Q2 2010 Earnings Call Transcript," August 3, 2010, last accessed May 10, 2014, available at http://seekingalpha.com/article/218349-freshdel-monte-produce-inc-q2-2010-earnings-call-transcript.

5 Stephanie Balaouras, *The State of Business Continuity Preparedness*, Disaster Recovery Journal, page 20 (Winter 2012).

6 Committee of Sponsoring Organizations (COSO) of the Treadway Commission, *Enterprise Risk Management: Integrated Framework Document* (2004).

7 *ibid.*

8 Robert Kaplan and Anette Mikes, *Managing Risks: A New Framework*, Harvard Business Review Blog (2012).

9 See U.S. Food and Drug Administration website for product recall press releases, last accessed May 10, 2014, available at http://www.fda.gov/Safety/Recalls/ucm332787.htm.

10 Source: SCM World CSCO 2012 Survey, n = 1,312.

11 Avery Fellow, *Investors Demand Climate-Risk Disclosure in 2013 Proxies*, Bloomberg Sustainability (February 25, 2013), last accessed May 10, 2014, available at http://www.bloomberg.com/news/2013-02-25/investors-demand-climate-risk-disclosure-in-2013-proxies.html.

12 Adapted from *Treating Water – Sector Report For Engagement: Water Exposure of Food and Beverage Companies*, Robeco Asset Management & World Resources Institute (April 2009).

13 SEC Rel. No. 33-9106 (Feb. 2, 2010), 75 FR 6290, page 9, last accessed May 10, 2014, available at http://www.sec.gov/rules/interp/2010/33-9106.pdf.

14 For a sector-specific discussion of physical risks from climate change, see *Physical Risks from Climate Change: A Guide for Companies and Investors on Disclosure and Management of Climate Impacts*, Oxfam America, Calvert Investments, Ceres, page 6 (May 2012), last accessed May 10, 2014, available at http://www.calvert.com/NRC/literature/documents/sr_Physical-Risks-from-Climate-Change.pdf.

15 SEC Rel. No. 33-9106 (Feb. 2, 2010), 75 FR 6290, page 9, last accessed May 10, 2014, available at http://www.sec.gov/rules/interp/2010/33-9106.pdf.

16 *Collaborative Action on Climate Risk*, Supply Chain Report 2013–14, Accenture & Climate Disclosure Project, page 17 (2014).

17 Lavell, A., M. Oppenheimer, C. Diop, J. Hess, R. Lempert, J. Li, R. Muir-Wood, and S. Myeong, *2012: Climate Change: New Dimensions in Disaster Risk, Exposure, Vulnerability, and Resilience*, in: MANAGING THE RISKS OF EXTREME EVENTS AND DISASTERS TO ADVANCE CLIMATE CHANGE ADAPTATION [Field, C.B., V. Barros, T.F. Stocker, D. Qin, D.J. Dokken, K.L. Ebi, M.D. Mastrandrea, K.J. Mach, G.-K. Plattner, S.K. Allen, M. Tignor, and P.M. Midgley (eds.)], A SPECIAL REPORT OF WORKING GROUPS I AND II OF THE INTERGOVERNMENTAL PANEL ON CLIMATE CHANGE (IPCC). Cambridge University Press, Cambridge, UK, and New York, NY, USA, pp. 25–64.

18 Paul J. H. Schoemaker, *Scenario Planning: A Tool for Strategic Thinking*, MIT Sloan Review (January 15, 1995).

19 Cardona, O.D., M.K. van Aalst, J. Birkmann, M. Fordham, G. McGregor, R. Perez, R.S. Pulwarty, E.L.F. Schipper, and B.T. Sinh, *2012: Determinants of Risk: Exposure and Vulnerability*, in: MANAGING THE RISKS OF EXTREME EVENTS AND DISASTERS TO ADVANCE CLIMATE CHANGE ADAPTATION [Field, C.B., V. Barros, T.F. Stocker, D. Qin, D.J. Dokken, K.L. Ebi, M.D. Mastrandrea, K.J. Mach, G.-K. Plattner, S.K. Allen, M. Tignor, and P.M. Midgley (eds.)], A SPECIAL REPORT OF WORKING GROUPS I AND II OF THE INTERGOVERNMENTAL PANEL ON CLIMATE CHANGE (IPCC), Cambridge University Press, Cambridge, UK, and New York, NY, USA, pp. 65–108.

20 KPMG, Fauna & Flora International & ACCA, *Is Natural Capital a Material Issue? An Evaluation of the Relevance of Biodiversity and Ecosystem Services to Accountancy Professionals and the Private Sector*, page 34 (September 2013).

21 See the Materiality Matrix of Ford Motor Company, *Collaborative Action on Climate Risk, Supply Chain Report 2013–14*, Accenture & Climate Disclosure Project, page 17 (2014).

[22] Cardona, O.D., M.K. van Aalst, J. Birkmann, M. Fordham, G. McGregor, R. Perez, R.S. Pulwarty, E.L.F. Schipper, and B.T. Sinh, *2012: Determinants of Risk: Exposure and Vulnerability*, in: MANAGING THE RISKS OF EXTREME EVENTS AND DISASTERS TO ADVANCE CLIMATE CHANGE ADAPTATION [Field, C.B., V. Barros, T.F. Stocker, D. Qin, D.J. Dokken, K.L. Ebi, M.D. Mastrandrea, K.J. Mach, G.-K. Plattner, S.K. Allen, M. Tignor, and P.M. Midgley (eds.)], A SPECIAL REPORT OF WORKING GROUPS I AND II OF THE INTERGOVERNMENTAL PANEL ON CLIMATE CHANGE (IPCC), Cambridge University Press, Cambridge, UK, and New York, NY, USA, pp. 65–108.

[23] U.S. System Task Team on the Post-2015 U.N. Development Agenda, *Disaster Risk and Resilience*, page 6 (2012).

[24] Lavell, A., M. Oppenheimer, C. Diop, J. Hess, R. Lempert, J. Li, R. Muir-Wood, and S. Myeong, *2012: Climate Change: New Dimensions in Disaster Risk, Exposure, Vulnerability, and Resilience*, in: MANAGING THE RISKS OF EXTREME EVENTS AND DISASTERS TO ADVANCE CLIMATE CHANGE ADAPTATION [Field, C.B., V. Barros, T.F. Stocker, D. Qin, D.J. Dokken, K.L. Ebi, M.D. Mastrandrea, K.J. Mach, G.-K. Plattner, S.K. Allen, M. Tignor, and P.M. Midgley (eds.)], A SPECIAL REPORT OF WORKING GROUPS I AND II OF THE INTERGOVERNMENTAL PANEL ON CLIMATE CHANGE (IPCC). Cambridge University Press, Cambridge, UK, and New York, NY, USA, pp. 25–64, 43.

[25] See the United Nations' website on the CEO Water Mandate, last accessed May 10, 2014, available at http://ceowatermandate.org/water-assessment-tools-methods/accounting-needs-functions/risk-assessment-and-identification/.

[26] For risk sharing alternatives, see Chapter 7 of Clifford F. Gray & Erik W. Larson, PROJECT MANAGEMENT: THE MANAGERIAL PROCESS, McGraw-Hill (2011).

[27] According to Carbon Disclosure Project, *Water Disclosure 2010 Global Report*, page 15.

[28] *See* Evan Mills, "The Greening of Insurance," Vol. 338 *Science* No. 6113, pages 1424–1425 (December 2012).

[29] *ibid.*

[30] See the page for Business Continuity Plan at Ready.gov, in collaboration with the Federal Emergency Management Agency, last accessed May 10, 2014, available at http://www.ready.gov/business/implementation/continuity.

[31] Stephanie Balaouras, *The State of Business Continuity Preparedness*, Disaster Recovery Journal, page 24 (Winter 2012).

[32] Brian Walker & David Salt, *Resilience Practice: Building Capacity to Absorb Disturbance and Maintain Function* (Island Press 2012).

[33] Jenny Gold, *Flu Wave Stresses Out Hospitals*, National Public Radio, January 15, 2013.

PART III

Implementation

CHAPTER 7

Marketing

FROM SUPERBOWL ADS TO VIRAL VIDEOS

One of the most highly televised events in the United States is the Super Bowl, the championship match-up concluding the National Football League season. Television commercial spots begin at $3,000,000 with an average viewership of 111,000,000 people, providing the greatest possible exposure any advertising executive could hope for. In 2011, German-based BMW took out an advertisement spot during the televising of Super Bowl XLV. The commercial was intended to showcase the diesel-powered 2011 BMW 3-series and distinguish this new diesel engine from those of the 1980's, which spouted soot from their tailpipes and had engine noise issues. Although BMW's diesel technology means cleaner burning, environmentally superior fuel with better mileage, the commercial focused primarily on the sporty aesthetics of the new edition. The sleek, new diesel 3-series is shown powering past an older model spewing dark clouds and struggling to move. The advertising established that the "greener" version of BMW's latest car was just as high-performing and luxurious as gasoline-based models. This was a key marketing strategy as some consumer segments still think *green* means poor quality and less functionality. BMW's international green marketing provided valuable information to a United States audience about new changes to diesel technology that even an inebriated Super Bowl viewing party-goer could process.

A completely different sustainable marketing ad comes from TOMS Shoes, in the form of a Christmas-themed philanthropic campaign. The company paid virtually nothing to publicize its campaign, but rather developed a short YouTube video with the intention of making it go viral; that is, the content was so compelling that viewers would go out of their way to share the advertisement with others through social media networks, creating broad exposure based on goodwill rather than paid media. The video is a digital animation of shoes and snowflakes with dramatically-rendered

"We need to harness the creativity and the sophistication of marketing, and its methodologies, for human health and environmental sustainability."

—*Ed Mayo*, **CHIEF EXECUTIVE, NATIONAL CONSUMER COUNCIL (2005)**[1]

"Organizations bear economic, legal, and ethical obligations to provide useful information about the risks and benefits of their products, policies, and services. [...] Financial analysts estimate that 70% of a typical private firm's assets are intangibles, like goodwill, that can be lost when communications fail."

—*U.S. Food and Drug Administration*[2]

189

LEARNING OBJECTIVES

After completing this chapter, you should be able to:

1. Understand the role of marketing in sustainable business, and explain sustainable marketing trends affecting SMEs.
2. Understand the legal and ethical boundaries of marketing sustainability.
3. Explain the development of a business strategy for marketing sustainability.
4. Explain the purpose of third-party certification of marketing claims.

versions of Christmas carol melodies playing in the background. The video explains that TOMS will donate one pair of shoes for every pair they sell for the Project Holiday campaign. The goal for the campaign was to provide 30,000 pairs of shoes to children in Ethiopia. These donated shoes would help prevent the soil-transmitted disease Podoconiosis, affecting more than 1,000,000 people in Ethiopia caused by walking barefoot in soil that is rich in volcanic silica. Silica is a fine glass that can penetrate the lymphatic system and cause swelling in the feet and legs, ulcers, and ultimately infections. The video concludes with suggestions for how the viewer can become personally involved in the campaign - in addition to simply purchasing a pair of TOMS Shoes. This form of sustainable marketing appeals to the viewer's sense of social responsibility and depends upon the collaborative response of viewers to disseminate the message far and wide. The campaign goal was exceeded by 23% and through earned social media. TOMS Shoes, in collaboration with conscientious consumers, were able to substantially improve the quality of life for thousands of children in poverty with an advertisement that cost them virtually nothing.

The examples of BMW and TOMS Shoes demonstrate the spectrum of strategies companies can use to market sustainability. Whether it is the environmental attributes of products or the social causes of a company, sustainability marketing is the critical step of communicating information about sustainable performance to potential consumers. However, marketing sustainability is different from conventional marketing in many important ways, and there are a number of unique opportunities and challenges presented by these differences.

7.1 Introduction: Marketing Sustainability

Marketing Introducing an offering to the market in such a way as to inform prospective customers of the attributes of the product or service and inducing them to purchasing it.

Marketing Sustainability Addressing the benefits of a product or service and consumer expectations about the company's social, economic, and environmental responsibility.

Marketing a product or service means introducing an offering to the market in such a way as to inform prospective customers of the attributes of the product or service and inducing them into purchasing it. Marketing is the link between innovation and profitability, connecting new products and services with potential buyers. It involves creating consumer demand by persuading potential consumers that the product or service would be beneficial to them in some way. It also involves satisfying consumer demand by informing the target audience as to how new products and services address specific needs.

Sustainable marketing has similar goals as traditional marketing - to encourage sales. However, it differs in important aspects because of the unique claims made by companies offering sustainable products or services. **Marketing sustainability** means addressing the benefits of a product or service and consumer expectations about the company's social, economic, or environmental responsibility.

7.1.1 Conventional Marketing Versus Marketing Sustainability

Marketing sustainability differs in a few substantial ways from conventional marketing. First, sustainable or green attributes can't stand alone. Customers need other reasons to buy, such as price, quality, and service. The green attribute is just another incentive. Consider Chiquita, which certifies bananas through the Rainforest Alliance program, discussed in Section 7.4: Certification Programs. The certification is a valuable attribute for environmentally conscious consumers, but the bananas still have to look and taste top notch in order to drive sales.

Second, although we know from corporate strategy that revenue can be raised through either increasing volume of sales or increasing price, when selling sustainable products raising price is not always an available option—only a small segment of the market for sustainable products is willing to pay a price premium.

Third, the issue of market segmentation and talking to different niches is especially important in marketing sustainability. Numerous companies have developed different pitches to reach different niches for the same product line. For example, Office Depot developed a catalog dedicated just to selling green products, but these products also appear in the general catalog. To see how different market niches may be approached, consider the contrasting assumptions between conventional marketing and marketing sustainability shown in Table 7.1.

TABLE 7.1

Conventional Marketing v. Marketing Sustainability

Conventional Marketing	Marketing Sustainability
• Environmentally superior products do not function as effectively as ones made with traditional practices.	• Today's green products are healthier, less toxic, more practical and convenient, and better for future generations.
• Green consumers are predominantly women between ages of 30 and 49 with children and better-than-average education.	• 83% of the United States population can be classified as involved in green values, activities, and purchasing habits.
• The company communicates with customers through unilateral paid advertising, highlighting product benefits to end users.	• The company actively solicits consumer feedback and advertises word of mouth, highlighting the values that went into their product or service.
• The company sells, acting in a secretive manner, competing, departmentalized, and driven by short-term profit maximization.	• The company educates, acting in a transparent manner, cooperating, holistic, and driven by the long-term triple bottom line.
• Products are viewed from cradle to grave, globally sourced, and made one-size-fits-all.	• Products are viewed from cradle to cradle, locally sourced, and tailored to suit nuances between regions.
• Marketing is reactive.	• Marketing is proactive.

Source: Adapted from Jacquelyn Ottman, *The New Rules of Green Marketing: Strategies, Tools, and Inspiration for Sustainable Branding*, 22–23 (2011). Used by permission of J. Ottman Consulting.

MANAGERIAL INSIGHT: The Emerging Market for Sustainability, by Jonathan M. Estes[3]

"With the combination of growing global concern for the environment, increasing energy costs and more informed consumers, entrepreneurs and investors are attracted to the new opportunities enabled by the emerging green movement. There are still many significant gaps in products and services in every industry, generating a vacuum of supply[.]"

The approach needed to market the sustainable performance of a company and its products or services will employ substantially different assumptions when compared with conventional marketing strategies.

7.1.2 Segmenting the Market for Sustainable Products

Are consumers actually interested in sustainable products? If so, which consumer segments? What aspects of the complex field of sustainability appeal to each consumer segment? This section answers these questions.

The demand for green products in the United States emerged with the cultural revolution of the 1960–70s, driven predominantly by middle-age women with children and better-than-average education. This demographic still leads in influence over the green market today because, in many households, the female makes most of the decisions with respect to which products to bring home from the store. Marketing a business's products or services that are based on principles of sustainability appeals to the largely female demographic for two primary reasons: men tend to be less responsive than women to information regarding threats to general safety, health, and environmental degradation,[4] and historically women have predominantly expressed nurturing instincts oriented toward the next generation.[5]

It would be incorrect to think the only consumers to which a sustainable company could successfully market is middle-age well-educated mothers, although this segment largely fueled the emergence of environmentally- and socially-conscientious consumerism. Today, approximately 83% of the adult consumer population of the United States is one of four shades of green, with different reasons for preferring sustainable products and services.[6]

The Natural Marketing Institute found that adult consumers across developed countries can be segmented according to their attitude toward sustainability issues into the following categories: (1) **Lifestyle of Health and Sustainability (LOHAS)**; (2) **Naturalites**; (3) **Drifters**; (4) **Conventionals**; and (5) **Unconcerneds**.[7]

In the United States in particular, sustainably created products now appeal to over 80% of the adult population for one or more reasons, with all but the Unconcerneds segment providing unique sustainable marketing opportunities. These characteristics are shown in Table 7.2.

Lifestyle of Health and Sustainability Consumer segment consisting of early adopters of sustainable products who are loyal to brand, influential in their community, and choose green for planet's sake.

Naturalites Consumer segment consisting of those who seek safer product alternatives for household safety.

Drifters Consumer segment consisting of those merely driven by trends with no integration of values into lifestyle or purchases.

Conventionals Consumer segment consisting of those who pursue recycling, reusing, repurposing, and reducing waste as a form of cutting costs.

Unconcerneds Consumer segment consisting of those who are unlikely to care about sustainability.

TABLE 7.2

U.S. Consumer Segmentation According to Sustainability Concerns

Consumer Segmentation	Lifestyle of Health and Sustainability (19% = 43 million)	Naturalites (15% = 34 million)	Drifters (25% = 57 million)	Conventionals (24% = 53 million)	Unconcerneds (17% = 39 million)
DEMOGRAPHICS: (AT LEAST 50% OF EACH SEGMENT)	Married, educated, middle-age, female across the U.S.	Least college educated, lowest income, Southern U.S., African American	Younger, middle-class, concentrated in coastal cities, larger families	Males in mid-to-late forties, highest incomes, some retired, good credit	Young males, Southern U.S., below-average income, low education levels
MOTIVATION:	Less sensitive to price for green products, skeptical of paid media, deeply committed to global causes	See the connection between environmental protection and personal health, seek to avoid exposure to chemicals	Half wish they did more to advance sustainability, get satisfaction from joining a cause	Driven by practical reasons, green for the sake of reduced costs, ingenuity and heartland values	Least concerned consumer, least likely to boycott a brand, no sense of responsibility
BEHAVIOR:	Early adopters, loyal to brand, influential in community, green for planet's sake	Seek safer product alternatives, attitudinal-behavioral disconnect exists because of income	Driven by trends, no integration of values into lifestyle or purchases	Recycling, reusing, repurposing, reducing waste and cutting costs	Less than a quarter recycle, unlikely to promote sustainability

Source: Adapted from Natural Marketing Institute (NMI), *2009 LOHAS Consumer Trends Database*® (All Rights Reserved).

According to the Natural Marketing Institute, the consumer segments LOHAS, Naturalites, Drifters, Conventionals, and Unconcerneds exist in many developed countries across the world, including Brazil, the United Kingdom, France, Germany, Italy, Russia, and Japan.[8] Although demographics change from nation to nation, the motivation and behavior of these segments is common wherever they are found.

Bear in mind that a company can market the same product to different segments of consumers at the same time, simply by emphasizing the product attributes that appeal to each consumer. Non-overlapping marketing channels—television, internet, satellite radio, and so on—allow companies to market to different consumer groups using different messaging and emphasizing different features. Indeed, some businesses even downplay the sustainable nature of products so that consumers will not infer that product quality was somehow traded off for environmental protection. For example, an organic winery may omit *organic* from their bottles just to prevent the mistaken consumer from thinking that product quality was sacrificed in exchange for organic growing practices.

When developing marketing material, it is critical to bear in mind the need for unique messaging for each consumer segment.

ETHICAL DECISIONS: "Dissing" Competitors for Lacking Sustainability

If a company goes all-in on sustainability, it will likely want to leverage those investments into marketing advantages, specifically product differentiation, brand enhancement, and price premiums. Consider the case of chicken eggs. Factory farming techniques enable large companies to produce eggs at massive scales through industrialized processes and conditions. This allows the larger farms to undercut smaller farms on product price. In order to remain competitive, smaller farms that engage in sustainable practices can point out the differences in how they do business. That said, is it ethical for a sustainable company to run an advertisement that discourages its customers from purchasing from its unsustainable competitors? An excerpt from the product packaging for a dozen eggs from the family-owned egg company, Pete and Gerry's Eggs, illustrates how one company has handled this question.

Our "cage-free hens live in clean, spacious barns with access to pasture during the warmer months," whereas, "by contrast, most of America's eggs are produced on giant factory farms, where millions of hens spend their lives confined in small cages. We think that's an unhappy and unhealthy way to live."[9]

7.1.3 Trends In Marketing Sustainability: Avenues for SMEs

Clearly, much has changed about the market for sustainable products and services, the demographics of which will be explored in the Section 7.2. For now, note a few general trends about sustainability marketing.[10]

Tough financial times flowing from the lingering global economic recession of 2008, unemployment, and austerity have encouraged many people to reconsider what they truly need, and products characterized by value and responsibility can appear more fetching in the eyes of budget-conscious consumers. The combination of a depressed economy with growing environmental awareness serves to accentuate the appeal of sustainable products and services. The vast majority of adult U.S. consumers are interested in protecting their health, environment, and surrounding society,[11] creating opportunities for green marketing.

CROSS-LINKAGE

For more on the rapid growth of markets for sustainable products and services, see Chapter 1: Introduction to Sustainable Business.

While there are pockets of consumer apathy about sustainability, this attitude is clearly in the minority. Environmentally friendly packaging has already become an important concern to the majority of consumers.[12] Actions such as using reusable canvas bags instead of taking the "paper or plastic" option at grocery checkout are becoming routine across the United States.[13] The majority of consumers in the United States aim to be more conservative with their domestic energy use and consumption levels,[14] suggesting that (1) sustainable practices are being incorporated into consumer lifestyles and therefore consumers are more literate about the issues of sustainability and the ways in which energy use and resource consumption impacts their livelihood, and (2) sustainable conduct reduces costs not just for multinational organizations but also at the smallest scale, the single family unit.

Consumers, NGOs, and elected officials have begun to seek greater environmental leadership from corporations, and assurances that the processes and practices of companies do not sacrifice the welfare of people or the environment. To ameliorate these concerns, tangible proof of sustainability is key, which can be provided in a number of ways. Advertising in various media, publication of in-house reports, and undergoing independent certification programs can demonstrate the sustainability performance of a company.

Consumers have developed sophistication about sustainability – demonstrating greater understanding of its scope, depth, and implications. Yet, consumers in each segment are generally driven by just one primary concern - for instance, fair labor, pollution, product safety, or value. Products that offer sustainability benefits are growing in market share across the consumer landscape in part because they involve fewer trade-offs than previous generations of the eco-friendly labeled products of the 1990s.

The majority of consumers promote sustainability with personal action such as recycling, using alternative transportation, donating to sustainability non-profits, purchasing offsets, and myriad other efforts to reduce individual and family impacts and to promote sustainable businesses. Corporate and public-interest informational campaigns have permeated across product markets (vehicles, home appliances, apparel, personal care products, food, cleaning products, etc.) and across service markets (transportation, entertainment, logistics, supply chain management, etc.). Sustainable products now compete in all of these markets and the vast majority of consumers are informed to an appreciable extent about sustainability.

These trends point to a transforming marketplace for goods and services where sustainability is a driver of consumer purchasing. Growth in market share for sustainable products and services creates a variety of opportunities for small- and mid-sized enterprises (SMEs). See Table 7.3.

The **Internet age** has created entire new marketplaces for ideas, products, and services. Social networking websites such as Facebook allow businesses to promote products and services to other members, track trends, and interact with customers, gaining valuable feedback in the process. The most dynamic aspect of the Internet is that transaction costs for communication are virtually zero. Businesses can produce a short video and publicize it online—if customers think it's funny, they might share it through their social networks, where the promotion can proliferate at no additional expense to the original promoter.

Thanks to online social media platforms, marketing content can end up **going viral** in this fashion, with the possibility that an advertisement can generate millions

Internet Age Demarcates the emergence of a digital marketplaces for ideas, products, and services made possible by Internet access.

Going Viral When Internet content circulates spontaneously through social networks, generating millions of hits in a short period.

MANAGERIAL INSIGHT: Market Trends for Small Businesses[15]

The first major study of sustainable business from the perspective of small business owners, including microbusinesses of 5 or fewer employees, was conducted in 2013. According to that survey of over 1,300 U.S.-based small businesses in a wide range of industries, there are growing opportunities for sustainable marketing and operating practices in food, consumer products, construction, finance, energy, and transportation, though challenges remain due to poor market positioning.

TABLE 7.3

SME Sustainability Opportunities by Sector

Sector Innovation	Opportunity
Food – Organic	Home delivery, restaurants, Community-Supported Agriculture; farmer's markets; wholesale; institutional purchasing; packaged food production.
Consumer Products – Organic	Production of organic products; importing, growing, processing, and distributing sustainable raw materials; product design using sustainable materials.
Construction – Source and Design	Resource-efficient system design, construction, and installation for roofs; solar photovoltaic panels; plumbing; and lighting.
Finance – Socially Responsible Investing	Financial planning services; crowd-sourced funding; increased demand for clean capital.
Energy – Renewables	Design, production and maintenance of renewable energy systems for residential and commercial facilities, including solar panels, geothermal wells, wind turbines, and biofuel engines.
Transportation – Hybrids	Supply of renewable raw materials for vehicle components; hybrid car parts production.
Food – Fair Labor Practices	Sourcing and importing products from fair labor certified farms and production facilities.

Source: Small Business Sustainability Report, 2013: The Big Green Opportunity for Small Business in the U.S., Green America, Association for Enterprise Opportunity, and Ecoventures International, page 25–31 (2013).

of views in a short time period. The popularity of online video-streaming websites like YouTube and Hulu provide additional marketing channels to consumers who are spending more time surfing the web. The direct access to consumers and low cost of social media and Internet venues make them excellent methods for marketing SMEs.

7.1.4 Rewards of Sustainable Marketing

Consumer demand for sustainable products and services has grown over the last several years. This has created opportunities for companies to create new products and services that are comparatively superior on sustainability dimensions, building top line sales, enhancing a firm's reputation, and delivering a host of other benefits, such as operational efficiency and superior supply chain relationships. The main sources of value for marketing sustainability is that many consumers prefer a sustainable product to a traditional one if comparably priced, and some are even willing to pay a premium for sustainable products. These purchases are becoming more standard as technology and innovation have enabled sustainable products to compete with existing offerings according to the traditional criteria of price and function.

Improving sustainability performance also helps companies avoid the barbs of advocacy groups when information about their performance is disclosed in an ever more transparent world. Improving sustainable marketing research helps companies develop and sell products and services that address their customers' specific sustainability concerns. Companies that understand their own sustainability performance are in a much better position to respond to these concerns, and to reap the benefits of engaging this emerging market.

The virtue of sustainable products is that they continue to offer the same benefits as mainstream products, plus any value added through more environmentally friendly and socially equitable procurement, manufacture, packaging, or labor use. For instance, hybrid cars can be just as capable of transporting people to and fro as regular cars, but they also offer a quieter ride and lower fuel costs. Natural cleaning products are just as capable of removing a smudge from the surface of a kitchen counter, but they have the added benefit of reduced indoor air pollution and fewer harsh effects when exposure with skin occurs or residues of the product escape into the environment. These added benefits differentiate sustainable products from competitors and lend justification to marginally higher prices.

As an example of the wealth-creating effect of sustainable product design, consider a 14-year global event study of "green" vehicle development and innovation.[16] This research found that when an automaker announces an environmental innovation, there is a generally positive market reaction with variation in excess returns influenced by profitability, debt-equity ratio, and oil price. This is consistent with prior research on the wealth effects of innovation announcements. Sustainability can command price premiums when it is associated with innovation, but also when associated with quality, value, durability, status, personal health, and moral satisfaction.

There are other benefits of green marketing in addition to wealth-creating effects of green product design. The **halo effect** describes the tendency of consumers to make inferences about a company's sustainability on the basis of very limited information, or to use an observable attribute to infer an unobservable one. Recent studies confirm what has previously just been speculation about the halo effect.[17] Namely, when consumers are aware of sustainable performance in the environmental domain of corporate conduct (say, recycling waste), this will positively influence their perceptions of sustainability performance within that domain where they have little to no information (say, energy efficiency). Further, the halo effect applies across domains: where consumers have information about corporate sustainability in the environmental domain (say, eco-friendly packaging), they will make positive inferences about corporate conduct in the social domain (say, fair labor practices or community engagement).

Halo Effect The tendency of consumers to make inferences about a company's sustainability on the basis of very limited information, or to use an observable attribute to infer an unobservable one.

The halo effect strengthens the business case for sustainability. When a company does right by the environment, consumers assume that company is also doing right by its employees; when a company does right by reducing water impacts, consumers assume that company also does right by reducing energy use.

Of course, the halo effect can be exploited by tricking consumers into thinking the company is performing better on sustainability indicators than it actually is. The line between benefiting from a true halo and profiting from unethical and perhaps illegal greenwashing will be discussed in Section 7.2.4: What Is Greenwashing?. One way to provide objective, reliable information about the sustainability of a company's products or processes is to procure independent, third-party certification, discussed later.

7.2 Legal and Ethical Boundaries

7.2.1 Truth-In-Advertising Rules

Deception Policy Statement
An ad is deceptive if it contains (or omits) information that is likely to *mislead* consumers acting reasonably under the circumstances, and it is *material* in the sense that the deceptive information is important to a consumer's decision to buy or use the product.

Unfairness Policy Statement
An ad or business practice is unfair if it is likely to cause substantial consumer injury that a consumer could not reasonably avoid, and the risk of injury is not outweighed by the benefit to consumers.

Companies advertising in the United States must comply with the rules set forth by the Federal Trade Commission (FTC). A set of rules and regulations apply to all commercial speech that limits what can be said in an advertisement. It is unlawful for any person, partnership, or corporation to disseminate an unfair, deceptive, or false advertisement by any means for the purpose of inducing the purchase of food, drugs, devices, services, or cosmetics.[18]

So, what are the rules for fair and truthful marketing? Under the Federal Trade Commission Act, advertising must be truthful, non-deceptive, backed up by evidence, and fair. Under the FTC's **Deception Policy Statement**, an ad is deceptive if it contains (or omits) information that is likely to mislead consumers acting reasonably under the circumstances, and it is material in the sense that the deceptive information is important to a consumer's decision to buy or use the product. Under the FTC's **Unfairness Policy Statement**, an ad or a business practice is unfair if it is likely to cause substantial consumer injury that a consumer could not reasonably avoid, and the risk of injury is not outweighed by the benefit to consumers.

Beginning in 2009, the FTC began to send warning letters to four major retailers that they were mislabeling products as environmentally friendly when in actuality they had a toxic life cycle.[19] The manufacturers for Sears, Amazon, Macy's, and Max Studio (Leon Max) used bamboo fiber to make textile, but used the same chemical process used to make rayon, which generates hazardous air pollutants. The retailers were selling the resulting textiles as "environmentally friendly," "organic," and "pure bamboo" crib sheets and t-shirts. In January, 2013, those companies agreed to a $1.26 million settlement with the FTC, but neither admitted nor denied the allegations. Nonetheless, the companies agreed to a compliance monitoring and reporting regimen. Retailers can be at risk of liability for misrepresenting the sustainability profiles of their products, even if another party manufactures them. According to Stuart Delery, head of the Justice Department's civil division,

CROSS-LINKAGE

For more on the role of law in sustainable business, see Chapter 4: Legal Frameworks.

MANAGERIAL INSIGHT: Does Red Bull Really Give You Wings?

The energy-drink maker Red Bull uses humorous cartoons to boast of the stimulating effects experienced by those who consume their product. Each cartoon concludes with a literally false slogan: "Red Bull gives you wings," and usually one of the cartoon characters sprouts white, swan-like wings from their shoulders soon after taking their first sip from Red Bull's signature skinny can. Although the statement is literally false, it is not (legally speaking) deceptive advertising, because a reasonable consumer, under the circumstances, would not be mislead into thinking that a sports beverage would drastically alter their anatomical structure. Businesses can use humor to market their products or services without violating truth-in-advertising guidelines.

"Consumers pay a premium for products labeled and advertised as being made from bamboo because they believe that the product is made from a renewable resource and is good for the environment."[20] Liability for these retailers hinged on the frustration of consumer's reasonable expectations of product sustainability, caused by their word choices in advertising.

7.2.2 Guidelines for Marketing Environmental Attributes

The FTC has published guidance to address marketing claims specifically related to environmental performance of companies and the products they sell. These are more specific than the basic truth-in-advertising rules discussed above and are organized into different types of environmental claims aimed to prevent greenwashing, or misleading advertisements related to environmental performance. FTC Chairman Jon Leibowitz claimed these standards would "bring substantial change to the marketplace," while Joel Makower, executive editor of Greenbiz.com, was more reserved: "They represent a low bar that's only going to head off the worst of the worst."[21] FTC green marketing regulations represent a regulatory floor, creating a minimum threshold that companies must meet in order to advertise their sustainability efforts.

A small subset of these guidelines is shown in Table 7.4.

For example, in general environmental claims, a marketing campaign saying "Green, made with recycled content" may be deceptive if the environmental costs of using recycled content outweigh the environmental benefits of using it. Also, marketers should qualify renewable materials claims unless an item is made entirely

TABLE 7.4

Sample Guidelines for Environmental Marketing

Type of Claim	FTC Guidance
General Environmental Benefits	Marketers should not make broad, unqualified general environmental benefit claims like "green" or "eco-friendly."
"Free-Of"	It would be deceptive to claim that a product is "free-of" a substance if it includes another substance that poses a similar environmental risk.
Non-Toxic	Marketers who claim that their product is non-toxic need competent and reliable scientific evidence that the product is safe for both people and the environment.
Recycled Content	Marketers should qualify claims for products or packages made partly from recycled material – for example, "Made from 30% recycled material."
Made with Renewable Materials	Marketers should qualify renewable materials claims unless an item is made entirely with renewable materials, except for minor and incidental components.

LEADERSHIP: SME Markets Organic Eggs[22]

The family-owned company, Pete & Gerry's Organic Eggs (discussed in Section 7.1.2) uses a variety of marketing strategies to differentiate their product from traditional egg farm competitors. Instead of the paper-fiber egg carton, Pete & Gerry's uses a clear recycled plastic container for the dozen, allowing shoppers to see the unique brown speckled eggshells. The package contains the following labels: "Certified USDA Organic. No Pesticides. No Antibiotics. Cage Free. Recycled package." Inside the egg carton, the lid is lined with an explanation of the recycled claim, thereby satisfying FTC marketing guidelines. The thorough explanation given to the recycled claim goes above and beyond what is required: "This recycled egg carton is more environmentally friendly than paper[.] We use recycled plastic bottles that have been collected, washed, melted and reformed to make our egg cartons. ... The process uses far less energy and water than paper, and uses no harsh chemicals."

---

with renewable materials, except for minor and incidental components. An example of acceptable sustainable marketing would be, "Our flooring is made from 100% bamboo, which grows at the same rate, or faster, than we use it." Another example of acceptable green marketing is a statement such as, "This package is made from 50% plant-based renewable materials. Because we turn fast-growing plants into bio-plastics, only half of our packaging is made from petroleum-based materials."

7.2.3 Product/Process Information Distinction

Product-Related Information
Facts about a product's attributes, such as whether it is safe, whether performs its intended purpose, what ingredients it contains, and how much it costs.

Process-Related Information
Facts about the methods and labor practices that went into producing a consumer good.

There is a conceptual distinction to be made between **product-related information** (such as whether a product poses a risk to the consumer) and **process-related information** (such as whether the production of a consumer good harmed laborers, the environment, or animals).

Ruthless, unregulated marketing could conceal potential risks posed by product ingredients or attributes in order to avoid scaring away buyers. With the development of product liability law, manufacturers and sellers are now responsible for unreasonable risks arising from the foreseeable use of their products. For instance, an exploding soda bottle frustrates the reasonable expectations of the purchaser and could subject the soda bottling company to liability for the resulting damages. Carbonated beverages now include disclaimers warning against the risk of exploding bottles, and cautioning consumers to point the bottle away from their face before opening. This means that manufacturers and sellers rely on the disclosure of product-related risk information to consumers in order to defend against product liability lawsuits. Informed consumers who know the risks ahead of time and yet engage in the risky conduct are unlikely to prevail against a manufacturer who went out of their way to caution the consumer against the product risks. Greater accountability for risks in product-related information disclosure is the result of the first generation of consumer activism of the 1970's.

The sustainability trend of today concerns process-related information. Now that it is firmly established that consumers are entitled to product-related information that affects their health, safety, or satisfaction with the product, consumers are beginning to look beyond their own use of the product to consider what happened

> **MANAGERIAL INSIGHT:** Doug Kysar: Process Information and Consumer Preferences[23]
>
> Process information about a product includes labor conditions for workers in that product's supply chain, environmental pollution from manufacturing, and "any number of other social, economic, or environmental circumstances that are related causally to a consumer product, but that do not necessarily manifest themselves in the product itself." In addition to product information that bears on the function, performance, and safety of a product, process information can and does "influence the willingness of consumers to purchase the product. Consumers, in other words, often have 'preferences for processes.'"

earlier in the products' supply chain. Manufacturers are now asked to disclose information related to the process by which their consumer goods were brought into existence. Did the manufacturing process use toxic chemicals? When the product's efficacy was tested, were any animals harmed? Did the manufacturer use harsh labor conditions when making this product? Greater accountability for risks in process-related information disclosures is the growing trend resulting from the sustainability movement.

Many policymakers in law and business have argued that the product/process distinction should serve as the basis for limiting consumer access to information. That is, some think that consumers should have access only to information about the product itself and have no legitimate claim to access information about production processes. The assumption behind this argument is that information about production methods is an illegitimate basis for consumers to differentiate between products. In other words, consumers should choose between products based exclusively on product information such as price, quality, appearance, safety, or function, and are not entitled to know about the life cycle of or supply chain behind those products. Those taking this position do not deny that consumers care about process information—rather, they argue that consumers simply are not entitled to such information, and product producers should have no obligation to disclose process information. This argument has taken hold in many forums, leading to a tangible shift in the marketplace for consumer goods where consumers are permitted to consider only functional characteristics of products, and ethical or environmental impacts of production processes are not subject to mandatory disclosure by government regulation.

In the United States, process information is for the most part immune from mandatory disclosure laws unless the lawmaking institution bases the disclosure requirements on proven environmental, health, or safety effects; government cannot require producers to provide process information against their will if the only basis for doing so is to satisfy consumer curiosity.[24] However, because many consumers do in fact care about the ethical and environmental implications of products about which product information alone reveals little, several companies have taken to voluntary disclosure of process information regardless of the fact that government regulations typically do not require them to do so. For an in-depth example of the product/process distinction in action, see the case *Nike, Inc. v. Kasky* at the conclusion of this chapter.

7.2.4 What Is Greenwashing?

Greenwashing Using marketing to promote the idea that a company is more socially or environmentally responsible than it actually is.

Greenwashing is the term used to describe the representation that a product or service is more socially or environmentally friendly than it actually is. The term greenwashing was coined by the environmentalist Jay Westerveld who criticized the practice of hotels encouraging guests to save water by declining fresh towels while making no effort to conserve resources as a company such as by recycling grey water or improving energy efficiency.

Collaboration between EnviroMedia Social Marketing and the University of Oregon developed the Greenwashing Index. This defines greenwashing as the act of a company or organization spending more time and money trying to convince customers that they are "green" than actually implementing business practices that minimize their environmental impact.

There are several dimensions to greenwashing. A product could be advertised as an environmentally superior alternative when it in fact has a substantially similar environmental footprint compared to competing versions. A product's environmentally friendly ingredients could be outweighed by the manufacturing processes or packaging. A company that has a business model inherently degrading to the environment, such as fossil fuel resource extraction, may promote one sustainability initiative while ignoring a long track record of environmental harms that remains ongoing. This leads to a situation where advocates complain about a company's ongoing impacts, and criticize the company's efforts to capitalize on side-issue sustainability improvements. Greenwashing is a risk of marketing sustainability efforts inappropriately.

Carbon Negative When the carbon emissions from production, packaging, and shipment of a product are more than offset by other carbon mitigation projects.

In addition to the reputational fallout from perceived greenwashing, a substantial marketing risk for sellers of are federal and state truth-in-advertising laws, which were

---

ETHICAL DECISIONS: FIJI Water Battles With Greenwashing

The company FIJI Water underwent a period marred by controversies surrounding alleged greenwashing activities. FIJI Water claims that its product, the iconic square bottle of water, is actually **carbon negative**, which means that the production, packaging and shipment of the water removes more carbon pollution from the atmosphere than it releases into it. Green marketing claims such as "carbon neutral" or "carbon negative" distinguish a product or company from its competitors by signaling an ambitious commitment to fighting climate change. FIJI Water generally enjoys the reputation as a sustainable company and is the beverage of choice for illustrious televised events. As discussed earlier in this chapter, some consumers are willing to pay a price premium for products distinguished in this way. However, for precisely this reason, the company engaged in these marketing tactics must be able to support such claims with an adequate scientific basis. FIJI Water Company has been named as a defendant in a class action lawsuit alleging that the company has profited by greenwashing. The lawsuit seeks restitution for the allegedly false claim that leads to substantial profits from a larger market share. According to one of the attorneys for the plaintiffs, "This case is very simple: Defendants convince consumers to buy their 'FIJI' brand of bottled water—and to pay more for FIJI than for competing brands—by advertising and labeling FIJI as 'The World's Only CARBON NEGATIVE bottled water.'"[25] The problem is that carbon reductions are only potential, not actual. The company has a plan to plant trees to offset the carbon emissions from their operations. For some consumers, this was misleading.

enacted to govern the emergence of spurious marketing claims about the environmental attributes of products and materials.

Being accused of greenwashing by environmentalists, the media, consumer groups, competitors, regulators, or members of the scientific community can have long-lasting impacts to a company's reputation. These examples point to the importance of transparency and integrity in marketing the sustainability status of a company. Failure to do so can lead to liability or reputational harm, which few companies can afford and all would prefer to live without.

7.3 Strategy for Marketing Sustainability

What can marketing employees do to ensure that consumers are informed about what their company is doing right, and how can marketing translate sustainable conduct into increased financial performance? To do so requires marketing strategy. Because marketing sustainable performance, products, and services is substantially different from traditional marketing, marketing strategies need to reflect these differences. We discuss principles of sustainable marketing strategy, then challenges faced by marketers of sustainable products and services that strategies must address, as well as the unique challenges faced when marketing to an international audience.

7.3.1 Sustainability Marketing Principles

There are at least seven principles that should be followed for marketing sustainability strategy to succeed.[26]

1. Perform market research to discern the environmental and social concerns of the company's customers. Address these concerns in long-term planning to align corporate conduct with the values and beliefs of customers. For more on the demographics of sustainable consumers, consider the earlier discussion in Section 7.1.2: Segmenting the Market for Sustainable Products.
2. Develop products and services that have superior social and environmental performance relative to industry standards. The key is to strike the right balance between quality, convenience, and affordability, and to conduct a life cycle analysis when developing new offerings. For more on product development, see Section 7.3.2: Brand Development. For more on life cycle analysis, see Chapter 3: Metrics and Tools.
3. Instead of trying to convince consumers to buy things they don't need, develop brands with clear practical benefits related to important issues affecting their life. Consumer literacy can be improved by engaging consumer's preferences and incorporating their values in the product and service development process.
4. Strive for transparency, and communicate clearly the company's commitment to sustainability. Shore up credibility by obtaining third-party certification. For more on transparency, see Section 7.4 on Certification Programs.
5. Instead of reacting to environmental or social problems when they become crises, proactively seek out these issues and make reasonable efforts to resolving them. Being proactive here means creating competitive advantage in the process of managing risks.

6. Develop a holistic, systems-based perspective on the company's situation, integrating corporate inputs and outputs with the social, economic, and environmental systems and resulting feedback loops.

7. Design more sustainable products and services, promote responsible product use, and facilitate disposal practices. Continuously improve corporate sustainability performance until the company reaches net zero impacts through a combination of material improvements and offsets, striving for permaculture.

Sustainable marketing strategy should include market research, innovative product and service developments that provide practical benefits, transparent supply chains, proactive risk management, a systems-based perspective on the market, and continuous improvement.

7.3.2 Brand Development

When a company launches a sustainability brand, it can develop that brand further in a variety of ways, either through line extension, brand extension, multi-brand, and new brand developments. Approaches to brand development are shown in Figure 7.1. Brand development enables a company to take advantage of the halo effect created by their sustainability initiatives, as well as to expand their sustainable offerings into entirely new markets and product categories.

To develop the brand for a sustainable product, we apply the general principles of brand development to the unique attributes of the product offered.[27]

Line extension means a company introduces new items in the same category under the same brand. The fashion label American Apparel made its mark on sustainability by counteracting the industry trend to outsource apparel manufacture to countries with poor labor standards. Offering a wealth of employee benefits for their domestic manufacturing operations and using environmentally friendly sourcing of materials, the company extended their line of sustainable products from basic cotton knitwear such as underwear to include a range of fashionable outer garments for men, women, and children.

Brand extension means using a successful brand to launch new or modified products in a different category. The cosmetics company Natura has pioneered sustainability in cosmetics for decades, using certified environmentally and socially responsible ingredients and practices. The company has extended their brand into lotion, perfume, and other personal care product categories.

The **multi-brand** approach involves two or more sustainability brands within the same product category. The electronic appliance company Philips introduced long-lasting energy-efficient light bulbs which reduce pollution and consumption. Their multi-brand approach included distinct bulb life-spans at different price points.

Line Extension When a company introduces new items in the same category under the same brand.

Brand Extension Using a successful brand to launch new or modified products in a different category.

Multi-Brand Launching two or more sustainable brands within the same product category.

FIGURE 7.1 Approaches to Brand Development

Source: Adapted from Kotler, P. & Armstrong, G., 1, The Principles of Marketing, page 296, 10th Ed. (2004).

		Product Category	
		Existing	*New*
Brand Name	*Existing*	**Line Extension**	**Brand Extension**
	New	**Multi-Brand**	**New Brand**

Introducing a **new brand** is entering a new product category with a new product. The retailer Coop has introduced new sustainable brands in separate categories including food and textiles.

Keep in mind that companies can market the same brand to multiple consumer segments by utilizing alternative media, and by emphasizing distinct product or service attributes that cater to unique segment preferences.

New Brand Entering a new product category with a new product.

7.3.3 Stages of Marketing Sustainability

Despite the substantial shift in approaches necessary for companies specifically marketing the sustainability attributes of their products or services, not all companies have made the same amount of progress along the path toward sustainability. As a result, marketing strategies must reflect the differences in sustainability performance actually achieved.

Marketing sustainability can take on three stages of separation from conventional marketing, ranging from the companies that have begun to take steps toward sustainability to companies that have transformed entire markets with sustainable innovations. These are shown in Figure 7.2.

At **Stage I**, businesses set the example within their industry by achieving improved standards for environmental performance and market the benefits of their services or products by comparison with the performance of competitors.[28] A company sets an example of sustainability by providing substantiated claims of superiority within their product or service category. Credible partnerships with an independent group such as a non-profit environmental organization authenticate sustainability claims. At this stage, companies create value by marketing the benefits of products vis-à-vis the competition.

At **Stage II**, businesses collaborate with clients to develop sustainable products and services, sharing the responsibility with consumers who voluntarily change their behavior.[29] Businesses must develop the market for their products and services by educating consumers about the problems addressed by the company's sustainability initiatives. Tribal brands can be *exclusive* by creating the impression of an "in-group" drawn to celebrity endorsements, or *inclusive* by creating a sense of community brought together by a common cause. At this stage, companies create value by encouraging customers to switch to their products or services for a cause.

At **Stage III**, businesses enable breakthroughs in sustainable design and technology that have the potential to reshape markets.[30] New business concepts introduced by social entrepreneurs can turn a market on its head by transforming what was previously considered property owned by individuals—such as the automobile—into a service—such as ZipCar's car sharing service. Trojan Horse ideas are revolutionary products or services that disguise their disruptive quality with a culturally acceptable wrapping. To continue with the car-sharing example, the efficiency and flexibility of sharing transportation serve as the wrapping to make the radical idea—lack of ownership—more palatable. At this stage, companies create value by challenging the premise of consumer culture—the idea that status is conferred through ownership, especially the ownership of ever-newer and ever-pricier products. Consumer culture drives the make-take-waste process that has proven to be unsustainable. By creating durable, high-quality products that can appreciate over time, and by providing services that can be shared, companies reduce waste and resource consumption.

Stage I Businesses set the example within their industry by achieving improved standards for environmental performance, and market the benefits of their services or products by comparison with the performance of competitors.

Stage II Businesses collaborate with clients to develop sustainable products and services, sharing the responsibility with consumers who voluntarily change their behavior.

Stage III Businesses enable breakthroughs in sustainable design and technology that have the potential to reshape markets.

	Stage I	Stage II	Stage III
Public Company & Markets	*Setting Examples*	*Developing the Market*	*New Business Concepts*
Social Brands & Belonging	*Credible Partners*	*Tribal Brands*	*Trojan Horse Ideas*
Personal Products & Habits	*Marketing Benefits*	*Changing Usage*	*Challenging Consumption*
	Set New Standards & Communicate	**Share Responsibility & Collaborate**	**Support Innovation & Reshape Culture**

FIGURE 7.2 Stages of Marketing Sustainability

Source: Adapted from John Grant, *The Green Marketing Manifesto* (2007).

7.3.4 International Marketing

How consumers perceive and respond to marketing claims, and sustainability claims in particular, differs depending on cultural expectations and the regulatory environment of regional governments.[31] Sustainability tends to be an **explicit element of corporate policy** in liberal market economies such as the United States. That means companies tend to be vocal about what efforts they happen to be making toward sustainability. In liberal market economies, national institutions tend to encourage individualism, implement policies that provide discretion to the regulated parties, and promote incentives for responsive parties.

Sustainability tends to be an **implicit element of the institutional frameworks** surrounding corporations in coordinated market economies such as in Europe. That means companies do not take credit for engaging in sustainable conduct because they are built-in requirements either in the laws or culture where they operate. In coordinated market economies, national institutions tend to encourage collectivism, provide incentives for program-driven actions, and promote policies creating obligations for the regulated parties. The context for corporate sustainability depends upon the culture and regulatory environment in which a company operates.

For sustainable marketing to be successful, it must take these location-sensitive variables into account. Different cultures will have different social responsibilities that they expect of the companies doing business with them. In a culture that expects fairness, it will do little good to advertise that your company treats its workers fairly. This is already an expectation and not something that would distinguish that company from existing ones. Indeed, such an advertisement could sow the seeds of mistrust by coming off as defensive in tone.

Because of the explicit/implicit distinction of corporate sustainability frameworks in the United States and Europe, respectively, the old imperative to know your audience is especially true in the context of marketing for international companies. In Europe, sustainable marketing could be perceived as corporate spin or mere window-dressing whereas the same messaging in the United States could be perceived as a significant investment of resources dedicated towards the public interest. McDonald's, the global fast-food restaurant famous for its cheeseburgers, has enjoyed a leadership role in the United States' corporate sustainability movement, whereas in Europe it is routinely criticized for dodging implicit sustainability norms in European labor law.

Explicit Element of Corporate Policy When companies are vocal about what efforts they happen to be making toward sustainability.

Implicit Element of Institutional Frameworks When companies do not take credit for engaging in sustainable conduct because they are built-in requirements either in the laws or culture where they operate.

On the other side of the Atlantic, Bayer, the global health care product maker famous for its headache medicine, enjoys the reputation of a responsible company even while facing lawsuits for violating explicit product safety concerns in the United States. These two examples show how important it is to be sensitive to whether sustainability policies are explicit or implicit in the national institutions in which one is doing business.

7.3.5 Challenges to Marketing Sustainability[32]

Marketing the accomplishments of a company is an important part of claiming value from sustainable innovation, and therefore a critical ingredient in the business case for sustainability. After all, while using recyclable materials may be good for the planet, unless this action is associated with a price premium or reputational benefit, it would not be untoward for a business manager to ask why it is worth the effort. However, marketing can pose its own risks. Paid advertising can create skepticism among savvy consumers. Marketing can backfire when a company is too self-aggrandizing in taking credit for sustainability-related improvements when they pale in comparison to that company's aggregate adverse social, economic, and environmental impacts.

Explaining the benefits of a brand, product, or service to customers is crucial for any company to succeed. When a brand, product, or service is distinguished from competitors by environmental, social, or economic attributes, it is even more important to communicate these features effectively in order for sustainability to pay off. The opportunities for marketing departments to promote corporate sustainable initiatives abound—through educational campaigns, product differentiation, price premiums, stakeholder engagement and feedback, social impact causes, NGO-corporate partnerships, as well as all of the traditional marketing tools that promote customer interest and increase sales. However, sustainable marketing poses challenges that traditional marketing does not. Depending upon the audience, potential customers will respond differently to certain claims about, say, sustainable product ingredients, and will be driven to make a purchase for different reasons.

The variability between people's responses to sustainable marketing claims requires marketers to design their product or service messaging with care and to perform substantial market research in order to avoid wasted expenditures for advertisements because they either gave the right reason for a purchase to the wrong person, or the wrong reason to the right person. The risk of greenwashing, discussed above, may also discourage some companies from making an effort toward sustainable marketing, even if they are genuinely committed to sustainable operations. This section assumes that a company has already resolved to promote sustainability, and is deciding whether and how to capture the value created by these efforts through marketing.

Failing to communicate how one's company is overtly oriented toward the public's and planet's interest can be a mistake. Neglecting to label an organic product as such could mean customers and other stakeholders will assume the product is made with the same harmful chemicals as competitors' brands and will decline to pay any increase in price that may have resulted from the product's organic status. If a company invests time, effort, or money in differentiating their products or services, they had better also invest in effectively communicating the emergent differences to potential customers. This is subject to the caveat that some customers may still have the traditional view on sustainable products; for instance, some customers could assume that organic food doesn't taste as good. Accordingly, businesses must weigh the costs and benefits of labeling.

The sustainable company that fails to market itself as such could lose sales to competitors. The risks of no investment into sustainability on one hand, and the risks of no marketing of sustainability on the other, form the proverbial rock and a hard place. The way to pass through this dilemma is to invest into sustainable innovation as well as sustainable marketing. This is not without its own challenges, which will be discussed in this section. Namely, sustainable product marketing must overcome challenges posed by indirect benefits, trade-offs, defining the target audience, cost, salience, and credibility.

Indirect Benefits[33] Suppose a large multinational business, such as the bank HSBC, has reduced its carbon emissions substantially beyond levels achieved by competitors over a decades long voluntary process of carbon management. By doing this, the company has reduced their contribution to global climate change, a laudable act of responsibility and leadership. However, most of the company's customers do not directly see the benefit of reduced risks of climate change because the resulting incremental reduction in risk to them is extremely difficult to measure or explain to any particular customer. Without effective marketing, or the recognition by the United States Environmental Protection Agency in the form of the 2007 Climate Protection Award, the result of sustainability efforts made by HSBC may have gone unnoticed by customers of the bank because they are only indirectly beneficial. Indeed, the heroic accomplishment of carbon neutrality in 2006 across a global array of branch offices did not in and of itself enhance the satisfaction of HSBC customers as far as their banking experiences are concerned. All other things being equal in terms of the customer service and financial products offered by banks, the average customer may not be able to discern that one bank is a global sustainability leader and another has done very little to reduce climate change impacts. That is because environmental and social commitments of various sorts create **indirect benefits** that may be intangible or insignificant to primary customers.

> **Challenge of Indirect Benefits**
> When the social, economic, or environmental benefits of a company's sustainability commitments do not directly benefit primary customers or clients.

When a company pays a living wage to their employees in factories abroad, domestic customers will probably lack that information and fail to be directly benefited. As a result, customers may not be willing to pay a premium for products produced under fair pay conditions if they are not apprised of the moral superiority of such employment practices. When a company reduces the amount of waste generated in a manufacturing process, customers do not automatically perceive how this tends to increase the capacity of surrounding landfills because they may have never been cognizant of the extent of manufacturing waste in the first place. Without a baseline against which to compare sustainable improvements, customers can easily be at a loss as to what a company has actually accomplished by their sustainability efforts.

When a company sources only from businesses that use humane labor practices, customers may not notice anything significant in terms of the attributes of rendered products or services. To the fiancée that is unaware that the diamond in her engagement ring was procured from a region torn apart by internecine conflict over those precious stones, a diamond is still forever, and just as valuable as a diamond sourced from less bloody grounds. The intangible benefits of many sustainable products or services (i.e., less pollution across a large geographic region, or better treatment of people on the other side of the planet) are harder to sell to end-users than traditional product or service attributes because they are not intrinsic to the item purchased by the customer. A carbon-neutral bank still charges interest on credit card accounts. Where the values created by sustainable innovation are not experienced directly by a company's customers, marketers must find new ways of communicating about these values to customers.

The strategies for green marketing discussed in this chapter, such as values laden messaging, can help companies turn indirect benefits resulting from their sustainable initiatives into greater revenue by convincing customers to choose a sustainably made product or service over traditionally made competitors, even when the similarity between company offerings means there is not a direct benefit to the customer from doing so.

Trade-Offs[34] A sustainably made product or service is usually not the same as traditionally made competitors in terms of product or service attributes. In these situations, the marketing challenge becomes one of justifying trade-offs in the attributes of the company's offering.

When a product or service has been intrinsically changed in order to accomplish sustainability goals, it is not simply the means by which the product or service was created that is modified. In such situations, the benefits to customers from the innovation are direct, but may involve trading off certain product or service attributes against others. Sustainable products or services can be less expensive to own, more convenient to use, and of higher quality in construction than traditional products or services. Alternatively, some sustainable products can be more expensive to own, more time-consuming to use, or less attractive than traditional products or services. For example, toilet paper made from virgin forest tree pulp tends to be significantly softer than toilet paper made from recycled pulp material, however the recycled version is significantly less expensive. With the toilet paper example, customers are required to make trade-offs between price and comfort, and it is the job of the marketer to justify the extent of this trade-off. Effectively marketing indirect benefits (such as the reduction in deforestation allowed by recycling pulp) can help a customer justify choosing the greener product even when the product's intrinsic attributes (such as lower cost) were not enough to convince the customer not to resort to the traditionally made competitor product.

Ideally, marketers will calibrate the extent of these attribute trade-offs in such a way as to keep the product or service within the zone of the familiar—not departing too radically from customer expectations. **Trade-Offs** in product attributes must be justifiable. Sustainably grown coffee that is extra expensive, tastes awful and which does not contain as much caffeine is not likely to sell very well because it requires too drastic of a trade-off between its environmental profile and its quality when compared with traditionally grown coffee. Sustainably grown coffee that tastes substantially similar to traditionally grown coffee, which has a substantially superior environmental profile, and which provides a substantially similar amount of caffeine relative to traditionally grown coffee is likely to do well on the shelves because it is characterized by intelligent and justified trade-offs in product attributes.

Challenge of Trade-Offs
When a sustainable product sacrifices attributes of traditional products (such as price) in favor of special attributes (such as environmental impact).

Target Audience[35] Conventional demographics-based market segmentation allows marketers to speak the same message effectively to a broad set of potential customers with apparently similar preferences. For instance, homeowners in the northeast are more likely to need portable electricity generators than those who live in apartments in the southwest. This is because owning a home involves a set of responsibilities for maintenance and care for the property that is not present with the apartment-dweller who can rely on the maintenance staff of the complex to restore power in case of an outage. Further, geographic location says a lot about what kinds of products or services are likely to be in demand—weather patterns largely determine whether an area will need a product such as a portable electricity generator, with areas historically experiencing greater frequency of freezing conditions predictably experiencing greater demand for portable power.

By contrast, sustainable marketing requires a more nuanced understanding of the **target audience** than traditional marketing. When it comes to marketing sustainable products and services that offer indirect benefits, or trade-offs, relative to traditional products and services, it is sometimes necessary to look deeper than mere demographic information. Without at least a rudimentary understanding of the inner values—not just demographic information—of the customer, it is difficult to induce demand for sustainable products and services. Lifestyle-based marketing provides customers an independent basis for preferring sustainably made products or services to traditional competitors, especially when the sustainable product involves indirect benefits and substantial tradeoffs in product attributes.

> **Challenge of Target Audience** When marketing for a product or service is tailored to specific subsets of potential customers rather than advertised to the general population.

Cost[36] Branding a company as sustainable can be a costly undertaking. The cost required to ramp up an effective sustainable marketing campaign may be too much for a small start-up company to afford. It can be downright overwhelming for a new company to dive directly into customer education, transaction costs associated with changing suppliers, learning time needed for employees to adjust to new processes, and the changing salience of certain sustainable product or service attributes. For these reasons it is important for marketers to get the biggest bang for their buck, so to speak, ensuring that marketing expenditures are prudently allocated between education, research, fostering trust among regulators and winning over members of the consumer base.

> **Challenge of Cost** When sustainable branding imposes costs in excess of traditional marketing costs.

Salience[37] Reasons for committing to sustainability—whether it be supplier labor concerns, climate change, water shortage, toxic pollution, etc.—will come into and out of popularity with customers. Some homeowners purchase solar panels for their house because they want to fit in with the Jones's, while others will add solar panels to their house because they want to reduce their long-term cost of ownership by minimizing energy expenditures. The **salience** of sought-after advantages of sustainably made products and services shift with the season, political tides, and cultural trends. Changes in customer preferences also affect the salience of certain sustainability issues. For example, organic produce was originally preferred because it was perceived as posing fewer health risks than traditional produce bathed in chemicals, but now organic produce is preferred largely because it is perceived to have superior flavor. There are usually multiple advantages associated with a sustainably made product or service, but typically only one of these advantages will have winning

> **Challenge of Salience** Selecting the right product or service attribute that is most pertinent to potential customers at the point of sale.

appeal to a specific consumer segment, and even that segment's preferences will change with time. It is critical for marketing professionals to keep up to speed with shifting customer preferences in order to ensure marketing efforts highlight product or service attributes that are salient at the time to the target audience.

Credibility[38] In general, when the subject is environmental matters, consumers trust industry far less than NGOs or government entities for accurate information. In order to enjoy marketing benefits from actual sustainability gains, a company must have credibility when they assert claims of progress, and must back up such claims with independent verification and quality data. Basing claims of sustainability progress on empirical and objective metrics is not just for establishing credibility, but also for avoiding allegations of deceptive advertising.

CROSS-LINKAGE

For more on measuring and reporting sustainability indicators, see Chapter 5: Metrics, Tools, and Reporting: The Role of Finance and Accounting.

One of the most important features of **credibility** in sustainable marketing is the perception that the efforts made are actually significant and sincere. Sustainable marketing claims must appear significant either (1) relative to the overall environmental impact of the company making those claims, or (2) relative to the nature of the problem that the company's efforts address.

Challenge of Credibility
Aligning marketing claims with actual corporate conduct so these claims are both significant and sincere.

For an example of the first situation, if a company is responsible for substantial amounts of water pollution but then proceeds to launch a PR campaign about their efforts to reduce the amount of paper used in their office, that company's efforts are likely to be met with skepticism or criticism because these paper-reduction efforts come off as insignificant. Conversely, if a company is responsible for substantial air pollution, their claims about efforts to reduce air pollution are likely to be met with a more appreciative audience because they deal with an issue of actual significance. For an example of the second situation, marketing claims about rainforest habitat conservation that deal solely with the habitat of an endangered butterfly are going to be perceived as insignificant relative to the nature of the problem of deforestation. Conversely, marketing claims about freshwater conservation that deal with the health of a major regional aquifer will be perceived as engaging with significant issues of the day.

In addition to making sustainable marketing claims significant (in both senses of the word discussed above), they must be sincere. A company that actively lobbies for weakening the stringency of environmental laws and fights tooth-and-nail against the enforcement of environmental regulations cannot sincerely claim to promote environmental protection. However, a company that actively collaborates with non-profits to reduce their supply chain's environmental impacts can sincerely claim to promote environmental protection.

7.4 Certification Programs

One of the challenges faced by marketers is that many customers are simply overloaded with information and want some simple proxy to indicate that a product is sustainable, without having to do time-consuming or technical research to make that call.

Certification Verification of sustainable marketing claims provided by qualified, independent, third-party entities.

In addition to providing credibility, **certification** programs also save customers the time and effort of having to scrutinize the marketing claims of companies. Government officials and consumers are wary of self-aggrandizing claims made by some businesses about their own sustainable performance. Credibility, honesty, evidence, and values laden messaging are as important as ever to successfully market sustainable products and services. To overcome the appearance of partiality and self-serving bias, many companies have sought out third-party certification of their sustainability performance.

In order to respond to increasing demand for clear, impartial, and objective communication of sustainable performance, companies can use reliable metrics, third-party verification, independent standards, codes, labels, and indices to substantiate their claims. In general, sustainable certification programs quantify a company's impacts (and benchmark progress made to reduce those impacts) on the environment and communities where the company does business.

CROSS-LINKAGE

For more on independent, third-party verification of sustainable performance, see Chapter 5: Metrics, Tools, and Reporting: The Role of Finance and Accounting.

7.4.1 Guidelines for Third-Party Certification Programs

The Federal Trade Commission (FTC) may consider third-party seals of approval or certifications to be endorsements, enabling the agency to regulate these marketing arrangements in conjunction with the truth-in-advertising rules and restrictions on environmental claims discussed in this chapter. According to the FTC's *Endorsement Guides*:

Endorsement Guides Guidelines prepared by the FTC that apply truth-in-advertising restrictions to third-party seals of approval or third-party certifications.

- Marketers should disclose any material connections to the certifying organization. A material connection is one that could affect the credibility of the endorsement, such as a conflict of interest.
- Marketers should not use environmental certifications or seals that do not clearly convey the basis for the certification, because the seals or certifications are likely to convey general environmental benefits.
- To prevent deception, marketers using seals or certifications that don't convey the basis for the certification should identify, clearly and prominently, specific environmental benefits.
- Marketers can qualify certifications based on attributes that are too numerous to disclose by saying, "Virtually all products impact the environment. For details on which attributes we evaluated, go to [a website that discusses this product]." The marketer should make sure that the website provides the referenced information, and that the information is truthful and accurate.
- A marketer with a third-party certification still must substantiate all express and implied claims.

In general, a certification label does not substitute for properly substantiated claims of environmental benefit. As always, the marketing company must be able to back up claims with hard facts. Without these guidelines in place, certification providers would have an incentive to sell labels without regard to actual sustainable performance.

7.4.2 **Types of Certification Programs**

There are three types of certification programs: voluntary, standards-based, and mandatory. For a range of existing certification programs, see Figure 7.3.

There are few certification programs that track social performance because of the difficulty in standardizing what it means to be good for the community in which a business operates. Whether a company makes a positive difference in its community depends in large part on what the standard of living is in that community, what sorts of natural and cultural resources are available there, and what sorts of labor practices are typical there. On the other hand, environmental performance is easier to track in an objective manner. The volume of waste or toxic pollutants can be monitored and reduced regardless of the location of operations. Cultural preferences and what consumers expect of businesses vary greatly from region to region, but in all parts of the globe, fresh water, clean air, fertile soil, and healthy ecosystems are desirable. For these reasons, the field of sustainable certification programs is predominantly comprised of environmental performance indicators, with social performance indicators available in a few of the prominent sources of metrics, such as the Global Reporting Initiative.

> **CROSS-LINKAGE**
>
> For more on sustainable performance metrics, see Chapter 5: Metrics, Tools and Reporting: The Role of Finance and Accounting.

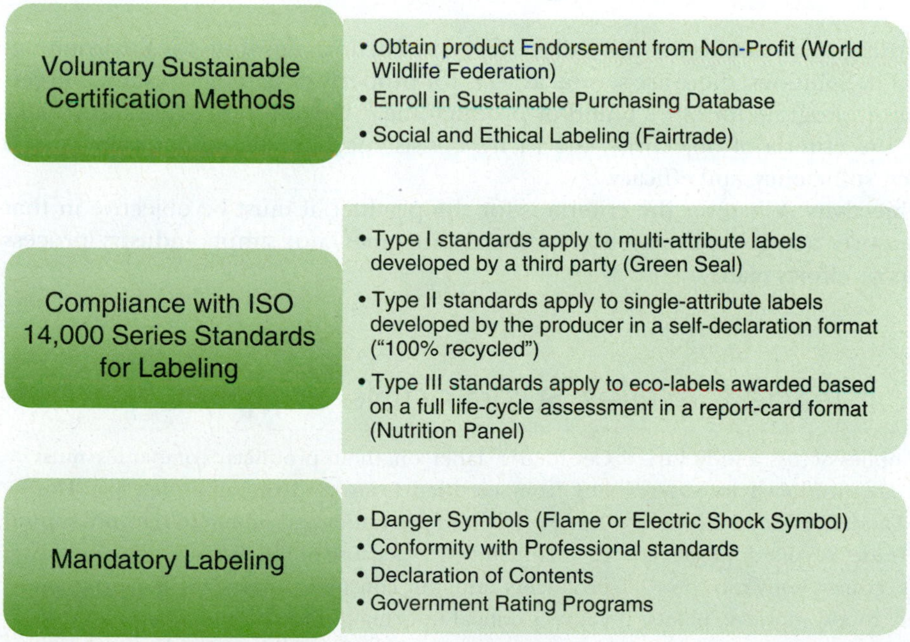

Voluntary Sustainable Certification Methods
- Obtain product Endorsement from Non-Profit (World Wildlife Federation)
- Enroll in Sustainable Purchasing Database
- Social and Ethical Labeling (Fairtrade)

Compliance with ISO 14,000 Series Standards for Labeling
- Type I standards apply to multi-attribute labels developed by a third party (Green Seal)
- Type II standards apply to single-attribute labels developed by the producer in a self-declaration format ("100% recycled")
- Type III standards apply to eco-labels awarded based on a full life-cycle assessment in a report-card format (Nutrition Panel)

Mandatory Labeling
- Danger Symbols (Flame or Electric Shock Symbol)
- Conformity with Professional standards
- Declaration of Contents
- Government Rating Programs

FIGURE 7.3 Categories of Sustainable Certification Programs[39]

Source: Adapted from Ralph E. Horne, *Limits to Labels: The Role of Eco-Labels in the Assessment of Product Sustainability and Routes to Sustainable Consumption*, 33 International Journal of Consumer Studies 175–182, 177 (2009).

Voluntary certification procured from a partnering non-profit organization, based on objective international standards, is helpful for companies interested in credible and clear means of communicating sustainable performance. Certification is helpful in ensuring traceability and transparency of supply chains as well as informing customers that their purchase of a certified product actually has the advertised beneficial social or environmental impact. One of the most famous examples of product certification is **Fair Trade** certified products, an example of which is Starbucks coffee. In addition to independent certification, Starbucks also implements an in-house sustainable supply chain program, discussed in the Chapter Opener for Chapter 8: Supply Chain Management.

Another certification provider that focuses on sustainable coffee is the Rainforest Alliance. The **Rainforest Alliance** assists forestry and agricultural sectors to conserve biodiversity and improve livelihoods of workers by promoting and evaluating the implementation of sustainability standards.[40] There are over 118,000 coffee farms currently Rainforest Alliance Certified to meet best practices in social and environmental sustainability. In 2012, Rainforest Alliance Certified coffee beans represented 4.5% of global coffee bean production, a 45% increase from 2011.[41] In the US and Canada, the fast food company McDonald's now requires its suppliers to source 100% of their espresso coffee beans from Rainforest Alliance Certified farms, and in Australia, New Zealand, and most of Europe, all of McDonald's coffee products must be from certified farms.

7.4.3 Certification Design

According to researchers at the Duke University Nicholas Institute for Environmental Policy Solutions, there are several aspects for properly designing a sustainable certification program for one's brand or product line.[43] Certification programs should meet the criteria of objectivity, specificity, consistency, functional equivalency, relevancy, sufficiency, and efficacy.

Objectivity. Whatever the criteria is for the product, it must be objective in that it measures actual environmental or social outcomes, not simply industry process inputs or efforts made.

Fair Trade Product label that verifies agricultural ingredients come from environmentally certified farms and organizations that pay fair prices to laborers and which submit to rigorous supply chain audits.

Rainforest Alliance Assists forestry and agricultural sectors conserve biodiversity and improve livelihoods of workers by promoting and evaluating the implementation of sustainability standards

Objectivity Based on facts rather than intentions.

GLOBAL INSIGHTS: Fair Trade Certifies Sustainable Supply Chains

The Fair Trade certification applies across a wide variety of consumer goods that are produced in lesser-developed regions of the world and distributed through global supply chains. Fair Trade certified products include apparel, linens, beans, grains, body care products, cocoa, coffee, packaged foods, flowers, plants, fruits, vegetables, honey, herbs, spices, nuts, oilseeds, spirits, sports balls, sugar, tea, and wine. "To earn a license from Fair Trade USA to use the Fair Trade Certified™ label on their products, companies must buy from certified farms and organizations, pay Fair Trade prices and premiums and submit to rigorous supply chain audits."[42] Because of the distance between the producers and the consumers, this labeling program conveys critical information to consumers who want to make sure they are supporting those who deserve it and that their purchases are not lining the pockets of exploitive employers.

Specificity. Key terms such as *eco-friendly* or *fair* must be defined specifically and consistently throughout the certification process to avoid equivocation or ambiguity. When comparing one product to others, product boundaries must be demarcated to ensure accurate comparisons.

> **Specificity** Criteria are defined clearly to avoid ambiguity.

Consistency. The certification process must be defined using the same method and time frame so that updates can be made and so the certification means the same thing today as it does in the future. Otherwise certifications can become quickly outdated, arbitrary, or less meaningful over time.

> **Consistency** Criteria are the same across time.

Functional Equivalency. In order to gauge the consumer demand and market share for certified goods, a market analysis should be performed that analyzes functionally equivalent goods across environmental metrics. In general, a product with an effective sustainable label will compete against functionally equivalent goods without sustainable certification.

> **Functional Equivalency** Comparisons are made between like-in-kind products only.

Relevancy. When it comes to product labeling, designers need to strike a balance between information value and information cost. An eye-catching simple label with a green check mark may help turn products better than a panel of fine-print; even though the latter contains a great deal more information, it comes at a cost to the consumer in terms of time and effort. The impact of a sustainable label is exponentially higher when the information it contains is accessible to the consumer. Relevant information is more important than lots of information.

> **Relevancy** Certification contains only information that is relevant to the customer.

Sufficiency. Certifications should avoid information overload; whether a sustainable certification is effective depends upon the consumer's ability to understand and act upon the information it contains. Labels promote informed consumer choice by providing sufficient information to differentiate the sustainable brand from others, but excessive information can overwhelm or confuse consumers.

> **Sufficiency** Certification contains no more information than is necessary to avoid information overload.

Efficacy. Because consumers are task-oriented rather than information-seeking, labels should tell consumers what purchasing the product will do, rather than how purchasing that product will do it. In other words, the label, "Each product sold saves one gum tree," would be more effective at reaching a conscientious consumer than the label, "This product is made with a gum tree sap alternative."

> **Efficacy** Certification allows consumers to incorporate information into purchasing decisions in real time.

For examples of certification labels, see Figure 7.4.

Agricultural certification programs help farmers grow superior crops and yield greater income while providing enhanced protection of the natural resources and workers. For instance, UTZ-certification is based on "strict requirements [that] assure good agricultural practices and management, safe and healthy working conditions,

FIGURE 7.4 Examples of Sustainability Certification

no child labor and protection of the environment."[45] UTZ certifies raw materials sourced by consumer product companies Mars, IKEA, and Nestlé.

When it came time to address the sustainability problems associated with palm oil, the **Roundtable on Sustainable Palm Oil (RSPO)** was formed to promote the growth and use of sustainable oil palm products through credible global standards and engagement of stakeholders. RSPO retained UTZ Certification to develop a traceability system to ensure transparency, disclosure, clarity and efficiency in the physical trading of certified sustainable palm oil through the global supply chain of over 400 businesses affiliated with RSPO. This example demonstrates the importance of industry partnerships with non-profits to promote and successfully market sustainability.

> **Roundtable on Sustainable Palm Oil (RSPO)** Formed to promote the growth and use of sustainable oil palm products through credible global standards and engagement of stakeholders.

7.4.4 Challenges to Sustainable Certification

There are many benefits of certification and labeling demonstrations of a company's commitment to sustainability. These include brand strengthening, addressing consumer demand for sustainable products, competitive advantage for early adopters within a product category, reduced risk of attack from advocacy groups (unless the label is arguably greenwashing), satisfaction of investor concerns, raising sustainability awareness within consumers, influencing sustainability performance within an entire industry, and the ancillary benefits of a resilient supply chain that come with monitoring and collaborating with suppliers.

That said, there are reasons to be skeptical of the efficacy of certification programs. Managers have expressed skepticism over whether eco-labels are worth the effort because labels can lack credibility if they are not based on demonstrated improved outcomes, rigorous criteria that would not be easy for just any product to meet, and integrity in the certification procedures to ensure the process and product being certified represents what the company is actually selling.[46]

Further, certification providers may risk getting into the business of "selling stickers" instead of improving outcomes as these certification providers compete with one another over the market share.[47] This kind of competition can create a conflict of interest for the certification provider because they compete with other providers not over integrity but rather over price and speed of delivery. This competition means a race to the bottom can take place between providers where labels are based on increasingly less stringent criteria and delivered without thorough assessment. Under these conditions, an eco-labeled product means eco-labels were sold to a company instead of meaning that a sustainable product was sold to a consumer.

The two fundamental concerns with sustainable certification is the lack of consensus on criteria and resulting consumer confusion. Moving to objective, universal standards for what constitutes social, economic, and environmentally beneficial performance can ameliorate many of the problems and concerns with sustainable certification.

Key Terms

Marketing   190
Marketing
  Sustainability   190
Lifestyle of
  Health and
  Sustainability   192
Naturalites   192
Drifters   192
Conventionals   192
Unconcerneds   192
Internet Age   195
Going Viral   195
Halo Effect   197
Deception Policy
  Statement   198

Unfairness Policy
  Statement   198
Product-Related
  Information   200
Process-Related
  Information   200
Greenwashing   202
Carbon Negative   202
Line Extension   204
Brand Extension   204
Multi-Brand   204
New Brand   205
Stage I   205
Stage II   205
Stage III   205

Explicit Element of
  Corporate Policy   206
Implicit Element of
  Institutional
  Frameworks   206
Challenge of Indirect
  Benefits   208
Challenge of
  Trade-Offs   209
Challenge of Target
  Audience   210
Challenge of Cost   210
Challenge of Salience   210
Challenge of
  Credibility   211

Certification   212
Endorsement Guides   212
Fair Trade   214
Rainforest Alliance   214
Objectivity   214
Specificity   215
Consistency   215
Functional
  Equivalency   215
Relevancy   215
Sufficiency   215
Efficacy   215
Roundtable on
  Sustainable Palm Oil
  (RSPO)   216

Discussion Questions

1. You work for Alphadora, a company that produces personal care products such as shampoo and hair conditioner. Your company has historically competed on cost within its market segment. Under new leadership, Alphadora is incorporating sustainability into product development.

   A. With the newly designed sustainable product line, how should the company's marketing strategy differ from its original marketing strategy?

   B. How should the marketing sustainability strategy be tailored for each of the five categories of consumers described in this chapter?

2. Select a sustainable product and describe its packaging. What positive inferences have you made about the product from the packaging? Are these inferences justified or is this an example of the halo effect in action?

| CASE 1 | **Marketing Sustainable Dinner Ware** |

Benito Montiego is an associate in the Division of Marketing for a container company. His team was given an assignment to develop a new line of home kitchen products made of plastic to serve as lower-price alternatives to glass and metal wares. Benito is trying to earn a promotion and wants to take this opportunity to demonstrate his ability to

(continues)

be creative and to create value for his company. Read the following passage and answer the questions at the end.

Bisphenol-A, or BPA, is an estrogen-mimicking industrial chemical used in plastic containers and food packaging. Since the 1960s, manufacturers have used BPA to produce hard plastic bottles, cups for toddlers, and the linings of food and beverage cans, including those that hold infant formula and soda. Research shows that BPA has found its way into the bloodstreams of more than 90 percent of the population at levels that have shown harm in animal studies. Studies have also detected BPA in breast milk, the blood of pregnant women, and umbilical cord blood. BPA leaches from containers into the stored food or beverage, whereby it is ingested with the product, and in the case of pregnant women, it can be passed on to the fetus.

In July of 2012, the United States Food and Drug Administration (U.S. F.D.A.) announced the ban on BPA in baby bottles and children's drinking cups.[48] The announcement came in response to a petition by the American Chemistry Council, the main trade association of the chemical industry, to prohibit the chemical on the grounds that manufacturers had already abandoned its use. A formal prohibition codified the latest update in industry practice and was intended to boost consumer confidence about the safety of children's food and beverage containers. The Deputy Commissioner for Foods at the U.S. F.D.A. confirmed that the decision merely reflected steps the industry had taken in response to consumers demand, and therefore did not reflect agency concerns about the safety of BPA in these products.

More than 200 scientific studies show clear links between tiny amounts of exposure to BPA and subsequent increased risk of health impacts, from early puberty, breast cancer, childhood obesity, autism, hyperactivity, cancer, diabetes, and reproductive, neurological, and developmental disorders. When reports began to surface about potential adverse health impacts from BPA, its use in consumer products fell into disrepute among concerned parents and advocacy groups, leading to a significant decline in consumer confidence and demand for products containing the chemical. Fetuses, infants and children metabolize BPA more slowly than adults, increasing the risks of exposure.

In 2010, the agency expressed concerns about the health risks of BPA, saying there was "some concern about the potential effects of BPA on the brain, behavior and prostate gland of fetuses, infants and children." Yet, the latest announcement specifically avoided any discussion of these potential health effects. The U.S. F.D.A.'s prohibition will provide limited protection from BPA amongst the most sensitive members of the population. While public health advocates praised the agency's decision, they said the chemical still presented risks to human health. According to the president of the National Research Center for Women and Families, "The F.D.A. is slowly making progress on this issue, but they are doing the bare minimum here."

Almost all other plastic containers may continue to use BPA, including baby food formula containers. The leaching of BPA into food and beverage products can occur whether the container is a sippy cup or a tin can. Indeed, BPA is used to provide the gloss to cash register receipts, as fillings in dental work, and as a sealant. Public health advocates are not content with the latest ban, seeking instead the prohibition of BPA from all products that can be ingested by humans.

The federal regulation from the U.S. F.D.A. is modeled after a ban that was enacted by the state of California. Interests of the chemical and formula industries lobbied hard at the state level to oppose the ban, in order to enable continued use of BPA in baby formula packaging and other products for infants. In a measure of compromise, advocates weakened the ban from a complete prohibition to one restricting the use of BPA in baby bottles and sippy cups. The industry fought against consumer safety measures to water them down, then championed those same weakened measures to promote consumer confidence in their products. When the industry petitioned the U.S. F.D.A., it created the appearance that the industry was ahead of the curve by taking a proactive approach to consumer safety, when just the opposite is true.

The issue of BPA in consumer products highlights the ethical grey area when it comes to complying with consumer protection regulations. Sometimes laws and regulations that purport to protect consumers are empty gestures that merely serve to protect the interests of the industry that is supposedly being regulated. Merely complying with regulations usually does not amount to promoting social, economic, or environmental sustainability.

Case 1 Questions

1. Can Benito make a business case for green product design that would convince the rest of his marketing team?

2. How can Benito use sustainable marketing to avoid greenwashing his company's kitchen products?

3. Is it appropriate for manufacturers to continue using BPA in consumer products aside from those in which it is prohibited? Assume Benito's competitor companies are using BPA in their dinnerware products. Is this something Benito should make use of for his company's marketing strategy?

4. In general, what role should the industry play in researching, informing and engaging consumers about the potential adverse health impacts of the chemicals they use?

> **CASE 2**

Nike, Inc. v. Kasky[49]

Nike Inc. has had its share of criticism for exploitative labor practices in their supply chain. To defend itself against the charge that they ran "sweatshop" manufacturing operations abroad, Nike proceeded to launch a CSR publicity campaign in the late 1990s, claiming to be a socially responsible employer. The state of California at the time had a consumer protection law that allowed "any person acting for the interest of … the general public" to sue for equitable relief against false and misleading advertisements.[50] Marc Kasky, a fair labor activist, sued the company under claims of false advertising. The case turned on whether Nike's claims about socially responsible labor practices were "commercial speech" that could be regulated strictly to prevent deception, or "noncommercial speech" about matters of public concern that required intentional deception to be unlawful. Commercial speech is expression solely related to the economic interests of the speaker and its audience, so whether 'process information' such as the fair treatment of laborers counts as commercial speech depends in large part upon whether such statements primarily shape consumers' purchasing decisions or only tenuously influence how consumers behave.

The trial court rejected Nike's argument that their advertising campaign was noncommercial speech, holding: "when a corporation, to maintain and increase its sales and profits, makes public statements defending labor practices and working conditions at factories where its products are made, those public statements are commercial speech that may be regulated to prevent consumer deception."[51] In reaching this decision, the California trial court reasoned that, unlike general corporate discussions about the value of globalization, factual statements about how Nike makes its products are (1) designed to appeal to consumers, are (2) motivated by the prospect of economic gain, and (3) constitute an important factor in consumer decision-making. The trial court rejected the notion that companies only had to tell the truth about 'product information.' Accordingly. Statements made about production processes were also subject to truth in advertising law.

Nike appealed the court's decision to the California Supreme Court, arguing that commercial speech (where truth was required) should include only statements about the qualities of a *product as such*, as in, the product's price, whether it was available in stores, and whether it was suitable to the purposes for which it was advertised. In a sense, Nike took the position that information about business operations, manufacturing processes, supply chain issues, and the like are not subject to truth in advertising law. Three advertising trade groups also filed briefs to the California Supreme Court, arguing that the only legitimate concern for consumers was the price of the product and whether it works as it should. The implication of these arguments is that consumers attempting to make purchasing decisions based on ethical, environmental, or social considerations were not entitled to such information in the first place, yet if companies did voluntarily provided such information, they need not tell the truth when doing so because it was not "commercial speech." Several scholars and members of the U.S. Congress

(*continues*)

| CASE 2 | *(Continued)* |

disagreed with Nike's position, because refusing to acknowledge 'process information' as legitimate items of consumer concern in the transactional context was an unduly narrow view of corporate commercial speech and its role in today's market-based society. Indeed, more and more, consumer good purchases are based on satisfying the consumer's concerns that those products are made sustainably.

The California Supreme Court never ruled on whether process-related information that was voluntarily given constituted commercial speech, so we do not yet know whether such statements are subject to truth-in-advertising rules. The issue was not resolved as a matter of law in this case because it settled out of court, with Nike agreeing to donate $1.5 million to a worker's rights organization.[52]

Case 2 Questions

1. Explain the difference between commercial and noncommercial speech.

2. Explain the difference between "product information" and "process information."

3. Should companies be truthful when volunteering information about production processes?

4. Is the distinction between product and process information a legitimate basis for requiring truth in advertising? What about the distinction between commercial and noncommercial speech?

5. What is your opinion about how Nike resolved the Kasky lawsuit?

Further Research

Steve Howard, Chief Sustainability Officer at IKEA, provides this TED-Talk about selling sustainable products, materials, and practices to a global customer base: "Let's Go All-In On Selling Sustainability."

Harvard Business Review Case: Rebecca Henderson & Frederik Neilemann, *Sustainable Tea at Unilever*, Prod. #: 712438-PDF-ENG (December 8, 2011).

Harvard Business Review Case: Rosabeth Moss Kanter, Rakesh Khurana, Rajiv Lal & Eric Baldwin, *PepsiCo, Performance with a Purpose, Achieving the Right Global Balance*, Prod. #: 412079-PDF-ENG (October 24, 2011).

Endnotes

1. In Anthony Kleanthous and Jules Peck, "Let Them Eat Cake: Satisfying the New Consumer Appetite for Responsible Brands," World Wildlife Fund report, 2007.

2. U.S. Food and Drug Administration, *Communicating Risks and Benefits: An Evidence-Based User's Guide*, page 1 (2011).

3. Jonathan M. Estes, *Smart Green: How to Implement Sustainable Business Practices in Any Industry—and Make Money*, xv (2009).

4. Natural Marketing Institute, *A Look at Key Sustainability Trends in the U.S.* (2011).

5. ibid.

6. According to the market segmentation based on Natural Marketing Institute (NMI), *2009 LOHAS Consumer Trends Database* interviews with over 4,000 U.S. adults.

7. *2010 GLOBAL LOHAS Report*, Natural Marketing Institute.

8. ibid.

9. See Pete and Gerry's website, last accessed May 13, 2014, available at www.peteandgerrys.com.

10. Natural Marketing Institute (NMI), *2009 LOHAS Consumer Trends Database*.

11. Natural Marketing Institute, *A Look at Key Sustainability Trends in the U.S.* (2011).

12. Natural Marketing Institute (NMI), *2009 LOHAS Consumer Trends Database*.

13. ibid.

14. ibid.

15 *Small Business Sustainability Report, 2013: The Big Green Opportunity for Small Business in the U.S.*, Green America, Association for Enterprise Opportunity, and Ecoventures International, page 5 (2013).

16 Sulin Ba, Ling Lei Lisic, Qindong Liu, and Jan Stallaert, *Market Reaction to Green Vehicle Innovation* (January 10, 2012), last accessed May 13, 2014, available at http://ssrn.com/abstract=1982854 .

17 N. Craig Smith, Daniel Read, and Sofia López-Rodríguez, *Consumer Perceptions of Corporate Social Responsibility: The CSR Halo Effect*, INSEAD Working Paper No. 2010/16/INSEAD Social Innovation Centre (March 23, 2010).

18 15 USC § 52(a)–(b).

19 Tom Shoenberg, *Amazon.Com, Macy's, Sears Settle FTC Mislabelling Claims*, Bloomberg (January 3, 2013).

20 *ibid.*

21 *FTC Toughens Standards on Products' "Green" Claims*, USA Today, 10.2.2012, 2B ("Money" Section).

22 See the web site for Pete & Gerry's Organic Eggs, available at www.peteandgerrys.com.

23 Douglas A. Kysar, *Preferences for Processes: The Process/Product Distinction and the Regulation of Consumer Choice*, 118 Harvard Law Review 525, 529–30 (2004).

24 *Int'l Dairy Foods Ass'n v. Amestoy*, 92 F.3d 67 (2d Cir. 1996).

25 *Fiji Water Targeted in 'Greenwashing' Class Action Suit*, Environmental Leader (December 29, 2010), last accessed May 13, 2014, available at http://www.environmentalleader.com/2010/12/29/fiji-water-targeted-in-greenwashing-class-action-suit/.

26 *See* Jacquelyn Ottman, THE NEW RULES OF GREEN MARKETING: STRATEGIES, TOOLS, AND INSPIRATION FOR SUSTAINABLE BRANDING, 47 (2011).

27 Examples of sustainable brand development are from Frank-Martin Belz & Ken Peattie, *Sustainability Marketing: A Global Perspective*, pages 167–169 (2009).

28 Adapted from John Grant, *The Green Marketing Manifesto* (2007).

29 *ibid.*

30 *ibid.*

31 *See* Dirk Matten and Jeremy Moon, *'Implicit' and 'Explicit' CSR: A Conceptual Framework for a Comparative Understanding of Corporate Social Responsibility*, Academy of Management Review, 9, 21–22 (2007).

32 *See* Jacquelyn Ottman, THE NEW RULES OF GREEN MARKETING: STRATEGIES, TOOLS, AND INSPIRATION FOR SUSTAINABLE BRANDING (2011).

33 *ibid*

34 *ibid.*

35 *ibid.*

36 *ibid.*

37 *ibid.*

38 *ibid.*

39 Adapted from Ralph E. Horne, *Limits to Labels: The Role of Eco-Labels in the Assessment of Product Sustainability and Routes to Sustainable Consumption*, 33 International Journal of Consumer Studies 175–182, 177 (2009).

40 See the Rainforest Alliance web page on Certification, Verification, and Validation Services, last accessed May 13, 2014, available at http://www.rainforest-alliance.org/certification-verification.

41 *Rainforest Alliance Certified Coffee Reached 4.5% of Global Market*, Environmental Leader (April 12, 2013), last accessed May 13, 2014, available at http://www.environmentalleader.com/2013/04/12/rainforest-alliance-certified-coffee-reached-4-5-of-global-market/.

42 See Fair Trade USA's website on Certification and Your Business, last accessed May 13, 2014, available at http://fairtrade-usa.org/certification.

43 *An Overview of Ecolabels and Sustainability Certifications in the Global Marketplace*, pages 11–12, Nicholas Institute for Environmental Policy Solutions, Corporate Sustainability Initiative, Duke University (October 2010).

44 See the UTZ Certified website on traceability services for palm oil, last accessed May 13, 2014, available at http://www.utzcertified.org/en/traceabilityservices/palmoil.

45 *ibid.*

46 Ralf W. Seifert and Joana M. Comas, *Have Ecolabels Had Their Day? The Truth Behind Sustainability Labels From the People Who Integrate Them*, IMD, May 2012.

47 *ibid.*

48 *See* Sabrina Tavernise, *F.D.A. Makes It Official: BPA Can't Be Used in Baby Bottles and Cups*, The New York Times, July 17, 2012.

49 Douglas A. Kysar, *Preferences for Processes: The Process/Product Distinction and the Regulation of Consumer Choice*, 118 Harvard Law Review 525, 574 (2004).

50 CAL. BUS. & PROF. CODE § 17204 (West 1997).

51 *See Nike, Inc. v. Kasky*, 45 P.3d 243, 262 (Cal. 2002).

52 William McCall, *Nike Free-Speech Case Settled for $1.5 Million*, SEATTLE TIMES, Sept. 13, 2003, at C1.

CHAPTER 8

Supply Chain Management

BUILDING A SUSTAINABLE SUPPLY CHAIN: LESSONS FROM STARBUCKS[1]

Most of us have had the experience of sitting at a Starbucks coffee shop enjoying our coffee, a frappuccino, or perhaps a pumpkin spiced latte. We may have noticed that Starbucks' coffee beans come from all across the globe, including Guatemala, Sumatra, Brazil, Kenya, Mexico, and Ethiopia. However, we have probably not given much thought to the complexity of decisions and coordination required to make sure that we, the customer, receive the beverage we enjoy. In fact, for Starbucks to be able to deliver such a high quality, consistent, and broad product offering to more than 15,000 store locations across 40 countries, it must manage an extensive global network of trading partners, from coffee growers to bean roasting facilities to coffee distributors. Part and parcel of this leadership in global supply chain management is Starbucks' commitment to sustainability.

In 2004 Starbucks launched an in-house sustainable supply chain program called Coffee and Farmer Equity (C.A.F.E.) Practices. The program includes a set of social, environmental, economic, and quality objectives that provide specific guidelines for the production and processing of coffee. Consider that in 2011 alone, Starbucks purchased 367 million pounds of coffee—or 86 percent of their global purchases—through its C.A.F.E. Practices program. That means the vast majority of Starbucks coffee is procured sustainably. This in-house program is separate from, but consistent with, the company's participation in the *Fair Trade Certification* process, discussed in Chapter 7.

Starbucks utilizes a strategy of developing mutually beneficial relationships with suppliers. Some of these efforts include: maintaining price disclosures with suppliers, extending credit to growers, facilitating economic development in growing regions of the world, promoting environmental sensitivity at farms in terms of soil quality and

> *"All the benefits of sustainability are only possible if you tackle the issues of the supply chain. If not, it's greenwashing."*
>
> —*Dierk Peters,* **FORMER INTERNATIONAL MARKETING MANAGER, UNILEVER**

> *"You can't possibly source everything sustainably, as Unilever has declared as a 2020 goal, unless you engage thousands and thousands of people around the world. You'll need technical innovations, management innovations, process innovations, and cultural innovations."*
>
> —*Peter Senge,* **PROFESSOR AT MIT SLOAN SCHOOL OF MANAGEMENT**

LEARNING OBJECTIVES

After completing this chapter, you should be able to:

1. Explain the role of supply chain management (SCM) in sustainable business.
2. Explain the role of life-cycle assessment in sustainable supply chain management.
3. Identify sustainability issues involved in managing the supply chain infrastructure.
4. Explain the management of external supply chain stakeholders.

biodiversity protection, and even offering social support to farm worker families. This commitment has extended sustainability through the entire supply chain, from "bean to cup."

So have these efforts been effective? The issue of setting standards and measuring performance is a key to sustainability, and supply chain management is no exception. To provide verification, in 2009 Conservation International, an independent non-profit organization, began to produce annual global reports assessing these sustainability efforts. It conducted independent field surveys with farmers participating in Starbucks' C.A.F.E. Practices and farmers not participating in the program in two sample regions, Guatemala and Colombia. The results of the independent assessment show a highly effective sustainable supply chain management program.[2]

Through this process Starbucks has learned a few lessons about sustainable supply chain management. Building sustainability into the supply chain is a long-term competitive business strategy. Sustainability practices are not just good for public relations, but are good business. The benefits to Starbucks have been excellent and consistent product quality, delivery, access to local knowledge, and improved profitability.

8.1 Sustainable Supply Chain Management in Context

According to a survey of over 700 professionals working on the forefront of sustainable business, the most significant developments of 2013 were supply chain disruptions and supplier labor conditions.[3] The most salient tragedy of the year was the Rana Plaza disaster, where a shoddily constructed 8-story commercial building that housed garment factories collapsed while workers were present inside. The top four floors of the building were constructed without a permit, and the concrete structure was not reinforced with steel; as a result of failed regulatory oversight and substandard construction methods, more than 1,100 people died and over 1,000 others were maimed and injured.[4] The resulting international outcry "shamed many international clothing companies into pledging to help finance safety improvements in other Bangladeshi factories."[5]

In a global economy characterized by Western consumption from Eastern production, the Rana Plaza disaster puts into stark contrast the working conditions in developed versus developing nations. Social and environmental impacts that take place deep in a supply chain are no less real than those that result directly from a company's own activities.

8.1.1 **The Role of SCM in Sustainability**

In **Chapter 7**, we discussed the role of consumer preferences and demands in shaping the social and environmental profile of products and services. This chapter explains how the product and service supply chain can meet consumer demand for sustainability. The major reasons for sustainable supply chain management are risk reduction, cost avoidance, efficiency improvements, reputation, and product innovation.

Supply chain management (SCM) is the design and management of flows of products, information, and funds throughout the network of all entities involved in producing and delivering a finished product to the final customer. It involves the coordination and management of all the activities of a supply chain, from supplier to end customer, as shown in Figure 8.1. This includes sourcing and transporting raw materials, manufacturing and assembling the products, storing goods in warehouses, order entry and tracking, distribution to retailers, and delivery to the final customer.

Another way of describing supply chain management is the expression, "source, make, move, and sell," used to describe the roles of the various entities within a supply chain. See Figure 8.2.

The flows through the supply chain begin with **suppliers** who supply and transport raw materials and components to producers or manufacturers. **Manufacturers** transform these materials into finished products that are then shipped either to the manufacturer's own distribution centres or to wholesale **distributors**. Next, the products are shipped to **retailers** who sell the product to final **customers**.

Consider the Starbucks' supply chain discussed in the Chapter Opener. At the beginning of the supply chain are coffee farmers at various locations across the globe that grow the coffee beans. The coffee beans are picked, packaged in burlap bags, and transported to coffee roasters, entities that roast the beans. The roasted beans are then sent to coffee distributors, who then sort, package, and move the beans to retailer outlets such as Starbucks' cafés, to be purchased by the consumer.

> **Supply Chain Management** The design and management of flows of products, information, and funds throughout the network of all entities involved in producing and delivering a finished product to the final customer.
>
> **Suppliers** Companies that provide raw materials and components to producers or manufacturers.
>
> **Manufacturers** Companies that transform raw materials into finished products.
>
> **Distributors** Companies that receive product shipments in bulk from manufacturers at centralized storage locations, and in turn supply smaller batches to retailers.
>
> **Retailers** Companies that sell to end users of products.
>
> **Customers** Any downstream company in a supply chain, as well as the final consumer.

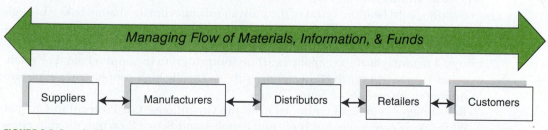

FIGURE 8.1 Supply Chain Management

FIGURE 8.2 Source, Make, Move, Sell

Sustainable supply chain management is the "strategic, transparent integration and achievement of an organization's social, environmental, and economic goals in the systemic coordination of key inter-organizational business processes for improving the long-term economic performance of the individual company and its supply chains."[6]

In theory, we can combine the triple-bottom-line perspective and the life-cycle perspective in order to illustrate the social, economic, and environmental impacts of supply chains.[7] Supply managers must exercise influence over supplier, manufacturer, distributor, and customer behavior when it comes to reducing the life cycle impacts of products.

The United States Environmental Protection Agency recommends a four-step sustainable supply chain decision framework called **The Lean and Green Supply Chain**:[8] (1) Identify environmental costs within your processes or facilities; (2) Determine opportunities that would yield significant cost savings and reduce environmental impact; (3) Calculate the benefits of your proposed alternatives; and (4) Decide, implement and monitor sustainability innovations. This framework is equally applicable to social and economic impacts of supply chain activities.

Sustainable supply chain practices run the gamut, including sustainable design (marketing and engineering); procurement practices (certifying supplier labor, purchasing environmentally sound materials and products); total quality environmental management (internal performance measurement, pollution prevention); environmentally friendly packaging and transportation; and the various product end-of-life practices such as reduction, reuse, remanufacturing, and recycling of materials.[9]

To be clear, committing to sustainability and developing a sustainable supply chain are two different issues. By 2008, a majority of worldwide firms surveyed by *The Economist* had implemented a Corporate Social Responsibility policy; however, only half of these firms extended this policy to their supply chains.[10] When Accenture surveyed CEOs in 2010, 88% of the members of the United Nations Global Compact on sustainable business practices considered supply chains an area of specific importance to sustainability, but actual implementation of sustainable supply chain practices continued to lag nonetheless.[11]

Supply chains bear the brunt of the most significant climate change risks (through resource scarcity and supply disruption), and supply chains are responsible for most of the emissions that exacerbate climate change impacts. For instance, "up to 60 percent of a manufacturing company's carbon footprint is in its supply chain. For retailers, that figure is closer to 80 percent – with an equally high supply chain exposure to human rights and social issues."[12]

Recall the taxonomy of emissions from the Greenhouse Gas Protocol in Chapter 5. While many companies are reporting Scope 1 and Scope 2 carbon dioxide emissions (direct and indirect emissions from internal operations and power consumption, respectively), few companies are yet reporting Scope 3 emissions—that is, emissions from their supply chain—even thought that is the major source of global greenhouse gas emissions.[13] Indeed, 86% of greenhouse gas emissions come from supply chain activities, not internal operations.[14] According to an Ernst & Young survey, only 36% of companies are working directly with suppliers to

CROSS-LINKAGE

For more on carbon footprinting metrics and tools for supply chains, see Chapter 5: Metrics, Tools, and Reporting: The Role of Finance and Accounting.

reduce the supply chain carbon footprint.[15] Clearly, while sustainable supply chain management is an important policy ambition, there is still work to be done.

8.1.2 Managing Supply Chain Risks: Going Beyond the First Tier

Environmental concerns, including climate change, energy use, environmental contamination, and resource depletion, have substantial impacts on supply chain management by interfering with resource inputs or disrupting logistics. According to a World Economic Forum survey on supply chain and transport risk, 59% of supply chain experts cited natural disasters as the greatest trigger of global supply chain disruption.[16] For instance, the Mississippi River is a major shipping lane through the continental United States. However, the mighty Mississippi has reached historic lows after record droughts, and the low waters have already interrupted the flow of billions of dollars worth of commodities. A shutdown of the river could affect more than 8,000 jobs and interrupt the shipping of 7.2 million tons of commodities worth about $2.8 billion.[17]

Environmental risks can pose major supply chain disruption challenges. Only **resilient supply chains** can withstand system shocks from environmental disasters. "The degree of supply chain resilience is typically assessed by the extent to which value is reduced or harm is caused, and the speed with which normal operations can be restored."[18] Relational supply chains are better poised to bear risks from environmental threats than arm's-length transactional supply chains because the former involves superior communication, collaboration, and risk-sharing.

Resilient Supply Chains Can absorb system shocks from environmental disasters in order to avoid supply chain disruptions and resume normal operations.

According to the World Economic Forum on supply chain risk, over half of respondents cited a handful of issues as the least effectively managed supply chain risk and sources of vulnerability: (1) over-reliance on oil to power supply chain activities, (2) lack of transparency and information sharing, (3) fragmentation along the value chain, (4) extensive subcontracting, and (5) supplier visibility.[19] The overall theme is that global supply chains are multi-layered, complex, and opaque. According to Nick Wildgoose, the Supply Chain Product Leader for Global Corporate at Zurich Financial Services, the lack of visibility is troubling: "Given the impact that a supply chain failure can have on the performance and reputation of an organization, it is no longer good enough in respect of critical supply chains just to look at tier one suppliers."[20]

CROSS-LINKAGE

For more on environmental risks and resilience, see Chapter 6: Risk Management.

It is difficult to ensure suppliers' compliance with corporate codes of conduct when the supplier sub-contracts production to another firm. We discuss examples of supplier audits in the following section. Increasing transparency and accountability through second and even third-tier suppliers is a critical ingredient in sustainable supply chain management. Doing so ensures that life cycle costs are accounted for, that laborers are treated with human dignity, and that supply chain risks are predicted and to the extent feasible, managed. Assessing adverse impacts and risks must go beyond the consumer-facing brand and the first tier suppliers, and must look deeper into the supply chain.

8.1.3 Traceability and Increased Supply Chain Transparency

As we learned in Chapter 5, measuring and reporting sustainability performance can satisfy investors and customers, but it also provides the information necessary to improve transparency and communication across product supply chains.

For example, The Sustainability Consortium designs and implements credible, transparent and scalable science-based measurement and reporting systems accessible to all producers, retailers, and users of consumer products.[23] The mission of TSC is to develop methodologies, tools, and strategies to drive a new generation of products and supply networks that address environmental, social, and economic imperatives. TSC has formed working groups to tailor metrics and reporting best practices to specific industries or focus areas, including textiles, electronics, forestry, agriculture, personal care products, packaging, retail, and toys.

TSC is pioneering a standardized framework for communicating sustainability-related information throughout product supply chains, called the **Sustainability Measurement and Reporting System** (SMRS). The SMRS "enables rigorous product level Life Cycle Assessments to be done at a fraction of today's time and cost, and provides a platform for sustainability-related data sharing across the supply chain."[24] Sustainability-related data sharing will make it easier for companies to "effectively manage the sustainability of upstream supplies and suppliers, and communicate product sustainability downstream to consumers."[25]

Information sharing is essential for transparency measures, such as traceability. The Global Compact Advisory Group on Supply Chain Sustainability established a task force on traceability in February 2013. **Traceability** is defined in the ISO 9000 series standard for quality management as "the ability to retrace the history, use or location of an entity by means of recorded identification." Traceability means

Sustainability Measurement and Reporting System A standardized framework for communicating sustainability-related information throughout product supply chains, developed by The Sustainability Consortium.

Traceability The ability to retrace the history, use or location of a product or component by means of recorded identification.

tracking "a product from its raw materials to its final placement in the market and ultimately its end-of-life disposal."[26]

As discussed in Chapter 4: Legal Frameworks, a variety of laws require supply chain transparency. The U.S. Dodd-Frank Act requires companies doing business in the United States to provide chain of custody information about conflict minerals. Additionally, the state of California passed a law requiring major importers to disclose efforts to eradicate human trafficking from their supply chains. In addition to legal compliance, companies should strive for improved transparency in supply chains for all of the reasons discussed in the earlier section on managing risks. Traceability provides "access to accurate data across the entire supply chain to support proactive risk assessment and mitigation; safeguards public health and safety by streamlining related product recalls; and increases brand equity and consumer satisfaction by ensuring product integrity and quality throughout the supply chain."[27]

Because of the expense of traceability programs, supply chain collaboration is an essential ingredient in implementing transparency programs through supply chains. We discuss supply chain collaboration in the section on managing suppliers in Section 8.4.

8.1.4 Business Benefits of Sustainable SCM

Making sustainability an integral part of SCM decisions is not an altruistic effort but rather is smart business. In fact, there are four documented types of payoffs that come with improving a company's sustainability performance. The first are **financial payoffs** that include reduced operating costs, increased revenue, lower administrative costs, lower capital costs, and stock market premiums. Next are **customer-related payoffs** that include increased customer satisfaction, product innovation, market share increase, improved reputation, and new market opportunities. **Operational payoffs** are those that result from process innovation, productivity gains, reduced cycle times, improved resource yields, and waste minimization. Lastly, **organizational payoffs** include employee satisfaction, improved stakeholder relationships, reduced regulatory intervention, reduced risk, and increased organizational learning. Supply chain management in particular promises benefits in the form of risk management, brand improvement, increased revenues, and cost reduction.[28]

Supply chains are under increasing financial pressure, and stages that do not add value to the supply chain are quickly bypassed or eliminated. For this reason, a supply chain is often called a **value chain** or a value network. Today's concept of the supply chain evolved from the concept of a value chain, introduced by Harvard Business School professor Michael Porter in the 1980s.

Porter explained that a company's competitive advantage comes from the many discrete activities that a firm performs and that each of these activities contributes to the firm's total cost position. With the rise of outsourcing, the value chain concept has evolved into optimization of supply chain management. Now the calculation to determine the value of each stage of the supply chain increasingly includes issues of sustainability, not just financial costs and benefits. Half of the survey respondents

Financial Payoffs Reduced operating costs, increased revenue, lower administrative costs, lower capital costs, and stock market premiums.

Customer-Related Payoffs Increased customer satisfaction, product innovation, market share increase, improved reputation, and new market opportunities.

Operational Payoffs Process innovation, productivity gains, reduced cycle times, improved resource yields, and waste minimization.

Organizational Payoffs Employee satisfaction, improved stakeholder relationships, reduced regulatory intervention, reduced risk, and increased organizational learning.

Value Chain The various value-adding activities performed by an organization to deliver a product or service to the market.

for PricewaterhouseCooper's 2013 Global Supply Chain survey indicated that sustainability is an important or very important supply chain value driver.[29]

8.1.5 Water-Related Supply Chain Risks

Supply of natural resources, particularly water, is critical for virtually every sector of the economy. For that reason, shortcomings in availability and quality of freshwater are a growing source of risk for businesses around the world, as discussed in Chapter 6: Risk Management. By 2030, every sector will see increased water demand at the same time global shortfall between demand and supply is expected to reach 40%.[30] There are several water-shortage risks for supply chains. See Table 8.1.

Unless a company works in manufacturing or raw material production where access to water is essential for day-to-day business, they are probably not completely aware of their water footprint, and may neglect to factor in water-related risks to their overall risk management program. Nonetheless, water risks impact not just the material processors or the manufacturers, but all of the businesses reliant on their products and services. Increased operating costs from water scarcity, pollution, and other threats to water supplies will be passed along the supply chain, increasing the costs of goods for business-to-business transactions as well as for end-users.

8.1.6 Human Rights, Child Labor, and Occupational Safety in Global Supply Chains

Academic research into sustainable supply chains has primarily focused on either supplier management for environmental risks and performance, or using supply chains to create environmentally superior products.[31] For the most part, "research is still dominated by green/environmental issues[, while] social aspects and also the integration of the three dimensions of sustainability are still rare."[32] Perhaps this is

---

TABLE 8.1

Water-Related Supply Chain Risks

Supply Chain Area	Water-Related Risk
Raw Material Production	Production of food crops, fibers, and metals has a substantial water footprint. Water scarcity, pollution, and climate change threaten to decrease yield and increase commodity costs.
Suppliers	Apparel, electronics, and food sectors may experience supply disruption, as raw material production is limited. If a supplier lacks access to water, it may be difficult to meet fulfillment requests.
Direct Operations	Manufacturing that depends upon water quality is limited by pollution, which may require expensive filtration technology to prevent operational disruption.
End Product	If customers are located in a water-stressed region, demand for water-intensive or water-polluting products will be limited.

Source: UN Global Compact, CEO Water Mandate: Risks in the Value Chain, available at http://ceowatermandate.org/business-case/risks-in-the-value-chain/.

due in part to the limited visibility on the part of supplier labor. For these reasons, this section highlights issues related to human rights and occupational safety and health in global supply chains.

Human Rights Companies that participate in the **United Nations Global Compact** "are expected to know and show that they are respecting human rights, and when people are harmed by business activities, that there is both adequate accountability and effective redress."[33]

While adverse impacts must be accounted for, at the same time, "companies are encouraged to explore what positive impacts they can have on human rights; as both a business opportunity, including improved reputation, consumer solidarity and innovation; and to maintain the social license to operate."[34] Because they are uniquely vulnerable to human rights abuses, special attention should be given to women, children, indigenous peoples, minorities, and people with disabilities.[35]

Child Labor **Child labor** is a serious concern when sourcing labor from developing countries where worker protection oversight is minimal or non-existent.

According to the International Labor Organization (ILO), by 2012 there were 168 million child laborers worldwide (down from 246 million in 2000); with 85 million children exposed to hazardous working conditions (down from 171 million in 2000).[36] See Table 8.2. Of the approximate 1.5 billion children in the world, over 10% were involved in child labor, and over 5% were involved in hazardous working conditions.[37]

Child labor does not include children engaged in permissible light work for only a few hours per week. Hazardous work by children refers to activities that lead to adverse effects on the child's safety, health, and moral development, including long hours, night shifts, all forms of abuse, physically dangerous working conditions, and heavy loads, among other things.[38]

Occupational Safety and Health According to ILO statistics, approximately 337 million people are victims of workplace accidents annually, and 2.3 million people die every year from occupational injuries and work-related diseases.[39] That means one worker dies from a work-related accident or disease, and 160 workers suffer a work-related accident, every 15 seconds. Better Work, a joint initiative between the ILO and the International Finance Corporation, found a 75% non-compliance rate

> **United Nations Global Compact** Calls for participating companies to know and show that they are respecting human rights, and when people are harmed by business activities, that there is both adequate accountability and effective redress.
>
> **Child Labor** Age-inappropriate and hazardous work by children.

TABLE 8.2

Child Laborers by Region (2012)

Asia and the Pacific	78 million
Sub-Saharan Africa	59 million
Latin America and the Caribbean	13 million
Middle East and North Africa	9.2 million

Source: Marking Progress Against Child Labor: Global Estimates and Trends 2000–2012, International Labour Office, pages 4–6 (2013), available at http://www.ilo.org/wcmsp5/groups/public/—ed_norm/—ipec/documents/publication/wcms_221513.pdf.

ETHICAL DECISIONS: Taking Responsibility for Supplier Labor Conditions[42]

The **Rana Plaza disaster**, discussed in the Chapter Opener, was a building collapse in Bangladesh that constituted the largest disaster in the history of the garment industry.

The supply chain for garment fabrication is heavily dependent upon labor from Bangladesh, which is home to more than 4,000 garment factories. One of the ethical questions posed by these disasters is whether companies that source from a high-risk area have any responsibility over the people put in harm's way while fulfilling orders. Some apparel companies took complete responsibility for their role in the Rana Plaza disaster.

When Bangladeshi labor groups found Benetton clothing labels in the rubble of the Rana Plaza, the company denied that it used any of the factories in the building. However, more clothing labels and even supply orders from Benetton were found as site cleanup proceeded. The company ultimately revised its position, distancing itself from the disaster by claiming that it had put in only a one-time order.

Meanwhile, the apparel retailer Primark immediately acknowledged that it used a supplier in the Rana Plaza building, and pledged to provide compensation to employees of their supplier and their families, in the form of long-term financial aid for children who lost parents, payments to surviving family members, and assistance to those injured. According to Primark, "We are fully aware of our responsibility. We urge these other retailers to come forward and offer assistance."

Rana Plaza Disaster The largest disaster in the history of the garment industry, involving a collapsed manufacturing building in Bangladesh.

of occupational safety and health regulations in the garment sector, creating risks from toxic cleaning solvents, lack of personal protective equipment, blocked or lack of access to factory emergency exists, and inadequate toilets and sanitation facilities at factories.[40]

Manufacturers and buyers invite business risks by allowing occupational health and safety problems to fester. Workplace injuries can be tragic, reducing morale, and productivity from remaining workers, while increasing the likelihood of turnover and liabilities. Companies that adopt health and safety management systems enjoy reduced costs, lowered rates of absenteeism, fewer accidents, higher employee retention, and increased productivity from workers by reducing fatigue and improving employee satisfaction.[41]

8.2 Managing the Entire Product Life Cycle

CROSS-LINKAGE

For more information on life cycle analysis and other sustainability metrics and tools, see Chapter 5: Metrics, Tools, and Reporting: The Role of Finance and Accounting.

SCM has tremendous opportunity to impact sustainability given its cross-functional and cross-enterprise nature. The basic idea of sustainable business is to reduce costs while helping the environment and benefiting affected communities. The critical question for sustainable supply chain management becomes how to define *costs*. In the past, most companies were focused on reducing unit costs. Many companies later evolved into looking at total landed costs with the on-set of global trade. Companies also started looking at the usage costs with a piece of equipment (e.g., what are the costs per copy when using a copier). A more complete accounting of costs comes from the **life cycle costs**, which assess social, economic, and environmental impacts of a product throughout its entire supply chain. We discuss means to manage the product life cycle from design to disposal in this section.

> **Life Cycle Costs** The social, economic, and environmental impacts of a product throughout its entire supply chain.

8.2.1 Life Cycle Assessment and Cradle-to-Cradle Design

Life Cycle Assessment (LCA) involves looking at the life-cycle of a product, service or process from raw material extraction, through manufacture and distribution to ultimate consumption.

> **Life Cycle Assessment** A technique to assess environmental impacts associated with all the stages of a product's life.

Life cycle assessment is a technique to assess environmental impacts associated with all the stages of a product's life (i.e., from raw material extraction through materials processing, manufacture, distribution, use, repair and maintenance, disposal, and recycling). LCA considers key environmental impacts, such as amount of carbon dioxide released, smog formation, oxygen depletion, and solid waste generation. LCA can help avoid a narrow outlook on environmental concerns that would arise by looking at the product only at one stage of its life. LCA does so by compiling an inventory of relevant energy and material inputs and environmental releases; evaluating the potential impacts associated with identified inputs and releases; and interpreting the results to enable the company to make a more informed decision.

LCA can substantially improve the environmental performance of processes and systems. In LCA, the environmental impacts of a product or service are analyzed through all phases of its life, with the objective of reducing environmental damage, in part by enhancing resources conservation and efficiency. Also, LCA is part of the ISO 14,000 family of standards on environmental management put out by the International Organization for Standards (ISO). These standards document what a company is doing to minimize their effects on the environment caused by its activities and to achieve continual improvement of its environmental performance.

> **CROSS-LINKAGE**
>
> For more information on life cycle, carbon footprint, water footprint analysis, and ISO standards, see Chapter 5: Metrics, Tools, and Reporting: The Role of Finance and Accounting. Life cycle assessment is also discussed in Chapter 9: Operations Management.

To develop a holistic and comprehensive understanding of environmental impacts, the full life cycle of a product or process need to be considered. In particular, it is the early stages of product development, where the product concept itself is devised, that are of particular importance for sustainability. Retrofitting after the fact results in incremental changes which can offer only limited benefits. LCA examines existing processes for consumption of energy and other resources, as well as environmental discharges of material and energy wastes and considers design alternatives.

LCA can enable cradle-to-cradle design, discussed in the next section, by illuminating the impacts of materials, processes, reuse, recycling, and final disposal.

8.2.2 Product Design

Cradle-to-Cradle Design The process of using environmentally friendly inputs and transforming these inputs through change agents - whose byproducts can improve or be recycled within the existing environment.

Cradle-to-cradle design is "the process of using environmentally friendly inputs and transforming these inputs through change agents - whose byproducts can improve or be recycled within the existing environment. This process develops outputs that can be reclaimed and re-used at the end of their life-cycle."[43] If a company wants to introduce a product with sustainability principles in mind, it needs to consider how its design creates life cycle impacts, and select the design that minimizes the environmental impacts identified by this analysis.

Innovations in product design can significantly improve environmental and social sustainability performance.[44] Changes in product design affect use of material, sourcing, and disposal. Often companies are not aware that some of their components are harmful to the environment. For example, one of the most distinctive features of Nike shoes, aside from the dramatic swooping check that identifies the brand, is the air-bubble in the heel of Nike Air sneakers. However, the company only recently became aware that the pocket contained a gas known as sulphur hexafluoride, or SF6, which is actually a potent greenhouse gas. As part of Nike's sustainability initiative, Nike replaced SF6 with nitrogen, which breaks up more readily upon release, and is not a greenhouse gas. An apparently small change such as this can have significant environmental impact in the aggregate.

Some environmentally friendly innovations in product design can actually transform the business model, as happened with Interface Inc., the world's largest carpet manufacturer (discussed in Chapter 1). Originally, Interface was in the business of selling carpets to clients. When the carpet was worn out, Interface would replace the entire carpet. Now, Interface installs carpets in modular form, giving clients the opportunity to inspect carpet tiles for wear on a monthly basis, replacing only the tiles that are worn out. This business model transformation provides a savings to clients and is better for the environment. The policy also requires less pollution and energy consumption than the original model of replacing the entire product.

In a recent study that ranks 36 different phones based on the relative concentration and presence of toxic chemicals by the Ecology Center and ifixit.com, cellular phones were ranked on a scale of "Low," "Medium," and "High."[45] A lower score indicates that fewer toxic chemicals were present, while a higher score signals a more toxic profile. Ten mobile phone manufacturers, including Apple, Motorola, Hewlett-Packard, LG Electronics, Nokia, and Samsung were included in the study. The Ecology Center study looked at levels of toxins such as mercury and lead in components such as the screen, soldering, and computer processor. While Apple showed the greatest improvement of any manufacturer in the study among phone models released in the last five years, none of the phones tested was completely free of toxic chemicals. Samsung phones had the highest average rating of all phones tested.

8.2.3 Packaging

Sustainable Packaging Product containers that are sourced, manufactured, transported, and recycled using renewable energy; which optimize the use of renewable or recycled source materials; are manufactured using clean production technologies; are physically designed to optimize energy and materials used; and are effectively recovered using biological or closed loop cycles.

Packaging offers an excellent opportunity to significantly impact the sustainability of a supply chain. **Sustainable packaging** is beneficial, safe and healthy for individuals and communities throughout its life cycle; is sourced, manufactured, transported,

GLOBAL PERSPECTIVES: Talking on Toxic Cell Phones?[46]

"Even the best phones from our study are still loaded with chemical hazards," said Jeff Gearhart, research director at the Ecology Center and founder of Healthy-Stuff.org. "These chemicals, which are linked to birth defects, impaired learning and other serious health problems, have been found in soils [at high levels] at e-waste recycling sites in China."

Sustainable product design would require redesigning products to use safer materials, such as less hazardous resins, and replacing PVC in cabling and other applications. It also means simplifying design to avoid the need for high-risk materials, and moving to less toxic substances, such as using mercury-free LCD displays and arsenic-free glass. These product design choices have ramifications for the entire supply chain of cell phone manufacturers. "Consumer demand for more sustainable mobile phones is driving companies to produce better products," said Gearhart. Better products ultimately require more transparent, environmentally benign supply chains.

and recycled using renewable energy; optimizes the use of renewable or recycled source materials; is manufactured using clean production technologies; is physically designed to optimize energy and materials used; and is effectively recovered using biological or closed loop cycles.[47]

For example, Proctor & Gamble reduced the negative environmental consequences of product packaging by designing a toothpaste tube that can be shipped and displayed for retail without any paper packaging.[48] Also, Nestlé Waters North America has created its Eco-Shape bottle that uses 25% less plastic compared to earlier bottles.[49] Similarly, Nestlé decided to use smaller labels on the outside of their water bottles in order to save paper; in five years, the company saved an estimated 20 million pounds of paper. Product packaging is so important that Walmart has developed an environmental sustainability scorecard to evaluate product packaging used by its vendors.[50] The criteria include GHG emissions from packaging production, product-to-packaging ratio, recycled packaging content, and emissions from transporting the packaging.

Sustainable packaging innovation is taking the form of **active packaging**, which can absorb food odors, retard oxygen migration, and preserve food longer than traditional packaging. This helps reduce food waste, prevent foodborne illnesses, improve product quality, lengthen shelf life, and increase distribution channels. One of the concerns with the new types of plastics being invented for active packaging is whether they can be recycled.

Wayne Wegner is Director of Sustainability for Bemis, Co., and a leading expert in packaging sustainability initiatives. According to Wegner, there are a few active packaging products "designed for recyclability that we believe can be more efficiently managed through existing recycling facilities. Also, as polymers sourced from renewable feedstocks become more cost competitive and their performance is improved, preliminary life cycle assessments have shown that these will improve the sustainability of the package."[51]

Product packaging can serve multiple purposes. It takes just a little bit of imagination to envision a further use for a package that would otherwise end up in a landfill. Innovations in use of product packaging can lead to considerable environmental

Active Packaging Food product containers which can absorb food odors, retard oxygen migration, and preserve food in order to reduce food waste, prevent foodborne illnesses, improved product quality, increase shelf life, and increase distribution channels.

and economic savings. For example, Stony-Field Farms, a dairy company famous for its green policies, has implemented a zero-waste concept that significantly reduces pollution. The company has a policy of take-back for the yogurt cups it sells. These plastic yogurt cups are then used to manufacture toothbrushes.[52] Other companies use aluminium cans to make office furniture.

Companies can also work together in partnerships to take advantage of each other's talents in creating sustainable consumer products. Consider India Proctor & Gamble, which decided to offer Pantene shampoo in single-serve packages for $0.02 each to low-income communities.[53] The goal is to allow individuals at the very **bottom of the pyramid** to access product markets typically only available to consumers in developed countries.

Of course, single serve packaging creates the problem of disposing of the packaging. Cargill and Dow Chemical researchers developed biodegradable packages for these mini-products to avoid excess waste. P&G's low-income market-penetrating product offerings combined with Dow's low-impact environmental packaging exemplifies how collaboration between supply chain partners can lead to innovations that promote social and environmental sustainability.

8.2.4 Sourcing

Sourcing practices can dramatically impact sustainability. Selecting suppliers that follow sustainability practices – and finding ways to monitor their compliance – are a large issue for companies. The sustainability performance of suppliers differs around the globe. According to the *Carbon Disclosure Project*, suppliers in Europe and Asia have superior climate change performance than those in North America or the rest of the world, measured in terms of having set an emissions reduction target, having a climate change communications strategy, and having accrued monetary savings from greenhouse gas emissions reductions.[54]

Improvements in sourcing do not have to be revolutionary to be effective. Even incremental or piecemeal improvements in sourcing count for something. For example, instead of overhauling all products, Ben & Jerry's simply released a new product line called For A Change, which procures cocoa, vanilla, and coffee beans from farmers who participate in cooperative farmers' associations that ensure these farmers a fair price for their beans.

Deciding how to evaluate, select, and monitor suppliers is a critical task. A structured screening process can help companies choose suppliers who meet sustainability criteria. For example, Nike developed a **New Source Selection Process** to determine whether to acquire a new factory.[55] The criteria include inspection results along environmental, safety, and health dimensions, as well as a third-party labor audit. This helps ensure that company expansion is consistent with principles of environmental and social sustainability.

Some companies rely on contracting to mandate certain practices from their suppliers. In order to ensure compliance with labor standards, L'Oréal uses a supplier selection process that begins with contract language requiring compliance from suppliers and supplier subcontractors.[56] L'Oréal enforces these social sustainability initiatives by monitoring compliance through surprise audits involving plant inspections,

Bottom of the Pyramid The largest, poorest socioeconomic group of the population, consisting of some 4 billion people living on less than $2.50 per day.

New Source Selection Process Used by Nike to determine whether to acquire a new factory by assessing criteria such as inspection results along environmental, safety, and health dimensions, as well as a third-party labor audit.

document review, and interviews with supplier employees. When audit results fail on a rated scale, L'Oréal takes necessary corrective measures.

Other companies rely on third-party audits to monitor sustainability compliance. For example, Unilever, the world's largest tea company, has committed to sustainable sourcing for all tealeaves. In collaboration with Rainforest Alliance, Unilever sees to it that all tea-growing estates are audited assuring sustainable growth and fair trade of the product. Like Unilever, Walmart has partnered with an oversight organization to ensure sustainable sourcing. Walmart plans to purchase all wild-caught seafood from sustainable fisheries certified by the Marine Stewardship Council. This helps prevent overfishing, as well as keep fish containing unhealthy toxins like mercury off the shelves. To be sure, the reliance on third-party certification is not without its challenges, discussed in Chapter 5.[57]

In addition to selecting and monitoring supplier sustainability practices, some companies offer training programs to their suppliers to continue improving.

8.2.5 Process Design

Redesign of organizational processes can go a long way toward improving the environmental and social sustainability of a supply chain without incurring prohibitive economic costs—indeed, process design that reconciles the triple bottom line may be essential to remain competitive.[58] Consider Kingfisher—Europe's leading home-improvement retailer and third largest in the world—which uses an evaluation system that provides actions for each operating company to undertake in order to meet corporate sustainability policy.[59] The program is called **Steps to Responsible Growth** with formal evaluations taking place two times each year to monitor progress. Similarly, the Swedish hotel chain Scandic Hotels created the Resource Hunt program to incentivize employees to improve their use of resources to yield efficiency gains.[60] Hotel employees receive a part of the savings from a reduction in energy and water consumption, as well reduction in waste. Through these measures Scandic Hotels was able to save over a million dollars over just a few years.

> **Steps to Responsible Growth** Kingfisher's formal evaluation system that provides actions for each operating company to undertake in order to meet corporate sustainability policy.

Process improvements that address disposal of equipment are an important part of sustainability. Technology equipment can contain environmentally-damaging materials that are relatively impervious to natural biodegradation. Improper technology equipment disposal can pose serious environmental consequences. In light of this, Hewlett-Packard implemented a product end-of-life or take back procedure.[61] This enabled Hewlett-Packard to recycle over 70,000 tons of computer products, which were then refurbished to be resold or donated. In one procedural move, Hewlett-Packard reduced environmentally damaging waste, increased profits by creating a secondary market for used equipment, and promoted social sustainability by donating computers.

To provide a simple illustration of what a sustainability analysis would include, consider the logistics decision of locating a chemical processing facility. Initially, the choice of location would be determined considering economic factors, such as real estate cost or transportation. However, sustainability

> **CROSS-LINKAGE**
>
> For more on product take-back and extended producer responsibility, see Chapter 4: Legal Frameworks.

TABLE **8.3**

SCM Decisions and Related Environmental Effects

SCM Decision	Adverse Impact	Sustainability Tactic
Facility Location	• Negative consequences of siting on natural habitats (ecosystems) and habitat destruction. • Negative effect on humans and animals, from increased noise pollution and energy consumption; contamination of air and water.	• Minimize total material and personnel travel distances to and from the facility. • Avoid runoff from construction activity and new pavement. • Abate noise pollution. • Reduce the air pollution effects on the community.
Product Packaging	• Non-biodegradable and non-recyclable packaging leads to landfill clutter and harm to wildlife.	• Eliminate or reduce product packaging. • Rely on biodegradable and recyclable materials.
Material Flow	• Modes of transportation used to move materials have significant effects on energy consumption, traffic congestion, and pollution.	• Reduce the number of shipments. • Source locally. • Strategically locate warehouses. • Consolidate shipments. • Select transportation modes wisely.
Inventory Control	• Increased energy use, increased motor vehicle congestion.	• Minimize total material movement to and from the facility by delivery consolidation and accepting the carrying of larger inventory quantities.

Source: From SCM Decisions and Related Environmental Effects. Benita M. Beamon, Environmental and Sustainability Ethics in Supply Chain Management, Vol. 11 Science and Engineering Ethics 221–234 (2005). Reprinted with kind permission from Springer Science and Business Media.

requires an analysis of environmental and social factors that go well beyond these basic economic considerations, as shown in Table 8.3.

A chemical factory may affect nearby plant and animal populations as well as local human health by introducing air, water, and noise pollution. Further, the choice of location may implicate job availability and commuter behavior, while requiring decisions about wages for local employees.

8.3 Managing the Supply Chain Infrastructure

A critical aspect of supply chain management is the design and management of the physical infrastructure. This includes managing the network of suppliers, warehouses, distribution centers, wholesalers, retailers, and the physical movement of goods between them, which can have a substantial impact on sustainability.

8.3.1 Logistics

Logistics The movement and storage of product inventories throughout the supply chain.

The business function responsible for transporting and delivering products to the right place at the right time throughout the supply chain is **logistics**. Logistics is about movement and storage of product inventories throughout the chain. It is a critical function that supports supply chain management by being responsible for inventory flows both upstream and downstream, as without it materials would not arrive when and where they are needed.

The function of logistics is complex and requires a great deal of coordination. This includes organizing and managing the entire distribution network, including location of warehouses, distribution centers and plants, and coordinating the modes of transportation between them. It also includes the design and management of operations throughout the network for efficient storage and quick movement of goods.

Traditionally the role of logistics has been to develop the supply chain's physical infrastructure and to orchestrate delivery of the right items at the right place when needed, minimizing cost and maximizing service delivery. However, increasingly research has focused on minimizing environmental and other sustainability impacts from logistics.[62] While transporting goods to where they are most valued makes economic sense, there are major social and environmental implications. For example, trucking product by road may lead to congestion and pollution. However, by packing a vehicle more densely, we can reduce both congestion and pollution, thus creating a more sustainable supply chain. Also, logistics is a key element to comprehensive carbon reduction efforts due to its unique role in the supply chain.

There are a number of efforts logistics can put in place to significantly impact sustainability. One is effective design of the physical supply chain network, such as selecting suppliers and locations of warehouses to optimize transportation concerns. Another is to utilize new vehicles and technologies that reduce emissions and help create optimal routes and network designs that minimize sustainability metrics, such as carbon emissions. Yet another strategy is increasing collaboration between supply chain partners, even competitors, to promote sustainability and reduce the environmental footprint, such as carbon-emission. CO_2 labeling, which allows customers to compare green products based on climate change impacts, may increasingly become standardized. Transparent policies raise customer confidence that their choices have real environmental benefits.

8.3.2 Reverse Logistics

Reverse logistics is the process of moving products upstream from the customer back toward manufacturers and suppliers. This is the reverse direction from the way materials typically flow through a supply chain. This occurs for a variety of reasons; such as returns of damaged products or items the customer did not want.

Just as when products flow downstream, logistics has to organize the transporting, storage, receiving, inspecting, sorting, and all other activities, to ensure efficient flow upstream. Sometimes the items are returned directly to the manufacturer from the customer, as shown in Figure 8.3. Other times a third-party logistics provider (3PL) may be used to handle returned items and arrange for repairs bypassing the manufacturer as shown in Figure 8.4.

Reverse logistics is especially challenging to design, as this flow traditionally has not directly added value. There are many different types of items returned to many different locations: it may be a damaged product being returned for repairs, an overstock item that can be sold elsewhere, or an item that has been recalled or has failed and needs to be disposed of in an environmentally safe manner. It is up to reverse logistics to arrange for efficient upstream flow of returned products.

Reverse Logistics The process of moving products upstream from the customer back toward manufacturers and suppliers.

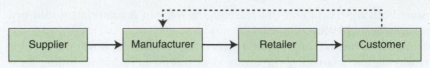

FIGURE 8.3 Reverse Logistics with Returns to the Manufacturer

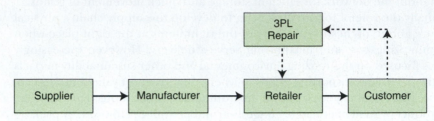

FIGURE 8.4 Reverse Logistics with Returns to a 3PL for Repairs

There are a number of issues that add complexity to reverse logistics. One is handling the financials and the cash flows once items are returned. Another is arranging for warehouse and storage space in the reverse order that does not confuse or take away from flow in the usual downstream manner. Yet another is abiding by green laws in countries that have them, which may require returning certain toxic materials for proper disposal, such as electronic waste.

The role of reverse logistics in sustainable business has become especially important. The reason is that companies are under increasing pressure to improve customer service and have made it ever easier for customers to return goods. This is especially prevalent in retail and Internet sales, where ease of returns is a major selling feature. The ability to easily return goods is becoming an order qualifier in much of retail sales. Therefore, it is imperative to innovate in reverse logistics to break away from the traditional model that fails to add value to the supply chain. Sustainable reverse logistics can both eliminate waste as well as add value. **Sustainable reverse logistics** "'closes the loop' of a typical forward supply chain and includes reuse, remanufacturing, and/or recycling of materials into new materials or other products with value in the marketplace."[63] Reverse logistics is necessary to implement cradle-to-cradle design (discussed in Section 8.2) via processing returned items that would otherwise be waste products.

Through sustainable reverse logistics, companies can cut out inefficient returns processes that result in unnecessary transportation moves, helping to reduce carbon emissions and improve air quality. The key is to manage reverse logistics processes so they are friendly to both the environment and the bottom line. Refurbishing and reusing products, especially hardware-heavy consumer electronics and home appliances, allows companies to reduce material input costs and create secondary markets for returned products.

Reverse logistics has a variety of transportation and carbon footprint implications. Refurbishing goods but ignoring transportation concerns makes for an incomplete strategy that fails to capture all of the carbon emissions from the logistics process. The procedures required to ensure timely processing and turnaround of returns directly

Sustainable Reverse Logistics The logistical functions that support cradle-to-cradle design, which close the loop of a typical forward supply chain via reuse, remanufacturing, and/or recycling.

affect emissions from transportation. One strategy is to use centralized returns processes in order to decrease multiple shipments and product location transfers. Shipping consolidated lots instead of piecemeal deliveries results in carbon footprint reductions and decreased fuel costs.[64]

8.3.3 Transportation

Transportation is probably the most important task logistics performs as it moves products throughout the supply chain. It is also an especially costly task given the high cost of transportation and distribution network design. Consider that some modes of transportation are less expensive than others, such as rail, but others are faster, such as air. Some also have much higher emission of pollutants than others, ranging from combustion of fossil fuels to noise pollution. However, these are not simple decisions.

On the expensive end, air is the most fuel-intensive mode; on the low end, pipelines are significantly limited in what they can carry. In the middle of the spectrum fall ocean, inland waterways, rail, and truck. Moving freight by rail is estimated to emit three times less nitrogen oxide and particulates per ton-mile than highway transportation. In fact, railroads are the most environmentally friendly way to move freight across land. However, trucks carry an estimated 70% of the freight that moves in the United States, while railroads cannot reach 80% of communities across the country.[65]

The decision of which mode of transportation to use is directly tied to the consideration of the distance a product has to be moved, the cost of the transportation, and its sustainability impacts. There are also other factors to consider, such as product characteristics. Perishable products, such as bananas, may need climate controlled transportation. Highly innovative products, such as Apple's iPad, may need to be delivered quickly. Products of very high value, such as diamonds, may need high security. The best strategy is to use a multimode transportation strategy that minimizes a bundle of costs, including environmental impact.

The ultimate question is how to make the entire supply chain greener. It involves also making changes to the entire system. Some ways logistics and transportation are being modified to address sustainability include the following:[66]

- relying on newer more energy efficient vehicles
- limiting idling times for vehicles
- installing properly inflated lower resistance tires
- using lighter, more aerodynamic trailers
- reducing speeds to conserve fuel
- using routing tools to reduce out-of-route miles
- cutting 'empty miles'
- making better use of fleet assets to fill empty miles
- reducing packaging to lighten loads
- reducing time drivers spend waiting to load and unload
- better dock planning
- improving routing
- creating smaller distribution centers closer to the end market

Transportation The physical means by which products and materials are moved through a supply chain.

> ### LEADERSHIP: United Parcel Service (UPS) Greens Transportation Fleet[67]
>
> We all recognize the signature brown aluminum frame oversize delivery vans used by UPS ground transportation crews. In Q4 of 2012, we might have seen a new van bearing the UPS logo. By utilizing powertrain technology, overall vehicle weight reduction, and new body aerodynamics, UPS has achieved a 40% increase in fuel efficiency in the new CV-23 vehicle.
>
> UPS added 150 of these new cleaner diesel vans developed with a chassis by carmaker Isuzu and a composite body designed by Utilimaster. Before rolling out the CV-23, UPS tested composite vans for one year in five locations to determine its ability to handle diverse climate conditions. "The areas were: Lincoln, Neb.
>
> with its rough back roads; Albany, NY for its tough winter conditions; Tucson, Ariz. for its extreme desert heat; Flint, Mich., a long urban route near Isuzu headquarters; and Acworth, Ga., a high-mileage route with close access for the UPS corporate automotive department."
>
> UPS claims the CV-23s are durable and easy to maintain and repair when compared to comparable sized vehicles in their fleet, with only a small reduction in payload capacity due to the smaller size (from 700 to 630 cubic feet). To maximize the positive environmental and cost-saving impacts of these vehicles, UPS will operate them on high-mileage delivery routes.

Understand that transportation and logistics have a huge impact on the sustainable supply chain and that there have been huge changes in consumer transportation, from gas-electric hybrid vehicles, alternative fuels, to straight electric-powered vehicles. Compared with other industries, third-party logistics (3PL) companies are already ahead of the game. Many large 3PL providers increased their respective commitments to developing more sustainability programs during that time, according to a separate report this year. FedEx, UPS, and DHL have all invested in more fuel-efficient vehicles and converted existing trucks to cleaner emission models.

8.3.4 Facility Location

Facility Location Choosing the parcel upon which capital assets and corporate activities will be take place.

Logistics is also involved in determining best location of warehouses, distribution centers, and other storage areas in relation to manufacturing facilities, customers, and suppliers. Decisions on **facility location** have a direct impact on difficulty of movement of products, distances of travel, and ultimately customer satisfaction. Optimal locations of distribution centers, for example, can have a dramatic impact on how quickly deliveries can be received at retail locations. Location decisions also have a huge impact on transportation costs and inventory levels. It is up to logistics to determine the best locations of these facilities, considering modes of transportation to move goods between them and to the final customer.

Location of warehouses and distribution centers are important decisions for logistics managers to make. An optimal location will ease distribution of goods in a timely manner, whereas a poor location will make it more difficult. There are a number of factors that must be considered in a facility location decision.

The first important factor to consider is proximity to customers or manufacturing facilities. It is important that the location be selected to be able to serve the largest geographic market size on the same or next day basis. Directly related to this is the availability of infrastructure and access to transportation. This includes convenient access to highway or rail, presence of a major airport, and proximity to inland or ocean port facilities. Ease of access and use of transportation coupled with customer proximity are key factors that must work together.

For labor-intensive operations, such as most warehouses and distribution centers, the cost and availability of labor is another important factor. This includes considering levels of unemployment in the area, labor skills levels, productivity, work ethic, and degree of unionization. These important factors must be considered carefully. Other considerations are business and personal taxes, as they have a significant impact on the cost of doing business. Also important is the overall business climate and whether it is welcoming to new business.

There are a number of techniques that can be used to help determine where to locate warehouses and distribution centers. Some of these are quantitative models that compute distances between locations and try to find the optimal balance between costs and geographic coverage. Other methods are qualitative in nature and help the decision maker evaluate the benefits of each location. One of the more popular techniques is called **Factor Rating** and involves evaluating multiple facility location alternatives based on a number of selected factors. It is a helpful procedure as it can give structure to a seemingly chaotic process when many location factors need to be considered simultaneously.

Next we look at how factor rating can be used to make a location decision.

> **Factor Rating** A facility location optimization tool that involves evaluating multiple alternative locations based on a number of relevant factors.

Steps in Factor Rating:

Step 1:   Identify key decision factors (e.g., proximity to customers, minimization of transportation, infrastructure, taxes)

Step 2:   Assign weights to each factor based on its importance; factor weights must add to 100.

Step 3:   Establish a scale for evaluating each location relative to each factor. The most common is scale is a 5-point scale, with 1 being poor and 5 excellent.

Step 4:   Evaluate each location based on the factors selected, using the scale set up in Step 3.

Step 5:   Compute a score for each location by multiplying the weight of the factor by the score for that factor and summing the results of each alternative.

Step 6:   Select location with the highest score.

Example Urban Apparel is deciding on where to locate its distribution center to serve its northeast retail stores. It has identified six factors it considers most important and has decided to use Factor Rating to evaluate the two location alternatives based on a 5-point scale, with 1 being poor and 5 excellent. The weights assigned to each factor for each location are shown in Table 8.4, as well as the factor score for each site. We can see that location 2 has a higher total score than location 1 and, therefore, appears to be a better location based on the set factors. See Table 8.4.

In order to incorporate sustainability into location decisions, simply add salient social, economic, and environmental factors with corresponding weights to the table. Site-specific evaluations of sustainability impacts and benefits are added to the overall factor rating score for each location. One site might involve dredging portions of

TABLE 8.4

Factor Rating for Urban Apparel's Two DC Location Alternatives

Factor	Factor Weight	Factor Score at Each Location		Weight Score for Each Location (Factor Weight x Factor Score)	
		Location 1	Location 2	Location 1	Location 2
Proximity To Stores	30	2	5	60	150
Access to Highway	30	5	3	150	90
Labor Availability	20	4	5	80	100
Taxes	10	4	3	40	30
Building Cost	10	3	4	30	40
Total	100			360	410

a wetland, whereas the alternative site might involve environmental remediation of a brownfield. Although some of these considerations may already be included in the Building Cost factor, many elements such as community impact and environmental impacts might otherwise be ignored by traditional factor rating for location analysis. Adding a Sustainability factor to the location analysis enables decision-makers to align facility location choices with the company's overall sustainability strategy.

8.4 Managing Supply Chain Stakeholders

Supply chain management has always been about managing relationships with supply chain partners, including suppliers and customers. Typically, relationships have been between external suppliers, manufacturing plants, distributors, retailers, and customers. Today's supply chains, however, are much larger and complex and involve designing, planning, and optimizing a complex global network of suppliers, consumers, and third-party logistics suppliers (3PLs).

The focus on sustainable supply chains has added many more parties deserving and demanding management attention, from various consumer groups, to NGOs, to remanufacturers, waste management companies, and recycling companies, to government entities. This large number of external stakeholders has created pressures that can significantly affect a supply chain's performance and its value proposition.

CROSS-LINKAGE

For more on stakeholder theory, see Chapter 2: Perspectives and Chapter 3: Leadership, Change Management, and Corporate Governance.

Legislation may determine, for example, what new logistics infrastructure projects (seaports, airports, warehouses, plants, etc.) may be completed; politics may influence economically but not environmentally optimum location decisions, and decisions on new suppliers and service providers; new regulations may incur rising procurement, logistics, and transport cost increases, while industrial relations may create environmental pressures, such as through strikes, that may shift options in suppliers.

Stakeholder management for sustainability involves stakeholder engagement and consultation, issues and conflict management, and credibility and trust between parties.[68]

8.4.1 Suppliers

The extent and nature of supplier relationships is multifaceted. The sustainability potential of supplier relations depends on the level of integration with suppliers. Is this a single-sourcing supplier? Is that your first tier supplier for A-parts? Is it a commodity, a function, or an innovative product that you are sourcing? The more influence your supplier has in the long-term decisions affecting your supply chain, the greater should be your attention and willingness to cooperate. "By working proactively on sustainability issues with their suppliers and contractors, a company can help assure that critical supplies and services will be available on an ongoing basis and that supply chain costs are properly controlled."[69]

Arguably, between a powerful supply chain master and a relatively weaker supplier, the stronger entity has a moral if not legal responsibility to exert positive influence over the weaker entity through codes of conduct, culture training, or otherwise.[70] Power disparities between a company in a developed country and a supplier in a developing country can actually incentivize better labor practices on the part of the supplier.[71] The moral authority of a supply chain master may actually ameliorate some of the concerns about the effects of globalization, discussed in Chapter 2: Perspectives. To wit, if a supply chain master can improve labor conditions on the part of the supplier, we have less reason to be concerned that arm's-length subcontracting relationships in globalized production networks inevitably lead to diminished labor standards in the developing nation because of the power disparity and lack of government regulation. That said, regulatory differences between geographic regions can pose tricky compliance issues for the supply chain managers.

> **CROSS-LINKAGE**
>
> For more on the sustainability challenges of globalization, as well as cross-cultural ethical issues, see Chapter 2: Perspectives.

> **CROSS-LINKAGE**
>
> For more on certification processes, see Chapter 7: Marketing.

The primary issue in managing overseas transactions is compliance and transparency in supply chain processes. Manufacturers are being increasingly held responsible for the products and services – including social impacts – of suppliers; therefore, companies need to ensure supplier compliance with corporate sustainability policy. This can be done through third-party certification of supplier performance.

There are significant challenges in the implementation of compliance in supplier relations. First, there is a lack of legal requirements and common standards covering specific issues for environmental and social impacts. Second, there are cultural differences within international supply chains that can impede smooth company-wide rollout of social and environmental standards, especially in large corporations.

Third, great effort is required to verify implementation, particularly compliance at distant supplier locations.

Leading companies maintain a global perspective and track developments across divisions and nations, and understand differences between sector-specific regulatory requirements and industry standards. Best practice companies try to develop incentives and to motivate their suppliers to invest in and comply with standards, especially the more visible first-tier suppliers. Leading companies also motivate their first-tier suppliers to implement the same compliance culture and awareness, and extend it to the second and subsequent tiers of the supply chain. Lastly, it is imperative to verify the results of supplier sustainability initiatives; this way you can prove whether or not the suppliers are applying the given standards in practice.

> **Supply Chain Collaboration** Building task-oriented long-term relationships between buyers and suppliers.

Supply chain collaboration is emerging as key to sustainable supply chain management. Supply chain actors can collaboratively manage transactions, events, and processes.[72] "Supply chain trends show a move away from agnostic outsourcing towards long-term partnerships. In such relationships, resilience can be built via improved security, information sharing and knowledge exchange."[73] Long-term relationships characterized by a high degree of collaboration provide sustainable competitive advantages.[74] Collaborative long-term relationships between buyers and suppliers also reduce supply chain management risks and help promote sustainability policies through the supply chain.[75]

> **Shared Value Creation** Where the line between supplier and buyer is blurred by treating the supply arrangement as if both parties were part of the same operation, or as if they were co-owned.

One of the themes of supply chain collaboration is **shared value creation**. In situations of shared value creation, the line between supplier and buyer is blurred in a number of ways: treating the supply arrangement as if both parties were part of the same operation, treating the two parties as if they were co-owned, and focusing on the best common solutions to issues, rather than self-serving solutions.[76] Even when the benefits of sharing value are not distributed evenly between the buyers and suppliers, participation usually provides sufficient advantages to both parties that it is worthwhile.[77]

According to strategy expert Michael Porter, creating shared value—as a general strategy in a market that is shying away from traditional capital exploitation—is an important strategy not just for helping to alleviate poverty, but also assuring the supply of raw materials that supply chain masters need.[78]

8.4.2 Consumers

> **Creating Shared Value** Nestlé's rural development program to help cocoa and coffee suppliers financially while benefiting local communities.

Consumers are in a much stronger situation than in the past, and demand more and more information about product and service content, and information on use, disposal, recyclability, and environmental impacts, such as embodied Carbon Dioxide in products, Carbon Dioxide emissions for vehicles, or services such as airline flights. The tools for calculating greenhouse gas emissions are still in their infancy, and the trend of emissions disclosure is likely to increase as the tools for measuring them increase in maturity.

Consumers are increasingly able to compare products and services, supported by NGOs (see Section 8.4.3), consumer protection authorities and commercial online

GLOBAL INSIGHT: Nestlé Creates "Shared Value" for Rural Suppliers[79]

Hundreds of thousands of farmers in the developing world are caught in a vicious cycle of poverty. Low incomes mean they cannot afford new investment, which in turn limits productivity growth and keeps incomes low. As the world's leading food company, spending billions of dollars a year on commodities such as milk, cocoa and coffee, Nestlé is in a strong position to tackle this problem. Critics argue that the company should simply pay farmers higher prices for their produce, but this strategy alone can be counter-productive by causing oversupply.

In 2009, Nestlé set up its **Creating Shared Value** (CSV) initiative to find ways to improve water quality, nutrition and rural development. CSV goes beyond compliance by identifying areas of benefit for both local communities and Nestlé shareholders. On rural development, Nestlé's long-term commitment to improve the lives of its raw material suppliers has taken several forms, including:

- Purchasing directly from farmers to avoid middlemen skimming profits.
- Lowering farmers' production costs and improving productivity, for example, through the use of disease-resistant plants.
- Providing other sources of incomes, through employment at milk processing and coffee-roasting plants, and offering training to local people.
- Assisting rural farmers with investment finance and buying insurance on their behalf.

Many challenges remain in Nestlé's supply chain, not least of which is addressing the root causes of child labor in Africa and elsewhere, finding appropriate ways to share the value created, and partnering with other companies to enable initiatives to be scaled up so that they help more farmers.[80]

MANAGERIAL INSIGHT: The Role of Retailers in Sustainable SCM

Positioned near the end of the product supply chain, retailers deliver end-use products to consumers. Contrary to first appearances, retailers are not passive in the sustainable supply chain effort. Rather, "retailers are increasingly dictating to upstream suppliers their own environmental requirements for the content and packaging" of products vended at the retail outlet.[81] Therefore, the integration of sustainability into product supply chains can come from both supply chain managers and retailers. This illustrates that policies can be integrated in both upstream and downstream directions, as long as there is supply chain coordination. Whether coordination is upstream, intra-firm, or downstream, it has long been understood that environmental purchasing efforts are facilitated as a result.[82]

comparison facilities. They are increasingly demanding products, packaging, and services that are competitive in being friendly to the environment and to society; this is particularly evident in specific sectors and products such as food, toys, clothes, and cosmetics. Some consumers are also willing to pay higher prices for environmentally and socially sound products.

CROSS-LINKAGE

For more information on marketing sustainability to distinct consumer segments, see Chapter 7: Marketing.

8.4.3 Non-Governmental Organizations (NGOs) and Non-Profits

Worldwide there are many thousand national and international NGOs dealing with social, economic, and environmental issues. Many large NGOs and non-profits have established themselves as multinational organizations with wide reach and influence. Well known examples include Greenpeace, the Environmental Defense Fund, the National Resource Defense Council, to name a few.

NGOs follow many different paths to achieve their missions. These can vary between fully confrontational litigation on one hand, to cooperative, partnership-based routes on the other. Along the confrontational route, for example, many NGOs and non-profits call for new regulations or standards that may be opposed by industry. Some groups, such as Earthjustice and the Natural Resources Defense Council, use high-profile litigation against companies to enforce federal environmental and public health laws and to set industry-wide precedent for corporate conduct.

Adopting a more collaborative stance, NGOs and non-profits may support industry by helping develop and promote best practices through partnerships aiming to collaboratively develop new technologies. For example, in 2000, FedEx and the Environmental Defense Fund joined forces to develop a diesel-electric hybrid delivery truck that dramatically cut emissions while increasing fuel economy. This was an ideal application for hybrid technology, given the frequent stops and starts of FedEx's 30,000-strong parcel delivery truck fleet. FedEx and the Environmental Defense Fund shared common objectives, and the latter was the catalyst in developing a competitive process for manufacturers to develop innovative technology.

Whether the non-profit or NGO uses litigation or collaboration, one thing they tend to have in common is subject-matter expertise and the ability to perform impartial quantitative analysis. Business can glean insights into their own operations by working with non-business entities that have a different perspective on the business model. For instance, Coca-Cola partnered with the World Wildlife Fund to reduce the water demands of their soda value chain, realizing that much of the water impacts resulted from the growing practices used to develop the sugar cane used to sweeten their beverages, rather than from the fizzy soda itself.

Even if NGOs and non-profit companies were generally antagonistic to industry, business depends upon these entities to add credibility to their sustainability initiatives.

8.4.4 Governmental Agencies and Regulation

Supply chain management is a cross-company and cross-industry function, hence the regulations and standards affecting them at process, managerial, and technical levels are numerous and diverse. Examples of government regulations concerning sustainability issues for supply chains are the transport of hazardous substances, handling of consumer goods, safe working conditions, and pollution prevention. Besides these complexities there is also a growing variety of regulatory instruments directly or indirectly related to logistics and transport: laws, directives, technical specifications, bans, rules, and emissions trading.

At the product level, some of the responsibilities of supply chain managers include end-to-end traceability, inventory control, reducing excess volume, avoiding obsolescence costs, ensuring supply chain compliance at first to n-tier suppliers, and fulfilling contractual obligations and liabilities related to legislative compliance. Third party logistics (3PL) service providers face additional challenges in this regard. Typically, 3PL deal with the products of different industries, and therefore must tackle different product-related regulations and regulatory overlaps, such as those that prohibit specific product combinations in transport and storage. Although compliance with product related regulations—such as the EU directive Restriction of Hazardous Substances (RoHS)—is primarily the responsibility of manufacturing departments, such regulations still present big challenges for supply chain managers.

At supply chain network level, the main regulatory issues concerning supply chain managers in larger firms, as well as exporters, are raised by the diversity of regulations in different countries. Sustainability is not always easy to attain by multinational companies (MNCs) competing in the capitalist world order because the global reach of their supply chains pose monitoring and enforcement challenges. In order to protect their brand name, MNCs may be pressured to take responsibility for the behavior of suppliers even if it is beyond their control or outside of their purview. The geographic range of governmental regulation extends from local planning commissions via regional, state, and national governments to global, supranational, and intergovernmental organizations such as the United Nations or European Union.

> **CROSS-LINKAGE**
>
> For more on the role of government in sustainable supply chain management, see Chapter 4: Legal Frameworks.

Government also plays a key role in supply chain resilience. The World Economic Forum recommends that governments use their powers carefully when intervening during times of environmental catastrophes. "A government's ability to intervene *in extremis* should be calibrated to avoid rewarding poor risk preparation or too-big-to-fail supply chain developments."[83] Governments can also maintain resilient public infrastructure such as roads and shipping corridors that withstand system shocks from floods and the like. The principles of resilience are discussed in Chapter 6. When infrastructure is compromised, responding with increased capacity is time-consuming, so the best strategy is utilizing alternative means of transportation. Therefore, "governments have a responsibility to encourage the development of alternatives to potential choke points."[84]

8.4.5 Competitors

In the context of supply chain sustainability, competitors represent a two-edged sword. On the one hand they may be willing to cooperate in certain logistics processes—transport and distribution, for instance—to create win-win situations; on the other hand, competitors can become environmental technology or process leaders who may set industry norms, increasing the level of competition by introducing new measures of success. Increasingly stringent standards for conduct provide a competitive advantage to businesses already pursuing sustainability.

While competition breeds excellence, competition between companies for market share should not involve trade-offs between company profit and stakeholder welfare. The increasing complexity of the business environment and the increasingly rapid pace of change has given priority to **multi-stakeholder partnerships**.

Networks of governments, civic groups, and businesses drive multi-stakeholder partnerships that seek to bridge multilateral best practices and local action.[85] Staying with the carbon emission issue, the Greenhouse Gas Protocol (GHG Protocol), a widely used tool by government and business leaders to quantify and manage greenhouse gas emissions, demonstrates how businesses can benefit by collaborating with competitors. The GHG Protocol is a multi-stakeholder process involving participants from business, policymakers, NGOs, academics and other experts from around the world dedicated to developing a new standard for supply chain GHG emissions measurement and reporting. By agreeing to a common standard, competitors can ensure a level playing field. Even in competitive markets, collaboration has a strong role in promoting sustainability.

> **Multi-Stakeholder Partnerships** Networks of governments, civic groups, and businesses that seek to connect corporate priorities with local action.

8.4.6 Communities

Many large companies have used their supply chain practices to promote sustainable development in low-income parts of the world, specifically by engaging SMEs.[86] Granting SMEs in developing countries to supply contracts can make a substantial difference on the ground by providing economic opportunities for business owners and employment opportunities in low-income areas. As long as these contracts are consistent with sustainable principles and fair labor practices are observed, including SMEs in supply chains can add worthwhile diversity to supplier portfolios.

The communities that live in physical proximity to the early stages in a supply chain—specifically, raw materials production and manufacturing—should be included as stakeholders in the decision-making process of buyers. The unique challenges facing these communities can become risks to buyers when exacerbated by supplier conduct. For example, in an area suffering a water shortage, suppliers

---

MANAGERIAL INSIGHT: Herman Miller Engages Over 200 Suppliers[87]

The Herman Miller Perfect Vision campaign, launched in 2003, includes goals such as no landfill waste, no hazardous waste, no air emissions and no water emissions from manufacturing, and the use of 100% green energy, all by the year 2020. According to CEO Brian Walker, "These are stringent targets our company cannot reach without engaging over 200 materials and components suppliers in the ongoing task of greening our global supply chain." Collaborating with various participants in the global supply chain is necessary to see sustainability improvements end-to-end. "It's far too large and complex an undertaking for any organization to go it alone and be truly effective. You know the saying, 'It takes a village to raise a child.' Well, it takes an entire supply chain to green a company."

engaged in industrial water use can always point to buyers as the reason for on-going water withdrawals. As far as public perceptions go, the unsustainable behavior of the supplier is easily imputed to the buyer. Instead of creating risks for the communities affected by supply chain practices, supply chain managers should look for ways to benefit all of the stakeholders affected by the various activities in the value chain, including local communities.

Tesco, a large food retailer, developed sustainability efforts that stem from their primary business model, which is to provide food to families. These programs are geared toward various actors in their supply chain, including employees, suppliers, and customers. The three goals are to address youth unemployment, obesity, and food waste. Tesco's vast scale and sprawling supply chains mean it can have a substantial impact on global sustainability, while delivering direct community benefits. Tesco is using its scale in order to build deep, long-term relationships with suppliers who can provide sustainably sourced, high quality, affordable food products that benefit its customers.

LEADERSHIP: Tesco Tries to Feed the World Sustainably[88]

Tesco, one of the largest food retailers, is trying to use its size and corporate ethos to make the world a better place. From being a good corporate neighbor, a good boss, and an environmentally-sensitive global concern, Tesco's three ambitions of 2013 relate directly to the triple-bottom-line of sustainability: economic, social, and environmental development.

The 75 million young people facing unemployment around the world pose a threat to the economic stability of various regions. Tesco's Ambition 1 is "to create new opportunities for millions of young people around the world" by inspiring, equipping, and enabling youth to succeed in the workplace through school outreach. Preparing the next generation to lead productive lives is critical for ensuring future economic viability.

Obesity is a threat to social sustainability, posing severe human health risks including potentially fatal diabetes, heart disease, and stroke. Many consumers recognize they are not living as healthy a lifestyle as they would like and expect their grocers to provide healthy options for them. Fifty-four percent of United Kingdom consumers are actively looking for supermarkets to take a lead in helping them to become healthier. Tesco's Ambition 2 is "to improve health and through this help tackle the global obesity crisis" by helping and encouraging Tesco's 500,000 colleagues and 50 million customers to live healthier lives. This is accomplished by encouraging physical activity among employees, labeling food for vital health and nutritional information, creating store environments that encourage healthier habits, and providing free information tailored to the health needs of customers.

Food waste, like all kinds of waste, is an environmental problem because it signals sub-optimal resource use and inefficient supply. Wasted food symbolizes wasted water, soil nutrients, energy, fertilizer, labor, transport, and refrigeration—all the resources that went into producing the food that was ultimately discarded. Approximately one-third of all food produced the world over is never eaten, either being tossed out or left to rot. Global populations will increase over the next 10 years, adding strain to already over-burdened agricultural resources. Every ton of food waste prevented will eliminate approximately 4.2 tons of CO_2 emissions. Tesco's Ambition 3 is "to lead in reducing food waste globally" by working with producers and suppliers and helping customers find ways to reduce food waste. This includes developing metrics to determine where the most food waste occurs, so that efforts to reduce this waste are tailored strategically.

Key Terms

Discussion Questions

1. Describe the supply chain of your company. What role does your company play in the supply chain?

2. What kinds of risks has your company's supply chain faced in the past? What kinds of risks do you expect it will face in the next few years? How can these supply chain risks be managed?

3. Has your company extended sustainability policies to its supply chain?

END-OF-CHAPTER CASES

There are more slaves alive today than at any time in human history. The non-governmental organization Free The Slaves estimates there are as many as 27 million people in modern-day slavery around the world.

Recall the California Transparency in Supply Chains Act from Chapter 4: Legal Frameworks. The legislation affects thousands of national and international manufacturers and retailers. The law mandates specific disclosures, such as whether the company has pursued 3rd party verification of risk, independent and unannounced supply chain auditing, certification of compliance from direct suppliers, internal accountability mechanisms, and provision of employee/partnership training. Keep the California Transparency in Supply Chains Act in mind as you read the following cases.

CASE 1 Gone Fishing: Human Trafficking on the High Seas[89]

This is a story about unethical labor practices in the global seafood supply chain. The human slaves are Indonesian workers hired by South Korean fishing companies to supply to New Zealand seafood distributors for United States companies selling to U.S. consumers. These workers are hired onto foreign charter vessels (FCVs) to be exploited by a process called 'debt bondage' whereby they are required to put up all of their assets as collateral for "satisfactory" performance of their job as fishers. A Bloomberg Business-Week article followed the story of Yusril, who was taken out to sea aboard the *Melilla 203* for 8 months, physically and sexually abused by his captor-employer, denied adequate medical care for his multiple injuries, grossly underpaid, and ultimately threatened that if he abandoned the ship he would not be paid anything for his toil. Tragically, Yusril's story is not unique.

As recently as November 2011, fish from the *Melilla 203* and other suspect vessels were bought and processed by United Fisheries, New Zealand's eighth-largest seafood company, which sold the same kinds of fish in the same time period to distributors operating in the U.S. Because the U.S. imports 86% of its seafood, distributors in turn have likely sold fish procured through slavery to major U.S. companies, including Safeway, Walmart, Sam's Club, Costco, Whole Foods Market, and P.F. Chang's. When the Bloomberg BusinessWeek story came to press, each of these companies began investigating their seafood suppliers for deviations from their corporate code of conduct.

Although New Zealand authorities repeatedly fined or seized the *Melilla* ships for ecological infractions (such as oil spills) over the last decade, crimes against humanity were a secondary concern at best. Yusril said that when he once whispered a plea for help to an onboard government observer, the reply was that it was "not my job" to provide assistance. Although crewmembers were entitled to certain minimum standards of treatment under New Zealand law including pay of at least $12 per hour, when deductions, agency fees, and a manipulated exchange rate differential were subtracted, the fishermen were averaging around $1 per hour.

Not all New Zealand fishing companies rely on exploitation for tough high-seas labor. "New Zealand seafood enjoys a hard-earned and world-leading reputation as a responsible fisheries manager, with a product range and quality to match," says Andrew Talley, Director of Talley's Group, the third-largest fishing company in New Zealand. Talley's Group submits to third-party social responsibility audits on its labor standards, a condition of spelled out in their contract to supply hoki for McDonald's Filet-O-Fish sandwiches.

Case 1 Questions:

1. Which business norms ought to apply to supply chain activities on the high seas? Does your answer depend on whether you are the employee, the supplier, the distributor, the retailer, or the consumer?

2. Assume no human trafficking laws apply to you.

   A. As a consumer, would knowledge that a consumer product was sourced using human trafficking discourage you from purchasing that product?

   B. As a retailer, would knowledge that a supplier used human trafficking affect your purchasing decision from that supplier? What if the products were priced substantially cheaper relative to ethically sourced competitors?

3. Assume you manage the supply chain for a major seafood distributor doing business in Los Angeles, California.

   A. Could you make a business case for paying a premium to ensure the fish served in your restaurant come from a sustainable-certified fishery/supplier?

   B. What would you do to ensure compliance with the California Transparency in Supply Chains Act?

<table><tr><td>CASE 2</td></tr></table> **iSlave: Labor Conditions at Consumer Technology Parts Suppliers[90]**

In 2010 Apple Inc. faced accusations that they relied on poorly treated, over-worked, and under-paid laborers in their supplier's Chinese factories. Foxconn, once the sole supplier of Apple's iPhones and iPads, required long hours from migrant laborers, paid minimal wages, and provided severely cramped quarters on the manufacturing-site campus. After a rash of employee suicides, Foxconn installed safety nets to prevent employees from throwing themselves off balconies.

Audits conducted internally since labor practices within Apple's supply chain became publicly suspect have discovered instances of underage workers, discrimination,

(continues)

and wage problems throughout Apple's sprawling global supply chains. Tim Cook, the Chief Executive taking control after founder Steve Jobs stepped down in 2011, has made commitments to improve supply chain transparency through extensive internal audits and to comply with an independent audit by the Fair Labor Association. While continuing to work with Foxconn, Apple has since shifted a portion of its supply chain toward Pegatron.

Senior Vice President of Operations Jeff Williams says the company has increased focus on their most challenging issues: ensuring there are no child workers in its supply chain and limiting working hours to 60 hours per week. Smaller suppliers face less oversight than the larger suppliers, and have earned greater scrutiny from Apple, which has either brought them into compliance or fired them. "We go deep in the supply chain to find it," Williams said. "And when we do find it, we ensure that the underage workers are taken care of, the suppliers are dealt with."

In 2013, Apple is focusing on student internships within suppliers in China, where many colleges mandate students to complete a business internship in order to graduate. The situation lends itself to intern abuse, where employers can threaten or mistreat student interns whose education and future careers are dependent upon completing the internship.

Case 2 Questions:

1. Assume you are the Supply Chain Manager for a computer manufacturing company that receives portions of its components from an overseas supplier that you suspect uses unfair labor practices. After conducting a supply chain audit, you determine that the supplier has failed to take action on past instances of sexual harassment and hazing style abuse of student interns, some of them as young as 16 years old.

   A. Is the supplier guilty of human trafficking?

   B. Would you (1) do nothing, (2) fire the supplier, or (3) engage the supplier in ongoing training to improve their labor standards? Why?

2. Assume your first tier supplier has recently merged with another company with a bad environmental track record. One of the newly-acquired legacy facilities caused a massive spill of hazardous waste, and workers have developed respiratory illnesses caused by poor indoor air quality and exposure to toxins.

   A. Does the supplier's environmental record pose a supply chain risk to your company?

   B. Would you (1) do nothing, (2) fire the supplier, or (3) engage the supplier in ongoing training to improve operating conditions? Why?

Further Research

Students can use this interactive website to calculate the extent of human trafficking involved in the products they buy: http://slaveryfootprint.org/.

For a discussion of human trafficking in consumer product supply chains, see Louis P. Masur, *How Many Slaves Work for You?*, The New York Times Op-Ed, (December 31, 2012).

To learn more about environmental impacts of the ocean-bound container shipping industry that provides transport for global supply chains, see the TED-Talk, "Inside the Secret Shipping Industry," by journalist Rose George.

To learn more about recycling and the life cycle of plastics from consumer products, see co-founder of MBA Polymers Mike Biddle's TED-Talk, "We Can Recycle Plastic." In addition, this talk also illustrates the environmental and human health impacts of regulatory arbitrage, discussed in Chapter 4: Legal Frameworks.

Harvard Business Review Case: Ray A. Goldberg & Jessica Droste Yagan, *McDonald's Corp.: Managing a Sustainable Supply Chain*, Prod. #: 907414-PDF-ENG (March 02, 2007).

Harvard Business Review Case: V. Kasturi Rangan & Nina Ann George, *Olam: Building a Sustainable Supply Chain in Cote d'Ivoire*, Prod. #: 514018-PDF-ENG (September 5, 2013).

Harvard Business Review Case: Gerry Yemen, Ronald G. Kamin & Karen Delchet-Cochet, *Sustainable Procurement at*

SNCF: An Impressionist's Approach to Transformation, Prod. #: UV6557-PDF-ENG (October 16, 2012).

Harvard Business School Case: David Robb, Ben Hopwood, Lei Wang & Jun Cheng, *Wal-Mart China: Sustainable Operations Strategy*, Prod. #: 908D09-PDF-ENG (January 21, 2009).

For a collection of cases involving supply chain strategy, see Balkan Cetinkaya, Richard Cuthbertson, Graham Ewer, Thorston Klaas-Wissing, Wojciech Piotrowicz & Christoph Tyssen, SUSTAINABLE SUPPLY CHAIN MANAGEMENT: PRACTICAL IDEAS FOR MOVING TOWARDS BEST PRACTICE, Chapter 9: Markets and Strategies Cases, page 191 (Springer 2011).

Endnotes

[1] Adapted from Elizabeth Baer, "Lessons from Starbucks: Building a Sustainable Supply Chain," Greenbiz.com (March 21, 2012).

[2] See Conservation International website on the Coffee and Farmer Equity (C.A.F.E.) Practices, last accessed May 16, 2014, available at http://www.conservation.org/campaigns/starbucks/Pages/CAFE_Practices_Results.aspx.

[3] State of Sustainable Business Survey, BSR & GlobeScan, page 6 (October 2013), available at https://www.bsr.org/reports/BSR_GlobeScan_Survey_2013.pdf.

[4] Ker Than, *Bangladesh Building Collapse Due to Shoddy Construction: The Deadly Catastrophe was Entirely Preventable, Experts Say*, National Geographic News (April 25, 2013).

[5] Jim Yardley, *After Bangladesh Factory Collapse, Bleak Struggle for Survivors*, The New York Times (December 18, 2013).

[6] C.R. Carter, D.S. Rogers, *A Framework of Sustainable Supply Chain Management: Moving Toward New Theory*, Vol. 38 No. 5 International Journal of Physical Distribution & Logistics Management, pages 360–387 (2008).

[7] E. Goncz, U. Skirke, H. Kleizen & M. Barber, *Increasing the Rate of Sustainable Change: A Call for a Redefinition of the Concept and the Model for its Implementation*, Vol. 15 No. 6 Journal of Cleaner Production, pages 525–537 (2007).

[8] US Environmental Protection Agency, *The Lean and Green Supply Chain: A Practical Guide for Materials Managers and Supply Chain Managers to Reduce Costs and Improve Environmental Performance* (2000), available at http://nepis.epa.gov/Exe/ZyPDF.cgi?Dockey=20000XKS.PDF.

[9] Aref A. Hervani & Marilyn M. Helms, *Performance Measurement for Green Supply Chain Management*, Vol. 12 No. 4 Benchmarking: An International Journal, pp. 330–353, 332 (2005).

[10] *Doing Good: Business and the Sustainability Challenge*, The Economist, page 4 (2008), available at http://graphics.eiu.com/upload/Sustainability_allsponsors.pdf.

[11] Gary L. Hanifan, Aditya E. Sharma & Paras Mehta, *Why a Sustainable Supply Chain is Good Business*, Accenture (October 2012).

[12] See the Ceres web page Sustainable Supply Chains, last accessed May 16, 2014, available at http://www.ceres.org/issues/supply-chain.

[13] Gary L. Hanifan, Aditya E. Sharma & Paras Mehta, *Why a Sustainable Supply Chain is Good Business*, Accenture (October 2012).

[14] H.S. Mathews, C.T. Hendrickson & C.L. Weber, *The Importance of Carbon Footprint Estimation Boundaries*, 42 Environmental Science and Technology 5839–5842 (2008).

[15] *Action Amid Uncertainty: Executing Climate Change Initiatives*, Ernst & Young (2010).

[16] World Economic Forum Supply Chain and Transport Risk Survey, 9 (2011).

[17] Karl Plume, *Mississippi River Nears Historic Lows, Shipping at Risk*, Reuters (January 2, 3013).

[18] *Building Resilience in Supply Chains*, World Economic Forum, page 21 (January 2013), last accessed May 16, 2014, available at http://www3.weforum.org/docs/WEF_RRN_MO_Building ResilienceSupplyChains_Report_2013.pdf.

[19] World Economic Forum Supply Chain and Transport Risk Survey, 11 (2011).

[20] *New Models for Addressing Supply Chain and Transport Risk*, World Economic Forum, page 11 (2012).

[21] Aref A. Hervani & Marilyn M. Helms, *Performance Measurement for Green Supply Chain Management*, Vol. 12 No. 4 Benchmarking: An International Journal, pp. 330–353, 338 (2005).

[22] *Supply Chain Sustainability: A Practical Guide for Continuous Improvement for Small and Medium Enterprises*, UN Global Compact & BSR, last accessed May 16, 2014, available at http://www.unglobalcompact.org/docs/issues_doc/supply_chain/Supply_Chain_Practical_Guide_SMEs.pdf

[23] The Sustainability Consortium, Sustainability Measurement and Reporting System (SMRS), last accessed May 16, 2014, available at http://www.sustainabilityconsortium.org/smrs

[24] *ibid.*

[25] *ibid.*

26 *Supply Chain Sustainability: Traceability Task Force Phase 1 – Scoping*, UN Global Compact, page 4 (2013), last accessed May 16, 2014, available at http://www.unglobalcompact.org/docs/issues_doc/supply_chain/Traceability/Research_Findings_Scoping_Recommendations_Phase1.pdf.

27 *ibid*, page 5.

28 Gary L. Hanifan, Aditya E. Sharma & Paras Mehta, *Why a Sustainable Supply Chain is Good Business*, Accenture (October 2012).

29 PwC, Global Supply Chain Survey, 16 (2013).

30 World Economic Forum web page on Water, last accessed May 16, 2014, available at http://www.weforum.org/issues/water#anote.

31 Stefan Seuring & Martin Muller, *From a Literature Review to a Conceptual Framework for Sustainable Supply Chain Management*, Journal of Cleaner Production, Volume 16 Issue 15 Pages 1699–1710 (October 2008).

32 *ibid*.

33 See United Nations Global Compact, Principles 1 and 2, last accessed May 16, 2014, available at http://www.unglobalcompact.org/AboutTheGC/TheTenPrinciples/humanRights.html.

34 *Supply Chain Sustainability: Traceability Task Force Phase 1 – Scoping*, UN Global Compact, page 8 (2013), last accessed May 16, 2014, available at http://www.unglobalcompact.org/docs/issues_doc/supply_chain/Traceability/Research_Findings_Scoping_Recommendations_Phase1.pdf.

35 See Women's Empowerment Principles, last accessed May 16, 2014, available at http://www.weprinciples.org/; Children's Rights and Business Principles, last accessed May 16, 2014, available at http://childrenandbusiness.org/; Business Reference Guide on Indigenous Peoples' Rights, last accessed May 16, 2014, available at http://www.unglobalcompact.org/Issues/human_rights/indigenous_peoples_rights.html.

36 *Marking Progress Against Child Labor: Global Estimates and Trends 2000–2012*, International Labour Office, pages 4–6 (2013), last accessed May 16, 2014, available at http://www.ilo.org/wcmsp5/groups/public/—ed_norm/—ipec/documents/publication/wcms_221513.pdf.

37 *ibid*, page 15.

38 *ibid*, page 16.

39 International Labour Organization web site, Safety and Health at Work, last accessed May 16, 2014, available at http://ilo.org/global/topics/safety-and-health-at-work/lang–en/index.htm.

40 *Occupational Safety and Health in the Supply Chain*, UN Global Compact, last accessed May 16, 2014, available at http://www.unglobalcompact.org/docs/issues_doc/labour/tools_guidance_materials/Occupational_Safety_Health_in_the_Supply_Chain.pdf.

41 *ibid*.

42 Steven Greenhouse, *Retailers Split on Contrition After Collapse of Factories*, The New York Times (April 30, 2013).

43 Patrick Penfield, THE GREEN SUPPLY CHAIN (2007).

44 T.E. Graedel and B.R. Allenby, DESIGN FOR ENVIRONMENT, Prentice Hall (1996).

45 Adapted from Lenika Cruz, *"How Toxic is the iPhone-5* (October 03, 2012), last accessed May 16, 2014, available at www.greenbiz.com.

46 *ibid*.

47 Environmental Leader-United Parcel Service Supply Chain DataBook, page 8 (2012).

48 See the Proctor & Gamble website, "Environmental Sustainability," last accessed May 16, 2014, available at http://www.pg.com/en_US/sustainability/environmental_sustainability/.

49 See the Nestle Waters website, "Innovation Timeline," last accessed May 16, 2014, available at http://www.nestle-watersna.com/en/water-sustainability/reducing-our-carbon-footprint/bottle-packaging-responsibility/innovationtimeline.

50 See Walmart's website, Sustainability Index, last accessed May 16, 2014, available at http://corporate.walmart.com/global-responsibility/environment-sustainability/sustainability-index.

51 Lisa McTigue Pierce, *Conference to Reveal Sustainable Innovations in Flexible Packaging*, Packaging Digest (January 25, 2014), last accessed May 16, 2014, available at http://www.packagingdigest.com/article/524054-Conference_to_reveal_sustainable_innovations_in_flexible_packaging.php.

52 See the Preserve website, Recycling Partners, last accessed May 16, 2014, available at https://www.preserveproducts.com/recycle/partners/340/stonyfield.

53 C.K. Prahalad, FORTUNE AT THE BOTTOM OF THE PYRAMID: ERADICATING POVERTY THROUGH PROFITS, 17 (Pearson 2005).

54 Environmental Leader-United Parcel Service, Supply Chain DataBook, page 12 (2012).

55 See the Nike website for potential licensees, last accessed May 16, 2014, available at https://www.nikeinclicensees.com/managing-your-factories/add-a-factory/.

56 See the L'Oréal supplier selection process, last accessed May 16, 2014, available at http://www.loreal.com/profiles/suppliers/our-evaluation-criteria.aspx.

57 Simon Clark & Heather Walsh, *Fair Trade Proving Anything But in Growing $6 Billion Market*, BloombergBusinessweek (January 04, 2012).

58 See, e.g., Michael E. Porter & Claas van der Linde, *Toward a New Conception of the Environment-Competitiveness Relationship*, Vol. 9 No. 4 The Journal of Economic Perspectives pp. 97–118 (Autumn 1995).

59 Kingfisher, *Steps to Responsible Growth: Kingfisher Social Responsibility Programme* (2006), last accessed May 16, 2014, available at http://www.kingfisher.com/files/sr_pdf/Steps_to_Res_Growth.pdf.

60 *A Natural Step Case Study: Scandic Hotels*, The Natural Step, page 5 (2008).

61 *HP Environmental History*, Hewlett-Packard pages 3–5 (February 2009), last accessed May 16, 2014, available at http://www.hp.com/canada/corporate/hp_info/environment/commitment/hp_environmental_history.pdf.

62 J. Quariguasi Frota Neto, J.M. Bloemhof-Ruwaard, J.A.E.E. van Nunen & H.W.G.M. van Heck, *Designing and Evaluating Sustainable Logistics Networks*, Erasmus Research Institute of Management (January 2006).

63 Aref A. Hervani & Marilyn M. Helms, *Performance Measurement for Green Supply Chain Management*, Vol. 12 No. 4 Benchmarking: An International Journal, pp. 330–353, 334 (2005).

64 Amy Roach Partridge, Full Circle: Reverse Logistics Keeps Products Green to the End, Inbound Logistics (June 2011).

65 Inbound Logistics, *Green on the Ground* (June 2011).

66 *ibid.*

67 See Environmental Leader, UPS Composite Body Vans are 40% More Fuel Efficient (6-22-2012), last accessed May 16, 2014, available at *http://www.environmentalleader.com/2012/06/22/ups-composite-body-vans-40-more-fuel-efficient/*.

68 Ann L. MacNaughton & John Stephens, *Achieving Sustainable Development: Meeting Economic Development, Environmental Protection, and Quality of Life Goals through Effective Stakeholder Management Systems*, Vol. 11, Issue 3 Corporate Environmental Strategy: International Journal for Sustainable Business 70–71 (March 2004).

69 William R. Blackburn, THE SUSTAINABILITY HANDBOOK: THE COMPLETE MANAGEMENT GUIDE TO ACHIEVING SOCIAL, ECONOMIC, AND ENVIRONMENTAL RESPONSIBILITY, page 86, Environmental Law Institute (2008).

70 Kenneth M. Amaeshi, Onyeka K. Osuji, and Paul Nnodim, *Corporate Social Responsibility in Supply Chains of Global Brands: A Boundaryless Responsibility? Clarifications, Exceptions and Implications* (2006).

71 Richard M. Locke, Greg Distelhorst, Timea Pal and Hiram M. Samel, *Production Goes Global, Standards Stay Local: Private Labor Regulation in the Global Electronics Industry* (January 3, 2012).

72 Judith M. Whipple & Dawn Russell, *Building Supply Chain Collaboration: A Typology of Collaborative Approaches*, Vol. 18 Iss. 2 International Journal of Logistics Management pages 174–196 (2007).

73 *Building Resilience in Supply Chains*, World Economic Forum, page 22 (January 2013), last accessed May 16, 2014, available at http://www3.weforum.org/docs/WEF_RRN_MO_Building ResilienceSupplyChains_Report_2013.pdf.

74 A. Cox, D. Chicksand, and M. Palmer, *Stairways to Heaven or Treadmills to Oblivion? Creating Sustainable Strategies in Red Meat Supply Chains*, Vol. 109 No. 9 British Food Journal pages 689–720 (2007).

75 H.L. Lee, *Embedding Sustainability: Lessons from the Frontline*, Vol. 8 International Commerce Review pages 10–20 (2008).

76 Soonhong Min, Anthony S. Roath, Patricia J. Daugherty, Stefan E. Genchev, Haozhe Chen, Aaron D. Arndt & R. Glenn Richey, *Supply Chain Collaboration: What's Happening?*, Vol. 16 Iss. 2 International Journal of Logistics Management, pages 237–256 (2005).

77 *ibid.*

78 Michael E. Porter & Mark R. Kramer, *Creating Shared Value*, Harvard Business Review (January 2011).

79 Nestle in Society: Creating Shared Value and Meeting Our Commitments in 2012.

80 Nina Kruschwitz (interviewing Nestlé's Hans Joehr), *Creating Shared Value at Nestlé*, MIT Sloan Management Review (September 10, 2013).

81 Leona E. Lewis, Karyn Schmidt, Mark N. Duvall, *Retailer Sustainability and the Supply Chain*, Vol. 26 No. 4, Natural Resources & Environment, American Bar Association (Spring 2012).

82 Carter, C. and J. R. Carter (1998) Inter-organizational Determinants of Environmental Purchasing. *Decision Sciences Journal,* Vol. 29, No. 3 (Summer): pp. 659–684.

83 *Building Resilience in Supply Chains*, World Economic Forum, page 23 (January 2013), last accessed May 16, 2014, available at http://www3.weforum.org/docs/WEF_RRN_MO_Building ResilienceSupplyChains_Report_2013.pdf.

84 *ibid.*

85 Karen Backstränd, *Multi-Stakeholder Partnerships for Sustainable Development: Rethinking Legitimacy, Accountability and Effectiveness*, 16 European Environment 290–306 (2006).

86 *Promoting Small and Medium Enterprises for Sustainable Development*, SNV & World Business Council for Sustainable Development, Page 3 (July 2007).

87 Brian Walker, *You Are Only As Green As Your Supply Chain*, HBR Green, February 6, 2008, last accessed May 16, 2014, available at http://www.hbrgreen.org/2008/02/you_are_only_as_green_as_your.html.

88 Tesco and Society Report (2013).

89 Adapted from E. Benjamin Skinner, *The Cruelest Catch: In the Waters Off New Zealand, Scores of Indentured Workers are Trawling for Seafood—And You May be Buying It*, Bloomberg BusinessWeek, 70–76 (Feb 27-March 4, 2012).

90 *Apple Labor Audits Uncover Underage Workers*, The New York Times (Jan. 25, 2013).

CHAPTER 9

Operations Management

ANCIENT AIR CONDITIONING IN MODERN BUILDING DESIGN[1]

The building home to the Pearl Academy of Fashion in Jaipur, Rajasthan (north-west India) does not have air conditioning. The summers reach high temperatures, especially in the industrial suburbs. Nonetheless, the Peal Academy building remains 20 degrees cooler inside than the surrounding climate. The building designers use a stepwell technique borrowed from ancient architecture to provide air conditioning without the use of electricity.

The **baoli** (Hindi word for stepwell) concept was invented over 1,500 years ago as a form of shelter from the desert heat. Today the stepwell design is described as a form of passive cooling, a technique for indoor climate control that does not rely on electricity consumption. The building design creates a microclimate within the structure by harnessing basic principles of natural elements. The base of the building contains a deep and wide pool of water enclosed by descending steps, with the entire structure raised above the stepwell on pillars, creating a shaded pavilion. The water absorbs heat from the incoming air and evaporates, lowering the ambient temperatures.

This sustainable building design impacts the triple bottom line. "We've been able to demonstrate that good green building is not only cheaper to run; it's not only more comfortable to live in –It's also cheaper to build," says Rastogi, "How did they think up something so elaborate and yet so simple?"

> *"Sustainable development is not rocket science. It is far more complicated and important than rocket science. Everyone in every society has a role to play, but the Facilities Management profession, with its immense influence to affect the way buildings and businesses operate, has an opportunity to make a difference."*
>
> —*Beyond 2000: A Sustainable Vision for FM*
> **JIM URE, DAVE HAMPTON & SONNY MASERO (1998).**

LEARNING OBJECTIVES

After completing this chapter, you should be able to:

1. Explain the role of operations management (OM) in sustainability.
2. Explain the Elements of an Operations Management Strategy.
3. Explain how product and process design influence sustainable performance.
4. Describe the role of operations planning and control in sustainable business.
5. Explain how facility and inventory management impact sustainability.

9.1 The Role of Operations Management in Sustainability

Operations management (OM) is the business function responsible for producing goods and services. In Section 9.1: The Role of Operations Management in Sustainability, we explain how operations management fits into overall sustainable business strategy, as well as the connections between the OM function and both Risk Management and Supply Chain Management (Chapters 6 and 8). In Section 9.2: Operations Strategy, we explain how sustainability policies can be integrated into traditional operations strategy so that sustainability becomes a competitive priority and source of advantage. Integrating environmental and social policies into operations strategy is also necessary for marketing purposes (Chapter 7).

The design of the operations function can be broken down into two categories of decisions. The first relate to *structure*: decisions related to the design of the production process, such as facilities, technology, and flow of goods and services through the facility. We discuss OM structure in Section 9.3: Operations Design. The second category of OM decisions concerns *infrastructure*: decisions related to the planning and control systems of the operation, such as organization of operations, skills and pay of workers, and quality measures. We discuss OM infrastructure in Section 9.4: Operations Planning and Control. This chapter concludes by discussing the role of facility management, facility layout, and so-called green building design in Section 9.5: Facility Management, Layout, and Design.

9.1.1 The OM Function

The domain of **operations management** covers the business functions responsible for producing a company's goods and services; in other words, OM refers to the process of transforming a company's inputs into outputs.

The classic transformation model of OM is shown in Figure 9.1.

In order to create the transformation process the OM function is responsible for planning, organizing, and managing all the inputs needed to produce a company's goods and services. These inputs include human resources, such as workers, staff, and managers; facilities and processes, such as buildings and equipment; as well as materials, technology, and information. In the traditional transformation model,

FIGURE 9.1 The Transformation Model of Operations Management

outputs are the goods and services a company produces. At a manufacturing plant the transformation is the physical change of raw materials into products, such as transforming leather and rubber into sneakers, denim into jeans, or plastic into toys. This is equally true of service organizations. At a hospital, OM is involved in organizing resources, such as doctors, medical equipment, and medications, to transform sick patients into healthy people.

In addition to these traditional outputs of OM, we also need to understand that goods and services are not the only outputs to be considered. Wastes, pollution emissions, employee injuries, and the impact of operations on local communities are also outputs of the transformation process that need to be controlled.

Sustainable operations management is the management of the transformational process to reduce resource consumption, pollution, and waste while benefiting employees, customers, and communities in order to reduce short-term risks and shore-up long-term cash flows. Sustainable operations management is the culmination of a multi-decade evolution in the field of OM that began in the 1960s, including Total Quality Management, Just-in-Time, Process Management, Efficient Consumer Response, Customer Relationship Management, Six Sigma, and Lean.[2] By incorporating external stakeholders and accounting for the entire life cycle of products, OM can play a central role in the overall sustainable enterprise.

As with all other disciplines discussed in this book, the themes of innovation, stewardship, and accountability permeate sustainable OM. However, OM's contribution to sustainability is unique from marketing, supply chain management, and other domains because of its "micro view of firms' processes and environment."[3]

> **Sustainable Operations Management** Guiding the transformational process to reduce resource consumption, pollution, and waste while benefiting employees, customers, and communities in order to reduce short-term risks and shore-up long-term cash flows.

LEADERSHIP: Avaya Takes on Climate Change Impacts from Operations[4]

The company Avaya provides enterprise communications systems to organizational clients around the world. After conducting an internal assessment of sustainable performance, the company decided it would take a lead on reducing its contribution to climate change. Instead of simply obtaining carbon offsets (discussed in Chapters 2 and 7), the company decided to implement operational changes within its own organization to mitigate carbon emissions. Accordingly, Avaya set a target to reduce Scope 1, 2, and 3 GHG emissions by 15% by 2015 when measured against the baseline of 2009 emissions. (For more on greenhouse gas metrics see Chapter 5.) This strategic decision to reduce greenhouse gas emissions from operations set into motion a series of design decisions affecting the company's processes, products, and facilities. Avaya re-vamped equipment to reduce energy consumption, started conducting energy audits, standardized temperatures in facilities, and consolidated data centers to make them more energy efficient. The company developed a phone system for customers that would reduce their customers' electricity consumption, and a virtual server platform that reduced electricity consumption and physical space requirements. The company began collecting greenhouse gas emissions data from all of the utilities consumed at its physical locations, and even includes employee business air travel in calculating its total greenhouse gas emissions.

9.1.2 How OM Impacts Sustainability

The design and management of OM strongly influences how much energy and material resources are consumed in order to manufacture goods or deliver a service. All aspects of operations that implicate water use have a direct bearing on sustainability—both in terms of risks to the company and external consequences for ecosystems and communities.

Small- and mid-sized enterprises (SMEs) can take many environmentally friendly steps to improve the sustainability of their operations. However, some have a faster return on investment (ROI) than others, and for small businesses with less capital to work with, fast ROI is important. Often, SME measures to improve the sustainability of operations can be funded by tax credits or government grants. See Table 9.1.

The transformation role of OM makes it the engine room of the organization; as a result, OM is directly responsible for many decisions and activities that give rise to environmental and social challenges.[5] OM decisions directly impact the extent of energy and material use, the ease of product recycling, and the characteristics and volume of pollution emitted from production activities. Operations, especially in manufacturing and production, are a significant source of employee accidents and occupational hazards. Therefore, solutions to many social and environmental challenges to business lie within the OM domain.

As discussed in Chapter 5, carbon footprinting is an analytical tool used to determine the extent of a company's contribution to climate change by measuring carbon emissions. The OM function is responsible for direct emissions through, for example, the operation of facilities, as well as indirect emissions from, for example, electricity supply companies that provide power for those operations. Using the Greenhouse Gas Protocol terms, OM is responsible for Scope 1 and Scope 2 emissions, whereas supply chain management (SCM) is responsible for Scope 3 emissions.

To understand the full impact of OM decisions, we need to consider the transformation process throughout the full life of the product—from material extraction to

---

TABLE 9.1

Top Ten Sustainable OM Innovations by Fastest ROI

1. Purchase energy-efficient equipment
2. Train staff to conserve energy
3. Install more efficient lighting
4. Recycle and reuse in-house plastics, paper, metals, glass
5. Redesign products to require less energy in production
6. Create employee incentives for reducing energy use
7. Enable energy saving settings on computers
8. Increase purchasing local products
9. Install energy efficient windows
10. Install solar photovoltaic panels

Source: Small Business Sustainability Report, 2013: The Big Green Opportunity for Small Business in the U.S., Green America, Association for Enterprise Opportunity, and Ecoventures International, page 37 (2013).

product use and disposal, and recycling. This is the principle of life cycle assessment (LCA), which requires that the social and environmental impacts of each stage of the product's life be considered. When extended to the product life cycle, operations decisions and activities impact waste, consumption, emissions, and labor conditions within a factory, but also the impacts associated with production upstream and downstream of operations. The transformation process can be understood as the physical connection between upstream suppliers and downstream consumers.

Developing a sustainable operating system for a company involves several elements:[6] developing new business models, which we discuss in Section 9.2.1; expanding the concept of operations as a total product system (discussed in the section on life cycle assessment); adhering to the applicable legal and regulatory regime (discussed in Chapter 4); setting sustainability performance goals and metrics (discussed in Chapter 5); and attending to the issues posed by each of the OM decision areas. Sections 9.2 – 9.5 of this chapter, respectively, address the latter issue: how can Operations Strategy, Design, Planning & Control, and Facilities Management address sustainability challenges? Before addressing these OM decision areas, we focus on a wide-spread risk to operations across a variety of sectors: water supply. How do water-related risks impact operations management?

> **CROSS-LINKAGE**
>
> For metrics to measure OM sustainability performance, see Chapter 5: Metrics, Tools, and Reporting: The Role of Finance and Accounting.

> **CROSS-LINKAGE**
>
> For more information on Life Cycle Assessment in sustainable supply chains, see Chapter 8: Sustainable Supply Chain Management.

9.1.3 Water-Related Operations Management Risks

Since the 1900s, global industrial impacts on water supplies (measured in terms of the amount of water extracted, consumed, and wasted) have increased steadily.[7] Water serves as an industrial coolant, solvent, cleaning fluid, sewage carrier, and critical input into a wide array of manufacturing processes. Limited water supplies can cause operational disruption or increased costs. Overburdening water supplies by withdrawing water excessively or wasting water can also damage ecosystems and create water use conflicts in the surrounding communities. The Global Issues Management Leader at The Dow Chemical Company, Peter Paul van de Wijs, says, "Forty percent of Dow sites around the world will experience some degree of freshwater stress by 2025."[8]

In order to manage water-related risks to operations, managers should identify at least three Key Performance Indicators (KPIs): (1) water use at all facilities owned and operated; (2) water use per unit of production; and (3) quality and quantity of wastewater discharged from facilities.[9] The first metric represents the burden placed on local water quantity (which could be a source of reputational problems if this conflicts with local needs), as well as the extent of dependency upon those water supplies (a potential liability which might need to be reported in case of drought). The second metric allows cross-industry comparisons and provides a baseline of water productivity. The third metric enables managers to comply with any applicable environmental laws related to water pollution and also provides a snapshot of the impact of the organization on local water quality.

> **CROSS-LINKAGE**
>
> For more on water-related risks to business, see **Chapter 6: Risk Management** and **Chapter 8: Supply Chain Management**.

MANAGERIAL INSIGHT: Water Is a "Critical Business Need" for Dow[10]

The chemical manufacturing company Dow operates over 200 factories in 37 countries, so capital exposure to water-related risks is substantial. Dow strives to improve water efficiency by reducing freshwater consumption and finding ways to maximize water reuse. According to Dow, the real critical business driver was not the cost of water, but rather, its continued availability. In general, the most affected operations are those located in water-stressed inland locations. When water quality is degraded beyond a certain point, is must be pre-treated before use, so poor water quality can cause business losses. Although technology changes, the outlook in 2010 was that water efficiency made more sense economically for initial facility designs than as a retrofit. In order to manage relationships with local stakeholders, companies with a large water footprint should engage in regional multi-party planning networks to ensure basin-wide stewardship of water resources. Water is perceived as the lifeblood of many communities, so it should come as no surprise that competing with local uses can cause reputational harm.

Operations Strategy The policies and plans for using the organization's resources to support its long-term competitive position while creating value for customers.

Sustainable OM Strategy Includes value creation for social and environmental stakeholders as a competitive priority.

9.2 Operations Strategy

Operations strategy specifies the policies and plans for using the organization's resources to support its long-term competitive position while creating value for customers. In pursuit of social and environmental improvements, OM strategy still should be based on a company's unique core competencies, resources, technologies, and supply network.

Sustainable OM strategy includes value creation for social and environmental stakeholders as a competitive priority. Together these elements create the building blocks of a firm's unique strategic sustainability architecture, or sustainable operating system.

Operations management, finance and accounting, and risk management practices intersect at the point of monitoring and reporting sustainability performance.[11] Specifically, businesses should measure their operations' environmental and social performance through metrics in order to support operations strategy with relevant information about emissions, waste, accidents, and so forth. Accurate monitoring enables accuracy in reporting and proactive risk management. Using sustainability metrics as KPIs, companies can optimize manufacturing and production beyond the traditional goal of cost reduction to one of shared value creation.

CROSS-LINKAGE

For more about sustainability performance metrics, see **Chapter 5: Metrics, Tools, and Reporting: The Role of Finance and Accounting**. For more on operational risks, see **Chapter 6: Risk Management**.

9.2.1 Sustainable Operations as a Competitive Priority

Operations strategy focuses on developing a company's competitive priorities. Competitive priorities determine the capabilities that provide competitive advantage. The most common competitive priorities include cost, quality, time, responsiveness, and flexibility. Increasingly companies are prioritizing sustainable performance as a significant source of competitive advantage. Companies are considering competitive priorities that simultaneously create environmental benefits and enhance product value, such as manufacturing products that consume less energy when being used.

Competitive priorities serve as a guideline when making trade-off decisions in the balancing of social, economic, and environmental factors.[12] For example, competing on cost means offering products at lower prices compared to that of competition by cutting costs in the production system, such as costs of labor, materials, and facilities. At the same time, cost cutting needs to be balanced with maintaining responsiveness to customer preferences. For example, customers may prefer lower-priced service, but not if it takes an inordinately long time to provide. Companies that decide to compete on cost should study their operations carefully to eliminate all waste and inefficiencies. They might focus their design efforts on maximizing productivity of resources and minimizing waste. Even though the goal is competing on cost, the ancillary benefit is a decreased environmental footprint from operations. Sustainable business leaders are not just competing on cost, but also on product quality, corporate ethos, and social responsibility.

In addition to the varieties of brand development choices discussed in Chapter 7: Marketing, companies can also innovate for sustainable improvements in terms of their business model. A focus on sustainability may require a reappraisal of a company's entire value system, and a resulting overhaul of operations strategy. **Reappraisal** means reconsidering potential stakeholder value creation and identifying new business opportunities, and developing business models and operations strategies to capture those opportunities.

Disintermediation means eliminating an intermediate process between the supplier and the end customer; **servicization** means replacing a physical product with a service, or a product-service system, such as ZipCar.[13] These business model changes can be used to lower net aggregate impacts of operations by cutting out unnecessary processes and replacing ownership with access.

CROSS-LINKAGE

For more on sustainable product design and marketing, see Chapter 7: Marketing.

Reappraisal Reconsidering potential stakeholder value creation and identifying new business opportunities, and developing business models and operations strategies to capture those opportunities.

Disintermediation Eliminating an intermediate process between the supplier and the end customer.

Servicization Replacing a physical product with a service, or a product-service system, to reduce environmental impacts.

9.2.2 Sustainable OM Strategy

The transformation process involves large opportunities for sustainable improvements by aligning operations decisions with sustainable policies, expanding the view of whom operations managers are accountable to, and striking the right balance between traditional and sustainable operations goals.

Alignment of Operations Decisions There are three levels of sustainable OM decisions, shown in Figure 9.2. Strategic, tactical, and operational decisions must be consistent with sustainability. At the very top are **strategic decisions**, which are long term and serve to set the direction for the entire organization and determine the value proposition of the company in terms of sustainable performance. Strategic decisions are broad in scope and authorize tactical and operational decisions. For example, a company may commit to specific greenhouse gas reduction goals through sustainable OM strategy.

Tactical decisions determine how resources and middle management will be deployed in furtherance of strategic decisions. An example is deciding to launch

Strategic Decisions Long term, broad in scope, authorizing tactical and operational decisions and serving to set the direction for the entire organization and determine the value proposition of the company.

Tactical Decisions Medium term, determining how resources and middle management will be deployed in furtherance of strategic decisions.

FIGURE 9.2 Alignment of Environmental Management Decisions

Source: R. P. Sroufe, et al., *Environmental Management Practices – A Framework*, Vol. 40 Greener Management International 23–44 (Winter 2002).

a sustainable product design in furtherance of the company-wide commitment to greenhouse gas reductions. Tactical decisions in turn drive the short-term **operational decisions** that involve day-to-day management and what goes on during production. Switching off machines while not in use in order to reduce total energy consumption is an example of an operational-level decision in furtherance of sustainable strategy.

The commitment to sustainability needs to start at the strategic level, which then will drive priorities and decisions at the tactical and operational levels. At the same time, tactical and operations decisions must be aligned with strategic decisions because they are the key to the company's effectiveness in the long run. Tactical and operational decisions provide feedback to the strategic decisions, which can be modified accordingly over time.

A dynamic model for the maturation process in sustainable operations strategy further illustrates how alignment can transform operations. See Table 9.2.

> **Operational Decisions** Short-term, day-to-day management of the production process to ensure alignment with tactical and strategic decisions.

> **CROSS-LINKAGE**
> For more on stakeholders and social license to operate, see Chapter 2: Perspectives.

TABLE 9.2

Stages of Sustainable Operations Strategy

Current Internal Strategy	• Employee engagement • Waste and pollution reduction • Energy and water conservation
Current External Strategy	• Choose materials by impact • Pursue closed-loop supply chains
Future-Looking Internal Strategy	• Chemical recovery capability • Substitute non-renewable inputs • Reduce material content of products • Reduce energy demand
Future-Looking External Strategy	• Develop entirely new core capacities, products, and processes • Engage supply chains for long-term shared value creation

Source: Paul R. Kleindorfer, Kalyan Singhal & Luk N. Van Wassenhove, *Sustainable Operations Management*, Vol. 14(4) Production and Operations Management 482–492, page 485 (2005).

9.2.3 **Stakeholder View of Operational Output**

To understand the full impact of operations on sustainability it is important to extend the concept of output in the transformation model. Traditionally, output is measured as the value derived by the customer from the goods and services delivered by the operation. To consider the full impacts of operations, however, it is important to consider a wider set of stakeholders beyond just customers. Stakeholders are individuals or groups with some sort of interest in the activity, including financiers, employees, government, NGOs, and customers. Applying stakeholder relationship management to operations can ensure facilities maintain their social license to operate.

> **CROSS-LINKAGE**
>
> For more information on social license to operate, see Chapter 4: Legal Frameworks. For more information on stakeholder management, see Chapter 8: Supply Chain Management.

9.2.4 **Striking the Right Balance through Quality Management**

Sustainable operations management requires a balancing act between the traditional concerns of operations—producing a marketable product or service—and the expanded concerns of stakeholders affected by operations. Sustainability may be difficult to achieve if a company's business model requires difficult trade-offs, for instance, where achievement of a social performance objective such as higher wages is only possible at the expense of an economic objective such as lower production costs. It should be company policy to explicitly balance the social, economic, and environmental attributes of products and services with traditional considerations of quality. Integrating sustainability into operations management begins with product and process quality improvements, known as quality management. See Table 9.3.

Quality as a competitive priority requires a company to implement quality measures in both product and process design. **Product quality** means the extent to which products are designed to meet the requirements of the customer. **Process quality** means designing a process to produce error-free products. This includes focusing on equipment, workers, materials, and every other aspect of the operation to make sure it works as intended. Companies that compete on quality have to address both of these issues: the product must be designed to meet customer needs and the process must produce the product exactly as it was designed.

> **Product Quality** The extent to which products are designed to meet the requirements of the customer.
>
> **Process Quality** The extent to which production creates error-free products.

> **CROSS-LINKAGE**
>
> For more on marketing sustainable products, see Chapter 7: Marketing.

TABLE 9.3

Quality Management Tools and Sustainable Performance

Quality Management	• Use of total quality management (TQM) tools to root out defects and waste.
	• Use of "plan, do, check, act" and continuous improvement frameworks.
	• Use lean operations strategies to efficiently steward resources inputs.

MANAGERIAL INSIGHT: Human Resource Management and SME Sustainability[14]

The International Labor Office published a study of SMEs in 2014 that found a positive causal relationship between good workplace practices and enterprise-level outcomes. Sustainable management of employees (such as amiable working conditions, protection from occupational hazards, fostering employee skills, and paying fair wages) causes increased productivity, reduced employee turnover, improved profitability, and higher levels of customer satisfaction.

Sustainable product and process quality goes beyond these traditional criterion for quality by addressing the social, economic, and environmental profile of the life cycle of the product or service. Even if a product has a minimal footprint on the environment, it would be inappropriate to market that product as sustainable quality if it is otherwise poor quality, lacking effectiveness, or produced in an environmentally degrading manner. A product designed to possess beneficial environmental attributes, but which depends on materials sourced from a supplier using harsh labor conditions, would be of questionable process quality. An expanded notion of quality in product design and production processes is imperative for producing sustainable products and services.

9.3. Operations Design

Operations design is concerned with both product and process design and their interactions. Sustainable operations design takes into account the entire product life cycle at the design stage. The two most important elements are the design of the product or service offering and the process used to create it. We look at the design of these elements next.

9.3.1 Product Design

> **Product Design** The process of specifying the exact features and characteristics of a product.

Product design is the process of specifying the exact features and characteristics of a company's product. Features of every product – from a Starbuck's café latte to Ikea's kitchen chairs to HP's DeskJet printer – were determined during product design. All of a product's features are determined by product design. This also includes the design of a complete and integrated bundle of goods and services, not just the goods element, such as the design of in-room dining at Marriott Hotels to shipping options at FedEx. The total package offering must be designed to deliver the required value and performance to customers and other stakeholders.

> **Sustainable Product Design** The philosophy of designing goods and services to comply with the principles of social, economic, and environmental sustainability.

Sustainable product design is the philosophy of designing goods and services to comply with the principles of social, economic, and environmental sustainability. Examples of sustainable product design include lowering the impact of materials by choosing non-toxic, renewable, or recycled materials. Another method is to focus on quality and durability, as longer-lasting and better-functioning products will have to be replaced less frequently, reducing the impacts of disposal. Design with reference to sustainability metrics—for instance, total carbon footprint, or volume of water per unit of production—allows empiric-based marketing.

Companies can use different product design strategies to create unique product attributes that appeal to distinct consumer segments. "New consumption patterns, new awareness of lifestyles, [new] energy source consumption, [new] purchasing methods and [new] consumption style … can be supported by design innovation, responding to expressed and unexpressed user needs."[15] There are many factors that go into sustainable product design. See Table 9.4.

When modifying product design for environmental improve-ments, like materials substitution, it is essential to retain com-petitiveness in terms of product performance. Product design with an eye toward sustainability can minimize the environmen-tal impacts of products through their entire product lifecycle (design to end-of-life disposal). Companies interested in cap-turing the growing consumer market for sustainable goods and services should begin by considering opportunities for sustain-able product design. We now look at specific issues to consider in the product design stage. After explaining the role of life cycle assessment in product design, we expand on the concept of biomimicry with examples of nature-based design.

> **CROSS-LINKAGE**
>
> For additional detail in consumer seg-mentation for sustainable product attri-butes, see Chapter 7: Marketing.

> **CROSS-LINKAGE**
>
> For more on biomimicry in product design, see Chapter 2: Perspectives.

Life Cycle Assessment The concept of cradle-to-cradle is relevant to sustainable product design. Design for reuse and recycling by considering the afterlife perfor-mance of a product helps close the supply chain loop. Cradle-to-cradle is consistent with biomimicry and both concepts helped influence the development of industrial ecology. The entire life cycle of a product should be attended to in the design stage. This includes raw materials acquisition, materials processing, manufacturing, distribu-tion, product use, packaging, and disposal. Within each stage of the product life cycle, there are several environmental factors to manage. See Table 9.5. When designing a product, these factors should influence how a product is both made and marketed.

Biomimicry Biomimicry is the design philosophy that mirrors the effects of natural evolution in product attributes. According to the non-profit research and consult-ing firm Biomimicry 3.8, "Mimicking these earth-savvy designs can help humans leapfrog to technologies that sip energy, shave material use, reject toxins, and work

TABLE **9.4**	
Elements of Sustainable Product Design	
Product Design	• How and where are product ingredients sourced?
	• Is there an impact of ingredients on consumer health?
	• Is there sourcing of conflict minerals?
	• Has the product design built-in planned obsolescence?
	• Has product design used concepts of green engineering?
	• What energy source does the product or process use?
	• Has recyclability been built into the design?

<table>
<tr><td colspan="2">**TABLE 9.5**</td></tr>
<tr><td colspan="2">**Life Cycle Considerations for Product Design**</td></tr>
<tr><td>*Raw Materials Acquisition and Processing*</td><td>Natural resource conservation;

Reliance on renewable resources;

Use of recycled and recyclable materials;

Limiting interference with natural habitats and endangered species;

Conservation of water and energy;

Minimization of waste and pollution;

Reduction or elimination of toxic ingredients and the release of toxics into air, water, and soil;

Transportation modes, distance traveled and fuel source used.</td></tr>
<tr><td>*Manufacturing and Distribution*</td><td>Reduction in materials use;

Minimize waste, pollution, use of toxics, and toxic releases;

Managing by-products of production;

Conserve energy and water resources;

Workplace safety and employee health.</td></tr>
<tr><td>*Product Use and Packaging*</td><td>Promoting energy and water efficiency;

Considering consumer health and environmental safety;

Efficient package design;

Packaging uses recycled materials;

Packages are recycled at high rates.</td></tr>
<tr><td>*After-Use and Disposal*</td><td>Recyclability, ease of use, remanufacture, and repair practices;

Waste minimization;

Durability;

Biodegradability or compostability;

Safety when incinerated or landfilled.</td></tr>
</table>

Source: Adapted from Jacquelyn Ottman, *The New Rules of Green Marketing: Strategies, Tools, and Inspiration for Sustainable Branding*, 58, 2011.

---

as a system to create conditions conducive to life."[16] Biomimicry principles of product and process design can stimulate innovation across a wide range of sectors and applications. See Figure 9.3.

Reduce Using fewer resources.

Value analysis Analyzes the functions of the materials that go into a product in an effort to reduce the cost and improve the performance.

The Four R's: Reduce, Reuse, Remanufacture, and Recycle **Reduce** simply means using fewer resources.

A useful tool in helping identify possible reductions is **value analysis**. It analyzes the functions of the parts that go into a product as well as the materials in an effort to reduce the cost and improve the performance. Value analysis repeatedly asks questions that include: Could a cheaper part or material be used? Is the function necessary? Can the function of two or more parts or components be performed by a single part of a lower cost? Can a part be simplified? Could product specifications be relaxed, and would this result in a lower price? Could

Materials	• Skin-inspired self-healing plastics • Leaf-inspired CO_2 conversion to biodegradable fiber
Water	• Cell-inspired desalination • Beetle-inspired fog capture
Manufacturing	• Spider silk-inspired benign, resilient fiber • Diatom-inspired benign computer chips
Transportation	• Penguin-inspired drag reduction for boats • Boxfish-inspired fuel-efficient Mercedes Benz
Health Care	• Shark-inspired antibacterials that defy resistance • Mosquito-inspired pain-free hypodermic needles
Buildings	• Cactus-inspired building skin that is self-cooling • Insect-inspired dehumidification for HVAC systems
Paints and Coatings	• Moth-eye-inspired coating for solar cells • Peacock-inspired color via structure rather than paint
Sensors	• Lobster-inspired water pollution source detectors • Locust-inspired collision avoidance technology
Energy	• Algae-inspired catalyst for solar hydrogen production • Bacteria-inspired platinum replacement in fuel cells
Business	• Detritivore-inspired cradle-to-cradle design • Ecosystem-inspired cooperative strategies in business

FIGURE 9.3 Use of Biomimicry in Product and Process Design

Source: Examples courtesy of Biomimicry 3.8, www .biomimicry.net | AskNature .org.

standard parts be substituted for nonstandard parts? The process continues until no further reductions are possible.

Reuse is the use of an item after it has already been used. This includes conventional reuse where the item is used again for the same function, and new-life reuse where it is used for a different function. In contrast to recycling, which involves breaking down the used item into raw materials for processing, reuse recovers the original product. By taking useful products and exchanging them, without reprocessing, reuse helps save time, money, energy, and resources. In broader economic terms, reuse offers quality products to people and organizations with limited means, while generating jobs and business activity that contribute to the economy.

Remanufacturing is a type of reuse that uses components of old products in the production of new ones.[17] It requires the operations of disassembly, repair or replacement of worn out or obsolete components and modules. It has significant environmental and cost benefits, as the remanufactured products can be a fraction of the price of their new counterparts. Remanufacturing is especially popular in the electronics industry, such as the production of computers and televisions.

Recycling is an important consideration for product design. It involves recovering materials for future use.[18] This applies not only to manufactured parts but also to materials used during production, such as lubricants and solvents. Reclaimed metal or plastic parts may be melted down and used to make different products.

Companies recycle for a variety of reasons, including cost savings, environmental concerns, and environmental regulation. It is interesting to note that companies that want to do business in the European Union (EU) must show that a specified proportion of their products are recyclable. The pressure to recycle has given rise to

Reuse The use of a product after it has already been used.

Remanufacturing A type of reuse that uses components of old products in the production of new ones.

Recycling Recovering raw materials for future use.

CROSS-LINKAGE

For more on legal requirements for sustainable product design, see Chapter 4: Legal Frameworks.

> ### LEADERSHIP: Hewlett-Packard Pioneers Recycled Hardware[19]
>
> Hewlett-Packard began recycling hardware in 1987, and has since recovered 2.3 billion pounds of their products for reuse, closed-loop recycling, and remanufacturing. Hewlett-Packard's product return program is geared to reduce the environmental impacts of their IT equipment that would otherwise generate substantial electronic waste. The company offers customers options for recycling, trading in, returning for cash, and donating all of their products, instead of just setting it out on the curb for garbage pick-up. Not only does this process reduce operating costs by providing low-cost feedstock and materials, it also diverts millions of tons of plastic and electronic waste from landfills.

Design for Recycling Product design that takes into account the ability to break down a used product to recover the recyclable components.

design for recycling, referring to product design that takes into account the ability to disassemble a used product to recover the recyclable parts.

9.3.2 Process Design

CROSS-LINKAGE

For more on consumer preferences and the product/process distinction, see Chapter 7: Marketing.

Process Design Developing a production process that can create the exact product that has been designed.

Sustainable Process Design The creation of goods and services using processes and systems that are non-polluting, ergonomically appropriate, safe from worker hazards, minimally consumptive of resources, and economically viable.

Sustainable product design is only part of the equation for sustainable operations. Improving the environmental attributes of a product is great, but the process by which that product is created must also be aligned with sustainable principles. Keep in mind, consumers have preferences for sustainable processes, not just products.

Process design means developing a production process that can create the exact product that has been designed. Different products – from a computer and its software to an aircraft jet engine – require different processes in order to be created. Some processes produce standardized off-the-shelf products while some work with customer feedback to customize products. Regardless of the type of production process used, it should be designed in accordance with principles of sustainability. See Table 9.6.

Product and process design interact. In fact, the product specifications determine the processes that must be undertaken in order to create the product. Sustainable design principles might be entertained first at the product design stage but they must continue into the process design stage. **Sustainable process design** is the creation of goods and services using processes and systems that are non-polluting, ergonomically appropriate, safe from worker hazards, minimally consumptive of resources, and economically viable.

TABLE 9.6

Principles of Sustainable Process Design

Process Design	• Efficient use of as few resources as possible.
	• Closed-loop so that if there is a waste product it can be fed back into the process.
	• Work system layout is sensitive to health and welfare of employees.

LEADERSHIP: The Rodon Group: Sustainable Plastics Manufacturing[20]

The Rodon Group exemplifies how a company can integrate sustainability into operations process design. The Rodon Group is the manufacturer of K'NEX, the famous plastic construction and building toys that made wooden blocks look like a thing of the past. The Rodon Group is a leader in the plastics industry through its commitment to environmental sustainability. They use manufacturing processes that reduce the use of packaging materials, transportation, waste, water, and energy. For instance, in the course of manufacturing the annual line of one K'NEX part, they recycle enough cardboard to spare over 300 cubic meters of landfill space. In order to avoid inefficient packaging when shipping parts to distributors, the Rodon Group uses servo robots that stack the parts precisely in each carton, allowing them to triple or quadruple the amount of parts that can be packed into each container to avoid using cardboard in the first place. Usually plastics-based manufacturing produces pieces of scrap, but the Rodon Group reuses and recycles all scrap, reducing waste. Further, they rely on non-toxic colorants, resins, lubricants and cleaners in the manufacturing process. Currently they are making headway to green their manufacturing plant by installing motion sensors and high-efficiency lighting to cut energy use. The Rodon Group is one of the first molding facilities in the world to be deemed a Landfill-Free Facility. The Rodon Group partners with Sustainable Waste Solutions, LLC, to use a cutting edge energy-from-waste resource recovery facility that generates enough electricity from the waste it receives to power tens of thousands of homes in the surrounding region.

9.3.3 Process Performance Metrics

An important way of ensuring that a process is functioning properly is to regularly measure its performance. **Process performance metrics** are measurements of different process characteristics that tell us how efficiently a process is performing. Just as accountants and finance managers use financial metrics, operations managers use process performance metrics to track the gains and losses of process efficiency over time.

There are many process performance metrics that focus on different aspects of operations. In this section, we will look at some common metrics used to evaluate the production process. See Table 9.7.

Process Performance Metrics
Measurements of different process characteristics that tell how efficiently a process is performing.

TABLE 9.7

Process Performance Metrics

Metric	Definition
Throughput Time	Average time product takes to move through system
Process Velocity = $\dfrac{Throughput\ Time}{Value\text{-}added\ Time}$	A measure of wasted time in the system
Productivity = $\dfrac{Output}{Input}$	A measure of how well a company uses its resources
Utilization = $\dfrac{Time\ a\ Resource\ Is\ Used}{Time\ a\ Resource\ Is\ Available}$	The proportion of time a resource is actually used

Throughput Time The average amount of time it takes a product to move through the production system.

These process performance metrics are generic in that they apply to operational efficiency in general. The simplest process performance metric is **throughput time**, which is the average amount of time it takes a product to move through the system. This includes the time someone is working on the product as well as the waiting time. A lower throughput time means that more products can move through the system. One goal of process improvement is to reduce throughput time.

Process Velocity How much wasted time exists in a process, computed as the ratio of throughput time to value-added time.

Process velocity is another important metric that measures how much wasted time exists in a process, computed as the ratio of throughput time to value-added time. Notice that the closer this ratio is to 1.00, the lower the amount of time the product spends on non-value-adding activities (e.g., waiting). Reducing idling times of trucks during, for example, loading and unloading cargo, is an example of process velocity improvement that impacts sustainability performance through decreased vehicle emissions.

Productivity The ratio of outputs to inputs.

A critical measure of efficiency is **productivity**, which is the ratio of outputs to inputs. Productivity measures how well a company converts its inputs to outputs and is a very important measure for sustainable performance. Low productivity means that resources are being wasted. Higher productivity means that resources are being utilized optimally.

Utilization The actual time that a resource (e.g., equipment or labor) is being used versus the amount of time it is available for use.

Resource **utilization** measures the actual time that a resource (e.g., equipment or labor) is being used versus the amount of time it is available for use. Utilization efficiency should strive to be a one-to-one match, such that resources are only made available when they are being used.

Sustainable operations reduce waste and increase efficiency in order to reduce the impact of operations on the natural environment and people and reduce operating costs. By introducing environmental metrics into these formulas for operating efficiency, you can quantify the sustainability performance of operations. For example, the productivity metric can be applied to water resources to determine how much water is used to develop each product, simply by dividing the total products created by the amount of water used to create them. Once productivity of a resource is determined, companies can use this number as a benchmark for future performance in order to track progress towards improved water efficiency. Other metrics for sustainable productivity could include greenhouse gas emissions, energy, employee accidents, and so on.

CROSS-LINKAGE

For more on sustainability performance metrics and analytical tools, see Chapter 5: Metrics, Tools, and Reporting: The Role of Finance and Accounting.

LEADERSHIP: Mountain Equipment Co-op Discloses Sustainable OM Metrics[21]

Mountain Equipment Co-op (MEC) reports on various metrics related to sustainable operations. One of the indicators is the percentage of materials they source from facilities that have Environmental Management Systems in place. Another indicator is the number of products they sell that are made from certified environmentally preferred materials. Operations are monitored by measuring carbon footprint and benchmarking against 2007 performance. The company also tracks the fate of all waste products they generate in order to meet their ambitious policy for diverting material from the waste stream.

9.4 Operations Planning & Control

Operations planning and control is concerned with operations decisions and improvements on a day-to-day basis. Decisions include scheduling individual workers, machines, or workstations; improving workflow; managing inventory levels; and monitoring quality and performance. Sometimes the relationship between efficiency and sustainability is not always direct and – as already discussed – trade-offs must be made. Many operations planning and control tools exist that can be modified to include principles of sustainability. We look to these next.

9.4.1 Inventory Management

Inventory management is the area of OM that deals with stocking levels, order policies, storage, and movement of goods. These decisions are all areas where significant gains in sustainability can be made for companies. Consider that modes of transportation used to move materials have significant effects on energy consumption, traffic congestion, and pollution. Decisions such as sourcing locally, reducing the number of shipments, and selecting transportation modes wisely can go a long way toward meeting sustainability goals. See Table 9.8.

> **Inventory management** The area of OM that deals with stocking levels, order policies, storage, and movement of goods.

If companies do not keep enough inventories in stock, they risk selling out during times of demand spikes, such as the days leading up to a storm. However, if companies keep too much inventory in stock, they must pay for the warehousing of excess and even risk losing inventory as waste in case of spoliation when the power goes out and perishable goods perish.

How much inventory should be kept available is an $8 trillion question. The world is sitting on about $8 trillion worth of inventory for sale,[22] which means that $8 trillion worth of consumer products are sitting on a shelf or in a refrigerator or in a warehouse or in a parking lot, waiting for a prospective purchaser to come along and move the good. This is a tremendous amount of capital languishing in storage, in a state of limbo between manufacture and sale. Each product is embedded with the energy, water, materials, and labor used to produce it. When these products sit idle, they depreciate, and the resources that went into their production risk being wasted.

Having zero inventory is impossible because no one can perfectly forecast the amount of inventory that will be sold in a given time period. Demand planning and demand sensing predicts needs and makes real time data analysis, respectively, for coordinating with a seller's supply chain. The error rate for consumer product vendors on predicting estimated versus actual sales is more than 40%.[23] If a company

---

TABLE 9.8

Issues with Inventory Management

Inventory Management	• Is extra inventory taking up storage space?
	• Are storage facilities energy intensive?
	• Is inventory distributed in locales easier to access by final consumers?
	• Do centralized warehouses lead to idling trucks, excessive truck traffic, and resulting cumulative emissions?

estimates that it will turn 1 million bottles of beer in 1 week, this error rate means that half the time the actual sales will be between 600,000 and 1.4 million bottles of beer, and half the time the actual sales will be somewhere outside of that range. This huge variation in actual sales causes substantial uncertainty for inventory managers with consequences for the cost of storage and the amount of waste generated. Going out of stock can lead to the termination of supplier contracts or lost customers, which is arguably worse than having overstock. For that reason, inventory managers maintain a safety stock as a buffer against selling out. Too much safety stock means wasted manufacture, distribution, and warehousing, all of which involve energy consumption, pollution, and waste.

One method for managing inventory sustainably is to compare centralized and decentralized inventory storage. Keeping freight at a **centralized storage facility** may require higher transportation costs (and therefore pollution, energy consumption, etc.) because goods must be delivered from the main warehouse to the point of sale in batches.

Decentralized inventory means storage takes place closer to the end customer, which allows the retailer to maintain lower amounts of safety stock and therefore generate less waste.

Sustainable inventory management involves comparing the cost of stock-out (including the social impacts this might cause by frustrating customers) to the cost of wasted overstock (including the energy and water footprint of the wasted goods). The right decision will balance social, economic, and environmental costs and benefits, given the capabilities of the suppliers and retailers, the nature of the products, and the needs of the customers.

9.4.2 Work System Design

Work system design is the area of OM decisions that involves designing jobs. A significant aspect of sustainability is the design of jobs and work with an eye toward minimizing harm to the laborer. This includes jobs within a company's own operations, as well as the job requirements made upon suppliers.

Ergonomics is the design of a job to protect workers from physical stress and environmental exposure.

Physical stressors can lead to cumulative trauma disorders and repetitive strain injuries.[24] One of the leading causes of lost workday injuries and employee illness is musculoskeletal disorders, or injuries to muscles, nerves, and tendons, such as carpal tunnel syndrome.[25] Lifting, bending, reaching, pushing, and pulling (1) heavy objects, (2) in a repetitive manner, or (3) using awkward body positions are contributing factors to the risk of musculoskeletal disorders. Indoor environmental exposure comes from poor air quality, excessive noise, and improper lighting.

Sick building syndrome, where a structure has systemic air quality problems from mold, toxins, poor circulation, and the like, causes occupants to suffer headaches, congestion, fatigue, and rashes. Bad lighting and excessive noise exposure can also cause long-term damage to vision and hearing, respectively.

At this point it might appear that occupational health and safety are mainly relevant to blue collar employees, manual laborers, assembly line workers, and the like.

Centralized Storage Facility A "mother ship" warehouse commonly used by distributors for receiving wholesale shipments from manufacturers and sending out batches of inventory to retailers.

Decentralized Inventory Storage that is smaller in size but geographically diffuse in order to maintain inventory closer to the end customer, allowing retailers to maintain lower amounts of safety stock.

Sustainable Inventory Management Balancing the risks of stock-out with the cost of wasted overstock given the social, economic, and environmental factors affected by each scenario.

Work system design The area of OM responsible for designing job descriptions.

Ergonomics The design of a job description to protect workers from physical stress and environmental exposure.

Sick Building Syndrome Where a structure has systemic air quality problems from mold, toxins, poor circulation, and the like, causing occupants to suffer headaches, congestion, fatigue, and rashes.

However, employees who work a desk job are not immune from occupational health impacts. Job designs that do not involve physical or environmental stress can nonetheless have significant adverse health impacts on employees by forcing them to remain sedentary throughout the shift. The health impacts of excessive sitting include increased risk of heart disease, type 2 diabetes, breast cancer and colon cancer.[26] In the United States, office workers sit on average for 9.3 hours per day, prompting the expression, "sitting is the smoking of our generation."[27] **Sustainable work system design** means designing jobs to protect employees from work hazards and to encourage healthy routines throughout the work-day.

One method for avoiding workplace injuries is to deploy **automation** to replace human workers in dangerous job descriptions. One of the main advantages of automation is the replacement of human workers with automated processes for tasks that are physically dangerous, such as exposure to extreme heat or toxic chemicals. Physically difficult or monotonous jobs can cause human worker fatigue, increasing error rate; in these situations, automation can improve process quality. In certain circumstances, automation can also increase operational capabilities while reducing risk of employee injuries by allowing work to be done in extreme conditions and extreme speeds.

Sustainable Work System Design Designing a working environment to protect employees from work hazards and to encourage healthy routines throughout the work-day.

Automation Replacing human workers in dangerous job descriptions with robotics.

9.4.3 Enterprise Resource Planning: Using Big Data Analytics

Enterprise Resource Planning (ERP) systems are now a major part of life for most businesses and their supply chains. When first implemented, the role of ERP was to manage a company's data and processes from a single system. Today, ERP have become increasingly important in managing sustainability.

As regulatory and environmental pressures grow, companies are now turning to ERP systems for help in executing and tracking the success of their sustainability initiatives. Remember that ERP systems are about managing resources, and measures of sustainability show how well a company uses these resources to achieve sustainable

Enterprise Resource Planning Management tool for executing and tracking the success of operational initiatives in terms of deployed resources.

GLOBAL INSIGHTS: Creating a Safe Working Environment at SMEs Overseas[28]

Human resources management at SMEs is a critical ingredient in making sustainability profitable. However, best practices must be deployed in a bundle, not piecemeal, to be effective. For example, T&T is a Vietnam-based washing and drying company that uses strong chemicals and large drying machines. In order to reduce occupational hazard exposure, the company provided employees with personal protective equipment to be used when handling chemicals. However, employees would not wear the protective equipment if the temperature at the facilities was too hot. By lowering the temperature of the building, T&T's workers were more likely to use proper protection when handling dangerous chemicals. This exemplifies how facility management and occupational safety are inter-connected.

performance. As a result, ERP systems are increasingly becoming platforms for sustainable performance analysis, providing accurate reports on items such as carbon footprints.

To meet this growing demand for ERP software, vendors such as SAP and Oracle are enhancing their software offering in the areas of sustainability reporting, planning, and management, and adding modules such as carbon management.[29] Using ERP systems to link organizational activities to sustainability metrics is such a growing trend that even small software vendors are developing these systems. These solutions involve expanding current ERP capability to include **big data analytics**, or gathering and analyzing enormous amounts of data and translating that into business intelligence.

ERP software that uses big data analytics could collect and analyze information from, among other things, sustainability metrics at the manufacturing, transport, product and SKU level. By synthesizing vast amounts of information, ERP systems enable companies to accurately track and report sustainability performance.

Big Data Analytics Gathering and analyzing enormous amounts of data to determine trends which can be translated into business intelligence.

CROSS-LINKAGE

For more on monitoring sustainable performance, see Chapter 5: Metrics, Tools, and Reporting: The Role of Finance and Accounting.

9.4.4 Healthy, Productive Employees: Scheduling

Scheduling techniques vary depending on the business and operating environment. Traditionally, employee scheduling is done according to **priority rules**, such as "the most productive workers are assigned to cover peak hours." Although such a rule may appear to be the most optimal allocation of human resources to satisfy operational objectives, this rule punishes productive employees with more demanding shifts, and can lead to breaking shifts and forcing workers into shifts that interrupt their personal life.

With the increasing push toward sustainability from customers and other stakeholders, these traditional priority rules and scheduling techniques need to be modified to help develop schedules that meet sustainability criteria. Scheduling has always been about staffing jobs with the right people with the right materials to do the job. We have to expand these rules to include meeting sustainability criteria,

Priority Rules A traditional method for worker scheduling that attempts to deploy the human resources optimally, such as "the most productive workers are assigned to cover peak hours."

LEADERSHIP: Major Sports Leagues Measure Footprint of Stadiums[30]

The Natural Resources Defense Council has produced software-based Greening Advisors for Major League Baseball, National Basketball Association, National Hockey League, Major League Soccer teams, and the United States Tennis Association. The NRDC Greening Advisor is a web-based environmental resource guide designed to help each team and facility operator identify what they can do in their specific city and facility to pursue environmentally superior operations and supply chain options. The Greening Advisor has helped professional sports teams reduce the electricity demand of their stadiums, reduce the water demand of their facilities, and procure merchandise and sports team jerseys from sustainable suppliers, among other things. The Greening Advisor won the EPA's Environmental Merit Award in 2008.

TABLE **9.9**	
Sustainable Workforce Scheduling	
Workforce Scheduling	• Respect cultural and ethnic sensitivity. • Ensure workforce diversity. • Promote happy labor force to enhance productivity. • Are employees encouraged to carpool or use public transit? • Are employees given a reasonable work life balance? • Are employees offered development opportunities?

by understanding the social and environmental impacts of workforce scheduling decisions. See Table 9.9.

In addition to traditional priority rules, **sustainable scheduling** decisions should include developing schedules to minimize carbon emission (i.e., from commuting), minimize energy use, lower material chemical content and other environmental pollutants, and maximize the use of recycled material. Job designs and worker schedules can also be developed to ensure fair treatment of workers. This concern also extends to how employees are treated by the employer, whether employees are consulted on schedule development, and the extent to which work demands and deadlines put the laborers of suppliers at risk.

Social sustainability requires management practices with respect to employees that should go above and beyond minimum requirements of health, safety, and nondiscrimination mandated by labor laws.

Sustainable scheduling also involves employing a diverse workforce with competitive wages and ample time away from work. Employment practices should maximize the productivity and quality of employees by fostering a culture of mutual respect, appreciation, and care. This involves redesigning difficult jobs, and moving away from long hours and poor pay.

Sustainable Scheduling
Assigning workers based on meeting social and environmental, in addition to operational, needs.

CROSS-LINKAGE

For more on occupational health and safety regulations, see Chapter 4: Legal Frameworks.

ETHICAL DECISIONS: OSHA Consultation for SMEs on Workplace Safety[31]

In the United States, workers have a right to a safe workplace. Under the Occupational Safety and Health Act (OSHA), employers must provide employees with working conditions that are free of known dangers. The agency responsible for administering these rules provides free assistance to SMEs in order to help assess working conditions, clarify compliance obligations, and assist in the development of workplace safety and injury prevention programs. OSHA provides confidential on-site consultation services that are separate from their enforcement activities. Because SME participation is voluntarily and intended to improve labor conditions, these inspections do not result in fines or citations if the inspection reveals unsafe conditions at the time. OSHA also recognizes SMEs who operate exemplary injury and illness prevention programs through a program called Safety and Health Achievement Recognition Program (SHARP).

Investing in employees, in the form of continuing education programs, leave time, childcare, and opportunities for advancement should be seen as investments in the company itself. The result is happier, healthier, more productive employees, and an enhanced reputation of the company. An excellent example of these benefits is the SAS Institute in North Carolina, a company consistently on the Fortune Magazine's top companies to work for. The company provides a superb work environment – from childcare to on-site massages – resulting in high productivity and almost no turnover.

9.5 Facility Management, Layout, & Design

This section addresses the management, layout, and design of the built structures that house operations activities.

9.5.1 Facility Management

Facility management professionals are poised to be environmental stewards of the physical workplace because it is within their area of responsibility to upgrade building equipment, materials, office space, and daily operations through sustainable procurement, design, maintenance, and workspace management strategies.[32] There are multiple avenues for facilities managers to pursue sustainability improvements within their organization.

Greenhouse Gas Tracking and Reduction Tracking the amount of greenhouse gases emitted by a facility and its employees is a critical step in reducing the total greenhouse gas footprint of a company's operations. Establishing a monitoring program can provide objective information regarding where the most substantial emissions come from (air conditioning, manufacturing processes, transportation, etc.) as well as where improvements are being made or need to be made.

Construction Construction activities allow a property owner to retrofit existing structures with energy efficiency improvements that significantly reduce operating costs of industrial, commercial, and residential facilities. Energy efficiency projects can decrease the volatility of returns on the investments made into property, and making the investment in energy efficiency prior to significant lease rollover maximizes these returns.

Energy Management Facilities need a system for energy management that controls the energy use for lighting and air-conditioning. The higher the cost of energy, the greater the payback of efficient energy management systems. The most efficient, least wasteful, and most environmentally friendly forms of lighting and interior climate control are natural light and natural ventilation such as the stepwell design discussed in the Chapter Opener. With respect to air conditioning, facilities managers may observe trade-offs between savings and comfort: during the summer, cooling increases operating costs but improves employee comfort; uncomfortable employees are less productive.

Food-Related Services Many companies have introduced a cafeteria into their office space in order to provide employees a place to dine on campus, saving time away from their work, as well as a forum to socialize with other employees. When a company provides food for its employees, it can also promote sustainability by sourcing locally, eliminating junk food and substituting it with nutritious organic food, utilizing biodegradable packaging, composting unused food to reduce waste, providing reusable containers, offering the option of using cloth bags instead of plastic bags when employees go out for lunch, and managing waste streams and water usage in the cafeteria.

Furnishings and Supplies Office furniture and stationary supplies should be procured from certified sustainable sources, and made from recycled and recyclable material. Printing should be avoided or done on both sides. Carpet can be replaced with hardwood for aesthetic, maintenance, and indoor air quality reasons.

Maintenance The way in which facilities are maintained, such as by cleaning with harsh chemicals, can adversely impact the environment as well as employee health by releasing volatile organic compounds into the indoor air conditioning system.

Landscaping and Grounds Keeping Any company with one or more large campuses can promote sustainability by landscaping the campus to create greenspace with ecosystem services for the company employees as well as local communities. Community gardens, parks, and arboretums are much more desirable than expansive paved parking lots.

Transportation Employees spend time, money, and energy commuting to work nearly every day. A sustainable business will find ways to make this easier by incentivizing public transit, carpooling, and walking and biking. This will reduce the overall energy and greenhouse gas footprint of the company by lowering the emissions required to get the staff to the office, and in the case of walking and biking, employees will benefit from improved health and fitness, ultimately contributing to their productivity.

9.5.2 Facility Layout

Facility layout is the physical arrangement of all resources within a facility. These resources include everything that is part of the operation: a work center, a machine, an entire office, or just the location of a desk. Facility layout has a significant impact on performance, especially production cost, time, and flexibility. Poor facility layout is a significant contributor to inefficiency and increased production cost as well as workplace injuries. For this reason, managers spend a great deal of effort ensuring that facility layouts are efficient and enhance workflow and employee safety.

Facility Layout The physical arrangement of all resources within a facility.

Physical layout and flow significantly impact resource efficiency; for instance, perhaps some process stages can be eliminated, reducing energy and material consumption. For example, positioning the loading docks near the storage space reduces the amount of carrying to-and-fro needed to manage inventory. Over time, given enough repetition, these small incremental improvements in facility layout can add up to substantial benefits. Not just operational efficiency but also the impact on working conditions and employee satisfaction must also be considered when making facility layout choices. See Table 9.10. This is closely related to work systems design. Facilities should be laid out to reduce the risk of employee injury.

In addition to promoting organizational efficiency, facility layout can play a significant role in improving organizational sustainability. Office spaces use large amounts of energy for lighting, heating, and air conditioning.

9.5.3 Facility Design

Recall the Dixon Golf example from Case 2, in Chapter 1: Introduction to Sustainable Business. Dixon's manufacturing plant was LEED certified, and incorporated a number of design features to minimize the environmetnal impact of the facility (especially water use in the Arizona desert), while harnessing the unique location (especially solar energy). Designing an office space with ample natural light, using cutting-edge insulation material and recycled building material can go a long way in reducing energy consumption and creating models of energy efficiency.

Sustainable Building Design
Creates structures that conserve energy, use renewable resources in an efficient manner, and provide healthy indoor environments for employees that are conducive to productivity, and which are resilient against natural disasters.

Sustainable building design creates structures that conserve energy, use renewable resources in an efficient manner, and provide healthy indoor environments for employees that are conducive to productivity, and which are resilient against natural disasters.[33] A company can retrofit an existing structure to improve its sustainability performance, and as it turns out, the cost of constructing a sustainable building design is essentially equal to that of a conventional building.[34]

The purpose of sustainable building design is not just to reduce the burden of the built environment on natural resources or climate impacts, but also to promote employee health and productivity.[35] See Table 9.11.

Traditionally, deep buildings were typical: the large cubic monolithic structure with inner offices ringed by hallways. Mostly lit by artificial lighting, deep building structures had poor air circulation and little natural light. However, researchers identified the optimal way to light a building to get the most employee comfort, health, and productivity: it involves coupling direct user-adjusted task lighting with indirect ambient daylight.[36] Now building designers using shallow designs and working with

---

TABLE 9.10

Issues with Facility Layout

Facility Layout	• Are facilities laid out so completing tasks does not risk employee injury?
	• When not in use are facilities powered down to conserve energy?
	• Are work stations positioned to improve efficiency?

> **TABLE 9.11**
>
> ## Issues with Facility Design
>
> Facility Design
> - Are facilities LEED certified?
> - Are lighting, air conditioning, and water systems efficiently designed?
> - Does the workplace atmosphere contribute to morale?
> - Do facilities waste energy or resources?
> - Are existing structures capable of being retrofitted?

glass exterior surfaces to expose more interior work areas to indirect sunlight, with implications for employee health, ergonomics, and productivity.[37]

Leadership in Energy and Environmental Design (LEED) certification is the recognized standard for measuring building sustainability. LEED certification can be obtained for new commercial construction, as well as major renovation projects, interior projects, and existing building retrofits. The LEED green building rating system is developed and administered by the U.S. Green Building Council, a non-profit coalition of building industry leaders.[38] The LEED system is designed to promote design and construction practices that increase profitability while reducing the negative social and environmental impacts of buildings.

> **Leadership in Energy and Environmental Design** Certification authorized by the U.S. Green Building Council, the recognized standard for measuring building sustainability.

The **LEED Rating System** is used to rank the extent of sustainable building design. LEED takes 100 possible base points and distributes them across five major credit categories: Sustainable Sites, Water Efficiency, Energy and Atmosphere, Materials and Resources, Indoor Environmental Quality, plus an additional 6 points for Innovation in Design and an additional 4 points for Regional Priority.[39] Buildings can qualify for four levels of certification: Certified (40–49 points), Silver (50–59 points), Gold (60–79 points), and Platinum (80 points and above).

> **LEED Rating System** Used to rank the extent of sustainable building design.

Not all certification programs are perfect. LEED judges the *design* of the facility, not necessarily its ongoing environmental performance. Ongoing monitoring of facility performance is necessary to ensure that LEED certification lives up to its promise.

> **CROSS-LINKAGE**
>
> For more on sustainable certification programs, see Chapter 7: Marketing.

Implementing a sustainable building design certification program can provide tax benefits and lowered overhead for the property owner. The often-attractive modern interiors and exteriors, as well as green roofs, can make a facility more enjoyable to work in. Properties are easier to re-sell if they are compliant with a bona fide certification program largely because the cost of ownership is reduced.

An alternative to LEED certification is the **Living Building Challenge**, a certification program developed by the International Living Future Institute. Living Buildings go beyond mere reductions of environmental impacts, and demonstrate that the built environment can improve the surrounding natural environment.[40] There are three types of building certifications available from the Living Building Challenge: Full Certification, Petal Recognition, and Net Zero Energy Building Certification.[41] The process involves documenting the construction project to fulfill the certification requirements, and submit to auditing before receiving a certificate.

> **Living Building Challenge** A certification program with metrics that go beyond mere reductions of environmental impacts, in order to demonstrate that the built environment can improve the surrounding natural environment.

> ### LEADERSHIP: Natural Resource Defense Council (NRDC) Greens Offices[42]
>
> An excellent example of savings that can be achieved through environmental layout design is seen in the offices of the Natural Resource Defense Council (NRDC). The NRDC, a nonprofit environmental advocacy organization, has been a pioneer in the area of sustainability and wanted to showcase environmental principles through the design of their own offices by incorporating sustainable facility design. Their New York City headquarters are located on the top three floors of a 12-story Art Deco building in Chelsea, selected for its abundance of natural light. Through LEED design, the New York Office cut energy consumption by 70%
>
> compared to conventional offices. Similar savings have been seen in their Washington, D.C. office, which showcases renewable building materials like countertops made of soybeans and recycled newspapers. The Chicago office achieved Petal Certification from the Living Building Challenge. The result of these green offices has been an annual operating cost savings of $65,000 and energy savings of more than $1 per square foot, as well as a reduction in annual pollution loads. This illustrates that layout design with an eye toward sustainability not only helps the environment but also has a direct positive impact on the bottom line.

Key Terms

Baoli 259
Operations
  Management 260
Sustainable Operations
  Management 261
Operations Strategy 264
Sustainable OM
  Strategy 264
Reappraisal 265
Disintermediation 265
Servicization 265
Strategic Decisions 265
Tactical Decisions 265
Operational Decisions 266
Product Quality 267
Process Quality 267

Product Design 268
Sustainable Product
  Design 268
Reduce 270
Value Analysis 270
Reuse 271
Remanufacturing 271
Recycling 271
Design for Recycling 272
Process Design 272
Sustainable Process
  Design 272
Process Performance
  Metrics 273
Throughput Time 274
Process Velocity 274

Productivity 274
Utilization 274
Inventory
  Management 275
Centralized Storage
  Facility 276
Decentralized
  Inventory 276
Sustainable Inventory
  Management 276
Work System Design 276
Ergonomics 276
Sick Building
  Syndrome 276
Sustainable Work System
  Design 277

Automation 277
Enterprise Resource
  Planning 277
Big Data Analytics 278
Priority Rules 278
Sustainable
  Scheduling 279
Facility Layout 281
Sustainable Building
  Design 282
Leadership in Energy
  and Environmental
  Design 283
LEED Rating System 283
Living Building
  Challenge 283

Discussion Questions

1. Identify major differences between a service and manufacturing operation. Do these different types of operations pose different sustainability challenges, or do they have issues in common?

2. Find a company you are familiar with and explain how it uses operations. How is its operations function

tied to its supply chain? Are the company's adverse impacts owing more to its own internal operations or to upstream actors within its supply chain?

3. Find an example of a process layout, work system design, and building design from a local business. How could your example be changed to promote sustainable OM?

Too Little or Too Much: Inventory Management During Environmental Crises[43]

In October of 2012, more than 60 million residents of the United States felt the impact of Hurricane Sandy, what meteorologists described as a perfect storm that slammed into New York, New Jersey, Maryland, the District of Columbia, Virginia, Connecticut, Pennsylvania, and many other states. The blustering combination of extremely high winds, torrential rain and blizzard-like snow caused major destruction of homes, stores, boats, and cars. The indirect losses are even greater, including lost wages, lost restaurant sales, lost tax revenue, canceled flights, and canceled cruises. The stock market on Wall Street was shut down for two entire days, freezing trade. Power outages and structural damages to infrastructure such as roads will take a long time to repair. An initial estimate of the economic losses imposed by Hurricane Sandy is about $35–$45 billion.

There were short term upsides for some businesses to the super storm as residents of the affected areas made runs on grocery and hardware stores in the days proceeding landfall—clearing out aisles containing batteries, flashlights, canned goods, toilet paper, ice, alcohol, snacks, bottled water, and other emergency items such as electric generators. The only arguable economic winners from the super storm were retail outlets. However, for many small businesses, catastrophic storms are mixed blessings. If a business experiences power loss, it may have to shut down because of inadequate lighting or climate control, inoperability of equipment, lost sales, flooding, repairs, and wasted inventory when products spoil without proper storage. Storms can lead to the involuntary creation of waste.

Imagine that you work for a general store in a small town and your manager has asked you to prepare an inventory needs estimate for the coming winter season. Meteorologists predict it is going to be a very cold, long, and harsh winter, with high probability of blizzard-like conditions that could knock out power for extended periods of time.

Questions for Case Study

1. How many perishable goods like meat and milk should be kept on site in the freezer? How many portable electric generators should be ordered from the manufacturer?

2. Given the high likelihood that local customers will make a run on the store in case of an ice storm—which can occur all of the sudden, offering you little time to prepare—how do you decide how much inventory to keep in stock?

3. Is it worthwhile to reach out to the local government and utility companies in order to prepare for harsh winter conditions and develop a disaster preparedness plan?

Further Research

An excellent integration of sustainability considerations with Operations Management is in the chapter by Alison Bettley & Stephen Burnley, *Towards Sustainable Operations Management: Integrating Sustainability Management into Operations Management Strategies and Practices*, in HANDBOOK OF PERFORMABILITY ENGINEERING, pages 875–904 (Springer, 2008).

For cases of successful on-site OSHA consultations and exemplary labor safety programs at small and medium sized enterprises (SMEs), see the Occupational Safety & Health Administration website.

The Chief Economist at General Electric Marco Annunziata discusses how technology is transforming industrial sectors throughout the global economy in the TED-Talk, "Welcome to the Age of the Industrial Internet."

For a discussion of innovation in building materials design, see the TED-Talk by Kevin Surace of Serious Materials: "Fixing Drywall to Heal the Planet."

Havard Business Review Case: Garima Sharma, Chris Laszlo, Eric Ahearn, Indrajeet Ghatge, *Tennant Company: Can "Chemical-Free" Be a Pathway to Competitive Advantage?*, Prod. #: W12808-PDF-ENG (March 19, 2012).

Harvard Business Review Case: Robert Klassen, Fraser P. Johnson & Asad Shafiq, *Building Sustainable Distribution at Wal-Mart Canada*, Prod. #: W13099-PDF-ENG (April 5, 2013).

Endnotes

1. Based on Nick Glass and George Webster, *Ancient 'Air-Conditioning' Cools Building Sustainably*, CNN, March 8, 2012.

2. For a brief historical overview, see Paul R. Kliendorfer, Kalyan Singhal, Luk N. Van Wassenhove, *Sustainable Operations Management*, Vol. 14 No. 4 Production and Operations Management 482–83 (Winter 2005).

3. David F. Drake & Stefan Spinler, *Sustainable Operations Management: An Enduring Stream or a Passing Fancy?*, Harvard Environmental Economics Program Discussion Paper 13–49, page 10 (July 2013).

4. Carbon Disclosure Project, Case Study on Avaya, last accessed May 17, 2014, available at https://www.cdp.net/en-US/What WeDo/Pages/Case-Study-Avaya.aspx.

5. Alison Bettley & Stephen Burnley, *Towards Sustainable Operations Management: Integrating Sustainability Management into Operations Management Strategies and Practices*, in HANDBOOK OF PERFORMABILITY ENGINEERING, pages 875–904, 876 (Springer, 2008).

6. Alison Bettley & Stephen Burnley, *Towards Sustainable Operations Management: Integrating Sustainability Management into Operations Management Strategies and Practices*, in HANDBOOK OF PERFORMABILITY ENGINEERING, pages 875–904, 885 (Springer, 2008).

7. E. Beinhocker, I. Davis, and L. Mendonca, *The 10 Trends You Have to Watch*, Harvard Business Review 55–60 (July–August 2009).

8. Dow Chemical, Understanding Our Water Risks—The GWT at Work (2010), last accessed May 17, 2014, available at http://www.wbcsd.org/web/projects/water/Dow.pdf.

9. CEO Water Mandate, Efficiency, Eco-Design, and Sustainable Manufacturing, last accessed May 17, 2014, available at http://ceowatermandate.org/water-assessment-tools-methods/accounting-needs-functions/efficiency-eco-design-sustainable-manufacturing/.

10. Dow Chemical, Understanding Our Water Risks—The GWT at Work (2010), last accessed May 17, 2014, available at http://www.wbcsd.org/web/projects/water/Dow.pdf.

11. See *Sustainability Framework 2.0:* Professional Accountants As Integrators, AccountAbility, International Federation of Accountants, last accessed May 17, 2014, available at http://www.accountability.org/images/content/4/3/435.pdf.

12. S.H. Byggeth & E. Handling, *Trade-Offs in Ecodesign Tools for Sustainable Product Development and Procurement*, Vol. 14 Journal of Cleaner Production 1420–1430 (2006).

13. O. Mont, *Reducing Life-Cycle Environmental Impacts Through Systems of Joint Use*, Vol. 45 Greener Management International 63–77 (Spring 2004).

14. Richard Coucher, Bianca Stumbitz, Michael Muinlan & Ian Vickers (eds.), CAN BETTER WORKING CONDITIONS IMPROVE THE PERFORMANCE OF SMEs?, International Labor Office (January 16, 2014).

15. F. Tosi, *Ergonomics and Sustainability in the Design of Everyday Use Products*, Vol. 41 Suppl. 1 Work 3878–82 (2012).

16. *See* Biomimicry 3.8 Website, last accessed May 17, 2014, *available at* http://biomimicry.net/about/biomimicry/a-biomimicry-primer/.

17. A.M. King & S.C. Burgess, *The Development of a Remanufacturing Platform Design: A Strategic Response to the Directive on Waste Electrical and Electronic Equipment*, Vol. 219 Proceedings of Institution of Mechanical Engineers Part B: Journal of Engineering Manufacture 623–631 (2005).

18. R. Geyer, T. Jackson, *Supply Loops and Their Constraints: The Industrial Ecology of Recycling and Reuse*, Vol. 46(2) California Management Review 55–73 (2004).

19. See Hewlett-Packard's web page on Global Citizenship: Product Return and Recycling, last accessed May 17, 2014, available at http://www8.hp.com/us/en/hp-information/environment/product-recycling.html#.UuCpbHn0DR0.

20. See the Rodon Group website, Sustainable Manufacturing, last accessed May 17, 2014, available at http://www.rodongroup.com/about-us/sustainability.

21. See Mountain Equipment Co-op, *2012 Accountability Report Summary* (2012), last accessed May 17, 2014, available at http://www.mec.ca/media/Images/pdf/accountability/accountability-2012-summaryreport_v2_m56577569831501421.pdf.

22. Andrew Winston, *Excess Inventory Wastes Carbon and Energy, Not Just Money*, Harvard Business Review Blog (August 8, 2011).

23. *ibid.*

24. Oklahoma State University EHS Safety Training website, Defining Ergonomics, last accessed May 17, 2014, available at http://ehs.okstate.edu/kopykit/ergo.htm.

25. See the Occupational Safety and Health Administration website on Ergonomics: Prevention of Musculoskeletal Disorders in the Workplace, last accessed May 17, 2014, available at https://www.osha.gov/SLTC/ergonomics/.

26. I.M. Lee, E.J. Shiroma, F. Lobelo, P. Puska, S.N. Blair, P.T. Katzmarzyk, *Effect of Physical Inactivity on Major Non-Communicable Diseases Worldwide: An Analysis of Burden of Disease and Life Expectancy*, Vol. 380(9838) Lancet 219–29 (July 2012).

27. Nolifer Merchant, *Sitting Is the Smoking of Our Generation*, Harvard Business Review Blog (January 14, 2013).

28. Richard Coucher, Bianca Stumbitz, Michael Muinlan & Ian Vickers (eds.), CAN BETTER WORKING CONDITIONS IMPROVE THE PERFORMANCE OF SMEs?, International Labor Office (January 16, 2014).

29 *Environmental Business Software: A Special Report on Selecting the Right Carbon, Environmental or Sustainability Accounting Tool for Your Organisation,* Environmental Data Services (August 2010).

30 See NRDC's Smarter Business website, Greening the Games, last accessed May 17, 2014, available at http://www.nrdc.org/greenbusiness/guides/sports/.

31 See the Occupational Safety & Health Administration website on On-Site Consultation for SMEs, last accessed May 17, 2014, available at https://www.osha.gov/dcsp/smallbusiness/consult.html.

32 See the International Facility Management Association website, Sustainability, last accessed May 17, 2014, available at http://www.ifma.org/know-base/browse/sustainability.

33 D. Kopec, HEALTH, SUSTAINABILITY AND THE BUILT ENVIRONMENT (Fairchild Books, 2009).

34 L. Forbes & S. Ahmed, MODERN CONSTRUCTION: LEAN PROJECT DELIVERY AND INTEGRATED PRACTICES (CRC Press, 2011).

35 L. Thomas, *Evaluating Design Strategies, Performance and Occupant Satisfaction: A Low Carbon Office Refurbishment,* Vol. 38(6) Building Research & Information 610–624 (2010).

36 A. Hedge, *Where Are We in Understanding the Effects of Where We Are?,* Vol. 43(7) Ergonomics 1019–1029 (2000).

37 K. Martin, S. Legg & C. Brown, *Designing for Sustainability: Ergonomics—Carpe Diem.,* Vol. 56(3) Ergonomics 365–388, 383 (2013).

38 See the U.S. Green Building Council website on LEED, last accessed May 17, 2014, available at http://www.usgbc.org/leed.

39 See the LEED Rating System, last accessed May 17, 2014, available at http://www.usgbc.org/leed/rating-systems.

40 See the Living Building Challenge website on Certified Projects, last accessed May 17, 2014, available at http://living-future.org/node/132.

41 See the Living Building Challenge website on the Certification Process, last accessed May 17, 2014, available at http://living-future.org/lbc/certification.

42 See the NRDC Smarter Business: Green Building website, NRDC's Green Offices, last accessed May 17, 2014, available at http://www.nrdc.org/cities/building/foffice.asp.

43 Marilyn Geewax, *Hurricane Sandy's Economic Impact Likely To Be Immense,* October 29, 2012, last accessed May 17, 2014, available at http://m.npr.org/news/front/163891993.

Chapter 1 Key Terms

Blue Ocean Strategy. The simultaneous pursuit of differentiation and low cost with the goal of rendering competitors irrelevant.

Global Living Planet Index. Scientific analysis of the health of the planet assesses the vitality of life systems given the burdens imposed by human activity.

Internalize. When the party that creates a risk ultimately bears that risk instead of externalizing it.

Natural Capital. The available stock of natural resources upon which human life and economic activities depend.

Negative Externality. A cost generated by business activity, which is shifted from the operator onto natural resources, populations, or third parties without consent or compensation.

Principle of Balance. The normative principle of balancing social, economic, and environmental factors when making business decisions.

Principle of Stewardship. The normative principle of maintaining natural resources at sufficient quality and quantity to remain viable for use by future generations.

Rio+20 Summit on Sustainability. International forum where private sector leaders committed to sustainable principles and practices.

Sustainable Business. The private sector trend of measuring and managing business success in terms of social, economic, and environmental performance.

Sustainable Economic Development. Economic activity that meets the needs of current generations without compromising the ability of future generations to meet their own needs.

Triple-Bottom-Line. Approach to measuring business performance that includes (1) the traditional financial bottom line measured in terms of profits and losses; (2) an account for social responsibility measured in terms of the organization's affect on people; and (3) an account for environmental stewardship measured by pollution and resource depletion.

Chapter 2 Key Terms

Anthropocentrism. Perspective in environmental ethics holding that only human beings are morally significant.

Biocapacity Deficit. When the human footprint exceeds the productivity and services that available land and sea provide.

Biocapacity Remainder. When the biocapacity of a given area exceeds the dependent population's ecological demand.

Biocentrism. Perspective in environmental ethics holding that protecting nature is necessary because all forms of life have intrinsic value; they are valuable in and of themselves.

Biomimicry. Finding practical commercial and industrial applications of biological features of plants and animals.

Conflicts of Cultural Tradition. Where local customs conflict with the attitudes and expectations of a newly arriving corporation.

Conflicts of Relative Development. Conflicts arising from differences in legal standards of the host country and the standards of the foreign corporation caused by differences in economic development.

Conservation. A process by which natural resources are managed to allow for exploitation of those resources in ways that do not jeopardize their long-term viability.

Conservation Easements. A form of property right that enables the holder of that right to limit the kinds of uses that are allowed on a specific parcel.

Corporate Social Responsibility. A form of self-regulation that integrates into the business strategy a process for monitoring and managing corporate conduct relative to external stakeholders.

Cradle-to-Cradle. Extends the cradle to grave metaphor by incorporating materials back as inputs into the production process rather than diverting them as waste products.

Cradle-to-Grave. From the point of origin for raw materials through the production process and on to the point of disposal at a landfill.

Cross-Country Ethical Dilemmas. Where a company does business in two countries with conflicting ethical standards.

CSR and Brand Differentiation. The benefits of CSR to brand differentiation such as creating a unique sales proposition.

CSR and Human Resources. The benefits of CSR to human resources functions such as employee recruiting, retention, and promotion.

CSR and Risk Management. The benefits of CSR to risk management functions such as maintaining corporate ethos and avoiding risks.

CSR and Social License to Operate. The role of CSR in meeting informal requirements of the community in which business activities take place.

Earth Systems Engineering. Large-scale engineering research into the function and stability of major natural systems of the planet and infrastructure that sustains civilization.

Ecological Engineering. Focuses on restoring ecological functions and service capabilities to natural systems.

Economies of Scale. Where marginal costs reduction is achieved by producing en masse.

Ecosystem Services. The benefits that humans realize because of healthy ecosystems, including productive yields, buffers against natural disasters, and biological filtration of air and water.

Environmental Justice. Providing meaningful involvement in the environmental decision-making affecting low-income minority communities, to address disproportionate burdens of environmental harm.

Environmental Kuznets Curve. The economic theory predicting that environmental degradation rises then falls in an inverted U-shaped function of income per capita.

Globalization. The spread of "western" political, economic, and cultural norms as the world's national and regional economies become integrated through information technology.

Green Engineering. Seeks to advance the sustainability of manufacturing processes, green building design, and public infrastructure by taking a systems or holistic approach.

Human Ecology. Interdisciplinary approach to understanding human-environmental systems that combines biophysical realities of human existence with social and psychological dimensions of human health and well-being.

Human Rights. The inherent dignity of all human beings deserving respect, enshrined in international treaties.

Industrial Ecology. The design of industrial infrastructures to function as inter-connected artificial ecosystems that sustainably interface with natural ecosystems.

Natural Capital Project. Aims to provide tools to corporate, government, and NGOs to facilitate incorporating natural capital into decision.

Offset. A means of compensating for environmental impacts of land use by purchasing a commensurate amount of land in a sensitive ecosystem to be set aside for preservation purposes.

Plantation Production Problem. Where under-regulated labor markets pose the risk of harsh labor conditions or human trafficking.

Preservation. A policy of maintaining nature in its pristine state, or at least in its condition prior to human intervention.

Race to the Bottom. When governments compete with one another for economic activity by deregulating a business environment, resulting in fewer environmental or worker protections.

Regenerative Capacity: the amount of useful biological material and industrial waste that an ecosystem can produce and absorb, respectively, given prevailing uses.

Regulatory Arbitrage. When a company shifts operations from one jurisdiction to another in order to dodge regulatory intervention as well as increased social license requirements.

Stakeholder Theory. Theory contending that business success requires creating value for customers, suppliers, employees, communities, and financiers.

Chapter 3 Key Terms

Articles of Incorporation. Legal agreements between shareholders and management that spell out the fiduciary duties owed by management personnel to the organization and which must be borne out in how the company is managed.

B-Corporation. A corporate form designed to deliver social, economic, and environmental benefits beyond shareholder profits (the 'B' stands for 'beneficial').

Carbon Leakage. Where a source of greenhouse gas emissions migrates from a regulated environment into an unregulated one in order to avoid compliance with emissions limits.

Change Management. Altering corporate behavior and processes in response to environmental influences in order to achieve a goal.

Changing. Step 2 in the classic change management process involving communication over various media within the organization—employee training, town hall meetings, and the like—to reinforce the new sustainability strategy.

Chief Sustainability Officer. A formal corporate leadership function positioned in the C-Suite, responsible for overseeing sustainability performance.

Collective Action Problem. Situation in which everyone in a given group has a choice between two alternatives—to maximize individual expected return or to cooperate with others to maximize aggregate return—and where, if everyone involved chooses to act individualistically self-serving, the outcome will be worse for everyone involved, in their own estimation, than it would be if they were all to choose a path of cooperation.

Corporate Governance Framework. The company's mission, strategy, objectives, culture, and leadership typically consisting of (1) Board of Directors and Committees, (2) Legal and Regulatory Compliance, (3) Organizational Hierarchy, (4) Monitoring and Internal Control, (6) Transparency and Accountability, and (7) Policies and Procedures.

Corporate Governance. The system of rules, practices and processes by which a company is directed and controlled, used to ensure all business units are working together to fulfill the corporate mission.

Cost Leadership and Differentiation. Offering a general portfolio of products that is lower in cost on average than competitors, while also offering a distinct product line that commands a price premium.

Cost Leadership. increasing profit margins by maintaining financial costs at levels lower than competitors while maintaining comparable levels of price and quality.

C-Suite. The collection of "Chief" officers near the top of an organizational hierarchy that exercise control over the various divisions of the company.

Differentiation. Offering a special product or service for which buyers are willing to pay price premiums.

Eco-entrepreneurialism. Innovation that involves enhancements in resource efficiency, environmental impacts, meeting unmet needs of society, and transforming waste into a valuable asset.

Eco-Innovation. Changing a firm's processes and responsibilities to reduce environmental impacts and support organization learning.

Enlightened Value Maximization View of Corporate Responsibility. Theory that business leaders should use social, economic, and environmental resources in the most efficient ways, while striving to maximize total value creation for all stakeholders.

Entrepreneurialism. The activation of opportunities to combine limited resources in order to create value and secure returns in new ways, brought about by problem solving practices under resource constraint and decision-making flexibility.

Environmental Management System. A voluntary regulatory structure that promotes internal environmental policies and strategies, with the goal of reducing the environmental impacts of industrial activity.

Executive Committees. Task-oriented subgroups consisting of Directors and Executives appointed to address specific themes or issues within the company.

Executive Compensation. The incentive package decided by executive committee and offered to business leaders to align behavior with the organizational mission and to compensate for excellent performance.

Focus. Selecting a small niche in geographic area, consumer segment, or specialty product or service.

Freerider. In a collective action scenario, when one party benefits from the cooperation of others, but is unwilling to reciprocate cooperation.

Independent Directors. An outside director determined by the Board of Directors to have no material relationship with the listed company prior to appointment.

Innovation. The investment of resources by a company into research and development (R&D) resulting in improvements upon current activities.

Leadership. The ability to make sound decisions on behalf of the company and to inspire the workforce to perform at their fullest potential.

Marketing Innovation. The development of a new marketing practice based on significant improvements to product design, packaging, product placement, promotional material, or price.

Minimizer. Providing goods or services in a method that reduces costs across the triple-bottom-line of financial, environmental, and social accounts, in order to increase profit margins without increasing prices.

Organizational Development. Change management approach using a planned change process that draws on behavioral sciences to systematically improve individual, interpersonal, and structural aspects of organizations.

Organizational Innovation. The implementation of a new method of business practice, workplace structure, or external relations.

Process Innovation. A new or significantly improved method of production or delivery, including modified production techniques or manufacturing equipment.

Product Innovation. The development of new or significantly improved goods or services through improved technical specifications, materials, software, use-friendliness, or other functional characteristic.

Public Goods. Resources which are non-rival and non-excludable, such as air.

Refreezing. Step 3 in the classic change management process where new behaviors and attitudes are adopted on the part of the organization's people toward the organization's sustainability strategy.

Responsible Care Management System. An integrated, structured approach to improve company performance in emergency response, employee health and safety, pollution prevention, and process and product safety developed by The American Chemistry Council.

Self-Regulation. Voluntary adherence to a firm- or industry-specific code of conduct.

Shareholder Resolutions. An accountability measure available to owners of voting stock in a publicly traded company that can influence corporate behavior.

Shareholder View of Corporate Responsibility. Theory that the sole objective of business leadership is to maximize shareholder value.

Stakeholder View of Corporate Responsibility. Theory that business leadership decision-making should include not just shareholder interests, but also any group or individual that can affect or be affected by corporate conduct.

Strategic Alignment. When a company has attained a fit between its core strategy, its organizational structure, and its competitive landscape through the performance of its employees and the consequences of its activities.

Sustainability Leadership Gap. The disconnect between where companies need to be and where they actually are in terms of sustainable performance.

Sustainable Business Leadership. The effective use of one's skill, knowledge, management style, and personality trait, given the internal and external context of one's business, to promote the sustainability mission of the company through certain activities.

Sustainable Corporate Governance. Using the mechanisms of corporate control to create long-term value that benefits internal and external stakeholders, contrasted with traditional corporate governance used to create short-term profits solely for the company's direct economic beneficiaries.

Sustainable Solutions. Providing goods and services that help solve real life problems, especially in emerging markets where consumer income and resources are limited.

Tragedy of the Commons. A scenario when a public good becomes rival but not excludable.

Transformer. Taking advantage of a discarded or undervalued resource (waste, pollution) by redeeming it into desirable goods through recycling, refurbishing, or repurposing.

Unfreezing. Step 1 in the classic change management process when managers inform employees that the status quo is no longer sustainable and that change is needed.

Wealth Inequality. Where a small percentage of people capture a disproportionate amount of a nation's wealth.

Chapter 4 Key Terms

1997 Kyoto Protocol on Climate Change. Unenforceable international agreement ratified by almost 200 nations, signaling a global commitment to reduce greenhouse gas emissions below specified baseline emissions rates.

Advantage. Attitude that sees law as a source of enforceable rights that can be leveraged to create value.

Article 3 of the United Nations' Trafficking in Persons Protocol. Defines human trafficking according to a rubric of illicit acts, methods, and purposes.

Article 5 of the United Nations' Trafficking in Persons Protocol. Calls upon UN member states to pass national legislation that criminalizes human trafficking.

Avoidance. Attitude that sees law as a barrier to economic growth and impediment to strategic planning.

Basel Convention. Successful international agreement to curb dumping of hazardous waste generated by developed nations into developing nations, requiring notice, consent, and tracking hazardous wastes across national boundaries.

Best Practicable Control Technology. Regulatory standard applied to mitigate water pollution through filtration or treatment before discharge.

Best System of Emissions Reduction. Standards that reflect the emission limits achievable considering cost, health impacts, environmental impacts, and the energy required to achieve the reductions.

Breach of Warranty. The seller's failure to fulfill the terms of a representation made regarding the quality of the product sold.

Citizens United v. Federal Election Commission. Landmark ruling by the US Supreme Court allowing unlimited political campaign contributions by corporations.

Clean Air Act. Regulates air pollution emissions from stationary and mobile sources.

Clean Water Act. Prohibits unpermitted point source discharges of any pollutant into the navigable waters of the United States.

Command-and-Control. Direct regulation of business by a government agency that determines what conduct is required and what conduct is illegal.

Compliance. Attitude that sees law as a source of unavoidable costs and obligations.

Conflict Minerals. Resources looted from a nation during times of armed conflict and human rights violations.

Design Defects. Foreseeable risks of harm created by a product that renders it unreasonably safe, which risks could have been avoided by adopting some reasonable alternative design.

Design. The process of transforming legal, technical, safety, functional, market or other requirements into the technical specification for a product.

Eco-Design of Energy-Using Products (EuP). EU Directive requiring manufacturers of 'energy-using products,' to design with the goal of reducing the energy consumption and negative environmental impacts attending the product life cycle.

Emergency Planning and Community Right-to-Know Act. Requires the U. S. EPA to publish a list of extremely hazardous substances, and the owner or operator of every facility where these listed substances are present must notify the state emergency planning commission of their presence at certain threshold quantities as well as any incident of their release into the environment.

Environmental Impact Statement. Require the government agency overseeing a land use permit decision to publish a record of the social, economic, and environmental impacts, both positive and negative, of a proposed change in land use.

Environmental Law. The subset of laws that define legal boundaries for pollution and risk-creation across all environmental media, protecting ecological integrity and public health.

Executive Branch. The enforcement arm of government.

Extended Producer Responsibility. Requires manufacturers to take responsibility for the disposal of waste from their products.

General Products Safety Directive. Seeks to ensure that products sold in the EU are only safe ones.

Green Marketing Guidelines. Require marketers using environmental claims to substantiate and specify these claims to prevent misleading consumers.

Greenwashing. Spending more on marketing environmental attributes than actually mitigating environmental impacts.

Hard Law. Civil and criminal laws that are enforceable and carry fines and penalties for noncompliance.

Hazardous Products Act. Sorts consumer products into lists of items that are banned, subject to regulation, subject to voluntary standards, or unregulated.

Human Trafficking. A criminal violation of human rights, generally involving kidnapping, physical abuse, slavery, and deprivation of basic needs.

Judicial Branch. The final arbiter of legal questions and common law claims within a government.

Law. System of rules that a particular community recognizes as regulating the actions of its members, and which government institutions can enforce.

Legal Environment of Business. The context of legal frameworks that provide the economic preconditions for efficient economic activity in the form of property, contract, and business law.

Legal Framework for Sustainable Business. Protective laws primarily designed to reduce the risk of adverse social, economic, environmental, and public health impacts resulting from economic activity.

Legal Hierarchy. The nested jurisdiction of government institutions that can regulate conduct at the international, regional, national, and local levels.

Legislative Branch. The lawmaking institution within government.

Lobbyist. Professional hired to influence public policy on a particular issue in favor of the client, especially through personal contact with legislators and staff members.

Manufacturing Defects. Where the product departs from its intended design, even if the manufacturer exercised all possible care for product quality and safety.

Mere Compliance. When a company seeks to comply with minimum standards for legal performance without going beyond these standards.

Misrepresentation. When the seller gives consumers false security regarding product safety, for instance by intentionally concealing potential hazards with statements that were relied upon by the consumer.

Mobile Source. Air pollution from a moving vehicle, such as a diesel powered heavy truck, tractor, or automobile.

Montreal Protocol. Successful measure to protect the Earth's ozone layer from destructive chlorofluorocarbons by establishing a system for monitoring and phasing out the production and use of ozone depleting substances in industrial processes.

National Ambient Air Quality Standards. Standards for protecting public health and welfare from a wide range of air pollutants, including hazardous air pollutants and ozone.

National Environmental Policy Act. For all major federal actions significantly affecting the quality of the human environment, federal agencies must prepare a detailed statement on the environmental impacts of the proposed action.

National Pollutant Discharge Elimination System. A pollution control program for point sources, based on water quality standards.

Negligence. When a company breaches their legal duty to exercise ordinary care, resulting in physical injury to a foreseeable victim.

Occupational Safety and Health Act. Enables standards to prevent workplace injury; require employers to provide employees with working conditions that are free of known dangers; and provide information, training and assistance to workers and employers.

Offset. Pollution emission reductions achieved in order to compensate for increased emissions from another source.

Oil Pollution Act. Creates liability for parties responsible for an oil spill.

Point Sources. Effluent water pollution from pipes or culverts that discharge pollutants from industrial, municipal, or other facilities into nearby surface water.

Pollution Prevention Act. Requires companies with annual toxic releases to report the quantity of the chemicals entering the waste stream prior to recycling, treatment, or disposal; the amount of each chemical treated and recycled; the source reduction practices used; and the amount of toxic chemicals released into the environment as a result of a catastrophic event.

Producer Responsibility. Electronic waste recycling programs where the manufacturer pays.

Production/Operations Management. Overseeing all stages of the process for transforming a design into a material object.

Recovery Fees. Electronic waste recycling programs where the consumer pays.

Registration, Evaluation, Authorization, and Restriction of Chemical Substances. Creates an open-access registration system for substances manufactured or imported into the EU.

Resource Conservation and Recovery Act. Governs the generation, transportation, treatment, storage, and disposal of solid waste, in particular hazardous waste.

Revolving Door. Where a leader in industry takes over as the chief regulator responsible for overseeing her prior industry, and vice versa—the chief regulator takes over as a director of the previously regulated industry.

SB 657: California Transparency in Supply Chains Act. Law requiring certain companies to disclose efforts taken to combat human trafficking in their supply chain.

Soft Law. Informal rules that lack legal status but still influence the behavior of other law-making bodies and the public.

Stationary Source. Air pollution from a fixed location, such as from a coal-fired power plant or factory.

Strict Liability. Allows anyone injured by a product to sue the manufacturer if they can prove the product was defective, which defect caused the injury, and which rendered the product unreasonably dangerous according to reasonable consumer expectations.

Sustainable Performance. When a company goes beyond mere compliance with the law to satisfy social, economic, and environmental objectives.

Sustainable Product Design. Improving the environmental performance of a product's life cycle by integrating environmental aspects into product design.

Sustainable Production/Operations. Reducing as much as feasible the use of harsh chemicals and toxic substances in products, ensuring the safety of employees, and reducing the emissions of pollution during the manufacture process.

Title XV of the Dodd-Frank Wall Street Reform and Consumer Protection Act. Requires companies to disclose dealings in conflict minerals as well as labor problems at mining operations.

Transformation. Attitude that sees law as an opportunity to transform the business and its value chain.

Transparency. When by law companies must produce and disclose information about social, economic, environmental, and governance issues affecting the company.

Under-Enforcement. Failure to take adequate legal actions to mandate compliance with laws such as fines, penalties, permit revocation, or prison for noncompliance.

U.S. Food and Drug Administration. Oversees the safety and effectiveness of pharmaceuticals, animal and veterinary drugs, food additives, and cosmetics sold in the United States.

Warning Defects. Inadequate user instructions that create product liability when the foreseeable risks of harm posed by a product could have been reduced by providing reasonable instructions or warnings, the omission of which renders the product unreasonably risky.

Waste Electrical and Electronic Equipment. Directive to reduce waste from the electronics sector, increase recovery and recycling rates, improve environmental performance throughout the life cycle of these products, and to extend producer responsibility over their disposal.

Chapter 5 Key Terms

Analytical Tools. Methods and devices that enable analysis and interpretation of information.

Aqueduct. An online global database of local and global water risk indicator metrics and reporting standards.

Balanced Scorecard. Financial and operational information integrated in a single dashboard that allows managers to identify the real-time relationship between market dynamics, sustainability initiatives, operation efficiency, and profit improvement.

Carbon Disclosure Project. A non-profit that collects climate change information from voluntary business disclosures, including emissions amounts and associated risks, on behalf of 475 institutional investors.

CEO Water Mandate. A public-private initiative designed to assist companies develop, implement, and disclose sustainable water policies and practices.

Collaborative Reporting. Reporting process between industry and nonprofit sustainability advocacy groups, as well as between nodes in a supply chain.

Commission Guidance Regarding Disclosure Related to Climate Change. Advises managers to provide future-oriented disclosures about known trends and uncertainties associated with climate change that are reasonably likely to have a material impact on a company's liquidity, capital resources, or operations.

Energy Productivity. Reveals how much energy per dollar of revenue the company is responsible for consuming.

Environmental Footprint Analysis. Used to determine aggregate or individualized impacts on climate change, air quality, water resources, forests, fisheries, and soil quality, among other environmental mediums.

Environmental Profit & Loss (EP&L). Metric developed by PUMA used to put environmental performance into financial terms.

External Data. Enables a business to establish situational awareness and assess external pressures.

Global Reporting Initiative. A non-profit providing comprehensive sustainability reporting frameworks for organizations to promote economic, environmental, and social sustainability.

Global Water Tool. Used to integrate corporate water use, discharge, and facility operational information with specific watershed and country-level data about water resources.

GoodGuide. A source of authoritative information for consumers about the health, environmental, and social performance of products and companies.

Greenhouse Gas Emissions. Indicate the company's contribution to climate change.

Greenhouse Gas Footprinting. A tool to determine aggregate climate change impacts from air pollution associated with a supply chain, a single facility, or a single product or service.

Greenhouse Gas Productivity. How much greenhouse gas emissions per dollar of revenue the company is responsible for generating.

Greenhouse Gas Protocol. An accounting tool used to understand, quantify, and manage greenhouse gas emissions, including guidance, frameworks, and calculation tools for virtually every greenhouse gas standard in the world.

Groundwater Footprint. The area required to sustain groundwater use and groundwater dependent ecosystem services.

Horizontal View. Reporting focused on the behavior and impacts of a single entity or organization, such as the end producer or the brand under which a product is sold.

Human Capital Value. Attributing capital value to intangible benefits derived from effective human resources management, instead of merely categorizing personnel as an expense on the balance sheet.

Independent, Third-Party Verification. Objective assessment and validation of sustainability reporting and marketing claims by an outside impartial entity.

Information-Driven Sustainable Business Model. A continual process of information gathering and disclosure that enables a company to be responsive to stakeholder concerns and environmental considerations while meeting its own performance goals.

Internal Analysis. Benchmarking progress and regress based on past and present performance data.

ISO 14000. A set of tools to identify and report on the adverse impacts of business, including environmental management systems that track energy use and water consumption at specific facilities; life cycle impact analysis of products in development; methods of communicating about sustainability; and auditing protocols.

ISO 26000. A set of standards emphasizing a process to ensure business decisions affecting society or the environment are made ethically and transparently.

Key Performance Indicator. Measures progress based upon data relating to the mission, stakeholders, and goals of an organization.

Life Cycle Assessment. Disclosure of the sum total of adverse impacts of all stages of a product system, from raw material acquisition or natural resource production to the disposal of the product at the end of its life, including extracting and processing of raw materials, manufacturing, distribution, use, re-use, maintenance, recycling and final disposal (i.e., cradle-to-grave).

Material. Information bearing a substantial likelihood that a reasonable investor would consider it important to an investment decision.

MD&A. SEC disclosure obligations that require a company to follow a specific process of management-level discussion and analysis of risks.

Metrics. Standards of measurement designed to capture critical information about corporate performance in the form of objective data.

Natural Capital Accounting. Measuring, managing, and reporting the environmental externalities of business in order to inform business decision-making with proper valuation of environmental assets.

Percent of Nature Mimicked. The use of ecosystem services to accomplish environmental remediation that would otherwise require major capital expenditure.

Public Disclosure. When the information gathered during internal analysis is put into context of relevant external data and published in an annual report.

Real-Estate Efficiency Ratio. Measures the amount of energy, water, and resources consumed per square foot of corporate-owned real estate.

Reporting. The forthright disclosure of relevant information regarding corporate conduct to affected stakeholders.

Revenue Share from Sustainable Products. The share of annual revenue derived from investments into sustainable products or services.

Safety Performance. An employee injury rate per hours of work time.

Sarbanes-Oxley Act. Enacted to protect investors by improving the accuracy and reliability of corporate disclosures, requiring senior management to certify the accuracy of financial information, and carrying severe penalties for fraudulent activity.

Scope 1 Emissions. Greenhouse gas metric bounded by direct emissions from internal operations.

Scope 2 Emissions. Greenhouse gas metric bounded by indirect emissions from other companies over which the reporting company has control, such as emissions generated by energy suppliers resulting from the reporting company's electricity consumption.

Scope 3 Emissions. Greenhouse gas metric bounded by indirect emissions caused by entities in the company's supply chain over which it has no control, such as second or third tier suppliers.

Stakeholder Feedback. The response to public disclosures from the various external stakeholders of an organization.

Sustainability Framework 2.0. The International Federation of Accountants' framework for measuring sustainable performance through accountancy by integrating environmental and social values into the economic structure of a firm.

Sustainability Metrics. Measures used to calculate the social, economic, and environmental impacts of services or products.

Sustainability Tools. Analytical frameworks for applying metrics to the social and environmental dimension of business performance.

Transparency. When those affected by corporate conduct - whether investors, regulators, customers, or communities impacted by business activities - are able to access information about such conduct.

Triple Bottom Line. To avoid social and environmental costs while reducing operating costs, and create financial value while benefiting communities and the environment.

Vertical View. Reporting focused on the impacts associated with a product life cycle, as measured through its entire value chain.

Waste Productivity. How much waste per dollar of revenue the company is responsible for generating.

Water Footprint Tools. Measures water use, polluted water discharge, and water-related business risks across a variety of geographic contexts and industry sectors.

Water Intensity Per Product Unit. Tracks water use through the entire supply chain and production process for a given time period and divides that total volume of water by units of production.

Water Productivity. How much water per dollar of revenue the company is responsible for consuming.

Water Sustainability Tools. Used to enable companies to build a corporate water strategy.

WFN Water Footprint. Methodology to measure the total volume of freshwater used to produce the goods and services consumed by any well-defined group of consumers, including a family, municipality, province, state, nation, or business/organization.

Chapter 6 Key Terms

Avoiding Risk. Reducing risk likelihood through behavior change.

Bearing Risk. Voluntarily assuming risk.

Business Continuity Planning. The process of anticipatory preparation for disruptions in business functions to avoid being caught by surprise.

Carbon Bubble Hypothesis. Theory that carbon assets are currently over-valued because of the failure to appreciate the risk of legal restrictions on future carbon emissions.

Control Activities. The procedures and protocols that an organization implements to make sure the path chosen in the risk response stage is actually carried out.

Enterprise Risk Management. A process that enables the organization to properly evaluate risks, prepare a response plan that is aligned with the company's objectives, and have a system in place to respond when needed.

Exposure. The extent of a system that would be impacted if an event was to occur.

Externality. When one party's activity generates a risk that another party bears without consent or compensation.

Financial Risk. Internal and external financial challenges arising from the management of company capital, debt, cash flow, and equity.

Hazard Risk. Random disruptions from wild card events.

Impact Mitigation. Reducing the severity of damage that exposure to external risk might cause.

Information and Communication. The identification of salient information about risks and the transmission of that information to those within a company responsible for managing those risks.

Internal Environment. The organization's culture, the ethical principles and values that define the character of an organization, how the core team of leaders responsible for critical functions view risk, and the extent to which leaders of a company desire risk.

Internalize Risk. When the party responsible for generating risk ultimately pays for the consequences if the risk materializes.

Magnitude of Harm. The extent of exposure and vulnerability, less the degree of resilience enjoyed by the impacted system.

Materiality. Qualitative assessment of whether a risk is high, medium, or low—in other words, whether the kind that needs to be addressed by management.

Mitigating Risk. Reducing risk impact through preparation.

Monitoring. Tracking risk performance through information technology (IT) and risk-related metrics.

Objective Setting. The process of determining what a company seeks to accomplish.

Operational Risk. Associated with managing a company's operation and its supply chain.

Preventable Risks. Can be prevented through careful planning and operational excellence.

Probabilistic Risk Analysis. Formulaic approach to determining the risk level of a given event.

Recovery. Ability to regain a degree of normality after a crisis or event.

Redundancy. Having excess capacity and back-up systems in place.

Regulatory Risk. When a government agency perceives that an industry is creating high risk levels, it may intercede in the market by imposing restrictions on a variety of commercial activities.

Reputational Risk. Impairs a company's brand through negative association.

Resilience. The ability of a system to adapt and survive in the event of a disaster.

Resourceful. Ability to adapt flexibly to crises.

Response. Ability to mobilize quickly in the face of crises.

Risk. Exposure to the chance of hazard.

Risk Appetite. An individual's or firm's preference for risk, lying along a spectrum between risk aversion and willingness to accept risk.

Risk Assessment. Determination of a potential adverse event's magnitude and likelihood.

Risk Identification. Identifying weaknesses of and threats to the company.

Risk Level Formula. A function of the vulnerability of exposed elements of the affected system, less the extent of resilience of that system, all of which is multiplied by the likelihood of the risk occurring.

Risk Management Frameworks. Descriptions of a specific set of functional activities and processes that an organization will use to manage risks.

Risk Management. The process of deciding which risks are worth addressing and the extent to which these risks should be avoided.

Risk Response. Determination of which risks are worth addressing and the means by which they should be addressed.

Robustness. Ability to absorb and withstand disturbances.

Scenario Planning. Serves to raise issues and provide context and perspective on the nature of risks and what strategic responses are available.

Sharing Risk. Spreading risk impact through contract.

Strategic Risk. Relates to decisions made by executive management that may be high risk but also high reward.

Uncontrollable Risks. Arise external to the company and outside the scope of the company's control.

Vulnerability. The capacity of a system to endure shocks to its environmental conditions.

Chapter 7 Key Terms

Brand Extension. Using a successful brand to launch new or modified products in a different category.

Carbon Negative. When the carbon emissions from production, packaging, and shipment of a product are more than offset by other carbon mitigation projects.

Certification. Verification of sustainable marketing claims provided by qualified, independent, third-party entities.

Challenge of Cost. When sustainable branding imposes costs in excess of traditional marketing costs.

Challenge of Credibility. Aligning marketing claims with actual corporate conduct so these claims are both significant and sincere.

Challenge of Indirect Benefits. When the social, economic, or environmental benefits of a company's sustainability commitments do not directly benefit primary customers or clients.

Challenge of Salience. Selecting the right product or service attribute that is most pertinent to potential customers at the point of sale.

Challenge of Target Audience. When marketing for a product or service is tailored to specific subsets of potential customers rather than advertised to the general population.

Challenge of Trade-Offs. When a sustainable product sacrifices attributes of traditional products (such as price) in favor of special attributes (such as environmental impact).

Consistency. Criteria are the same across time.

Conventionals. Consumer segment consisting of those who pursue recycling, reusing, repurposing, and reducing waste as a form of cutting costs.

Deception Policy Statement. An ad is deceptive if it contains (or omits) information that is likely to *mislead* consumers acting reasonably under the circumstances, and it is *material* in the sense that the deceptive information is important to a consumer's decision to buy or use the product.

Drifters. Consumer segment consisting of those merely driven by trends with no integration of values into lifestyle or purchases.

Efficacy. Certification allows consumers to incorporate information into purchasing decisions in real time.

Endorsement Guides. Guidelines prepared by the FTC that apply truth-in-advertising restrictions to third-party seals of approval or third-party certifications.

Explicit Element of Corporate Policy. When companies are vocal about what efforts they happen to be making toward sustainability.

Fair Trade. Product label that verifies agricultural ingredients come from environmentally certified farms and organizations that pay fair prices to laborers and which submit to rigorous supply chain audits.

Functional Equivalency. Comparisons are made between like-in-kind products only.

Going Viral. When internet content circulates spontaneously through social networks, generating millions of hits in a short period of time.

Greenwashing. Using marketing to promote the idea that a company is more socially or environmentally responsible than it actually is.

Halo Effect. The tendency of consumers to make inferences about a company's sustainability on the basis of very limited information, or to use an observable attribute to infer an unobservable one.

Implicit Element of Institutional Frameworks. When companies do not take credit for engaging in sustainable conduct because they are built-in requirements either in the laws or culture where they operate.

Internet Age. Demarcates the emergence of a digital marketplaces for ideas, products and services made possible by internet access.

Lifestyle of Health and Sustainability. Consumer segment consisting of early adopters of sustainable products who are loyal to brand, influential in their community, and choose green for planet's sake.

Line Extension. When a company introduces new items in the same category under the same brand.

Marketing. Introducing an offering to the market in such a way as to inform prospective customers of the attributes of the product or service and inducing them to purchasing it.

Marketing Sustainability. Addressing the benefits of a product or service and consumer expectations about the company's social, economic, and environmental responsibility.

Multi-Brand. Launching two or more sustainable brands within the same product category.

Naturalites. Consumer segment consisting of those who seek safer product alternatives for household safety.

New Brand. Entering a new product category with a new product.

Objectivity. Based on facts rather than intentions.

Process-Related Information. Facts about the methods and labor practices that went into producing a consumer good.

Product-Related Information. Facts about a product's attributes, such as whether it is safe, whether performs its intended purpose, what ingredients it contains, and how much it costs.

Rainforest Alliance. Assists forestry and agricultural sectors conserve biodiversity and improve livelihoods of workers by promoting and evaluating the implementation of sustainability standards.

Relevancy. Certification contains only information that is relevant to the customer.

Roundtable on Sustainable Palm Oil (RSPO). Formed to promote the growth and use of sustainable oil palm products through credible global standards and engagement of stakeholders.

Specificity. Criteria are defined clearly to avoid ambiguity.

Stage I. Businesses set the example within their industry by achieving improved standards for environmental performance, and market the benefits of their services or products by comparison with the performance of competitors.

Stage II. Businesses collaborate with clients to develop sustainable products and services, sharing the responsibility with consumers who voluntarily change their behavior.

Stage III. Businesses enable breakthroughs in sustainable design and technology that have the potential to reshape markets.

Sufficiency. Certification contains no more information than is necessary to avoid information overload.

Unconcerneds. Consumer segment consisting of those who are unlikely to care about sustainability.

Unfairness Policy Statement. An ad or business practice is unfair if it is likely to cause substantial consumer injury that a consumer could not reasonably avoid, and the risk of injury is not outweighed by the benefit to consumers.

Chapter 8 Key Terms

Active Packaging. Food product containers which can absorb food odors, retard oxygen migration, and preserve food in order to reduce food waste, prevent foodborne illnesses, improved product quality, increase shelf life, and increase distribution channels.

Bottom of the Pyramid. The largest, poorest socioeconomic group, consisting of some 4 billion people living on less than $2.50 per day.

Child Labor. Age-inappropriate and hazardous work by children.

Cradle-to-Cradle Design. The process of using environmentally friendly inputs and transforming these inputs through change agents - whose byproducts can improve or be recycled within the existing environment.

Creating Shared Value. Nestlé's rural development program to help cocoa and coffee suppliers financially while benefiting local communities.

Customer-Related Payoffs. Increased customer satisfaction, product innovation, market share increase, improved reputation, and new market opportunities.

Customers. Any downstream company in a supply chain, as well as the final consumer.

Distributors. Companies that receive product shipments in bulk from manufacturers at centralized storage locations, and in turn supply smaller batches to retailers.

Facility Location. Choosing the parcel upon which capital assets and corporate activities will be take place.

Factor Rating. A facility location optimization tool that involves evaluating multiple alternative locations based on a number of relevant factors.

Financial Payoffs. Reduced operating costs, increased revenue, lower administrative costs, lower capital costs, and stock market premiums.

Life Cycle Assessment. A technique to assess environmental impacts associated with all the stages of a product's life.

Life Cycle Costs. The social, economic, and environmental impacts of a product throughout its entire supply chain.

Logistics. The movement and storage of product inventories throughout the supply chain.

Manufacturers. Companies that transform raw materials into finished products.

Multi-Stakeholder Partnerships. Networks of governments, civic groups, and businesses that seek to connect corporate priorities with local action.

New Source Selection Process. Used by Nike to determine whether to acquire a new factory by assessing criteria such as inspection results along environmental, safety, and health dimensions, as well as a third-party labor audit.

Operational Payoffs. Process innovation, productivity gains, reduced cycle times, improved resource yields, and waste minimization.

Organizational Payoffs. Employee satisfaction, improved stakeholder relationships, reduced regulatory intervention, reduced risk, and increased organizational learning.

Rana Plaza Disaster. The largest disaster in the history of the garment industry, involving a collapsed manufacturing building in Bangladesh.

Resilient Supply Chains. Can absorb system shocks from environmental disasters in order to avoid supply chain disruptions and resume normal operations.

Retailers. Companies that sell to end users of products.

Reverse Logistics. The process of moving products upstream from the customer back toward manufacturers and suppliers.

Shared Value Creation. Where the line between supplier and buyer is blurred by treating the supply arrangement as if both parties were part of the same operation, or as if they were co-owned.

Steps to Responsible Growth. Kingfisher's formal evaluation system that provides actions for each operating company to undertake in order to meet corporate sustainability policy.

Suppliers. Companies that provide raw materials and components to producers or manufacturers.

Supply Chain Collaboration. Building task-oriented long-term relationships between buyers and suppliers.

Supply Chain Management. The design and management of flows of products, information, and funds throughout the network of all entities involved in producing and delivering a finished product to the final customer.

Sustainability Measurement and Reporting System. A standardized framework for communicating sustainability-related information throughout product supply chains, developed by The Sustainability Consortium.

Sustainable Packaging. Product containers that are sourced, manufactured, transported, and recycled using renewable energy; which optimize the use of renewable or recycled source materials; are manufactured using clean production technologies; are physically designed to optimize energy and materials used; and are effectively recovered using biological or closed loop cycles.

Sustainable Reverse Logistics. The logistical functions that support cradle-to-cradle design, which close the loop of a typical forward supply chain via reuse, remanufacturing, and/or recycling.

Sustainable Supply Chain Management. The strategic, transparent integration and achievement of an organization's social, environmental, and economic goals in the systemic coordination of key inter-organizational business processes for improving the long-term economic performance of the individual company and its supply chains.

The Lean and Green Supply Chain. Four-step framework for establishing a sustainable supply chain, developed by the US EPA.

Traceability. The ability to retrace the history, use or location of a product or component by means of recorded identification.

Transportation. The physical means by which products and materials are moved through a supply chain.

United Nations Global Compact. Calls for participating companies to know and show that they are respecting human rights, and when people are harmed by business activities, that there is both adequate accountability and effective redress.

Value Chain. The various value-adding activities performed by an organization to deliver a product or service to the market.

Chapter 9 Key Terms

Automation. Replacing human workers in dangerous job descriptions with robotics.

Baoli. Ancient architectural feature used to passively cool a structure without electricity by using a stepwell design.

Big Data Analytics. Gathering and analyzing enormous amounts of data to determine trends which can be translated into business intelligence.

Centralized Storage Facility. A "mother ship" warehouse commonly used by distributors for receiving wholesale shipments from manufacturers and sending out batches of inventory to retailers.

Decentralized Inventory. Storage that is smaller in size but geographically diffuse in order to maintain inventory closer to the end customer, allowing retailers to maintain lower amounts of safety stock.

Design for Recycling. Product design that takes into account the ability to break down a used product to recover the recyclable components.

Disintermediation. Eliminating an intermediate process between the supplier and the end customer.

Enterprise Resource Planning. Management tool for executing and tracking the success of operational initiatives in terms of deployed resources.

Ergonomics. The design of a job description to protect workers from physical stress and environmental exposure.

Facility Layout. The physical arrangement of all resources within a facility.

Inventory management. The area of OM that deals with stocking levels, order policies, storage, and movement of goods.

Leadership in Energy and Environmental Design. Certification authorized by the U. S. Green Building Council, the recognized standard for measuring building sustainability.

LEED Rating System. Used to rank the extent of sustainable building design.

Living Building Challenge. A certification program with metrics that go beyond mere reductions of environmental impacts, in order to demonstrate that the built environment can improve the surrounding natural environment.

Operational Decisions. Short term, day-to-day management of the production process to ensure alignment with tactical and strategic decisions.

Operations Management. The business functions responsible for producing a company's goods and services.

Operations Strategy. The policies and plans for using the organization's resources to support its long-term competitive position while creating value for customers.

Priority Rules. A traditional method for worker scheduling that attempts to deploy the human resources optimally, such as "the most productive workers are assigned to cover peak hours."

Process Design. Developing a production process that can create the exact product that has been designed.

Process Performance Metrics. Measurements of different process characteristics that tell how efficiently a process is performing.

Process Quality. The extent to which production creates error-free products.

Process Velocity. How much wasted time exists in a process, computed as the ratio of throughput time to value-added time.

Product Design. The process of specifying the exact features and characteristics of a product.

Product Quality. The extent to which products are designed to meet the requirements of the customer.

Productivity. The ratio of outputs to inputs.

Reappraisal. Reconsidering potential stakeholder value creation and identifying new business opportunities, and developing business models and operations strategies to capture those opportunities.

Recycling. Recovering raw materials for future use.

Reduce. Using fewer resources.

Remanufacturing. A type of reuse that uses components of old products in the production of new ones.

Reuse. The use of a product after it has already been used.

Servicization. Replacing a physical product with a service, or a product-service system, to reduce environmental impacts.

Sick Building Syndrome. Where a structure has systemic air quality problems from mold, toxins, poor circulation, and the like, causing occupants to suffer headaches, congestion, fatigue, and rashes.

Strategic Decisions. Long term, broad in scope, authorizing tactical and operational decisions and serving to set the direction for the entire organization and determine the value proposition of the company.

Sustainable Building Design. Creates structures that conserve energy, use renewable resources in an efficient manner, and provide healthy indoor environments for employees that are conducive to productivity, and which are resilient against natural disasters.

Sustainable Inventory Management. Balancing the risks of stock-out with the cost of wasted overstock given the social, economic, and environmental factors affected by each scenario.

Sustainable OM Strategy. Includes value creation for social and environmental stakeholders as a competitive priority.

Sustainable Operations Management. Guiding the transformational process to reduce resource consumption, pollution, and waste while benefiting employees, customers, and communities in order to reduce short-term risks and shore-up long-term cash flows.

Sustainable Process Design. The creation of goods and services using processes and systems that are non-polluting, ergonomically appropriate, safe from worker hazards, minimally consumptive of resources, and economically viable.

Sustainable Product Design. The philosophy of designing goods and services to comply with the principles of social, economic, and environmental sustainability.

Sustainable Scheduling. Assigning workers based on meeting social and environmental, in addition to operational, needs.

Sustainable Work System Design. Designing a working environment to protect employees from work hazards and to encourage healthy routines throughout the work-day.

Tactical Decisions. Medium term, determining how resources and middle management will be deployed in furtherance of strategic decisions.

Throughput Time. The average amount of time it takes a product to move through the production system.

Utilization. The actual time that a resource (e.g. equipment or labor) is being used versus the amount of time it is available for use.

Value analysis. Analyzes the functions of the materials that go into a product in an effort to reduce the cost and improve the performance.

Work system design. The area of OM responsible for designing job descriptions.